# European Union Governance and Policy Making

# European Union Governance and Policy Making:
## A Canadian Perspective

EDITED BY
Emmanuel Brunet-Jailly, Achim Hurrelmann,
and Amy Verdun

UNIVERSITY OF TORONTO PRESS

Toronto Buffalo London

LIBRARY AND ARCHIVES CANADA CATALOGUING IN PUBLICATION

European Union governance and policy making : a Canadian  perspective / edited by Emmanuel
Brunet-Jailly, Achim Hurrelmann, and Amy Verdun.

Includes bibliographical references and index.
Issued in print and electronic formats.

ISBN 978-1-4875-9358-2 (softcover).—ISBN 978-1-4875-9359-9 (hardcover).
—ISBN 978-1-4875-9360-5 (EPUB).—ISBN 978-1-4875-9361-2 (PDF)

1. European Union—Textbooks. 2. Textbooks. I. Verdun, Amy, 1968–, editor II. Brunet-Jailly,
Emmanuel, 1961–, editor  III. Hurrelmann, Achim, editor

JN30.E975 2018                    341.242′2          C2017-905329-9
                                                     C2017-905330-2

We welcome comments and suggestions regarding any aspect of our publications—please feel free to
contact us at news@utphighereducation.com or visit our Internet site at utorontopress.com.

*North America*
5201 Dufferin Street
North York, Ontario, Canada, M3H 5T8

2250 Military Road
Tonawanda, New York, USA, 14150

ORDERS PHONE: 1-800-565-9523
ORDERS FAX: 1-800-221-9985
ORDERS E-MAIL: utpbooks@utpress.utoronto.ca

*UK, Ireland, and continental Europe*
NBN International
Estover Road, Plymouth, PL6 7PY, UK
ORDERS PHONE: 44 (0) 1752 202301
ORDERS FAX: 44 (0) 1752 202333
ORDERS E-MAIL: enquiries@nbninternational.com

Every effort has been made to contact copyright holders; in the event of an error or omission,
please notify the publisher.

This book is printed on paper containing 100% post-consumer fibre.

The University of Toronto Press acknowledges the financial support for its publishing activities of
the Government of Canada through the Canada Book Fund.

Printed in Canada.

Funded by the Government of Canada    Financé par le gouvernement du Canada    Canada

# Contents

## Part III. Challenges

# Acknowledgments

THIS BOOK IS THE PRODUCT OF cooperation that lasted more than a decade. The idea to produce a textbook about the European Union (EU) for Canadian students first came in 2003, when Amy Verdun started coordinating a team-taught interdisciplinary course on European Studies at the University of Victoria, in which Emmanuel Brunet-Jailly and several of the contributors to this book were also involved.

The idea was further rekindled when European Studies experts from across Canada began cooperating more intensively in the mid-2000s. In 2005, Joan DeBardeleben at Carleton University, Amy Verdun at the University of Victoria, and representatives of three other EU Centres in Canada set up a "Policy Research Cluster on Canada-EU Relations" that was funded by the Public Diplomacy Fund of the European Commission, DG External Relations In 2008, the Canada–Europe Transatlantic Dialogue (CETD) was launched under the directorship of Joan DeBardeleben, funded by the Social Sciences and Humanities Research Council (SSHRC). This project, which lasted for nine years, brought together over a hundred Canadian and European scholars, including the editors and many contributors to this book.

In September 2009, Amy approached University of Toronto Press with the idea for this textbook, and they immediately expressed interest. Amy invited Emmanuel Brunet-Jailly to join her as co-editor. Shortly after, on May 2–3, 2010, the two organized a workshop in Victoria, BC, where the first versions of the chapters were presented. Revised versions of six of the papers were presented at panels of the European Community Studies Association–Canada (ECSA–C) in Ottawa on April 26–28, 2012. In 2015, the two editors invited Achim Hurrelmann to join their team. The project sped up, and further revised papers were presented at a workshop which Achim hosted at Carleton University in Ottawa on March 12, 2016.

Thus, this book benefited from the long-term relationships that have been built over many years, catered by the EU Centres in Canada (funded by the EU) and further developed through the activities of the CETD. The contributors have been extraordinarily responsive and willing to accommodate the many requests from the editors, often in a timely manner. The editors are hugely thankful to all contributors for their enthusiasm in contributing to this project.

The project has also benefited immensely from the various editors of the University of Toronto Press, first Daniel Quinlan, then Michael Harrison, Mark Thompson, and most recently Mat Buntin. The editors also are very grateful for the two sets of reviews that they received on the book proposal in 2012 and 2016, as well as the detailed comments from four anonymous reviewers on the entire manuscript in 2017.

This book project was further aided by research and technical assistance, supported by the Work Study program at the University of Victoria, Amy Verdun's SSHRC Insight Grant, the CETD, and Achim Hurrelmann's Jean Monnet Chair. Donna Wood and later Ivan Dumka assisted in the early stages. Ottilie Grisdale and Dara Marcus helped make the Carleton University workshop a success. In the process of putting the final manuscript together, Valerie D'Erman provided indispensable support, which included supervising two undergraduate students, Morgan Buckner and Alexa Lewis (both on work study positions), who worked on the glossary, the PowerPoint slides that accompany this book, as well as some copy editing. Valerie also assisted with the class exercises. Zoey Verdun provided research assistance in a final stage to streamline the entire document. The three editors are indebted to them all.

# Tables, Boxes, and Figures

## Tables

## Boxes

## Figures

## Map

# Acronyms

| | |
|---|---|
| 3Ms | Money, Markets, and Mobility |
| AA | Association Agreement |
| AAMS | Associated African and Malagasy States |
| ACP | African, Caribbean, and Pacific countries |
| AFSJ | Area of Freedom, Security, and Justice |
| ALDE | Alliance of Liberals and Democrats in Europe |
| AMIF | Asylum, Migration, and Integration Fund |
| AP | Association Partnership |
| ASA | Agricultural Stabilization Act |
| ASEAN | Association of Southeast Asian Nations |
| BC | British Columbia |
| Benelux | Belgium, the Netherlands, and Luxembourg |
| BRICS | Brazil, Russia, India, China, and South Africa |
| CAIS | Canadian Agricultural Income Stabilization Program |
| CAP | Common Agricultural Policy |
| CCP | Common Commercial Policy |
| CEAS | Common European Asylum System |
| CEE | Central and Eastern Europe |
| CEECs | Central and Eastern European Countries |
| CET | Common External Tariff |
| CETA | Comprehensive Economic and Trade Agreement |
| CFP | Common Fisheries Policy |
| CFSP | Common Foreign and Security Policy |
| CIVCOM | Committee for Civilian Aspects of Crisis Management |
| CJEU | Court of the Justice of the EU |
| $CO_2$ | Carbon dioxide |
| COP21 | 21st Conference of the Parties to the UN Framework Convention on Climate Change |
| COREPER | Committee of Permanent Representatives |
| CORINE | Coordination of Information on the Environment |
| CSDP | Common Security and Defence Policy |
| DCFTA | Deep and Comprehensive Free Trade Area Agreement |
| DG | Directorate-General |
| DGDEVCO | Directorate-General for International Cooperation and Development |

| | |
|---|---|
| DGNEAR | Directorate-General for Neighbourhood and Enlargement Negotiations |
| DGTRADE | Directorate-General for Trade |
| EAC | European Affairs Committee |
| EAGGF | European Agricultural Guidance and Guarantee Fund |
| EAP | Environmental Action Programme |
| EaP | Eastern Partnership |
| EAW | European Arrest Warrant |
| EC | European Community |
| ECB | European Central Bank |
| ECHR | European Convention on Human Rights |
| ECJ | European Court of Justice |
| ECOFIN | Council of Economic and Finance Ministers |
| ECSC | European Coal and Steel Community |
| ECR | European Conservatives and Reformists |
| ECU | European currency unit |
| EDC | European Defence Community |
| EEA | European Economic Area |
| EEAS | European External Action Service |
| EEC | European Economic Community |
| EES | European Employment Strategy |
| EFDD | Europe of Freedom and Direct Democracy |
| EFF | European Fisheries Fund |
| EFSF | European Financial Stability Facility |
| EFTA | European Free Trade Association |
| EI | Employment insurance |
| EMCO | Employment Committee |
| EMFF | European Maritime and Fisheries Fund |
| EMU | Economic and Monetary Union |
| EMS | European Monetary System |
| ENF | Europe of Nations and Freedoms |
| ENP | European Neighbourhood Policy |
| EP | European Parliament |
| EPA | European Partnership Agreement |
| EPC | European Political Cooperation |
| EPP | European People's Party |
| EPSCO | Employment, Social Policy, Health, and Consumer Affairs Council |
| ERM | Exchange Rate Mechanism |

| | |
|---|---|
| ESCB | European System of Central Banks |
| ESDP | European Security and Defence Policy |
| ESF | European Social Fund |
| ESM | European Stability Mechanism |
| ETS | Emissions Trading System |
| EU | European Union |
| EUBAM | EU Border Assistance Mission |
| EUFOR | European Union Force |
| EUL | Confederal Group of the European United Left |
| EULEX | European Union Rule of Law Mission (in Kosovo) |
| EUMC | EU Military Committee |
| EURATOM | European Atomic Energy Community |
| EUR-LEX | Official website of European Union law |
| EUROJUST | EU Judicial Cooperation Unit |
| EUROPOL | European Police Office |
| EUTM | EU Training Mission |
| FAO | Food and Agriculture Organization (of the United Nations) |
| FDI | Foreign Direct Investment |
| FIFG | Financial Instrument for Fisheries Guidance |
| FRONTEX | European Border and Coast Guard Agency |
| FTA | Free-trade agreement |
| GAC | General Affairs Council |
| GAMM | Global Approach to Migration and Mobility |
| GATT | General Agreement on Tariffs and Trade |
| GDI | Gross domestic income |
| GDP | Gross domestic product |
| GHG | Greenhouse gases |
| GI | Geographical indication |
| GNI | Gross national income |
| GUE/NGL | European United Left/Nordic Green Left |
| GWh | Gigawatt hours |
| HR | High Representative |
| IGC | Intergovernmental Conference |
| IMF | International Monetary Fund |
| IP | Intellectual property |
| IR | International relations |
| ISDS | Investor State Dispute Settlement |
| JHA | Justice and Home Affairs |
| MEDA | Euro-Mediterranean Partnership |

| MEP | Member of the European Parliament |
|---|---|
| MFF | Multiannual Financial Framework |
| MW | Megawatt |
| NA | Non-attached members |
| NAFO | North Atlantic Fisheries Organization |
| NATO | North Atlantic Treaty Organization |
| NGO | Non-governmental organization |
| NI | *Non-inscripts* (non-attached member to an EP Group) |
| OECD | Organisation for Economic Co-operation and Development |
| OLP | Ordinary legislative procedure |
| OMC | Open Method of Coordination |
| PCA | Partnership and Cooperation Agreement |
| PSC | Political and Security Committee |
| QMV | Qualified majority voting |
| R&D | Research and development |
| SAA | Stabilization and Association Agreement |
| SCC | Supreme Court of Canada |
| S&D | Progressive Alliance of Socialists and Democrats in the European Parliament |
| SEA | Single European Act |
| SFP | Single Farm Payment |
| SGP | Stability and Growth Pact |
| SPC | Social Protection Committee |
| SPRING | Support to Partnership, Reform, and Inclusive Growth |
| TAC | Total allowable catches |
| TACIS | Technical Aid to the Commonwealth of Independent States |
| TCA | Trade and cooperation agreement |
| TCN | Third country national |
| TEC | Treaty Establishing the European Community |
| TEEC | Treaty Establishing the European Economic Community |
| TEU | Treaty on European Union |
| TFEU | Treaty on the Functioning of the European Union |
| TPC | Trade Policy Committee |
| TTIP | Transatlantic Trade and Investment Partnership |
| UfM | Union for the Mediterranean |
| UK | United Kingdom |
| UKIP | United Kingdom Independence Party |
| UN | United Nations |
| UNCTAD | United Nations Conference on Trade and Development |
| US | United States |

| | |
|---|---|
| USSR | Union of Soviet Socialist Republics |
| VAT | Value-added tax |
| VP | Vice President |
| WGSA | Western Grain Stabilization Act |
| WTO | World Trade Organization |

# Contributors

**Emmanuel Brunet-Jailly,** Professor of Public Administration at the University of Victoria, Jean Monnet Chair in European Urban and Border Region Policy, Director of the European Union Centre for Excellence at the University of Victoria

**Gabriela Chira,** Head of Sector, European Commission Services. Holds a PhD in European Union law from the University of Nice and completed a postdoctoral fellowship at the University of Victoria.

**Constantin Chira-Pascanut,** Secretariat General, European Economic and Social Committee. Holds a PhD in history from the University of Victoria.

**Assem Dandashly,** Assistant Professor of Political Science at Maastricht University (Netherlands)

**Joan DeBardeleben,** Chancellor's Professor in the Institute of European, Russian and Eurasian Studies at Carleton University, Jean Monnet Chair in EU Relations with Russia and the Eastern Neighbourhood, Co-Director of the Centre for European Studies at Carleton University

**Valerie J. D'Erman,** postdoctoral researcher at the Department of Political Science, University of Victoria

**Achim Hurrelmann,** Associate Professor of Political Science at Carleton University; Jean Monnet Chair in Democracy in the European Union; Director of the Institute of European, Russian and Eurasian Studies; Co-Director of the Centre for European Studies at Carleton University

**Finn Laursen,** Honorary Professor in International Politics at the University of Southern Denmark, Jean Monnet Chair *ad personam*

**Heather MacRae,** Associate Professor of Political Science at York University, Jean Monnet Chair in European Integration

**Frédéric Mérand,** Professor of Political Science at the Université de Montréal, Director of the Centre d'études et de recherches internationales (CÉRIUM), and Co-Director of the Union Centre of Excellence Université de Montréal-McGill University

**Martha O'Brien,** Professor of Law at the University of Victoria

**Charles C. Pentland,** Professor emeritus of Political Studies at Queen's University

**Antoine Rayroux,** Assistant Professor of Political Science at Concordia University

**Oliver Schmidtke,** Professor of Political Science and Acting Vice President Research at the University of Victoria, Jean Monnet Chair in European History and Politics

**Paul Schure,** Associate Professor of Economics at the University of Victoria

**Ingeborg Tömmel,** Professor emerita of International Politics at the University of Osnabrück (Germany), Jean Monnet Chair in European Politics

**G. Cornelis van Kooten,** Professor of Economics and Canada Research Chair at the University of Victoria

**Amy Verdun,** Lansdowne Distinguished Fellow in European Integration, Professor of Political Science at the University of Victoria, Jean Monnet Chair *ad personam*

**Crina Viju,** Associate Professor in the Institute of European, Russian and Eurasian Studies at Carleton University

**Donna E. Wood,** Adjunct Assistant Professor of Political Science at the University of Victoria. Holds a PhD from the University of Edinburgh.

**Rebecca H. Wortzman,** MA student in economics at the University of Victoria

# 1
# Introduction

EMMANUEL BRUNET-JAILLY, ACHIM HURRELMANN,
AND AMY VERDUN

## Reader's Guide

This chapter provides an introduction to the textbook. It explains key milestones in the development of the European Union (EU), defines important terms and concepts in EU studies, and discusses some of the challenges that the EU currently faces. It clarifies that some aspects of the EU's development have been highly successful, whereas others are increasingly contested. The chapter also sets out the rationale and structure of the book and introduces three main themes related to the EU's policy portfolio, its institutional structure, and its political legitimation. These are taken up in the individual chapters.

## Introduction

In 2012, the European Union (EU) won the Nobel Peace Prize. The EU, argued the prize committee, has contributed to "the advancement of peace and reconciliation, democracy and human rights in Europe" and has thus "helped to transform most of Europe from a continent of war to a continent of peace" (Norwegian Nobel Committee, 2012). The Nobel Peace Prize was an unexpected recognition for an achievement that is indeed monumental. EU member states have collaborated since the early 1950s, overcoming historical disputes and avoiding wars among them, whereas the preceding centuries had been plagued by violent conflicts and destruction. The EU has set up common institutions with substantial powers to make binding decisions and has created a large range of common policies that have helped to abolish barriers to economic exchange and people's mobility between the member states. This process of establishing common institutions and policies, which brings European member states closer together, is called **European integration**.

The process of European integration has fundamentally transformed the political systems, economies, and societies of Europe. Six west European countries (Belgium, France, Italy, Luxembourg, the Netherlands, and West Germany) initiated the process. By 2013, the EU had grown to 28 member states (see Map 1.1). In addition to this geographic *widening*—the addition of more member states—the EU has also experienced a process of *deepening*, meaning that more and

**Map 1.1** Map of the EU and its member states (2017)

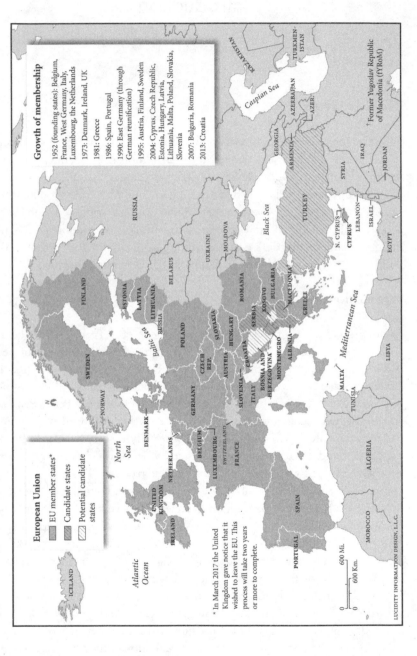

**European Union**

- EU member states*
- Candidate states
- Potential candidate states

* In March 2017 the United Kingdom gave notice that it wished to leave the EU. This process will take two years or more to complete.

**Growth of membership**

1952 (founding states): Belgium, France, West Germany, Italy, Luxembourg, the Netherlands

1973: Denmark, Ireland, UK

1981: Greece

1986: Spain, Portugal

1990: East Germany (through German reunification)

1995: Austria, Finland, Sweden

2004: Cyprus, Czech Republic, Estonia, Hungary, Latvia, Lithuania, Malta, Poland, Slovakia, Slovenia

2007: Bulgaria, Romania

2013: Croatia

† Former Yugoslav Republic of Macedonia (FYRoM)

LUCIDITY INFORMATION DESIGN, L.L.C.

0    600 Mi.
0    600 Km.

more powers have been shifted from the member states to the EU level. The EU now influences virtually all areas of policy-making. However, its powers vis-à-vis the member states are much more far-reaching in some areas (such as economic policy and trade) than in others (such as social policy or defence).

This creation of the EU and the dual process of its widening and deepening over time have produced many beneficial political developments. These include the establishment of an integrated **Single Market** with more than 500 million citizens, in which most internal economic barriers have been abolished. The Single Market provides many tangible benefits for Europeans, such as the ability to purchase goods and services from other member states without the imposition of customs duties or the right to take a job in another member state without applying for a work permit. It has also contributed to the economic prosperity of the member states. These achievements explain why so many European states have sought to join the EU, why there continues to be a queue of further applicants that seek to become members, even though there have also been European countries that have explicitly chosen not to join the EU. Furthermore, European integration has facilitated the peaceful reunification of the European continent after the end of the **Cold War**, during which Europe was split into a Western and an Eastern bloc. By admitting post-communist states of Central and Eastern Europe as EU members, the EU has aided these states in transitioning from non-democratic, one-party systems toward (in most cases) relatively well-functioning democracies.

At the same time, the EU has been affected by—and sometimes also contributed to—major political crises. Some of these have dominated the EU-related news in recent years. For instance, the 2008 financial crisis wreaked havoc on the European continent when numerous member states—especially those that had adopted the euro, the European single currency—experienced serious banking failure, sovereign debt crises, and subsequently severe economic recessions leading to unemployment figures that went as high as a quarter of the adult population in some member states (see Chapter 7). In the summer of 2015, Europe faced a new challenge when nearly one and a half million people—including nearly 120,000 unaccompanied children—from the Middle East, Africa, and Asia came into the EU seeking refuge, and the EU member states struggled to find a coordinated response (see Chapter 8). Most recently, the EU has been confronted with yet another challenge: the majority people of the United Kingdom (UK) voted in a referendum, held in June 2016, to leave the EU, an outcome (referred to as "**Brexit**") that the UK government has pledged to honour. These crises have constituted major challenges to the EU. Over the decades, the EU has seen numerous such challenges but has somehow overcome them. Thus, today's challenges, difficult and urgent as they are when they emerge, should not overshadow the EU's long-term achievements.

## The Purpose of This Book and the Three Themes

This book provides an introduction to the EU. It explains how the EU came about, how its institutions work, which major policies it has established, and what challenges it currently faces. This book is aimed at readers who have not previously studied European integration. More specifically, it is directed at those *outside Europe* who are studying the EU. More often than not, existing EU textbooks, though outstanding in their contents, assume a considerable amount of prior knowledge from their readers. European students may have this knowledge, as they can learn a lot about the EU simply from being exposed to it, but this situation applies much less to readers outside the EU. Furthermore, many of the existing textbooks end up having elaborate chapters on each of the policy areas, theories, and institutions, going into many details that often overwhelm first-time students of the EU.

Besides wanting to provide a textbook that neither assumes too much background knowledge nor offers too much detail, the editors and authors were keen to produce a book that is first and foremost written expressly for a *Canadian* audience. The chapters assume the typical background knowledge of students in a Canadian classroom. We attempt to draw explicit comparisons between the issue, policy, or institution at hand and the situation in Canada—although no prior knowledge of Canada is necessary for readers to use this textbook. We also discuss various aspects of the bilateral relationship between the EU and Canada (see Box 1.1).

Finally, as editors we felt that a textbook would benefit from being highly structured. Our chapters all start with a brief summary, followed by a short introduction, a main body of text that provides the general overview, a shorter section that discusses matters subject to current debate, and a conclusion. As already mentioned, each chapter furthermore has a section—in the form of a text box—that that offers a comparison with Canada; in particular, each of the policy-making chapters also has a text box detailing the EU budget specific to that policy issue. We have chosen a writing style that is very "light" on references. Each chapter closes with 20 sources for further reading and a few questions.

In order to guide our readers through the materials, we have organized the text around three major themes. The first theme is that the EU was created out of the ashes of World War II with the primary goal of never having another war again. This goal was achieved through a strategy of locking the member states into ever-closer economic and political interaction as well as setting up mechanisms to regulate economic exchange, thus creating strong common interests and establishing procedures to resolve conflicts peacefully. The second theme is that the EU, as it exists today, has more powers than a

**Box 1.1** Canada's relationship to the EU

In the first decades of the European integration process, Canada's relationship with Europe was dominated by its links to individual EU member states—especially the United Kingdom and France—as well as its membership in the North Atlantic Treaty Organization (NATO), the Western defence alliance. Relationships to the common European institutions became more important in the 1970s, when the Canadian government sought to diversify its economic relations to reduce dependence on the United States, and the integrated European trade bloc was an obvious partner. The 1976 Framework Agreement between Canada and the EU (then called the **European Economic Community**) was the first international agreement the EU concluded with another industrialized state. In the decades that followed, Canada maintained an interest in further deepening economic relations to the EU. The EU was initially reluctant, due to a preference for multi-country trade agreements, but eventually agreed to negotiations on an ambitious **Comprehensive Economic and Trade Agreement (CETA)**, which was signed in October 2016. At the time of writing, the CETA agreement is applied on a provisional basis, while still awaiting full ratification in the EU. This ratification will require the approval of all national and, in some cases, regional parliaments (38 in total). Canada has also been designated as one of 10 "strategic partners" of the EU (the others are Brazil, China, India, Japan, Mexico, Russia, South Africa, South Korea, and the United States).

typical international organization but falls short of being a state—even one that is organized as a federation. The EU, in other words, represents a *unique* form of cooperation among member states. The third and final theme is that the EU's legitimacy is increasingly subject to controversial debates. These debates concern both the EU's political achievements ("output") and the ability of citizens to exercise democratic control over EU decision-making ("input"). Let us turn to each of these three themes in turn.

## Theme 1: Peace-Building through Economic Cooperation in a Mixed Economy

As was mentioned previously, the predecessor institutions of the EU[1] were created in the early 1950s by six states: Belgium, France, Italy, Luxembourg, the Netherlands, and West Germany. Many of these countries—especially

France and Germany—had been enemies in World War II, as well as in numerous earlier military conflicts. They joined together to create a unique form of collaboration with the explicit purpose of not going to war again. The first step in the integration process was putting the production of coal and steel—the sectors of the economy that were essential for the production of tanks and cannons—under a joint regulatory authority. This first step was symptomatic for what would become the distinct peace-building strategy underlying the early European integration project. The idea was to build a community of states with strong economic cooperation and interdependence that therefore would not go to war with each other again. This strategy proved successful—so successful indeed, that the history of conflict between European states and the memories of World War II have receded deeper into the collective consciousness of European citizens. As a result, the origins of European integration as a *peace project* have become less obvious to younger generations, but they remain of central importance if one wants to understand the design of EU policies and institutions.

The model for regulating coal and steel production was expanded in the late 1950s to other sectors of the economy. By that time, Europe was fully engulfed in the Cold War, the confrontation between the capitalist democracies of the West (led by the United States) and the communist one-party states of the East (led by the Soviet Union). While the founding states of the EU were firmly anchored in the Western bloc, the competition with the East about which regime type was preferable made them acutely aware of the need to organize their economies in a way that produced high degrees of economic and social security for their citizens. The policies conducted in the EU framework were hence inspired by the idea that the European way would be one that is a *mixed system* (an economy that is neither state-controlled nor left to an unconstrained market), regulated with a view to social inclusion (see Table 1.1).

The mixed-economy model implied that the EU unfolded as an ambitious project of economic and political integration that combined market-making with selected initiatives of market correction. At the heart of the EU is the Single Market, a comprehensive plan to allow free circulation of goods, services, labour, and capital across all member states. However, as various chapters in this book illustrate, the construction of the Single Market coincided with initiatives that implement solidarity across various areas of policy, most importantly agriculture, regional development, and social affairs.

In addition to the creation of the Single Market, the first four decades of European integration (the 1950s to the 1980s) were characterized by the gradual growth of the EU from six to 12 member states (Denmark, Ireland,

**Table 1.1** The concept of a mixed economy

|  | State-controlled economy | Mixed economy | Free-market economy |
|---|---|---|---|
| **Ownership of the means of production (factories, machines, capital, etc.)** | State | Either mix of state and private or private | Private |
| **Core mechanism of economic coordination** | State planning | Market mechanism, but within constraints established by state | Market mechanism (supply and demand) |
| **Extent of state regulation of economic activities** | High: focused on process (working conditions, etc.) and outcome (products, etc.) | Medium: focused on process (working conditions, etc.), not outcome | Low |
| **Density of state programs to protect against social risks (unemployment, illness, etc.)** | High | Medium to high | Low |

and the United Kingdom joined in 1973; Greece in 1981; Spain and Portugal in 1986). Following this period of pioneering, ground-breaking, and incremental developments, a major qualitative shift in European integration occurred in the 1990s. This shift consisted of major—and simultaneous—*deepening and widening of European integration.* After the Single Market was declared to be largely "completed," the EU began to expand—and deepen—its competences into additional policy fields. In the economic realm, it set up a common currency, the euro. In non-economic fields, it developed institutions for a common foreign and defence policy as well as for common policies on home affairs, migration, and border control. The latter included the establishment of the so-called **Schengen Area** for borderless travel between EU member states (see Box 1.2). These developments led to deeper integration, but they also helped sow the seeds of what has become a *multi-speed* Europe. Not all member states were willing to participate in all of the new initiatives, and as a result, many negotiated selective **opt-outs**. For instance, the United Kingdom did not adopt the euro and has stayed outside of the Schengen Area, but it takes part in the common foreign and defence policy. Denmark has opted out of the euro and the EU's common defence policy, but it does form part of the Schengen Area.

**Box 1.2**   The reverse development of border formalities in Canada and the EU

The majority of EU member states (the exceptions being Bulgaria, Croatia, Cyprus, Ireland, Romania, and the United Kingdom), as well as some non-member states (Iceland, Liechtenstein, Norway, and Switzerland). have joined the so-called Schengen Area. Members of the Schengen Area have abandoned border controls among them; visitors from outside the EU have to abide by common visa rules. By contrast, following the terrorist attacks of September 2001 in the US, the Canada-US border became ever more difficult to cross. While for many decades a driver's licence sufficed as documentation for crossing the border, and few Canadian or US citizens held passports, they are now required to show a (biometric) passport to travel to each other's country.

The process of widening the EU that began in the early 1990s was triggered by the fall of the Berlin Wall in 1989, which marked the end of the Cold War. Both formerly neutral states (Austria, Finland, and Sweden) and countries in Central and Eastern Europe that used to be part of the Soviet bloc (Bulgaria, Czech Republic, Estonia, Hungary, Latvia, Lithuania, Poland, Romania, Slovakia, and Slovenia) were now seeking to join the EU. The former were admitted to the EU in 1995, the latter joined in 2004 and 2007 (along with Cyprus and Malta; Croatia followed in 2013). This peaceful reunification of the European continent under the EU umbrella can be seen as the crowning achievement of the peace-building strategy first initiated after World War II. At the same time, the widening process has implied new challenges for the EU's external relations (for instance in relations with Russia, now a direct neighbour of the EU) and internal policies (for instance in dealing with different interpretations of democracy and the rule of law in some of the newer member states). Most importantly perhaps, it has made the EU much more diverse both economically and in terms of political and social values, and as a result, policy-making for Europe's diverse and progressively more polarized economy has become more difficult.

## Theme 2: More than an International Organization, Less Than a State

While our first theme focused on the EU as a system of policy-making, our second theme examines the EU as a system of political institutions. The EU is a unique entity that is clearly more than an international organization but less than a state (even a federal one). Since December 2009, the EU has legal personality under international law. Its legal foundations have been its *founding treaties*, concluded between the member states, which have been elaborated further and revised in the decades following the EU's founding. Yet these international treaties have set up a political system that differs from conventional international organizations in a variety of ways.

The first major difference is the extensive scope of EU powers. Most international organizations deal with a relatively narrowly circumscribed range of issues. The EU, by contrast, has an encompassing range of policy responsibilities that is comparable to those of a state. In the exercise of these responsibilities, it is engaged in continuous European-level legislative production. As a result, the EU has become a legal giant; it has adopted so much legislation in the past six decades that it keeps the national parliaments of the member states—which have to discuss the implications of EU legislation for national law—busy for an estimated 50 per cent of their seating time. All the laws passed at the EU level are commonly referred to as the *acquis communautaire*, which purportedly consists of more than 170,000 pages of legal texts.

The second major difference between the EU and a conventional international organization lies in the legal quality of this law. Most international law is only binding in state-to-state relations, but does not have automatic effects on the citizens. By contrast, the **Court of Justice of the EU (CJEU)** has ruled that EU law has **direct effect**, meaning that it may directly create rights and obligations for the citizens. Most forms of EU law are binding on the member states and/or their citizens; EU law also enjoys **supremacy** over national law, which implies that in cases of conflict, the national law has to give way.

The third major difference concerns decision-making bodies and processes in the EU. While most international organizations are controlled by their member states, the EU combines institutions that speak for the member states and their governments (called **intergovernmental**) with institutions that represent the EU as a whole (called **supranational**). The most salient intergovernmental institutions are the **European Council** (where heads of states or governments of the member states decide on longer-term priorities of the EU or agree to new treaties) and the **Council of the EU** (where ministers of the member states meet to pass legislation). The main supranational institutions are the **European Commission** (the EU's executive body that represents the interests of the EU as a whole); the **European Parliament** (which is directly elected by the EU citizens and takes part in discussing and adopting EU legislation); the Court of Justice (which interprets EU law and settles legal disputes); and the **European Central Bank** (which aims at maintaining price stability of Europe's single currency, the euro).

Considering all of these differences with conventional international organizations, we can conclude that the EU has many state-like characteristics, especially if we compare it to states that are organized as a *federation*, composed of various regional subunits (such as the provinces in Canada) with their own institutions and responsibilities. Like federal states, it has a tripartite division of powers, with an executive (Commission), a **bicameral legislature** (Council of the EU representing the member states, European Parliament representing the citizens), and a judiciary (CJEU). It has policy competences in almost all areas of policy-making, even though in some fields its competence is either minimal or shared with the member states. The EU is also represented internationally; it has become a member in some international organizations and is represented abroad through the **European External Action Service (EEAS)**—the EU's diplomatic service (similar to national embassies or consulates). Since 1993, there even exists the concept of EU citizenship: citizens of the member states are automatically also citizens of the EU with a passport that provides them with some rights and duties much like citizens of a nation-state.

However, the EU has never described itself as a state, and there are certain important aspects in which it differs from the state model. First, the EU lacks certain critical powers of statehood, most importantly the power of raising its own revenue through taxation and the power to implement and enforce its own decisions. In both these domains, the EU depends on the member states, which finance the EU's operations and implement the vast majority its laws. The EU does not have institutions that directly interact on a regular basis with the citizens, let alone exercise a state-like monopoly of force. Second, the EU is also unable to define its own powers; it can exercise only powers explicitly conferred by the member states. It thus lacks a crucial component of state **sovereignty**. While large-scale transfers of competence from the national to the European level have occurred, the member states have explicitly withheld decision-making powers—or have insisted on a national veto—in policy fields that they consider particularly important to their own sovereignty, such as taxation or foreign and defence policy. Third, the legitimacy of the EU in the eyes of its citizens can be seen as more precarious than that of established federal states, because the citizens' EU-related identity and sense of belonging remain weak. In most federations, the majority of citizens identify first and foremost with federal level citizenship. In Canada, most people's identification with Canada is stronger than their identification with a province or region, whereas in the EU most citizens identify more with the "national" citizenship (feeling "French" or "German" rather than an "EU" citizen).

In other words, the EU has various elements that resemble a federal state, but it falls short of having all the characteristics of one (see Table 1.2). In a number

**Table 1.2**   The EU between international organization and state

|  | Typical international organization | EU | Typical state |
|---|---|---|---|
| **Policy responsibilities** | Task-specific, or limited range of tasks, powers controlled by member states | Encompassing range of tasks, but EU powers controlled by member states, often shared with them | Encompassing range of tasks, can determine its own powers |
| **Powers of common/ central institutions** | Limited (member state control) | Substantial (mix of supranational and intergovernmental decision-making) | High (in federations: divided between central government and subunits) |
| **Legislation** | Operates based on founding treaties; no legislative role | Legislative actor, law binding on member states | Legislative actor |
| **Policy implementation** | Dependent on member state agencies | Largely dependent on member state agencies (limited front-line implementation powers, plus oversight role) | Implements its own legislation |
| **Sources of finances** | Member state contributions | Primarily member-state contributions (no taxation power) but some income from tariffs | Primarily taxation |
| **Identification of citizens** | Weak | Weak to medium | Strong |

of ways it still resembles more an international organization, especially when it comes to areas where the member states have deliberately retained their powers. The chapters in this book lay out in greater detail the implications of this peculiar status of the EU—as being "in between" a conventional international organization and a federal state—and discuss how it influences the operation of EU institutions and the making of EU policy in different fields of activity.

## Theme 3: From Economic to Democratic Legitimation?

The third theme of the book approaches the EU from the perspective of political legitimation. The question here is how, and with what success, the EU attempts to generate support for its institutions and policies in the population. As was discussed above, the EU construction emerged from a postwar assumption that economic legitimacy trumps all. This assumption was behind the EU's original mixed-economy model. Since the very early days, the EU has been focusing on market integration, coupled with some measures aimed at increasing the welfare of EU citizens. This economic focus implied that other ways of legitimating politics—especially through mechanisms of democratic participation and accountability—were for a long time not considered particularly important.

Economic performance remains as essential for the EU's legitimation as it was in the 1950s. It represents what political scientists call *output legitimacy*, that is, legitimacy that derives from a polity's performance in safeguarding and improving the citizens' well-being. The EU has a mixed track record in this respect. On the one hand, most economists agree that EU membership has, on the whole, been beneficial for the participating member states. During the debate about the United Kingdom's withdrawal from the EU, the Organisation for Economic Co-operation and Development (OECD) estimated that Brexit will reduce that state's gross domestic product by 3 per cent over four years, equivalent to a cost per household of £2,200 (more than CA$3,500; OECD, 2016). On the other hand, the economic gains of EU membership are not equally distributed. Some parts of the population—especially less educated people, members of the working class, older people, and people living outside of metropolitan areas—perceive themselves as economic losers of the Single Market, since it implies more competition for resources and jobs.

In addition to ongoing discussions about the economic impacts of European integration, the past three decades have seen the emergence of a new line of debate, which focuses on the democratic quality of the EU. Calls for the EU to legitimate itself in democratic terms have never been entirely absent in the history of European integration. They explain, for instance, why the predecessor institution of today's European Parliament was created in the EU's founding treaties. However, democracy concerns—which represent what political scientists call *input legitimacy*, deriving from the participation of the citizens—were considered secondary to economic legitimation until the early 1990s. The main reason for this disregard for input legitimacy was the lack of widespread public interest in European integration. Yet this situation has changed in light of the deepening and widening of European integration. More and more citizens have voiced their concerns about political processes in the EU. These debates also witnessed the emergence of explicitly "Euroskeptic" political positions that are fundamentally opposed to European integration.

The EU has explicitly sought to address the criticism that it might not be sufficiently democratic, most importantly by increasing the power of the European Parliament, turning it into a fully coequal legislator on par with the Council of the EU. Yet although some of the **democratic deficit** has been rectified by these institutional amendments, these changes have not alleviated

**Figure 1.1** Support for European integration in the citizenry, 1973–2011

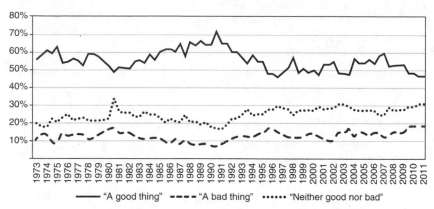

Question: "Generally speaking, do you think that (your country's) membership of the European Union is…?"
Source: Eurobarometer, 1973–2011

all of the concerns about the democratic quality of the EU. The people of various member states have expressed their dismay, *inter alia*, in an increasing number of referendums about EU-related issues. The referendums are usually organized by national governments in response to public pressure, and some of them have resulted in an explicit rejection of further European integration. The June 23, 2016, UK referendum on EU membership is the most prominent recent example. It demonstrates that policymakers in the member states and in the EU can no longer ignore the citizens' perceptions of European integration.

Public opinion research shows that the EU has not been equally popular among its citizens over time. It has experienced ebbs and flows in popularity. Yet looking at some of the statistics about support for the EU collected by Eurobarometer over the past decades, we see that a majority of EU citizens has consistently supported their country's EU membership. However, since 1991, support for membership has clearly declined (see Figure 1.1).

At the time of writing (spring 2017), the EU faces undeniable difficulties in securing both output and input legitimacy. Some EU citizens feel that the EU has made the wrong decisions in trading off regulation and redistribution versus market freedom. They also feel disconnected to how the EU makes such decisions and how they can influence it. The emergence of more active questions about what the EU is doing, questions about its direction, active national party political discussions about EU politics, or even outright vocal opposition to the EU, is referred to as *politicization* of the EU. It may be a trigger for further democratization, but may also lead to a stagnation of the integration process. Politicization may also influence EU institutions and EU policy-making in various fields.

## Structure of the Book

This book is subdivided into three parts. Part I, "Integration and Governance," looks at the institutional core of the EU. It starts with Chapter 2, a comprehensive overview of the history of the EU from World War II, in which Constantin Chira-Pascanut discusses how certain policies were developed earlier than others and how we can make sense of those developments. In Chapter 3, Finn Laursen describes how the EU works and discusses the major institutions and the legislative process. He also offers a look at how democratic input is infused into EU decision-making. Chapter 4, by Martha O'Brien, sheds light on legal integration—the functions of the Court of European Justice, but also the legal instruments and the role legal integration has played in the integration process. In Chapter 5, Ingeborg Tömmel provides an overview of governance and policy-making in the EU's **multilevel system**. She compares various types of EU policy to each other and also to what is typical in the member states. The final chapter in this part, Chapter 6, by Amy Verdun, focuses on the theories of European integration. It offers an introduction to the leading integration theories as well as more general political science theories that have become more frequently used in the analysis of European integration studies.

Part II, "Policies," encompasses 10 chapters that all concentrate on a specific area of policy-making. They each discuss the development of the policy in question from the EU's origins until the present. Chapter 7, by Paul Schure and Amy Verdun, offers an overview of the economic integration process, from the Single Market through the single currency to the recent developments to deal with the financial crisis and the UK referendum on the EU. Oliver Schmidtke, in Chapter 8, presents the policy development in the area of **Justice and Home Affairs**, including the more recent challenges to freedom and security in light of the migration and refugee flows and terrorist attacks. In Chapter 9, Frédéric Mérand and Antoine Rayroux offer an account of the way in which foreign, security, and defence policies have advanced from the early days till the present time. Heather MacRae and Donna E. Wood, in Chapter 10, provide an overview of social and employment policies. They explain the various mechanisms for governing social affairs, as well as the role of various levels of government in the EU multilevel system. Crina Viju, in Chapter 11, examines the EU's **Common Agricultural Policy (CAP)**, one of the earliest EU policies that has in recent years undergone far-reaching reforms. G. Cornelis van Kooten and Rebecca H. Wortzman, in

Chapter 12, look at energy and environment policy in the EU. They provide a historical overview and examine current challenges, including the fight against climate change and the establishment of a so-called **Energy Union**. Emmanuel Brunet-Jailly offers an account of **regional policy** since the early days in Chapter 13. He describes a policy set to alleviate the social impact of economic convergence, which has become the world's most ambitious **smart, sustainable, and inclusive growth** and development policy. The next chapter, by Valerie J. D'Erman (Chapter 14) recounts EU trade policy, one of the earliest truly supranational policies. The chapter also discusses the contents and challenges surrounding the Comprehensive Economic Trade Agreement (CETA) between Canada and the EU. Chapter 15, by Charles C. Pentland, offers an overview of the process of EU **enlargement** and the challenges that have accompanied each enlargement. He also looks at the states with which the EU is currently negotiating possible membership. The last policy chapter covers the European Neighbourhood Policy. In Chapter 16, Gabriela Chira and Assem Dandashly set out how the EU developed policies toward countries in the East and the South that are not EU members and what policies the EU uses to deal with them.

Part III, "Challenges," starts off with Chapter 17 by Achim Hurrelmann, who examines the various aspects of the democratization of the EU. The chapter deals with the EU's recent attempts to create more democratic legitimacy but also discusses the increasing politicization of European integration and the growth of **Euroskepticism**. Chapter 18, by Joan DeBardeleben, discusses the **geopolitics** of the EU. This chapter assesses the role of the EU in the world and examines a few of the large geopolitical issues dominating the EU domain over the past decades, including controversies about the relationship with Russia. The final chapter, by the three editors, returns to the three themes of this textbook and assesses what can be learned from the book on the EU's achievements and challenges in each respect.

## References and Further Reading

Bache, I., S. Bulmer, S. George, et al. 2014. *Politics in the European Union*. 4th ed. Oxford: Oxford University Press.

Brunet-Jailly, E., ed. 2007. *Borderlands: Comparing border security in North America and Europe*. Ottawa: University of Ottawa Press.

Cini, M., and N. Pérez-Solórzano Borragán, eds. 2015. *European Union politics*. 5th ed. Oxford: Oxford University Press.

Croci, O., and A. Verdun, eds. 2006. *The transatlantic divide: Foreign and security policies in the Atlantic alliance from Kosovo to Iraq*. Manchester: Manchester University Press.

Della Posta, P., M. Uvalic, and A. Verdun, eds. 2009. *Globalization, development and integration: A European perspective*. Basingstoke, UK: Palgrave Macmillan.

Dinan, D. 2014. *Europe recast: A history of European Union*. 2nd ed. Boulder, CO: Lynne Rienner.

Hosli, M., A. Kreppel, B. Plechanavová, and A. Verdun, eds. 2015. *Decision-making in the EU before and after the Lisbon Treaty*. London: Routledge.

Hurrelmann, A. 2014. "Democracy beyond the state: Some insights from the European Union." *Political Science Quarterly* 129 (1): 87–105. https://doi.org/10.1002/polq.12143.

Hurrelmann, A., A. Gora, and A. Wagner. 2015. "The politicization of European integration: More than an elite affair?" *Political Studies* 63 (1): 43–59. https://doi.org/10.1111/1467-9248.12090.

McCormick, J. 2014. *Understanding the European Union*. 6th ed. Basingstoke, UK: Palgrave Macmillan.

Norwegian Nobel Committee. 2012. "The Nobel Peace Prize for 2012. European Union." https://www.nobelprize.org/nobel_prizes/peace/laureates/2012/press.html

OECD. 2016, April. The economic consequences of Brexit: A taxing decision. *OECD Policy Paper No. 16*. http://www.oecd-ilibrary.org/economics/the-economic-consequences-of-brexit_5jm0lsvdkf6k-en.

Richardson, J., and S. Mazey, eds. 2015. *European Union: Power and policy-making*. 4th ed. London: Routledge.

Tömmel, I., and A. Verdun. 2009. *Innovative governance in the European Union: The politics of multilevel policy-making in the European Union*. Boulder, CO: Lynne Rienner.

Verdun, A. 1998. "The institutional design of EMU: A democratic deficit?" *Journal of Public Policy* 18 (2): 107–32. https://doi.org/10.1017/S0143814X98000063.

Verdun, A. 2000. *European responses to globalization and financial market integration: Perceptions of Economic and Monetary Union in Britain, France and Germany*. Basingstoke, UK: Palgrave-Macmillan. https://doi.org/10.1057/9780230535824.

Verdun, A. 2013. "Small states and the global economic crisis: An assessment." *European Political Science* 12 (3): 276–93. https://doi.org/10.1057/eps.2012.34.

Verdun, A. 2016. "The federal features of the EU: Lessons from Canada." *Politics and Governance* 4 (3): 100–10. https://doi.org/10.17645/pag.v4i3.598.

Verdun, A., and O. Croci, eds. 2005. *The European Union in the wake of eastern enlargement: Institutional and policy-making challenges*. Manchester: Manchester University Press.

Wallace, H., M. Pollack, and A. Young, eds. 2015. *Policy-making in the European Union*. 7th ed. Oxford: Oxford University Press.

Wood, D., and A. Verdun. 2011. "Canada and the European Union: A review of the literature from 1982 to 2010." *International Journal* 66 (1): 9–21. https://doi.org/10.1177/002070201106600102.

## Note

1    The EU itself, as well as some of its key institutions, have changed their names in the course of the European integration process. In order to keep matters simple, this introduction consistently uses current terminology, even when referring to a time period in which another term was used. Subsequent chapters provide more details on the changes in terminology over time.

PART I

# Integration and Governance

## Introduction to Part I

THE EUROPEAN UNION IS A UNIQUE ORGANIZATION WITHIN the international system. In 1985, Jacques Delors, the president of the **European Commission** at the time, called it an "unidentified political object." Its defining characteristic is the mixture of **intergovernmental** and **supranational** features. An organization is *intergovernmental* if decisions are controlled by the governments of the organization's member states and usually require unanimous approval by all of them. The EU has important intergovernmental features. The member states are the "masters of the treaties": all changes to the EU treaties must be approved and ratified by each of them. In addition, the member states are involved in every important legislative and executive decision at the EU level, control the EU's finances, and fulfill the crucial role of implementing EU law. However, at the same time the EU also has *supranational* features—aspects of its functioning that cannot be fully controlled by the member states. The EU has institutions of its own, which speak for the EU as a whole rather than for the individual member states, and its decisions are often taken through procedures in which all member states have representatives but a minority of states may be outvoted.

These processes of decision-making in the EU require that different institutions play different roles. The EU's main intergovernmental institutions—which fulfill different functions despite their similar-sounding names—are the **European Council** and the **Council of the EU**. A number of times a year, member state leaders meet in the European Council to decide the broad policy objectives of the EU. The other body, the Council of the EU (or "Council" for short), is one of the EU's two main legislative bodies, in which ministers from all member state governments meet to discuss and agree on proposed EU legislation. The usual procedure is such that the Council may make its decisions using a **qualified majority voting (QMV)** rule, where individual member states can be overruled. Nevertheless, the Council normally seeks to find consensus to please as many member states as possible.

In addition to the QMV rule, the EU also stands out from other international organizations because of the high importance attached to its supranational institutions. Such institutions are designed to give a collective voice to broader EU interests rather than to the sum of the interests of the individual member states. These institutions include the **European Parliament (EP)**, which is directly elected by European citizens every five years. Originally not more than a consultative institution, the EP is now the second main legislative institution of the EU, on par with the Council of the EU; the vast majority of legislative proposals must be approved by both bodies in order to become law. Another supranational institution is the European Commission, the EU's main executive and administrative actor, which oversees the implementation of EU law but, importantly, also has the unique power to initiate legislative proposals. Those working at the Commission all vow to serve the interests of the EU as a whole, *not* the interests of the member states to whom they belong, and to execute EU decisions, rules, and laws. The Commission is therefore also referred to as the "guardian of the treaties." The Court of Justice works in a similar way. Although judges and advocates-general are nominated by member states, when they assume office, they vow to support the EU as a whole and, specifically, to uphold the treaties. In so doing, they will not seek to be an advocate of any particular member state. Another supranational institution is the **European Central Bank**. The members of its governing board also represent the member states, but here again the ECB's goal is to protect the interests of the EU and to execute its mandate, which is to protect price stability and, notwithstanding that primary mandate, also ensure that the economic interests of the EU as a whole are safeguarded.

In this first part we introduce the EU system. As will become clear, the EU has developed very specific institutions that offer a governance system that in many ways is similar—but not identical—to an "ordinary" state (Theme 2 of this book). It has not replaced the member states, but at the same time it can make decisions that bind the member states. To clarify how the EU system works we first go over its history: where did the EU come from, and what is its driving force? We then look at the various institutional bodies, examine the legal system of the EU, and provide insights into how the EU passes legislation, and what policies are salient and why. Finally, we offer a brief overview of the theories that help us understand how the EU integration process has developed over time as well as how theorists have tried to explain which actors and mechanisms play important roles in **European integration**. When going through the chapters in this first part of the book, keep in mind that the EU has developed beyond a typical international organization but has not yet developed into a full-fledged state. Keeping in mind a comparison with Canada might make it easier to understand how the EU resembles and also differs from a state.

# 2
# A Short History of the European Union: From Rome to Lisbon

CONSTANTIN CHIRA-PASCANUT[1]

## Reader's Guide

European unification was a concept that had been advocated for centuries, but it was not until the post-1945 era that it took concrete shape. While many projects promoted idealist visions of a unified continent, the plan that laid the basis for the first European institutions was chiefly motivated by pragmatic objectives. Western European states were attracted to the idea of **European integration** for economic and political reasons. Since its inception, European cooperation has been a work in progress. This chapter focuses on how the European Union (EU) and its predecessor institutions were constructed, highlighting also the parallels with the formation of Canada.

## Introduction

What we today call the European Union (EU) is a complex construct, the result of more than half a century of cooperation between the European states. Even though the idea of establishing a united Europe had been explored in intellectual circles over the centuries, it was only after World War II that a project of this sort was implemented. While plans before 1950 envisaged the creation of a European federation, with a **supranational** government and assembly, making decisions for all of Europe, the organization established after the war had little in common with this type of political structure. Indeed, as discussed in the introductory chapter (and expressed as Theme 2 of this book), the EU is neither a full-fledged federal state, comparable to Canada or the United States, nor is it an international organization, such as the United Nations (UN). It has developed some quasi-federal characteristics, but it is best described as a unique entity governed by atypical institutions designed to ensure dialogue between its members and the functioning of the decision-making process.

The particularities of current European states were shaped over centuries. This is one of the main reasons why the construct was difficult from the beginning. Indeed, the EU has largely been a work in progress whose end goal is unclear. There have been different understandings of what the final shape of European integration could be. Some maintain that the establishment of a European federation is the end goal of European integration, while others would prefer **intergovernmental** cooperation—that is, decision-making by the governments of the member states—to advance integration gradually in specific fields. To this day, it seems that integration is walking the very fine line between these two ideas.

Not having legitimacy in its own right, the EU needed to acquire competence (power to legislate in a field) progressively, and it did so gradually but at the expense of the power of the member states. Over the years, in its different guises, the EU has extended its competence gradually. However, even within these fields the competence acquired by the EU is not always exclusive but is often shared with the member states (see Chapter 5). Transferring competence to the EU level has been the result of a process of ongoing bargaining—and with mixed results.

## European Integration: A Historical Overview

### The First Moves: The European Coal and Steel Community (1951), the European Economic Community (1957), and the European Atomic Energy Community (1957)

Throughout the centuries, Europeans have seen their territory ravaged by many conflicts. On numerous occasions, tensions between European states could not be solved diplomatically and led to war. The two world wars of the twentieth century both began in Europe, with Germany and France as the major adversaries. It is not surprising that in such a context, politicians, academics, journalists, and others sought solutions to avoid future wars and preserve peace in Europe. Given the long-standing Franco-German rivalry and the conflicts that it had generated, any ideas put forward to preserve peace in Europe would have to have a Franco-German reconciliation process at their core.

As early as the mid-eighteenth century, one of the main solutions considered in intellectual circles was the idea of a federal Europe, similar to the United States of America. This idea aimed to bind European states and to ensure dialogue between Europeans. In 1849, the French writer Victor Hugo proposed in his work *Pour les États-Unis d'Europe* the creation of a United States of Europe that would enforce dialogue between Europeans, develop a European identity, and rule out war as a means to resolve conflicts. The concept continued to appear over the next century when, at the beginning of the 1930s, two books with the same title—*The United States of Europe*—were published, one authored by a French politician, Édouard Herriot, and the other by a British civil servant, Arthur Salter.

The search for solutions intensified after World War I, which had shown that, as technology developed, the devastation of wars could be catastrophic. In the early 1920s, Count Richard Coudenhove-Kalergi established a Pan-European movement, gathering notable members (including Konrad Adenauer, Aristide Briand, Léon Blum, Albert Einstein, Sigmund Freud, Thomas Mann, and others) aiming to unify European states. The concept of a unified Europe continued to be developed in intellectual circles during the interwar period, when people such as Denis de Rougemont and Dusan Sidjanski argued for the federalization of Europe. In his *Vingt-huit siècles d'Europe*, de Rougemont argued that the concept of Europe was older than that of the nation-state. This intellectual effervescence did not remain without effect. In 1930, former French prime minister Aristide Briand proposed a plan to federate Europe under the umbrella of the League of Nations.

Since none of these ideas had been brought to fruition, the search for ideas on how to bring together European states continued during and after World War II. The first prominent move after the war, a mammoth congress in The Hague in May 1948, organized by European movements and chaired by Winston Churchill, achieved little to advance the federalist cause. Its main outcome was the establishment in May 1949 of a consultative assembly, the **Council of Europe**—an international organization that continues to exist but is institutionally unrelated to the current EU.

It was an idea more concrete and limited in scope that laid down the foundations of the first supranational European organization. In the late 1940s, a French businessman, Jean Monnet, drafted a plan focusing on economic cooperation of participating states in two key sectors of the postwar Western European economy, namely coal and steel. This plan had very little in common with the previous federalist projects postulated in intellectual and political circles. As spelled out in the introductory chapter, Monnet's plan was to secure peace in Europe by locking European states into a system of ever more extensive economic interactions (Theme 1 of this book). This project embodied Monnet's preoccupation with finding a concrete solution in order to ensure Franco-German reconciliation. During the war, he served as a member of the French National Liberation Committee (Charles de Gaulle's French government-in-exile in Algiers); he declared in 1943 that the only solution for finding peace in Europe was a European federation.

To explain Monnet's approach, one must consider his personality, experience, and world view. A businessman and a financier, never elected to public office, Monnet (1888–1979) was a pragmatic individual. The son of a famous

French cognac producer, he gave up university studies for more concrete endeavours—learning the art of business. In 1919, at the age of 31, he was appointed deputy secretary general of the League of Nations. Four years later he returned to his family business. As a result of wholesale trade of his brandy in the United States and Canada, he had established contacts with key players in the New World. According to Trygve Ugland (2011), while in Canada, Monnet was impressed by the Canadian federal system and considered it a possible model for a future federation in Europe. The economic benefits as well as the optimism of such an ethnically diverse people were the main features that caught his attention.

In the following years, he became involved in financial transactions in both Washington and New York. Owing to his extensive contacts, governments called upon him to conduct key missions, such as facilitating the purchase of war supplies from the United States by the United Kingdom in August 1940. After World War II, he was put in charge of preparing and implementing a plan for postwar reconstruction and modernization of the French economy. It was in this position that, in early 1950, he drafted his plan to pool French and German coal and steel production.

As somebody outside the political establishment, Monnet realized that he lacked the key political backing for his idea, without which his plan did not stand a chance of being accepted. At the beginning of May 1950, he secured the support of the French foreign minister, Robert Schuman, who was ready to take on the plan. Schuman had a personal interest in Franco-German reconciliation. Born a German citizen, he became a French citizen after the region in which he lived (Alsace-Lorraine) changed hands in 1919. Yet this was not the only reason why the politician agreed to offer political backing to Monnet's idea. As French foreign minister, Schuman was under a lot of pressure to propose a practical solution to ease the Franco-German relationship. The postwar policy toward West Germany, which offered a number of advantages to France, was going to be revised. Schuman was aware that the future Allied Conference, scheduled for May 10, 1950, was the deadline for France to come up with a constructive proposal for reconciling its relationship with Germany. In this context, the French minister welcomed Monnet's proposal, as it offered a response to the political deadlock. In addition, Monnet had the backing of influential US friends who held key positions in the post-1945 era, namely John J. McCloy (the American High Commissioner for Germany, arguably the most influential player in Germany) and Dean Acheson (the American secretary of state).

Monnet's idea, embodied in the **Schuman Plan**, was made public by the French foreign minister on May 9, 1950, and subsequently became the basis for negotiations on a future treaty between the representatives of six Western

European states (France, West Germany, Italy, Belgium, the Netherlands, and Luxembourg). Political, economic, and security concerns of the participant states shaped the negotiations. French representatives were concerned about their country's security as well as the defence of its economic interests. To a large extent, France's economy depended on the availability of German coal on advantageous terms. In addition to regaining control of their country's coal resources, West Germany's representatives aimed to restore their country's status in the international arena. Italian, Belgian, Dutch, and Luxembourgish representatives also adopted a realist approach, pursuing political and economic objectives.

The proposed institutional design was innovative and had little in common with those suggested by previous plans. It underlined the importance of establishing a High Authority, made up of independent experts, whose decisions would bind the participating states. Although the plan did not foresee any governmental involvement, at the end of the negotiations a Council of Ministers was to be established. Therefore, the High Authority was to become the guardian of the supranational principle, while the Council of Ministers safeguarded of the interests of national governments. The **Cold War** and the onset of the Korean War accelerated the conclusion of the negotiations under the patronage of the United States, which wanted to have a strong regional alliance in Western Europe. As a result, the Treaty establishing the **European Coal and Steel Community (ECSC)** was signed in Paris in 1951 (see Box 2.1).

In that context, the United States insisted on West German rearmament. Using the model of the ECSC, Jean Monnet proposed the establishment of a **European Defence Community (EDC)** aimed at containing any possible future rearmament of West Germany and at preventing it from becoming a North Atlantic Treaty Organization (NATO) member. Based on the example of his previous project, Jean Monnet sought political backing for his proposal, referring this time to the French premier and former defence minister, René Pleven. The project was designed to include the original ECSC member states. The draft treaty explicitly mentioned that the EDC was going to be supranational in character, with joint institutions, armed forces, and a budget. Underlining that its objectives were exclusively defensive, the projected EDC duplicated in some respects NATO's role, stating explicitly the common defence clause. Although the EDC treaty was signed in 1952, it was eventually rejected by the French National Assembly in 1954.

With the failure of the EDC, European integration in the mid-1950s seemed to have reached a deadlock. Those who believed that integration in the coal and steel sectors would spill over and stimulate the integration of other economic segments saw their hopes evaporating. Moreover, it seemed that economic cooperation would not spur political cooperation. It

**Box 2.1**   The European Coal and Steel Community (ECSC)

The 1951 Treaty of Paris established the ECSC on the basis of a proposal of the French foreign minister, Robert Schuman (May 9, 1950). The originator of the proposal was Jean Monnet. The founding member states were France, West Germany, Italy, Belgium, the Netherlands, and Luxembourg. It aimed to prevent war within Europe through regional integration of two chief economic sectors after the war. Coal and steel were primary resources for wars. By aiming to regulate and oversee the production of coal and steel at the Western European level and chiefly by involving West Germany and France, the organization sought to limit the possibilities of the signatories to wage war.

   Institutions:

- High Authority (the future **European Commission**), representing the supranational aspect of the organization, included nine members who were supposed to be independent and not represent their countries' interests. It exercised an executive role.
- The Council of Ministers, representing the intergovernmental aspect of the organization, included representatives of member states' governments. Its role was to scrutinize the HA. The presidency rotated between member states.
- The Common Assembly (now the European Parliament) included 78 representatives. Until 1979, when the first elections at the European level were organized, its representatives were elected by national parliaments. Its role was to monitor the HA, which it had the power to dismiss.
- The Court of Justice (seven judges) oversaw the application of ECSC law and its interpretation.
- The European Economic and Social Committee (30–50 members) was created in order to bring the input of professional associations (employers, employees, and other interests) in the decision-making process.

   The ECSC Treaty was valid for 50 years. Therefore, the ECSC ceased to exist in 2002, when its activities were transferred to the European Community.

was in this context that the foreign ministers of the six member states met in Messina, Italy, in June 1955 to discuss a program designed to revive European integration. Monnet took advantage of the moment and highlighted the importance of atomic energy to further European integration. At the same time, the Benelux countries came up with a plan that would expand integration aimed at creating a common European market.

Indeed, the Messina Conference provided a new impetus and, as a result, in 1957 two new treaties were signed in Rome: the Treaty establishing the **European Economic Community (EEC)** and the Treaty establishing **Euratom** (the **European Atomic Energy Community)**. The **Treaty of Rome** entered into force on January 1, 1958.[2] In addition to the establishment of a **Common Market** and an atomic energy community, it formalized a series of common policies, such as the **Common Agricultural Policy (CAP)** and the **Common Commercial Policy (CCP)**. Furthermore, the Treaty of Rome opened up the possibility of extending European competence to other policy fields. As a result, in the early 1970s the Community was allowed to take action in additional fields, including environmental, regional, social, and industrial policy (see Chapters 10, 12, 13).

## The 1960s: A Decade of Mixed Results

The 1960s showed that member states and their domestic interests could seriously impede European integration. Arguably the best examples of this were French President Charles de Gaulle's political moves with respect to the EEC. Despite the fact that France was one of the most important food producers in Europe, its prices were not competitive on the food market. By contrast, West Germany was a large importer of agricultural products. De Gaulle saw this situation as an opportunity to promote domestic interests and to use the EEC to strengthen the French economy. Therefore, during the negotiations on the implementation of the EEC Treaty, de Gaulle pushed for the establishment of a mechanism that would create a market for French agricultural products. At the beginning of 1962, a Common Market for agricultural products was established. The **Common Agricultural Policy (CAP)** ensured not only preference for Community agricultural products but also created a subsidy mechanism that encouraged production and export while protecting the European Community market from lower-priced products. As France was the main agricultural producer in the EEC, it was the one with the most to gain (see Chapter 11 for more details).

De Gaulle's bargaining continued in the years that followed, when he even threatened the whole edifice. According to the 1962 agreement, the CAP was to be revisited by the mid-1960s. This time de Gaulle expected the Community budget to subsidize further agricultural production. How-ever, as he did not get what he expected during the negotiations, he made use of French bargaining power. Also, he felt that France would lose its influence in the EEC once **qualified majority voting (QMV)** was introduced, offer-ing weighted votes to each member state according to its population size. QMV would be the dominant voting mode as of January 1966, in accordance with the EEC Treaty. Until then **unanimity** had been the only voting mechanism used at the EEC level. Indeed, France wanted to maintain the right to use its veto power to preserve its interests (for example, in the field of agriculture).

In this context the French president triggered one of the most serious crises ever faced by the EEC. France withdrew its representatives from the EEC in June 1965 and paralyzed the organization for about half a year. This period, referred to as the Empty Chair Crisis, lasted until January 1966, when the member states managed to find a satisfactory compromise for France: QMV would apply, but a member state could veto a decision if it felt that very important national interests were at stake (a solution known as the Luxembourg Compromise).

Agricultural concerns were at the core of EEC negotiations in the 1960s. Once again, they played a key part in de Gaulle's decision on two occasions (1963 and 1967) to veto Britain's application to join the EEC. He feared that Britain would favour Commonwealth agricultural products and would threaten the CAP, which principally served French interests. De Gaulle's use of unilateral policy as a bargaining tool in international negotiations demon-strates that the domestic preferences of EEC member states have had a major influence in shaping European integration (see Box 2.2).

## The 1970s: Facing Economic Crisis

As the 1960s drew to a close, new objectives were set for the EEC. The summit of The Hague (1969) defined the Community's primary objectives: further membership expansion and the establishment of an **Economic and Monetary Union (EMU)** (see Chapters 7 and 15). While the first was achieved in 1973, when the United Kingdom, Ireland, and Denmark joined (facilitated by de Gaulle's retirement in 1969), the outcomes of efforts to achieve the EMU were more modest.

Many saw the need for a common European monetary policy as an una-voidable consequence of the Common Market. For this purpose, the Coun-cil of Ministers appointed a committee headed by Pierre Werner (the prime minister and finance minister of Luxembourg), whose task was to draw up a plan for the establishment of EMU. The Werner group completed its work in the fall of 1970 and issued a plan that aimed at establishing the EMU in successive stages by 1980.

**Box 2.2**    The Empty Chair Crisis

The Empty Chair Crisis had its origin in two developments at the EEC level:

- The 1965 Hallstein Commission proposal to increase Commission's role as well as to enhance the European Parliament's budgetary powers with a view to developing the Communities' own financial resources.
- The upcoming third stage of the transitional period for the establishment of the Common Market (beginning in January 1966), which involved the application of QMV in the Council of Ministers.

This development worried de Gaulle, who feared that the CAP might be reformed against France's interests if it could no longer be protected by unanimous voting. As a compromise could not be reached, France withdrew its representative in the Council meetings on July 1, 1965, and refused to participate in Council's work, thus paralyzing decision-making at the EEC level.

After half a year of stalemate, the French government agreed to resume negotiations. In January 1966, Luxembourg's premier proposed a compromise. According to the proposal, should a member state feel that its vital national interests might be adversely affected, negotiations had to continue until all parties accepted the solution. In practice, this meant that member states could invoke the concept of vital national interests in order to block decisions in the Council. This practice remained in place until the conclusion of the Single European Act (SEA) in the 1980s.

However, the worsening international environment, marked by the onset of the oil crisis, drove the EEC member states' economies into recession. As a result, the main objectives of EEC member states became the stabilization of national currencies and financial discipline. In the first stage, member states tried to counter inflation by imposing limits on how much national currencies could fluctuate when pegged against each other (the "snake"). As this system failed to achieve its aims, it was abandoned in 1976 and replaced by the European Monetary System (EMS) in 1979. This mechanism maintained the fluctuation margins of national currencies (maximum ± 2.25 per cent for most currencies; ± 6 per cent for the weaker currencies, such as the Italian lira) but introduced a new reference—the European Currency Unit (ECU), a basket of the EEC member states' currencies. In the end, all attempts in this decade to create economic and monetary unification failed, and the EMU plans were eventually abandoned by the late 1980s.

## The 1980s and the 1990s: European Integration Reloaded

The deadlock of the 1970s was followed by an unprecedented advance of European integration driven by supranational institutions and bodies such as the Commission or the European Court of Justice (now **Court of Justice of the EU**). The recurring meetings of the heads of state and governments called "Summits" or "European Councils" gave the first impetus for this revival. In 1984 (Fontainebleau), European leaders reached an agreement on pending financial issues such as CAP spending and the British contribution to the EEC budget (Britain complained about not benefiting from the CAP and obtained a rebate). The Milan Summit (1985) paved the way for the first revision of the EEC Treaty. The Single European Act (SEA), signed in 1986, represented a major reinforcement of supranational institutions. The introduction of new decision-making procedures and the expansion of QMV made it more difficult for states to veto decisions. This feature became increasingly important as the number of member states increased (Greece became a member in 1981, Spain and Portugal in 1986). In addition, this treaty extended EEC competence to new policy fields, including social policy, research, and the environment.

The SEA was the result of extensive treaty reform preparations and negotiations, not only within the intergovernmental conference charged with the revision of the treaty but also during the first years of the Delors Commission. Jacques Delors, a French political leader who left a profound mark on European integration, became president of the Commission in January 1985. Only months after taking office, in June 1985, the Delors Commission published a key document, namely a white paper titled "Completing the Internal Market," aiming to achieve the creation of a **Single Market** by abolishing all physical, technical, and tax barriers in the Community. The SEA took on the content of this paper and provided the instruments for completing, as suggested in the 1985 document, the Single Market by the end of 1992.

The successful implementation of the Single Market project made the Delors Commission, and especially its president, more prone to undertaking bold decisions that moved European integration forward. For instance, at the request of the June 1988 **European Council**, an expert group of mostly central bank presidents headed by Delors issued a report that proposed the establishment of the EMU in three stages (between July 1, 1990, and January 1, 2002), ending with the introduction of the euro banknotes and coins

(Delors Report, 1989). The objective of establishing the EMU was incorporated into the **Maastricht Treaty** (1992).

The other objectives listed in this new treaty were to further expand EU competence especially in foreign and security policy (see Chapter 9) as well as **Justice and Home Affairs (JHA)** (see Chapter 8)—two areas considered particularly important for member state **sovereignty**—and to make decision-making easier and less time consuming. The price paid was high, since the reformed organization—now called the European Union—was divided into three "**pillars**" (see Table 2.1).

The creation of this system was the result of a compromise between states that wanted to give new powers to the EU and those reluctant to surrender national power in areas considered highly sensitive, such as **foreign policy**, security, or justice. The arrangement created an intergovernmental side of the EU, grouping on the one hand policies such as asylum, immigration, and judicial cooperation in civil and criminal matters and on the other hand foreign and security policy. Within the new arrangement, the Commission remained the leading body in Pillar I, while in the other two pillars the foremost institution was the Council of Ministers with the Commission, the **European Parliament (EP)**, and the European Court of Justice (ECJ) having much more limited powers.

The next revision of the treaties, namely the Treaty of Amsterdam (1997), further consolidated the powers of the supranational institutions such as the Commission, the EP, and the ECJ. This treaty not only extended the co-decision procedure (a legislative procedure that placed the Council and the Parliament on an equal footing, now called the **ordinary legislative procedure [OLP]**) but also made it more efficient by reducing its time span. Furthermore, it transferred most areas of the JHA pillar (such as asylum and immigration) into Pillar I and communitarized them (made them subject to supranational institutions) after a period of five years.

## The EU at the Beginning of the New Century

The integration trend, characterized by the expansion of the EU's areas of competence, continued throughout the last decade of the twentieth century and the beginning of the twenty-first century. Most of the period was marked by an unprecedented expansion of the EU borders. The demise of communism in Central and Eastern Europe represented not only an opportunity for the EU but, in many respects, was seen as an event which gave rise to a moral obligation to reunify Europe. Three previously neutral states—Austria, Sweden, and Finland—joined the EU in 1995. The following **enlargements**, which almost doubled the number of member states, had to be rigorously prepared for in advance (in 2004 the Czech Republic,

**Table 2.1**    The three EU pillars established in the Maastricht Treaty

| Pillar I<br>European<br>Communities: ECSC,<br>EEC, Euratom<br>(Community<br>integration method) | Pillar II<br>Common Foreign and<br>Security Policy<br>(intergovernmental<br>cooperation) | Pillar III<br>Justice and Home Affairs<br>(intergovernmental<br>cooperation) |
|---|---|---|
| • Common Market | • Foreign policy | • Asylum, immigration, and crossing of external borders |
| • **Customs Union** | • Coordinated position on international crises | • Combating drug addiction, fraud, and international crime |
| • Economic and Monetary Union | • Respect for the obligations of member states toward NATO | • Judicial cooperation in civil and criminal matters |
| • Competition | | • Customs cooperation |
| • Common Agricultural Policy | | • Police cooperation (**Europol**) |
| • Common Fisheries Policy | | |
| • Trans-European Networks | | |
| • Industrial policy | | |
| • Education and vocational training | | |
| • Youth | | |
| • Culture | | |
| • Environment | | |
| • Social policy | | |
| • Public health | | |
| • Consumer protection | | |
| • Nuclear power | | |
| • Energy | | |

Source: Centre Virtuel de la Connaissance sur l'Europe (http://www.cvce.eu/en/education/unit-content/-/unit/4b1b60b1-b97f-4d63-97f9-cbf26f66aa06/f3ec8cc7-560b-489a-a4af-281fde11e9ac/Resources#37b4b8c8-0f00-4c1c-bec8-bcdf4b26807d).

Poland, Hungary, Slovenia, Slovakia, Estonia, Latvia, Lithuania, Malta, and Cyprus became members; and in 2007 Romania and Bulgaria joined). In sum, all through the 1990s the EU leaders looked for ways to adapt the institutional mechanism to an enlarged EU (see Chapter 15).

Because the Amsterdam Treaty failed to a large extent to address this matter, enlargement continued to remain on the EU agenda at the beginning of the new century. In 2001, the Treaty of Nice clarified many details and paved the way for the accession of new member states. Also, this new treaty modification was taken as an opportunity to broaden EU competences and the powers of supranational institutions. The co-decision procedure, one of the main tools of supranational bodies, was extended to new areas at the expense of the member states' power. One of the main beneficiaries of this was the European Parliament, which saw its powers increasing. However, while this treaty provided the framework for the functioning of an enlarged EU, it fell short when it came to the simplification of the EU machinery. The overcomplicated three-pillar structure was maintained, together with the **opt-out** system (where some states obtained the right not to participate in certain policy areas). For example, the United Kingdom and Denmark preserved their right to decide when to adopt the euro, while all other states were obliged to join the **Euro Area** once they met the so-called **convergence criteria**.

The ink was barely dry on the text of the treaty when EU leaders adopted a declaration on the future of the EU (Laeken Declaration, December 15, 2001), which listed the simplification of the treaties as a paramount objective. The European Convention, convened to draw up a new treaty modification, addressed this issue. It crafted an agreement, officially called the Treaty Establishing a Constitution for Europe or, more colloquially, the European Constitutional Treaty, which aimed to achieve a comprehensive treaty revision by replacing the ECSC, EEC, and Euratom treaties with a consolidated and simplified text that gave up some of the complicated constructs such as the pillars. It integrated the Charter of Fundamental Rights of the European Union within its text, making its principles of fundamental rights mandatory for the EU member states, and introduced a number of EU symbols, such as the anthem and flag.

Despite the fact that the heads of state or governments of all EU member states had signed the European Constitutional Treaty on October 29, 2004, it could enter into force only after ratification by all EU member states' parliaments, which could be done after a national parliamentary vote and in some cases a national referendum (depending on member states' legal systems). Some states are obliged to put this kind of treaty to a referendum (Ireland, for instance), but the governments of other states chose to consult their citizens (for example, France and the Netherlands). As the French and Dutch people voted against the adoption of the Constitutional Treaty in May 2005, the ratification process was postponed in other countries. In the end, the Constitutional Treaty was never ratified.

After this outcome and a period of reflection on future steps, in mid-2007 European leaders decided to abandon the constitutional path and turn back to the more secure strategy of treaty amending. Following the subsequent negotiations, the **Lisbon Treaty** was drafted by incorporating many of the innovations of the Constitutional Treaty. What were some of these changes? The European Council and the European Central Bank became official EU institutions (see details in Chapters 3 and 7). The post of the High Representative of the Union for Foreign Affairs and Security Policy, heading the new **European External Action Service (EEAS)**, was established with the aim to give a single voice to the EU in international affairs (see Chapter 9). In an effort to address the **democratic deficit**, the treaty provided that national parliaments would be more involved in the legislative process (see Chapter 17).

The treaty reform also gave up the pillar system but preserved the intergovernmental character of the **Common Foreign and Security Policy (CFSP)**, where decisions still require unanimity. Furthermore, it expanded qualified majority voting to more policy areas, restraining the fields requiring unanimity. The Lisbon Treaty was signed in December 2007 and entered into force two years later after it was ratified by all member states. Once again, ratification was troublesome, as Irish nationals rejected the text in a first referendum. Only after Ireland had been granted a number of concessions, and following a second referendum, was the treaty ratified by Irish citizens.

## Debate: How Do Scholars Assess the Origins of European Integration?

While the creation of the European Union has some similarities with processes of state-building in federal states such as Canada, its progression and outcome are clearly unique (Box 2.3). As previously discussed, the idea of European unity had been put forward long before the first European supranational organization was created in 1951. Philosophers, politicians, and journalists had proposed plans that aimed at merging European states into some form of federation. Considering this context, one question arises: Did political ideas of unification or rational interests of the member states provide the main motivation of European integration? Two contradictory approaches have been taken in the literature of European integration to answer this question: the federalist and the state-centric schools of thought.

### The Federalist School of Thought

The first attempt to explain European integration focused on the role played by various thinkers and movements who, according to this school

**Box 2.3** Comparison with Canada

The historical process leading to the construction of the entity now called the European Union partly resembles and partly differs from that leading to the formation of Canada. One of the main differences between the EU and Canada is their respective political organization. While Canada is a federal state, the EU is a unique construct that is neither a federal state nor an international organization. The governance established in the 1950s at the ECSC/EEC/Euratom level was unique, while the Confederation of Canada had a typical federal institutional system from the outset. The 1950 ECSC plan provided for the establishment of a supranational institution, namely the High Authority, comprising independent European experts. Later, when the EEC and Euratom were created, this body became the **European Commission**. During the negotiations the initial plan was altered to create a Council of Ministers (now the **Council of the EU**) and later a Common Assembly.

Turning to the construction of the EU and Canada, in both cases a number of plans for unification were put forward. It is interesting to note that the first supranational European organization was based on economic cooperation, not political ideas of a federated Europe. Pragmatic considerations drove European states to get involved in the ECSC. Political, economic, and financial considerations convinced British colonies to attend the Charlottetown (1864), Quebec (1864), and London Conferences (1866) leading to the creation of the Confederation of Canada. External threats also played a role in both instances, namely Cold War tensions and the US doctrine of Manifest Destiny.

Increased economic cooperation constituted an important incentive in the case of both the post-1945 Western European states (the establishment of a Western European Common Market) and the colonies of British North America (the prospective inter-colony railroad across Canada). As in the case of Canada, which initially included only a few of the current provinces, the first three European Communities (ECSC, EEC, and Euratom) were established between a few European states only. The current EU, with its 28 member states, is the result of successive enlargements, just as Canada saw its borders expanding progressively. Important in this process in the case of both the EU and Canada were the high-level meetings organized at the EU level

*(continued)*

**Box 2.3**    (Continued)

between heads of state or government (European Council meetings) and the provincial-federal meetings in Canada (the First Ministers' Conferences). Held behind closed doors, the European and Canadian meetings address topical issues and help iron out differences between participants in an informal way.

While fundamentally different when it comes to institutional organization, the EU and Canada were established through processes that have a number of similarities, such as previous unsuccessful plans, initial limited membership, and successive territorial expansion, as well as pragmatic considerations motivating provinces or states to join the project.

of thought, gradually convinced statesmen that the system of nation-states was outdated and that only a federated Europe could prevent new wars between European states. These intellectuals and movements, it is claimed, contributed decisively to the process of defining the idea of European integration. In the end, according to this school of thought, the idea succeeded because policymakers had finally understood after World War II that the only solution to avoid war in Europe was to create a European federation. Therefore, the acknowledgment and endorsement of the idea by European leaders was considered the decisive factor in the postwar outcome.

The main representative of this school of thought was Walter Lipgens, who in his massive 1982 study *History of European Integration* argued that the establishment of the supranational European organization was the crowning glory of the activity of various federalist movements. By collecting an impressive amount of documents, speeches, and other information proving the devotion of the authors to the cause of European unity, Lipgens aimed to demonstrate that the creation of a supranational European entity was not a coincidence but rather the outcome of this intense ideological effort. In Lipgens' view, these protectors of the ideal of European unity, active all across Europe, kept alive its flame in times of crisis, such as World War II, until the policymakers of key powers were ready to accept it after 1945.

### State-Centric Approaches

The first, and main, challenge to the federalist view came in the early 1980s, when Alan S. Milward questioned both the origins of European cooperation and the factors that contributed to the creation of supranational European organizations. In *The Reconstruction of Western Europe* (1984), he put forward a state-centric view of the process of European integration, expanded later in *The European Rescue of the Nation-State* (1992), where he emphasized states' interests as the prime mover in European integration.

Milward also flatly contradicted the core argument of the federalists, based on the conversion of statesmen to the cause of European integration. In his view, Western European postwar cooperation was not a reaction to the weakness of the nation-state since, according to him, from 1945 on, Western Europe experienced a sustained economic boom. This phenomenon was the key, in his view, to explaining the desire for European integration, which was considered by the states' administrators as the best solution to cope with sustained economic expansion; indeed, Western European states seemed to have understood that cooperation was the only way forward in a period when large amounts of national income came from outside their national frontiers. Milward underlined that the perception that "sustained economic development required a larger market for their goods and services than that offered by the narrow confines of their national territories" (Milward, 1984, p. 492) convinced states to design a practical way to cooperate among themselves. The ECSC was going to ensure an institutionalized framework for this cooperation. As a result, the British historian does not see European integration as the product of intellectual movements or the actions of great men, assimilated to what he called *"European saints"* (Milward, 2000, p. 319). Rather, he considered integration to be the outcome of realist policies designed by national bureaucracies in response to the postwar realities.

Other studies promoting similar realist views of European integration appeared in the 1980s and the 1990s. For instance, edited volumes by Raymond Poidevin (1986) and Klaus Schwabe (1988) also adopted a state-centric approach to European integration. In the same vein, John Gillingham in his 1991 and 2003 studies considered national interests as paramount in the origins and development of European integration (Gillingham, 1991, 2003). In contrast to Milward, when examining the onset of EU integration, Gillingham assigned a key role to Monnet and the United States. Focusing mainly on the period after 1980, Gillingham painted EU history as a struggle between economic liberalism and state interventionism. He argued that "a federal Europe can be created democratically, functionally, and through the market—or not at all" (Gillingham, 2003, p. 496).

The state-centric approach was further reinforced by a study from a different academic field. In his 1998 work aimed at developing a liberal inter-governmentalist theory of European integration, political scientist Andrew Moravcsik suggested that national governments, based on a liberal model of preference formation that focused on societal actors, were the most important actors in determining the development of European Union institutions. According to him, this process of power transfer to EU institutions worked only when it served states' national interests (see Chapter 6 for more details).

When examining the question of the origins of European integration, opinions were divided in the literature. Federalists argued that European integration after 1945 succeeded because states acknowledged that integration was the only path to avoid war in Europe. Therefore, idealism contributed to keeping the idea alive until politicians finally understood the importance of European integration. While recognizing the prime role of states, realist approaches discarded idealism, highlighting instead states' realism—economic and political interests—in governments' decision to pursue European integration.

## Conclusion

The first six decades of European cooperation show that European integration was, and to a large extent still remains, a work in progress, whose final shape is unclear. The development of European cooperation shows that European integration has had little in common with the pre-1950 projects advocating a federal Europe. The plan that sketched the basis of the first European supranational organization focused on economic rather than political cooperation in two specific fields. Economics were also at the core of the EEC Treaty, whose main objective was the establishment of a Common Market. The Empty Chair Crisis and the crises of the 1970s demonstrated that European integration could be strongly influenced by the internal politics of member states and by international events.

The completion of the Single Market, the establishment of a common currency, the extension of EU competence to new fields, as well as the increase in the number of EU member states after 2000 have also been considered as significant advances in European integration. However, the failure to establish an EU constitution indicated that reforms that push the EU too much into a federal state–like direction generate considerable opposition. The last half-century has demonstrated that European integration did not and could not follow any established blueprint.

## References and Further Reading

Bitsch, M. 2001. *Histoire de la construction européenne: De la 1945 à nos jours*. 3rd ed. Charlottesville, VA: Éditions Complexe.

Desmond, D. 2006. "The historiography of European integration." In *The origins and evolution of the European Union*, edited by D. Desmond, 297–324. Oxford: Oxford University Press.

Gerbet, P. 1994. *La construction de l'Europe*. Paris: Imprimerie nationale.

Gillingham, J. 1991. *Coal, steel, and the rebirth of Europe, 1945–1955: The Germans and French from Ruhr conflict to economic community*. Cambridge: Cambridge University Press. https://doi.org/10.1017/CBO9780511583858.

Gillingham, J. 2003. *European integration, 1950–2003: Superstate or new market economy?* Cambridge: Cambridge University Press. https://doi.org/10.1017/CBO9780511610004.

Griffiths, T.R. 1986. *The Schuman plan negotiations: The economic clauses*. Brussels: European Commission Library.

Hackett, C.P., ed. 1995. *Monnet and the Americans: The father of a united Europe and his US supporters*. Washington, DC: Jean Monnet Council.

Kaiser, W., B. Leucht, and M. Rasmussen, eds. 2009. *The history of the European Union: Origins of a trans- and supranational polity 1950–72*. London: Routledge.

Lipgens, W., W. Loth, and A.S. Milward. 1982. *A history of European integration 1945–1947: The formation of the European unity movement*. Oxford: Clarendon Press.

Ludlow, P. 2010. "History aplenty: But still too isolated." In *Research agendas in EU studies: Stalking the elephant*, edited by M. Egan, N. Nugent, and W. Paterson, 14–36. Basingstoke, UK: Palgrave Macmillan. https://doi.org/10.1057/9780230279445_2.

Milward, A.S. 1984. *The reconstruction of Western Europe, 1945–51*. London: Methuen. https://doi.org/10.4324/9780203393130.

Milward, A.S. 2000. *The European rescue of the nation-state*. New York: Routledge.

Monnet, J. 1978. *Memoirs*. Translated by R. Mayne. London: Collins.

Moravcsik, A. 1998. *The choice for Europe: Social purpose and state power from Messina to Maastricht*. Ithaca, NY: Cornell University Press.

Poidevin, R. 1986. *Origins of European integration: March 1948–May 1950/Histoire des débuts de la construction européenne, mars 1948–mai 1950*. Brussels: Bruylant.

Schwabe, K. 1988. *The beginnings of the Schuman-Plan: Contributions to the Symposium in Aachen*. Baden-Baden, Germany: Nomos.

Ugland, T. 2011. *Jean Monnet and Canada: Early travels and the idea of European unity*. Toronto: University of Toronto Press.

Urwin, D.W. 1991. *The community of Europe: A history of European integration since 1945*. London: Longman.

Zorgbibe, C. 1993. *Histoire de la construction européenne*. Paris: Presses Universitaires de France.

## Review Questions

1. How was European Union constructed?

2. What are the main schools of thought regarding the history of European integration?

3. How was the first European supranational organization created?

4. To what extent have national interests influenced European integration?

## Exercises

1.  Select one EU member state and examine its relationship to the EU over time. What have been the costs and benefits of being a part of the EU for this country? What does this one country's experience tell you about the project of European integration?
2.  Select a different example of regional integration (e.g., NAFTA, ASEAN, MERCOSUR, etc.). What were the origins of this organization? Are there any parallels between the origins of the selected organization and the origins of the ECSC? What do the differences tell you about European integration?

## Notes

1   The views expressed in this paper are personal opinions of the author and do not in any way reflect those of the European Economic and Social Committee.
2   Both treaties together are often referred to as the Treaty—or Treaties—of Rome. In this book, we will consistently use the singular (Treaty of Rome) to refer to the institutional outcome of the Rome Conference.

# 3

# The Major Legislative and Executive Bodies of the European Union

FINN LAURSEN

## Reader's Guide

This chapter provides an overview of the main political institutions of the European Union (EU): the **European Parliament (EP)**, the **Council of the EU**, the **European Commission**, and the **European Council**. Legislative power in the EU is exercised by the EP and by the Council, which form a **bicameral legislature**. Yet legislation depends on a proposal from the Commission, which has the exclusive right to propose legislation. Executive power in the EU is mainly exercised by the Commission. The Council also has executive functions, especially during the implementation of legislation, as most implementation is done by the member states. The European Council, where the heads of state or government meet, sets guidelines, acts as an agenda-setter, and makes some decisions, but it does not have any immediate legislative or executive powers.

## Introduction

The European Union (EU) is in many ways a unique organization. This does not mean that it cannot be compared with other organizations. As the introductory chapter to this book spells out, the EU is less than a federal state, but more than an international organization or international regime (Theme 2 of this book; see also Wallace, 1983). In contrast to international organizations, the EU adopts legislation that is binding on citizens and businesses and the member states themselves. To adopt this legislation, the EU has a bicameral legislative system, in which both citizens and member states are represented. The citizens are represented in the EP; the member states are represented in the Council of the EU and the European Council. The EU also has an executive, the Commission, which in some ways can be compared to a government and its bureaucracy in a state, and which is clearly more than the secretariat that international organizations such as the United Nations (UN) will typically have.

In this chapter, the main legislative and executive institutions in the EU are described and analyzed. In addition to distinguishing legislative and executive functions, we also describe the composition of the main institutions, distinguishing **intergovernmental** institutions (representing the governments of the member states) from **supranational** institutions (representing the EU as a whole). Among the formal institutions covered, the Council of the EU (often shortened as "the Council") and the European Council are the intergovernmental institutions *par excellence*. Here politicians representing the member states meet, deliberate, negotiate, and make **recommendations** and decisions. The most prominent supranational institution is the European Commission (as well as the **Court of Justice of the European Union [CJEU]**, which is covered in Chapter 4). Once appointed, the Commission is formally independent and can make decisions without seeking approval from the member states. It is expected to represent the collective European interest. Since the EP also makes decisions without having to ask the member states, it too can be considered a supranational institution. However, national parties still play a role in selecting candidates for EP elections, and national governments still nominate the members of the Commission. The EU's political system is formed by intricate interactions between these bodies, and the borderline between what is intergovernmental and supranational can often be difficult to delineate (see Table 3.1).

## The European Parliament

The history of the EP goes back to the Common Assembly created for the **European Coal and Steel Community (ECSC)** in 1952 (see Chapter 2). An assembly was also created for each of the following two Communities, the **European Economic Community (EEC)** and the **European**

**Table 3.1**  The main legislative and executive bodies of the EU

|  | Function | Composition |
|---|---|---|
| **European Parliament** | Legislative | Elected parliamentarians (supranational) |
| **Council of the EU** | Legislative, some executive functions | Member state ministers (intergovernmental) |
| **European Commission** | Executive, some legislative functions | EU public servants (supranational) |
| **European Council** | Sets guidelines for legislative and executive action | Member state leaders (intergovernmental) |

**Atomic Energy Community (Euratom)** in 1958. However, it was decided in the Convention on Certain Institutions Common to the European Communities that there would be one single assembly for the three Communities. This assembly was consulted on legislation proposed by the Commission and adopted by the Council, but it could not reject or amend legislation. When it first met in 1958, it decided to call itself the European Parliamentary Assembly. In 1962 it changed its name to European Parliament (EP), a term that was formally confirmed by the Single European Act (SEA) in 1986 (see Box 3.1).

Direct elections were foreseen in the three founding treaties. The ECSC Treaty had mentioned it as a possibility (Article 20); the EEC Treaty made it an obligation (Article 138). But it was only the Paris summit in December 1974 that decided that direct elections should be arranged in the future. The first direct elections took place in June 1979. Until then, the members of the Assembly/Parliament were nominated by national parliaments from among their own members. Since 2014, the EP consists of 751 elected members. As the most populous member state, Germany has the maximum number of 96 Members of the European Parliament (MEPs). The minimum number of six MEPs goes to the member states with the smallest populations: Cyprus, Estonia, Luxembourg, and Malta. The apportionment of seats leads to a relative overrepresentation of the smaller member states (see Table 3.2). Malta has one seat per 70,000 inhabitants. Germany has one seat per 848,000 inhabitants. By giving the smaller countries relatively more seats, the EU ensures that different political views can be represented in all countries.

As mentioned, the EP started out as an advisory and consultative body in the 1950s. It could force the Commission to retire by a motion of no confidence, a power it still has. In 1980, the European Court of Justice (ECJ,

**Box 3.1**    Key roles of the European Parliament

1.  Passing laws together with the Council based on Commission proposals.
2.  Adopting the budget together with the Council.
3.  Deciding on international agreements and **enlargements**.
4.  Scrutiny of the executive institutions.
5.  Appointment and dismissal of the Commission.

Source: https://europa.eu/european-union/about-eu/institutions-bodies/european-parliament_en

**Table 3.2**  Seats in the European Parliament per member state, 2014 (total 751 seats)

| Germany | 96 |
|---|---|
| France | 74 |
| Italy | 73 |
| United Kingdom | 73 |
| Spain | 54 |
| Poland | 51 |
| Romania | 32 |
| Netherlands | 26 |
| Belgium | 21 |
| Czech Republic | 21 |
| Greece | 21 |
| Hungary | 21 |
| Portugal | 21 |
| Sweden | 20 |
| Austria | 18 |
| Bulgaria | 17 |
| Denmark | 13 |
| Finland | 13 |
| Slovakia | 13 |
| Croatia | 11 |
| Ireland | 11 |
| Lithuania | 11 |
| Latvia | 8 |
| Slovenia | 8 |
| Cyprus | 6 |
| Estonia | 6 |
| Luxembourg | 6 |
| Malta | 6 |

Source: http://europa.eu/about-eu/institutions-bodies/european-parliament/index_en.htm

now called Court of Justice of the EU) decided that the Council had to wait for the opinion of the EP where the treaties gave it the right to be consulted. The implication of this decision was that the EP could at least delay legislation, which gave the Council an interest in negotiating. The SEA then introduced the so-called cooperation procedure, which gave the EP a second reading on some legislation, especially regarding the **Single Market**. If the EP adopted an amendment at the second reading and this amendment was accepted by the Commission, then the Council could reject it only by **unanimity**. The SEA also introduced the assent procedure (now called consent procedure), which gave the EP the power to veto some legislation, especially association agreements and accession treaties. The next step in the empowerment of the EP was the introduction of the co-decision procedure by the **Maastricht Treaty**. Subsequent treaty reforms have expanded the application of this procedure, which was named the **ordinary legislative procedure (OLP)** in the Treaty of Lisbon. The Treaty of Lisbon has also put the EP on par with the Council in adopting the annual budget.

The internal organization of the EP is similar to that of national parliaments. It elects a president for two and a half years, at the beginning of and midway through its five-year term. In recent periods the two largest party groups, the European People's Party (Christian Democrats) (EPP) and the Progressive Alliance of Socialists and Democrats in the EP (S&D), have agreed to alternate the presidency between themselves. In exercising its legislative function, the EP works mostly through its 20 committees. Legislative proposals from the Commission go straight to the relevant committee, which appoints a *rapporteur* in charge of drafting a report. The draft reports are debated and voted on in the plenary, which most often accepts the committee report. EP plenary and committee meetings are public. Important meetings are attended by many stakeholders who are now eager to influence the EP's position. The plenary meets most often in Strasbourg, France. The committees, by contrast, normally meet in Brussels. Part of the secretariat is based in Luxembourg. These rather costly arrangements, which are relics from past political choices rather than budgetary rationality, are criticized by most MEPs, but defended strongly by France. Since this arrangement is mentioned in the treaty, France has a veto against moving all meetings to Brussels.

In addition to its legislative function, the EP also has a role in appointing the Commission. This role has been strengthened by recent treaty changes. The Treaty of Amsterdam (1997) gave it the right to approve the member states' nominee for president of the Commission. Since the Treaty of Lisbon (2007), the EP now "elects" the Commission president, on a proposal from the European Council. Article 17(7) of the **Treaty on European Union (TEU)** stipulates, "Taking into account the elections to the EP and after having held the appropriate consultations, the European Council, acting by a qualified majority, shall propose to the European Parliament a candidate for President of the Commission. The candidate shall be elected by the European Parliament by a majority of its component members." If the EP does not

elect the proposed candidate, the European Council has a month to come up
with another candidate. This provision was tested in the May 2014 elections,
where all the major party groups in the EP offered their candidates—known
by the German term *Spitzenkandidaten*, or "lead candidates"—for Commission president. The *Spitzenkandidat* for the European People's Party (EPP) was
Jean-Claude Juncker from Luxembourg. The candidate for the Socialists was
Martin Schulz of Germany, and the candidate for the Liberals was Guy Ver-
hofstadt from Belgium. Other parties proposed lesser-known candidates. Since
the EPP emerged as the largest group in the Parliament after the election, five
party groups decided to support Juncker's nomination. The European Council
hesitated, asking for time for to consult. Eventually, despite opposition from
the United Kingdom and Hungary, the European Council agreed formally to
nominate Juncker for the post, and he was then elected by the EP.

In the current Parliament, first elected in May 2014, eight party groups
have formed (Figure 3.1). There are also some non-attached members—
members not belonging to any political group. A political group must
have at least 25 MEPs from at least seven member states. This explains why
members from France's anti-EU Front National initially could not form
a group right after the May 2014 election, since other MEPs found them
too extreme. Later, in 2015, they did succeed in putting together the group

**Figure 3.1** Party groups in the 8th European Parliament (2014–2019), as of
December 2016

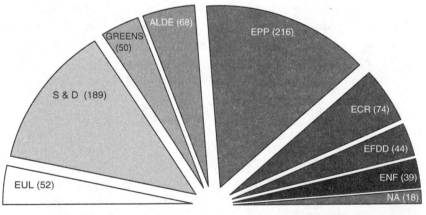

EPP: European People's Party (Christian Democrats); S&D: Progressive Alliance of Socialists and
Democrats in the European Parliament; ECR: European Conservatives and Reformists; ALDE: Al-
liance of Liberals and Democrats for Europe; EUL: Confederal Group of the European United
Left—Nordic Green Left; Greens: Greens/European Free Alliance; EFDD: Europe of Freedom and
Democracy; ENF: Europe of Nations and Freedom; NA: Non-attached members.
Source: Adapted from http://www.europarl.europa.eu/meps/en/crosstable.html

Europe of Nations and Freedom (ENF), which also includes MEPs from Italy's Northern League and the Austrian Freedom Party. The members from the other main anti-EU group, the United Kingdom Independence Party (UKIP), are in the EFDD.

Turnout at EP elections has been lower than in national elections. But worse than that, the turnout has been falling over the years (see Table 3.3). Despite the gradual empowerment of the EP, voters do not consider EP elections very important. Issues that citizens care about—jobs, health, education, and pensions—largely remain national responsibilities. Some scholars therefore have called EP elections "second-order" elections (see Chapter 17). It remains to be seen whether the increased influence of the EP in electing the Commission president will politicize the elections, giving voters the feeling that they are helping to decide who will head the next Commission (see Chapter 17 for a more detailed discussion).

## The Council of the EU

The body often referred to as the Council of Ministers officially became the Council of the EU in November 1993 after the Maastricht Treaty came into force. The treaties continue simply to call it "the Council." The Council is composed of "a representative of each Member State at the ministerial level." The purpose of this rule is to make sure that the representative can commit the member state to implement decisions. Since the Treaty of Lisbon, it is stipulated that the Council "jointly with the EP, exercise legislative and budgetary functions" (Article 16 TEU).

Originally each of the three Communities established in the 1950s had their own Council of Ministers. The Merger Treaty of 1965 brought these together. Today Council meetings take place in various (currently 10) configurations, which bring together different member state ministers, depending on their portfolios (see Box 3.2). The **General Affairs Council (GAC)** has a coordinating role. The most important Council configurations, such as the **Economic and Financial Affairs Council (ECOFIN)**, the Council of Agriculture and Fisheries Ministers, and the Foreign Affairs Council, usually meet once a month. The other Council configurations meet less frequently. In spite of its different configurations, the Council acts as one body in a legal sense. This means that any Council can vote on proposals that would normally be voted on in another configuration, which may speed up the legislative process. Since 1993, the Council meets in public when it legislates. This change was introduced to increase transparency.

Council meetings are prepared by the **Committee of Permanent Representatives (COREPER)**. It is composed of representatives of the

**Table 3.3**  EP election turnout (% eligible voters)

| | 1979 | 1981 | 1984 | 1987 | 1989 | 1994 | 1995 | 1996 | 1999 | 2004 | 2007 | 2009 | 2013 | 2014 |
|---|---|---|---|---|---|---|---|---|---|---|---|---|---|---|
| Belgium | 91 | | 92 | | 91 | 91 | | | 91 | 91 | | 90 | | 90 |
| France | 61 | | 57 | | 49 | 53 | | | 47 | 43 | | 41 | | 42 |
| Germany | 66 | | 57 | | 62 | 60 | | | 45 | 43 | | 43 | | 48 |
| Italy | 86 | | 82 | | 81 | 74 | | | 70 | 72 | | 65 | | 57 |
| Netherlands | 58 | | 51 | | 47 | 36 | | | 30 | 39 | | 37 | | 37 |
| Luxembourg | 89 | | 89 | | 87 | 99 | | | 87 | 91 | | 91 | | 86 |
| Denmark | 48 | | 52 | | 46 | 53 | | | 50 | 48 | | 60 | | 56 |
| Ireland | 64 | | 48 | | 68 | 44 | | | 50 | 59 | | 59 | | 52 |
| UK | 32 | | 33 | | 36 | 36 | | | 24 | 39 | | 35 | | 36 |
| Greece | | 81 | 81 | | 80 | 73 | | | 70 | 63 | | 53 | | 60 |
| Spain | | | | 69 | 55 | 59 | | | 63 | 45 | | 45 | | 44 |
| Portugal | | | | 74 | 51 | 36 | | | 40 | 39 | | 37 | | 34 |
| Sweden | | | | | | | 42 | | 39 | 38 | | 46 | | 51 |
| Austria | | | | | | | | 68 | 40 | 42 | | 46 | | 45 |
| Finland | | | | | | | | 58 | 30 | 39 | | 39 | | 39 |
| Cyprus | | | | | | | | | | 73 | | 50 | | 44 |
| Czech Rep. | | | | | | | | | | 28 | | 28 | | 18 |
| Estonia | | | | | | | | | | 27 | | 44 | | 37 |
| Hungary | | | | | | | | | | 39 | | 36 | | 28 |
| Latvia | | | | | | | | | | 41 | | 54 | | 30 |
| Lithuania | | | | | | | | | | 48 | | 21 | | 47 |
| Malta | | | | | | | | | | 82 | | 79 | | 75 |
| Slovakia | | | | | | | | | | 17 | | 20 | | 13 |
| Slovenia | | | | | | | | | | 28 | | 28 | | 25 |
| Poland | | | | | | | | | | 21 | | 25 | | 24 |
| Bulgaria | | | | | | | | | | | 29 | 39 | | 36 |
| Romania | | | | | | | | | | | 29 | 28 | | 32 |
| Croatia | | | | | | | | | | | | | 21 | 25 |
| **EU total** | **62** | | **59** | | **58** | **57** | | | **50** | **45** | | **43** | | **43** |

Source: http://www.europarl.europa.eu/pdf/elections_results/review.pdf

member states permanently located in Brussels. It meets in two configurations: COREPER I and COREPER II. The permanent representatives
(equivalent to ambassadors, but not called ambassadors, because that des-
ignation is associated with **diplomacy**) meet in COREPER II and their
deputies in COREPER I. COREPER II is responsible for General Affairs,

**Box 3.2**   Council configurations

General Affairs
Foreign Affairs
Economic and Financial Affairs
**Justice and Home Affairs**
Employment, Social Policy, Health, and Consumer Affairs
Competitiveness (internal market, industry, research, and space)
Transport, Telecommunications, and Energy
Agriculture and Fisheries
Environment
Education, Youth, Culture, and Sport

Source: http://www.consilium.europa.eu/en/council-eu/configurations

Foreign Affairs, Justice and Home Affairs, multiannual budget negotiations, structural and cohesion funds, institutional and horizontal questions, development policy and association agreements, accession, and intergovernmental conferences (IGCs). COREPER I is responsible for the internal market and competitiveness, conciliation under the ordinary legislative procedure, environment, employment, social policy, health and consumer affairs, transport, telecommunications, energy, fisheries, agriculture, education, youth, and culture. After receiving and deliberating legislative proposals, COREPER divides them into A and B points for the Council of Ministers. For A points, agreement is expected without debate in the Council. B points include issues where no agreement has been reached in COREPER. It will thus be up to the Council to seek an agreement.

A number of working groups of national experts, some permanent, some ad hoc, are an important part of the Council system. The Council also has a General Secretariat headed by a secretary general who can play an important role in difficult negotiations. The secretariat gives the Council a collective memory. The secretariat is housed in the Justus Lipsius building in Brussels, across from the Berlaymont building, where the Commission is based.

In the Council, the use of **qualified majority voting (QMV)** has now become the norm. This increases the efficiency of decision-making. A qualified majority is defined as "at least 55 per cent of the members of the Council, comprising at least 15 of them and representing member states comprising at least 65 per cent of the population of the Union" (Article 16[3] TEU). This new double majority system has replaced a cumbersome system of weighted votes that had existed before and where the weighting had become very controversial. There are some decisions, mostly procedural, that can be made by a simple majority; in these cases, each member state has one vote. Other decisions require unanimity, mostly those concerning **foreign policy** and defence, but also taxation issues. Abstention does not hinder unanimity. It is estimated that roughly 80 per cent of Council decisions now fall under QMV. But in reality there are relatively few votes, as a so-called culture of **consensus** leads member state representatives to seek mutually acceptable solutions whenever possible.

The presidency of the Council rotates every six months among the member states in a pre-established order. The president chairs the Council meetings, except for the Foreign Affairs Council, which is chaired by the High Representative for Foreign Affairs and Security Policy (when it does not deal with trade). The meetings are held in Brussels except in April, June, and October, when they are in Luxembourg. The Treaty of Lisbon attempted to increase cooperation between successive presidencies by creating a "trio" presidency. Three presidencies work together in 18-month periods. The pre-established order also determines the seating arrangement at the meeting table. At one end is the president, who does not vote. On his or her right side is another minister from the presidency country, who can vote, followed by representatives from the other member states, who sit around the table according to an agreed-upon order. The Commission representative sits across from the president.

The Council is a powerful body in the EU institutional setup; however, it has lost some power in recent years. One reason is that the European Council has become more important. The European Council increasingly sets the agenda and is the forum where many disputes are solved. As will be discussed later in this chapter, the Treaty of Lisbon has made it a formal institution of the EU with an elected president. Even more importantly, the EP has become a co-legislator, as well as a joint decision-maker on the budget.

Since the entry into force of the **Lisbon Treaty**, the OLP—in which the EP acts on part with the Council—has become the norm for most legislation. The OLP builds on the co-decision procedure introduced in the Maastricht Treaty, which for the first time made the EP a co-legislature for the policy areas covered (mostly the internal market at the time). The application of the co-decision procedure was successively expanded in subsequent treaty reform; the procedure was explicitly designated as the "ordinary" legislative procedure in the Treaty of Lisbon. In the OLP, a proposal for legislation from the Commission goes to both the Council and EP (see Figure 3.2). If they agree with the proposal it can be adopted after the first reading. This is where informal contacts, known as **"trilogues,"** between the Council

**Figure 3.2** Ordinary legislative procedure (OLP), simplified

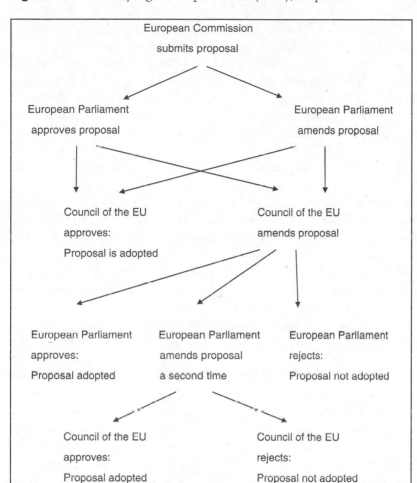

Source: Based on Art. 294 TFEU

presidency, the EP committee in charge, and the Commission may start. If trilogues do not succeed finding an agreement there will be a second reading. If there is still disagreement at that stage the conciliation procedure is initiated. Trilogues can take place throughout the different stages.

Co-decision in the OLP creates incentives for cooperation between the Council and the EP. This explains the trilogues. These have increased the efficiency of legislation but have also been criticized for limiting transparency and broader deliberation, and thus negatively affecting the democratic nature of the process. Trilogues take place in the EP and are chaired by the EP committee chair, which may give the EP some advantages logistically. The cooperation between the Council and EP has improved since the beginning of co-decision in 1993. Legislation is increasingly approved early and without conciliation. From 2004–09, nearly 70 per cent of all co-decision procedures were concluded at first reading. About 25 per cent went to a second reading, and 6 per cent went into conciliation. (In the previous legislature, 22 per cent went into conciliation.) This upward trend continued in the 2009–14 legislature, where almost 90 per cent of all legislative files under OLP were adopted at first reading.

## The European Commission

The main executive body of the EU is the European Commission. In a nation-state, it would largely be comparable to the cabinet of ministers. It dates back to the High Authority established for the ECSC in 1952. The two Communities—Euratom and the EEC—each established an executive called the Commission in 1958. In the Merger Treaty of 1965 (in force from 1967), the three executives were merged into a single Commission for the three European Communities.

The Commission consists of one commissioner per member state, so that the EU-28 today has 28 commissioners. However, the commissioners do not formally represent the member states. They are expected to promote the general interest of the Union and should be completely independent from their home state. They may not seek or take instructions from any government, which is why the Commission is considered a supranational body. Nonetheless, the member states feel that they are represented in an indirect way by someone who knows their country well. Smaller member states have often seen the Commission as a safeguard against the formation of a "directorate" of the large states.

Each commissioner has a portfolio of responsibilities. These can cut across the range of administrative **Directorates General (DGs)**. Currently there are more than 30 DGs. The College of Commissioners, comprised of the 28 commissioners, meets weekly, usually on Wednesday. Decisions can be made by a simple majority, but are usually by consensus. The commissioners and their cabinets (private staff) are housed in the Berlaymont building in Brussels, but most of the policy staff is spread out in Brussels over 70 different buildings, and some staff is in Luxembourg. In total, the Commission employs about 25,000 officials.

Since the Maastricht Treaty, the Commission has been appointed for a term of five years, which is aligned with the term of the EP. The Maastricht Treaty also made the Commission as a body subject to a vote of approval by the EP. The Treaty of Amsterdam introduced a separate earlier vote of approval of the president of the Commission. Until the Treaty of Nice (2001), appointments were by "common accord" of the member states, meaning a unanimous decision. The Treaty of Nice introduced QMV in the Council for the appointment of the Commission. The role of president of the Commission has been strengthened somewhat in recent years. The president lays down guidelines and decides the internal organization of the Commission.

As was discussed above, the Commission president is elected by the EP based on a nomination by the European Council. The president-elect together with the Council will adopt the list of proposed members of the Commission. Following that, "the President, the High Representative of the Union for Foreign Affairs and Security Policy and the other members of the Commission shall be subject as a body to a vote of consent by the EP" (Article 17[7] TEU). Before the vote, the EP holds hearings to vet Commission candidates. In the process, it has sometimes rejected candidates as unqualified, thus affirming its powers in respect to the formation of the new Commission. The EP can force the Commission to resign as a body by passing a so-called motion of censure. This has been used as a threat but so far has never been implemented. However, the voluntary resignation of the Commission in 1999, at the time presided over by Jacques Santer, probably pre-empted its use on that occasion.

The Commission has a mix of responsibilities: proposing legislation, proposing the budget and implementing it, administering policies, and making specific decisions, for instance in **competition policy**. It also negotiates agreements with third countries and represents the EU externally in economic policy matters (see Box 3.3).

**Box 3.3**   Key roles of the Council

1. Passing EU laws—jointly with the European Parliament in many policy areas.
2. Approving the EU's budget, jointly with the European Parliament.
3. Defining and implementing the EU's Common Foreign and Security Policy (CFSP) based on guidelines set by the European Council.
4. Coordinating the broad economic and social policies of the member states.
5. Concluding international agreements between the EU and other countries or international organizations.

Source: http://europa.eu/about-eu/institutions-bodies/council-eu/index_en.htm

When the Commission prepares legislative proposals it usually consults with experts as well as interest organizations and other stakeholders. Legislation in the form of **regulations** and **directives** require a proposal from the Commission before the Council and EP can adopt it. This "monopoly of initiative" allows the Commission to act both as an agenda-setter and as a gatekeeper. In the implementation of legislation, the Commission cooperates with, and monitors, the member states, whose bureaucratic agencies are usually tasked with the front-line implementation of EU laws. Since the member states play important roles in implementation, they are, in turn, represented in the Commission's activities in this respect through specialized committees (known as comitology committees). The Treaty of Lisbon introduced provisions on so-called delegated acts and implementing acts. They stipulate how the Commission, the Council, and the EP work together on implementation. The monopoly of initiative does not extend to **Common Foreign and Security Policy (CFSP)**, where the member states also have a right of initiative.

The original conception of the role of the High Authority/Commission was one of a supranational leader, which would actively articulate goals and visions, build coalitions of political actors and interest groups, exchanging concessions, engineering consent, and building support for the system. The extent to which the Commission has been able to play this role has varied over time. Recently, this leadership role has to some extent been taken over by the European Council and has thus moved from the supranational to the intergovernmental realm.

## The European Council

The European Council was created in 1974 on a proposal from the French president, Valéry Giscard d'Estaing. It is the meeting of heads of state or government, sometimes called the summit.[1] It was first mentioned explicitly in the SEA in 1986 but it has been a formal institution only since the Treaty of Lisbon. According to the current treaty, "The European Council shall provide the Union with the necessary impetus and shall define the general political directions and priorities thereof" (Article 15 TEU). The European Council has also been tasked with determining "the strategic interests and objectives of the Union" for its external action (Article 22[1] TEU). However, the European Council does not legislate. That role is left to the Council and the EP (see Box 3.4 and Box 3.5).

Problems that cannot be solved at the level of the Council sometimes end up on the agenda of the European Council. Officially the European Council now meets twice every six months, but in recent years meetings have taken

**Box 3.4**   Main tasks of the Presidency of the Council

1.   Planning and chairing meetings in the Council and its preparatory bodies. This includes efforts to drive forward the Council's work on EU legislation, ensuring cooperation among member states. To do this, the presidency tries to act as an honest and neutral broker.
2.   Representing the Council in relations with the other EU institutions. This role includes trying to reach agreement early on legislative files through so-called trilogues with the EP and Commission, as well as taking part in Conciliation Committee meetings.
3.   Working closely with the president of the European Council and the High Representative of the Union for Foreign Affairs and Security (including chairing the Foreign Affairs Council when it deals with trade issues).

Source: http://www.consilium.europa.eu/en/council-eu/presidency-council-eu/

**Box 3.5**   Key roles of the Commission

1.   Proposing legislation to the Parliament and the Council.
2.   Managing and implementing EU policies and the budget.
3.   Enforcing EU law (jointly with the Court of Justice).
4.   Representing the European Union on the international stage, for example, by negotiating agreements between the EU and other countries.

Source: http://europa.eu/about-eu/institutions-bodies/european-commission/index_en.htm

place more often. All meetings take place in Brussels. The European Council is assisted by the General Secretariat of the Council. Meetings are prepared by the COREPER and the GAC (see Box 3.6).

Until the Treaty of Lisbon, the meetings of the European Council were chaired by the rotating Council presidency. Since the entry into force of that treaty, there has been a separate, semi-permanent European Council president, first Herman van Rompuy (from Belgium) from 2009, and then Donald Tusk (from Poland) from 2014. In addition to the European Council president, the president of the European Commission and the

**Box 3.6**   Key roles of the European Council

1.  Deciding on the EU's overall direction and political priorities—but the European Council does not pass laws.
2.  Dealing with complex or sensitive issues that cannot be resolved at lower levels of intergovernmental cooperation.
3.  Defining the general guidelines for the EU's Common Foreign and Security Policy (CFSP), taking into account EU strategic interests and defence implications.
4.  Nominating and appointing candidates to certain high-profile EU-level roles, such as the presidency of the **European Central Bank (ECB)** and the Commission.

Source: http://europa.eu/about-eu/institutions-bodies/european-council/index_en.htm

High Representative of the Union for Foreign Affairs and Security Policy also take part in European Council meetings. The president of the EP is usually invited to address the European Council at the beginning, but is not a member. The secretary general of the Council takes part in the meetings.

The normal approach to decision-making in the European Council is consensus. But there are decisions that require a vote by unanimity, for instance the allocation of EP seats to the member states (which was previously determined in the treaty, but is now determined by the European Council by unanimity because of its importance). Some decisions require a simple majority; apart from rules of procedure, this includes decisions to convene or not to convene a convention to examine amendments to the treaty under the ordinary revision procedure (Article 48 TEU). Then there are decisions that require a qualified majority vote (QMV), especially appointments (Commission, High Representative, board of the European Central Bank). Decisions are communicated to the public through presidency conclusions and press conferences, not only by the president but also the national "heads," as they are usually called in Brussels.

## Debate: Efficiency, Solidarity, and Leadership

The founding fathers emphasized efficiency when they established the original Communities in the 1950s. The High Authority/Commission was supposed to play a lead role as the engine of **European integration**. Jean

Monnet's first proposal to the 1950 Paris Intergovernmental Conference, which negotiated the ECSC treaty, did not even have a Council. It did include a parliamentary assembly, but a weak one. The representatives of the Benelux countries, however, made a Council of Ministers a non-negotiable part of the initial institutional setup.

Subsequent treaties gradually increased the powers of the Council and, as we have seen, the European Council was added in 1974, first as an informal and then as a formal institution. These changes strengthened the intergovernmental institutions, arguably improving checks and balancing on the supranational Commission, but weakening it at the same time. In parallel, with some time lag, the EP started to become more of a real parliament with important budgetary and legislative powers. This empowerment of the EP has been explained by pointing to the need to provide more procedural (or input) legitimacy, as the functional scope of European integration increased and the role of national parliaments was reduced.

When the Danes first rejected the Maastricht Treaty in 1992 and the French barely accepted it in a referendum, it sparked a major debate about transparency and democracy in the EU. Several observers claimed that there was a **"democratic deficit"** (see Chapter 17). One approach to address this deficit was to include provisions on the role of national parliaments into the treaties. National parliaments are now supposed to oversee the application of the principle of subsidiarity, which prescribes that decisions must be taken at the lowest level where they can be "sufficiently achieved" (Article 5 TEU). It was argued that national parliaments, being closer to the people, were necessarily more legitimate than the EP.

However, increasing the powers of 28 national parliaments even more in the future will probably not increase the efficiency of decision-making in the EU. In reality, the EU has many decision-makers. Power is dispersed. For instance, making decisions during the **Euro Area financial crisis** was a cumbersome process, and arguably the necessary decisions to deal with the **refugee crisis** in Europe were slow to be taken because of too many national veto points.

This suggests that there is still an issue of efficiency in the current institutional set-up. It is a complex system, difficult to understand for EU citizens, and possibly even more difficult for citizens in third countries. However, the EU is a union of nation-states with long traditions of being in charge of their own affairs. Building up strong supranational institutions is therefore a difficult process. Nevertheless, many see it as necessary because of the high degree of interdependence between the European states. Therefore, there are forces that pull toward greater national autonomy, and at the same time, there are forces pulling in the direction of stronger, more efficient common institutions.

The decision-making in connection with the refugee crisis, which exploded in 2015, can serve as an example. Southern European states, Greece and Italy in particular, were overwhelmed by the number of refugees. Many of these refugees started travelling further north, especially to Germany and Scandinavia. Some countries closed their borders to refugees. The Commission stepped in and suggested reallocation schemes, according to which all member states should take certain quotas of refugees. Many member states opposed this quota system, especially the new member states in Central and Eastern Europe. It looks as if successive enlargements have made it more difficult to have sufficient solidarity among the member states to make difficult decisions (see Chapter 8 for more details).

The lack of solidarity, according to some observers, was also an issue during the Euro Area debt crisis, when the EU took very long time to agree on rescue packages for Eurozone member states at risk of bankruptcy. Richer member states worried about the conditions under which emergency financing and bailouts would take place. But the delay of decisions contributed to a worsening of the crisis, which in turn led to complaints about a lack of solidarity with the members hit hardest by that crisis, especially Greece. In the end, agreements were eventually made that, in many ways, have deepened integration.

It is exactly in crises that the EU's efficiency becomes decisive. After the June 2016 UK referendum on EU membership (**Brexit**), the other 27 members seem to have very different ideas about how to deal with the new situation (see Chapter 7 for more details). France and Italy seem to want "more Europe." Some countries, including the Central and Eastern European Countries (CEECs), seem to want "less Europe." Germany seems to be trying to be the pragmatic leader in between. Now and then we see Franco-German efforts to exercise joint leadership, which in the past has been important for European integration. The situation has become rather volatile. It is uncertain where we will end up. The fact that fewer refugees reach Europe through Turkey has eased the situation somewhat, but immigration remains a controversial issue in many of the member states.

The current crises have also tested the post-Lisbon decision-making system. The EU has many heads and leaders. It is sometimes unclear when it is the Commission and when it is the European Council that has to act. The first president of the European Council, Herman van Rompuy, played an important role in the **Euro Area financial crisis**. The current president of the European Council, Donald Tusk, has not been able to play a similar role in the refugee crisis. The Commission has tried, but it is meeting opposition from many member states. The conclusion can only be that efficient decision-making in the EU requires a high degree of solidarity as well as efficient leadership.

## Conclusion

As we have seen in this chapter, the EU's legislative and executive institutions have changed gradually over time. The Treaty of Lisbon introduced an elected president of the European Council. It also strengthened the role of the EP in the legislative process and in "electing" the president of the Commission. In legislation, co-decision has become the "ordinary legislative procedure," indicating that it is now the procedure used most often (see Figure 3.3).

With the reforms of the Lisbon Treaty, the political system of the EU has become more similar to that of a federal state like Canada—but key differences remain (see Box 3.7). In the post-Lisbon situation, we can ask whether a lasting "constitutional" settlement has been reached. There can be no doubt that EU political leaders are not eager to go into yet another relatively big treaty change, given the debacle of the Constitutional Treaty in 2005. But the question of legitimacy of the current arrangement remains. The EU keeps facing challenges. Will it succeed in solving the problems, or

**Figure 3.3** Central aspects of the EU's post-Lisbon institutional set-up

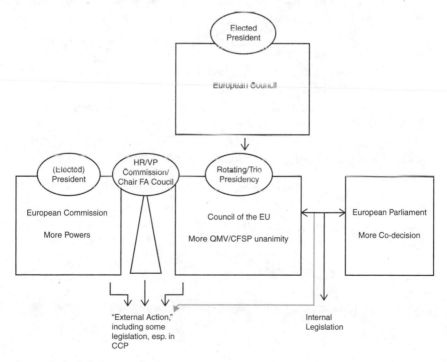

Source: Author's design

will it break up? In the latter case, will a "hard core" of states move ahead toward "an ever closer union among the peoples of Europe" (a phrase used in the treaty's preamble) and leave the laggards behind? That would increase the already considerable amount of differentiation and multi-speed integration, which may make decision-making more difficult.

Looking back, it seems fair to say that European integration has contributed to peace, security, and prosperity. The peace and security part is often taken for granted now, although events in Ukraine and the election of Donald Trump as US president have rekindled the discussion about security in Europe. An issue coming to the foreground in connection with Brexit and Trump's election is also the question of the distribution of the wealth created. Not all people feel they have benefited from open markets

**Box 3.7**   Comparison with Canada

If we compare the EU and Canada, they are both polities with legislative powers on at least two levels of governance. Both are fairly decentralized systems, but the member states in the EU play a much greater political role in decision-making at the central level than the provinces in Canada, especially because the Canadian provinces are not represented in a legislative chamber at the federal level. Executive leadership in the EU is more dispersed than in Canada, where the most powerful politician is the federal prime minister. In the EU the president of the Commission has to share the limelight with the president of the European Council and the rotating presidency of the Council. Canada has a purer parliamentary system than the EU, although the EU has been moving slightly in that direction with the EU now "electing" the president of the Commission.

|  | **The EU** | **Canada** |
|---|---|---|
| Executive leadership | The Commission is the main executive body. The president of the Commission can be compared with a prime minister in a nation-state. | The focus is clearly on the prime minister as the leading politician and head of the federal government → Focused executive leadership |

|  | The EU | Canada |
|---|---|---|
| Legislation | The president of the European Council might be seen as a kind of head of state. The rotating presidency of the Council also has executive functions → Dispersed executive leadership The EU now has a bicameral system, with both the Council and EP having legislative powers (ordinary legislative procedure). They also have equal powers in the budgetary process. (A better comparison than Canada would be the German federal system, with the directly elected *Bundestag* and the *Bundesrat*, where the 16 *Land* governments are represented, with the bigger *Länder* having more seats than the smaller ones.) | Canada does have a bicameral system (inspired by Britain), but the elected House of Commons has more powers than the appointed Senate. Bills will be considered and passed by the Senate, but only after passage by the House of Commons. The Canadian provinces do not have a legislative chamber at the federal level (which is rather exceptional for a federal system). |

Source: Compiled by author

and international trade. A turn toward more protectionism could be the next great challenge for the EU, both internally and externally.

## References and Further Reading

Best, E. 2014. *EU law-making in principle and practice.* London: Routledge.
Coombes, D.L. 1970. *Politics and bureaucracy in the European community: A portrait of the Commission of the E.E.C.* London: Allen & Unwin.
European Parliament. 2014. *Co-decision and conciliation: A guide to how the European Parliament co-legislates under the ordinary legislative procedure.* http://www.europarl.europa.eu/code/information/guide_en.pdf.
Hayes-Renshaw, F., and H. Wallace. 2006. *The Council of Ministers.* 3rd ed. Basingstoke, UK: Palgrave Macmillan.
Hayes-Renshaw, F. 2012. "The Council of Ministers." In *The institutions of the European Union,* 3rd ed., edited by J. Peterson and M. Shackleton, 68–85. Oxford: Oxford University Press.
Hix, S. 2008. *What's wrong with the European Union and how to fix it.* Cambridge: Polity Press.
Hix, S., and B.K. Høyland. 2011. *The political system of the European Union.* 3rd ed. Basingstoke, UK: Palgrave Macmillan.
Kassim, H., J. Peterson, M.W. Bauer, et al. 2013. *The European Commission of the twenty-first century.* Oxford: Oxford University Press. https://doi.org/10.1093/acprof:oso/9780199599523.001.0001.
Laursen, F. 1996. "The role of the Commission." In *The European Union: How democratic is it?* edited by S. Andersen and K. Eliassen, 119–41. London: SAGE Publications. https://doi.org/10.4135/9781446279434.n8.
Laursen, F. 2016. *Historical dictionary of the European Union.* Lanham, MD: Rowman & Littlefield.
Lelieveldt, H., and S. Princen. 2013. *The politics of the European Union.* Cambridge: Cambridge University Press.
Lindberg, L., and S. Scheingold. 1970. *Europe's would-be polity: Patterns of change in the European community.* Englewood Cliffs, NJ: Prentice-Hall.
Piris, J. 2010. *The Lisbon Treaty: A legal and political analysis.* Cambridge: Cambridge University Press. https://doi.org/10.1017/CBO9780511762529.
Puetter, U. 2014. *The European Council and the Council: New intergovernmentalism and institutional change.* Oxford: Oxford University Press. https://doi.org/10.1093/acprof:oso/9780198716242.001.0001.
Rittberger, B. 2005. *Building Europe's Parliament: Democratic representation beyond the nation-state.* Oxford: Oxford University Press. https://doi.org/10.1093/019927 3421.001.0001.
Scharpf, F. 1999. *Governing in Europe: Effective and democratic?* Oxford: Oxford University Press. https://doi.org/10.1093/acprof:oso/9780198295457.001.0001.
Shackleton, M. 2012. "The European Parliament." In *The institutions of the European Union,* 3rd ed., edited by J. Peterson and M. Shackleton, 124–47. Oxford: Oxford University Press.
Tallberg, J. 2006. *Leadership and negotiation in the European Union.* Cambridge: Cambridge University Press. https://doi.org/10.1017/CBO9780511492075.

Teasdale, A., and T. Bainbridge. 2012. *The Penguin companion to European Union*. 3rd ed. London: Penguin Books.

Wallace, W. 1983. "Less than a federation, more than a regime: The Community as a political system." In *Policy making in the European Communities*, 2nd ed., edited by H. Wallace, W. Wallace, and C. Webb, 403–36. London: John Wiley.

## Review Questions

1. What are the main legislative and executive institutions in the EU?
2. How is the Commission appointed?
3. Why do you think the turnout at EP elections has been declining?
4. Should the EU move toward a more federal system (possibly more like the Canadian system), or are there better models for the EU? Or should the system become more multi-speed or "differentiated"?

## Exercises

1. Do some research on the history of unanimous voting versus QMV in the Council. What are the strengths and weaknesses of using QMV? Draw a parallel to a familiar group setting in your own life (classroom, work setting, campus organization), and discuss: when should efficiency be prioritized, and when should representation be prioritized?
2. Compare the European Parliament to the Canadian House of Commons. What are the main similarities and differences? How does this translate to the idea of the EU being a quasi-federation?

## Note

1  Notice the word "or." Most countries send their prime minister (head of government), the federal chancellor in the case of Germany, but a few, especially France, send their president (head of state). The European Council should not be confused with the **Council of Europe**, a weaker intergovernmental organization created in 1949. Nor should it simply be called Council; that term is used to refer to the Council of the EU.

# 4

# Legal Integration and the Court of Justice of the European Union

MARTHA O'BRIEN

## Reader's Guide

This chapter is an introduction to the legal foundations of the European Union (EU), the EU's legislative and judicial methods for achieving legal integration, and the role of the **Court of Justice of the European Union (CJEU)** in the creation of the EU's legal system. The EU is recognized as having evolved its own legal system, unique among legal systems in the world, through which the national (and sub-national) laws of the member states are integrated with Union law. The body of law governing the EU and its member states and peoples is called the *acquis communautaire*. This chapter describes the sources of EU law, the types of EU legislation, and the role of the CJEU in interpreting and applying EU law.

## Introduction

The process of creating first a **Common Market** and later a union of member states and peoples is economic, political and, above all, legal. It can be argued that the progressive integration that has created the EU has always depended on legal evolution, both through legislative and judicial advances, as well as political impetus. The original treaties of the 1950s were broadly drafted and left many open questions as to how to attain their objectives. The creation of the EU of today depended not only on political will but also on a purposive judicial interpretation of the treaties and the legislation adopted by the institutions that could be enforced as law. Other efforts by neighbouring countries toward free trade and greater economic integration, such as in North America (NAFTA), East Asia (ASEAN), and South America (MERCOSUR) have not achieved anything resembling the degree of economic, political, and legal integration of the EU, at least in part because their objectives either did not include legal and judicial integration, or the political will to implement such a degree of integration was lacking. We can therefore ask what role the types of legal instruments and fundamental judicial decisions have played in advancing legal integration. Are there any specific points in the EU's legal history that can be seen as critical to the system that is in place today? How does legal evolution affect and respond to political context and events?

## Primary Law: The Treaties

The European Union is founded on two multilateral international conventions, the **Treaty on European Union (TEU)** and the **Treaty on the Functioning of the European Union (TFEU)**. The EU is therefore a creation of international law, and its actions and decisions are governed by and subject to the rule of law. The TEU and TFEU are the current names for the founding treaties as they have been added to and amended over the years since the original Treaty of Paris was agreed upon in 1951 (see Table 4.1).

The treaties play the role of a constitution for the EU, even though they are theoretically distinct from a constitution of a sovereign state. The treaties are the supreme law of the EU. This means that any action by either EU institutions or member states that is inconsistent with the treaties is in principle illegal and can be declared ineffective by the EU courts. The treaties lay out the fundamental principles of EU law. An example of an important EU legal principle is found in Article 5 TEU which establishes the "principle of conferral" (see Box 4.1). This principle—meaning that the EU cannot determine its own competences, but can exercise only powers explicitly delegated by the member states—is one of the factors that distinguishes the EU from a state (Theme 2 of this book).

**Table 4.1**    Development of EU primary law

| Agreement name, date | Result for primary law, entry into force |
|---|---|
| Treaty of Paris, 1951 | Created the **European Coal and Steel Community (ECSC)**, 1952 (lapsed 2002) |
| **Treaty of Rome**, 1957 | Created the **European Economic Community (EEC)** and the **European Atomic Energy Community (Euratom)**, 1958 |
| Single European Act, 1985 | Amended the EEC Treaty, 1987 |
| Treaty of Maastricht, 1992 | Created the Treaty on European Union (TEU); amended the EEC Treaty, renaming it the Treaty Establishing the European Community or TEC (EEC was renamed European Community or EC), 1993 |
| Treaty of Amsterdam, 1997 | Amended the TEC and the TEU, 1999 |
| Treaty of Nice, 2000 | Amended the TEU and the TEC, 2003 |
| Treaty of Lisbon, 2007 | Amended the TEU; amended the TEC and renamed it the Treaty on the Functioning of the European Union (TFEU); Charter of Fundamental Rights of the European Union brought into force, 2009 |

**Box 4.1**   The principle of conferral

**Article 5 TEU**

1.   The limits of Union competences are governed by the principle of conferral. The use of Union competences is governed by the principles of subsidiarity and proportionality.
2.   Under the principle of conferral, the Union shall act only within the limits of the competences conferred upon it by the Member States in the Treaties to attain the objectives set out therein. Competences not conferred upon the Union in the Treaties remain with the member states.

Also of great importance is the Charter of Fundamental Rights of the EU, which is of equal legal force with the treaties and which became part of the legal structure of the Union with the Treaty of Lisbon. However, long before the Charter was adopted, the Court of Justice of the EU (CJEU) had recognized certain general principles of EU law that protected fundamental human rights within the Union. For example, the CJEU acknowledged that the EU recognized the principle of equality and a general prohibition of discrimination at an early stage of the development of EU law. The role of the CJEU in developing a body of distinct EU law is examined in this chapter.

## Secondary Law: Acts of the EU Institutions

One of the innovative features of the EU, which distinguishes it from other international organizations such as the **World Trade Organization (WTO)** or the United Nations (UN), is that it has its own legislative institutions, empowered to adopt legislative "acts" (what we would call statutes or regulations in Canada), which directly or indirectly constitute enforceable law in the member states. The primary legislative institutions of the EU are the Commission, the **Council,** and the **European Parliament**. The main types of legislative act are provided for in Article 288 TFEU (see Box 4.2). Chapter 3 of this textbook describes in more detail the legislative procedures to be followed by the EU legislative institutions.

**Regulations** are "directly applicable." This means that from the time they come into force they are automatically enforceable law in the legal systems of the member states and do not need to be transposed. The national courts must apply a regulation as if it were part of the national law. The

**Box 4.2**   Types of EU legislative acts

**Article 288 TFEU**

To exercise the Union's competences, the institutions shall adopt regulations, directives, decisions, recommendations and opinions.

A regulation shall have general application. It shall be binding in its entirety and directly applicable in all Member States.

A directive shall be binding, as to the result to be achieved, upon each Member State to which it is addressed, but shall leave to the national authorities the choice of form and methods.

A decision shall be binding in its entirety. A decision that specifies those to whom it is addressed shall be binding only on them.

Recommendations and opinions shall have no binding force.

legislatures of the member states do not have to act to bring regulations into force on their territory; indeed, they are forbidden to do so. Legislation in force in a member state that is inconsistent with an EU regulation must be repealed. Regulations are commonly used for technical changes to existing policies, such as changes to prices or quotas under the **Common Agricultural Policy (CAP)**, but have also been used to put in place basic common rules for creating the **Single Market**, or to impose new rules and standards in any policy area (see Box 4.3 for an example).

**Box 4.3**   Example of a regulation

Regulation (EEC) No. 1612/68 on the free movement of workers within the Community, adopted by the Council in October 1968, is an example of a regulation enacting fundamental rules creating the Common Market. Article 1 of the Regulation provides:

> Any national of a Member State shall, irrespective of his place of residence, have the right to take up an activity as an employed person and to pursue such activity, within the territory of another Member State in accordance with the provisions laid down by law, regulation or administrative action governing the employment of nationals of that state.

**Directives** are commonly used to harmonize the member states' laws on a particular matter, a process also referred to as "approximation of laws." A directive sets out rules and standards that must be put in place in each member state, so that the same rules and standards apply uniformly throughout the EU. A period of time, usually two years, is prescribed in the directive during which the member states' legislatures must adopt the rules and standards as part of their national or sub-national legal systems, a process called "transposition" of a directive into national law (see Box 4.4). Failure to transpose the directive's provisions by the deadline, or failure to do so correctly, constitutes a breach of the member state's obligations under the treaties. The Commission is responsible to ensure that member states transpose directives, and may bring an action against a member state that fails to do so before the General Court (discussed below). After the deadline has passed for the member states to transpose the directive, the directive may have **direct effect**. That is, a private party (an individual, company, or other organization) can insist that the provisions of the directive that are clear, precise, and unconditional be applied, and, if necessary, enforced in a court of a member state, and any national rules or practices that are inconsistent with the directive be "disapplied." In addition, failure to transpose a directive may result in liability in damages of the member state to a person who has suffered loss as a result of the failure to transpose the directive.

**Decisions** are a third type of binding legislative act. A decision is a flexible and effective instrument that is very frequently used to create binding EU law in a wide range of circumstances and for varied purposes. The EU institution having competence in a policy area, usually the Council or the Commission, may adopt a decision as provided for in the treaties. For example, international agreements between the EU and third countries, such as the **Comprehensive Economic and Trade Agreement (CETA)** with

**Box 4.4**   Example of a directive

An example of a directive is Directive (EU) 2016/680, which protects the personal information of individuals and provides rules for the processing of such personal data by competent authorities for the purposes of the prevention, investigation, detection, or prosecution of criminal offences or the execution of criminal penalties, and on the free movement of such data. The directive was adopted by the Council and Parliament on April 27, 2016. The member states have until May 6, 2018, to transpose the directive into their national laws.

Canada, are approved by decision of the Council. The Commission may have been delegated the authority to make a decision providing details of implementation of a regulation or directive that sets out only a broad framework. Decisions are generally binding on everyone who is subject to EU law. If they are addressed to specific member states, individuals, companies, agencies, or institutions, they are binding only on those entities.

Article 288 TFEU also describes two non-binding types of act, the **recommendation** and the **opinion**. The Commission often makes recommendations to the member states, or to the other institutions, as to how to move forward to achieve policy goals in a particular area where binding legislation is either not within the EU's competence or the necessary support in Council or Parliament for a binding legislative act cannot be achieved. Opinions are occasionally issued by the CJEU in respect of proposed agreements between the EU and third countries. They are usually issued at the request of the Commission to ensure that the proposed international agreement will be effective and valid. The opinion is not binding, but if the CJEU rules that some or all of the obligations assumed in the agreement are beyond the competence of the EU, the agreement must be renegotiated so that it will not be vulnerable to challenge after it enters into force.

There are also certain "soft-law" instruments that may be used to shape policy in the absence of binding EU legislation. For example, the Commission uses communications to advise member states on how it intends to administer various policies or to suggest ways the member states may voluntarily remove impediments to the implementation of Union policies. Guidelines may be issued so that member states and private parties may align their actions and policies with the Commission's interpretation of a ruling of the CJEU or of a "hard law" EU act. The CJEU occasionally refers to such soft-law instruments and indicates the extent to which it agrees with the Commission's interpretation.

## The Court of Justice of the European Union: Overview

The CJEU derives its jurisdiction directly from the treaties. From a legal perspective, it is impossible to overstate the impact that the Court has had on the evolution of the EU. The judgments of the CJEU are a source of binding EU law and form part of the *acquis communautaire*. Because of its role as the final, supreme interpreter of EU law, the CJEU controls both EU institutions and the member states.

The CJEU has forcefully used its jurisdiction, often at the behest of the Commission or a private party, to "constitutionalize" the treaties. This means that it has interpreted the treaties in an expansive way in numerous fundamental rulings, thus creating a constitutional structure and set of norms based on the rule of law and the recognition of fundamental rights of individuals. It has firmly asserted its jurisdiction to review the validity of EU acts and control the exercise of power by the other EU institutions and ensure the application of EU law on the territory of the member states, and to delineate the division of competences between EU institutions and national legislatures.

The CJEU has grown immensely in size and importance, and its structure has been revised on several occasions since its creation in 1952. It was originally a single seven-judge panel for resolving disputes among the six founding member states of the European Coal and Steel Community (ECSC). After the European Economic Community (EEC) came into being in 1958, the jurisdiction of the Court of Justice expanded to include all policy areas, and its influence over the evolution of EU law and its legal system became definitive. The Court has demonstrated that it has a distinct view of its role as ensuring that the objectives of the Treaty of Rome (EEC Treaty) and its successor treaties are attained. It considers that it must ensure that the EU remains founded on and governed by law. In its judgments it has emphasized the protection of free movement rights and the fundamental human rights of individuals under EU law in order to give real effect to these rights.

The number of cases the Court heard each year increased quickly so that in 1988 the Council created a second level of court, the Court of First Instance, now called the General Court (see Box 4.5). The General Court originally had jurisdiction to hear appeals from decisions of the Commission in competition and state aid cases, and disputes between EU civil servants and their employer. Its jurisdiction has been broadened gradually with each

**Box 4.5**    Structure of EU courts

Article 19 TEU sets out the structure of the Union courts and the role of the Union judiciary, to uphold the rule of law within the EU:

1.   The Court of Justice of the European Union shall include the Court of Justice, the General Court and specialized courts. It shall ensure that in the interpretation and application of the Treaties the law is observed....
2.   The Court of Justice shall consist of one judge from each Member State. It shall be assisted by Advocates-General.

The General Court shall include at least one judge per Member State.

amendment of the treaties, but there are still certain types of cases reserved for the Court of Justice, the highest ranking court. In addition, the Court of Justice hears appeals from the General Court on a point of law, as well as the special categories of cases reserved to it. One specialized court, the Civil Service Tribunal, was established in 2005 and took over jurisdiction for disputes between the EU and its civil servants from the General Court.

As of 2017 there are 28 judges of the Court of Justice, one from each member state. The General Court is composed of at least one judge from each member state; in total there are currently 46 judges. Twenty-three official languages may be used at hearings. The Court of Justice also comprises 11 advocates general whose role is to give impartial, independent, but non-binding opinions on the cases that come before the Court of Justice. The advocates general have the same status and rank as the judges, and their opinions are very valuable in understanding the factual and legal context of the dispute and the opposing arguments presented in the cases. The Court of Justice usually, but by no means always, follows the opinion of the advocate general in deciding a case, and it may diverge in its reasoning even where it agrees with the advocate general's opinion as to the correct result.

In the next two sections, the most significant types of cases heard by the CJEU will be examined as a way of illustrating the role of the CJEU as a constitutionalizing and federalizing force in EU legal integration.

## The CJEU as a Constitutional Court for the European Union

### Ensuring Member State Compliance with EU Law: Direct Effect and Supremacy

Although the EU is not a federal state and does not have a constitution in the strict sense, the treaties have come to fulfill essentially the same role that a constitution plays in a federal state, and cannot be viewed merely as international agreements enforceable by the state parties in accordance with international law. Article 2 TEU expresses ideals that are commonly found in a national constitution: "The Union is founded on the values of respect for human dignity, freedom, democracy, equality, the rule of law and respect for human rights, including the rights of persons belonging to minorities. These values are common to the member states in a society in which pluralism, **non-discrimination**, tolerance, justice, solidarity and equality between women and men prevail."

In the early 1960s, the CJEU laid down the foundational EU legal principles of direct effect and **supremacy** of EU law over national law. At the time, the Common Market was in the process of creation, and member states were required to remove barriers in their laws to the free movement of goods, services, persons (free movement of workers and the right of establishment of self-employed individuals and of corporations and other business entities) and, to a lesser extent, capital. The Commission and Council were engaged in the early stages of the process of positive harmonization of member state laws through the adoption of regulations and directives.

The principle of direct effect holds that a treaty provision that is clear, precise, and unconditional can confer legal rights on individuals; these rights are enforceable in the courts of the member states. In the earliest days, the free movement of goods and the right of establishment were economic rights in the EEC Treaty that the Court recognized as having direct effect, so that laws of the member states that restricted these rights were, in principle, unenforceable, even where no harmonizing legislation had been adopted. Any person could bring action against such laws in the national courts to obtain a declaration that the national law restricting a right of free movement was unenforceable. In this way, private individuals and companies joined forces with the Commission to use judgments of the Court to help construct the Single Market, even where the necessary political will did not exist.

In 1963, in perhaps the Court's best-known judgment, *NV Algemene Transport en Expeditie Onderneming van Gend & Loos v. Netherlands Inland Revenue Administration* or "*Van Gend en Loos*," the CJEU ruled in favour of a private company that alleged that an increase in the import tariff applied by the Netherlands to certain goods imported from Germany violated the EEC Treaty's guarantees of free movement of goods between member states. The Netherlands government, supported by the governments of Belgium and West Germany, argued that the matter was one of Netherlands constitutional law, and that only the Commission could take action to enforce the EEC Treaty. The Court found that the treaty prohibition on increases in tariff rates was clear, precise, and unconditional and made far-reaching statements about the nature of the EU legal system, distinguishing it from the existing conception of the enforceability of treaties in international law:

> The objective of the EEC Treaty, which is to establish a Common Market, the functioning of which is of direct concern to interested parties in the Community, implies that this Treaty is more than an agreement which merely creates mutual obligations between the contracting states....
>
> ...the [European Economic] Community constitutes a new legal order of international law for the benefit of which the states have limited their sovereign rights, albeit within limited fields, and the subjects of which comprise not only Member States but also their nationals. Independently of the legislation of Member States, Community law therefore not only imposes obligations on individuals but is also intended to confer upon them rights which become part of their legal heritage.

In these famous words, the CJEU established the principle of direct effect, recognizing the right of the citizens of Europe to enforce their rights under EU law against laws made by their own governments and in their own courts.

Only a year after *Van Gend en Loos*, the Court laid down the principle of supremacy of EU law over inconsistent laws of the member states in the case of *Costa v. ENEL.* This was a challenge brought by a Mr. Costa to an Italian law, enacted in 1962, that nationalized electricity production and distribution companies into a single state-owned company, ENEL. The government of Italy defended the law, saying that under the Italian constitution, parliament had the power to pass a law that conflicted with its obligations under an international treaty, such as the EEC Treaty. As a matter of Italian constitutional law, the 1962 law was valid as a later enacted law, which is taken to be an implied repeal of the prior Italian law that ratified the treaty. Italy might be in breach of its obligations to the other member states as a matter of international law, but under Italian domestic law, applicable to private parties and entities such as Mr. Costa and ENEL, the 1962 law was valid and enforceable in the Italian courts. The Italian constitutional court held that the hierarchy of law according to Italian constitutional law applied, so that the treaty obligation could not prevent the Italian legislature from passing a valid and enforceable domestic law that contravened it.

In his opinion to the Court of Justice, the advocate general framed the issue this way: "The real problem is that of the co-existence of two rules of law which ... are incompatible but nevertheless both applicable within the internal order, the one derived from the [EEC] Treaty or the institutions of the Community, the other from [Italian] national law: which one should prevail?"

The advocate general acknowledged that it was for the national and/or constitutional courts of the member states to determine if the EEC Treaty was compatible with the constitution as a matter of national law. However, this reasoning would result in "near disastrous consequences" for the Common Market and the system established by the treaty. And, to prevent these disastrous consequences, he said that the treaty must prevail even over the constitution of a member state—if a judge of a constitutional court found a conflict between the two laws, the member state must either amend its constitution or renounce the EEC Treaty.

The Court of Justice made the following statements, excerpted from the judgment:

> By contrast with ordinary international treaties, the EEC Treaty has created its own legal system which, on the entry into force of the Treaty, became

an integral part of the legal systems of the Member States, and which their courts are bound to apply....

The integration into the laws of each Member State of provisions which derive from the Community, and more generally the terms and the spirit of the Treaty, make it impossible for the states, as a corollary, to accord precedence to a unilateral and subsequent measure over a legal system accepted by them on the basis of reciprocity. Such a measure cannot therefore be inconsistent with that legal system. The executive force of Community law cannot vary from one State to another in deference to subsequent domestic laws, without jeopardizing the attainment of the objectives of the Treaty...

It follows from all these observations that the law stemming from the Treaty, an independent source of law, could not, because of its special and original nature, be overridden by domestic legal provisions, however framed, without being deprived of its character as Community law and without the legal basis of the Community itself being called into question.

In making such clear statements in such forceful language about the relationship of EU law to national law, the CJEU established the doctrine of supremacy. The doctrine holds that member states may not enact or enforce laws that are inconsistent with the treaty or with secondary Community (now EU) law. The principles of Community law penetrate the national legal order, so that even the constitutional principles governing the national legal order of the member state concerned must give way. This is necessary to ensure that EU law is uniformly applicable throughout the EU and that the objectives of the EU can be attained.

The principle of supremacy (or primacy) was affirmed in Declaration 17 to the **Lisbon Treaty**: "The Conference recalls that, in accordance with well settled case law of the Court of Justice of the European Union, the Treaties and the law adopted by the Union on the basis of the Treaties have primacy over the law of Member States, under the conditions laid down by the said case law."

The principles of direct effect and supremacy are the fundamental building blocks on which the EU legal order is grounded; they are the core legal reason why the EU can be described as being more than a conventional international organization, though less than a state. Over the next decades, the CJEU repeatedly confirmed these principles, using a purposive interpretation of the treaties and insisting that adherence to these principles was necessary to attain the objectives of the treaties. The member states did not all immediately accept the principles of direct effect and supremacy. Particularly in Germany, the principle of supremacy of EU law in relation to the German constitution has been a matter of dispute that is only provisionally resolved.

In many instances, when the necessary majority to adopt harmonizing directives or regulations could not be attained in the Council, the CJEU did not hesitate to hold that member state laws that inhibited the exercise of free movement rights or were otherwise inconsistent with EU law were to be "disapplied." This encouraged both the Commission and individuals to challenge existing restrictions on the fundamental freedoms, very often with success. This judicial support for the Single Market project laid the path toward the greater political, economic, and monetary integration envisaged in the **Maastricht Treaty** of 1992.

As outlined above, the CJEU also developed a number of general principles of EU law, some of which were later added to the treaties as these were amended. Probably the most significant of the general principles is that the EU and its institutions are governed by international standards of fundamental human rights. This aspect of the Court's exercise of constitutional jurisdiction is discussed below.

### Enforcing EU Law in the CJEU

The CJEU ensures that the law is observed throughout the EU; this is an affirmation that the EU is governed by the rule of law. This role has two primary aspects: ensuring that the member states comply with their treaty obligations, and ensuring that the EU institutions carry out their roles in accordance with EU law and respect the limits of their powers as conferred by the treaties. The enforcement power of the CJEU results in **negative integration**, meaning that the judgments of the CJEU can only remove legal barriers to integration of EU law, rather than imposing positive rules and standards to advance legal integration.

There are two main legal actions, outlined in the TFEU, by which the laws and actions of the member states can be challenged in the CJEU. The first is initiated by the Commission against a member state, which the Commission claims has failed to fulfill its treaty obligations. In most cases, the member state is alleged to have failed to correctly transpose a directive into national law within the allowable time for doing so, or its existing law may be in conflict with a treaty provision or a regulation, or it may have failed to actually implement secondary EU law in a way that ensures it is applied and respected. The Commission will first advise the member state that it considers the latter to have infringed the treaties, providing detailed reasons. If the response of the member state is unsatisfactory, the Commission commences an action before the Court of Justice. If the Court rules that the member state has failed to fulfill its treaty obligations, the member state must comply with the Court's ruling as to how it must correct this.

Since the Maastricht Treaty came into force in 1993, the Commission has been able to go back to the Court to obtain a further judgment ordering the member state to pay a monetary penalty, sometimes totalling millions of euros, for failure to amend its law or properly implement EU policy after the first judgment of the Court that ruled that the member state was not in compliance with EU law.

The *Van Gend en Loos* and *Costa v. ENEL* cases are examples of the second form of legal action, the **reference for a preliminary ruling**. In these cases, a private party challenges the validity of a law of a member state on the basis that it is inconsistent with a provision of the treaty or of an act of EU secondary law by commencing an action in a national court of a member state. The national court has the power and the duty, as an organ of government of a member state, to uphold the EU law and declare the inconsistent national law to be inapplicable. If the national court has any doubt as to the correct interpretation of the EU law, it may refer the question to the Court of Justice, which will give a judgment called a "preliminary ruling." The case then goes back to the national court, which applies the preliminary ruling to decide the issues in the case. In this way, the correct interpretation of EU law as determined by the CJEU is transmitted to the national court for application within the member state. The goal is to ensure uniformity of interpretation and application of EU law throughout the Union. The courts of the other member states must also either apply the CJEU's interpretation to the domestic law of their own country, or at least refer a similar question relating to the issue of EU law to the CJEU to ensure they apply EU law correctly in their own national context. The power of citizens to bring actions in their local courts to enforce their rights under EU law, combined with the preliminary ruling procedure, is undoubtedly one of the most significant factors in the legal integration of the EU. The collaboration of national courts with the CJEU in making references for preliminary rulings, and then applying the interpretation given by the CJEU, ensures that consistent application of EU law throughout the EU "federalizes" the EU legal system.

The Commission's authority to take action against member states for failure to carry out their treaty obligations, combined with the right of citizens to directly enforce their EU legal rights in their local courts has been referred to as a system of "dual vigilance." The rulings of the Court in these cases have generally supported a broad and purposive interpretation of the obligations of member states, and upheld the EU legal rights of individuals, in particular in relation to the fundamental freedoms. The Court's rulings as a whole are an indication to the Commission of the parameters of EU competences and objectives as set out in the treaties, so that the Commission can draft proposals that are within the EU's legal powers in order to intensify positive legal integration. In this way, the Court of Justice shapes and controls policy-making in all the areas in which the EU has competence.

### The CJEU as a Court of Review of EU Secondary Legislation

The CJEU has jurisdiction to ensure that the acts of the EU institutions are within their powers as conferred by the treaties. This is a classic role for a federal constitutional court, like Canada's Supreme Court (see Box 4.6), as it allows the Union's judicial authorities to delineate the division of powers between the member states and the EU institutions, and to guard against procedural flaws, abuse of power, or other illegalities in the actions of the institutions. A member state, the Parliament, Commission and Council, and even private parties can bring an "action in annulment," asking the CJEU to review the legality of an act of an EU institutions. If the Court concludes that any act of an EU institution is not validly adopted, whether because the act is inconsistent with the treaties, the institution did not have the competence to act, or failed to follow the proper procedure, it will declare the act to be annulled.

A member state that has voted against a regulation or directive that has been adopted by qualified majority in the Council may challenge the validity of the act on the basis that **unanimity** was required, that the EU had no competence to adopt the act (because the subject matter was within

**Box 4.6**    The CJEU compared to Canada's Supreme Court

The Supreme Court of Canada (SCC) is the final court of appeal in Canada. In this role, it gives judgments that interpret and apply the constitution that must be followed by the lower courts. Parliament and the provincial legislatures may not enact legislation that is inconsistent with the constitution, and individuals may challenge such legislation as a violation of their constitutional rights, including their Charter rights. The SCC is empowered to determine whether a particular legislative power belongs to the federal or provincial governments, just as the CJEU is charged with determining whether a competence is to be exercised by the EU or the member states. The principles of interpretation employed by the SCC differ from those that apply in EU law, but the balancing of federal and provincial powers and the determination of whether a federal or provincial law is consistent with broader constitutional principle is similar to the role played by the CJEU.

the exclusive power of the member states), or that a step in the legislative procedure was not correctly followed. An example of this type of case is the *Tobacco Advertising* case, in which Germany challenged the legality of a directive regulating the advertising and sponsorship of tobacco products. The directive was adopted based on Article 114 TFEU which provides for the adoption of measures for the harmonization of member state laws with the object of the establishment or functioning of the internal market. The Court held that Article 114 could not support the directive's very extensive restriction of tobacco advertising and sponsorship, as it was not sufficiently connected to the internal market.

Sometimes one EU institution will challenge the validity of an act adopted by another institution. An early example is the *Tariff Preferences* case. The Commission alleged that a regulation adopted by the Council was illegal, because the treaty article on which it was based was not stated, and it was adopted by unanimity after consultation of the Parliament, rather than by **qualified majority voting (QMV)** under the **Common Commercial Policy**. The TEC provided (as does the TFEU) that all legislation had to state the legal basis (usually the treaty article) on which it was adopted. The regulation granted special preferences for import to the European Community to products from developing countries. This is a form of international development aid. At the time, there was no provision in the treaty that clearly granted competence to the Community to provide international development aid. However, the granting of import tariff preferences is also closely concerned with the common commercial policy, over which the Community had exclusive competence, and which required only qualified majority support in the Council. Further, no legal basis for the regulation was identified in it. The Court ruled that the regulation was invalid because it infringed the treaty requirement to state the legal basis for its adoption. It also ruled that the common trade policy included tariff preferences for development aid purposes, and that the regulation should have been adopted under that policy, by qualified majority, and was invalid for this reason as well.

Private parties can also challenge the legality of EU legislation that is addressed to them. This most frequently occurs when a corporation challenges a decision of the Commission finding that the corporation has engaged in anti-competitive behaviour prohibited by EU law. The action in annulment in this case is heard by the General Court.

The action in annulment allows the CJEU to ensure that the rule of law is observed not only by the member states, but by the EU institutions as well. The Council, Commission, and Parliament are equally bound by the treaties, and any act they make that is not in accordance with their treaty powers can be declared null and void by the Court.

## The Court's Defence of Fundamental Rights

As mentioned above, another classically constitutional role played by the Court is the protection of human rights, or fundamental rights, within the EU. The founding treaties of 1951 and 1957 did not mention human or fundamental rights, but as early as the late 1960s the CJEU began to recognize general principles of law that included the protection of fundamental rights. It has affirmed on many occasions the following statement regarding the status of fundamental rights within the EU legal order: "According to settled case-law, fundamental rights form an integral part of the general principles of law, whose observance the Court ensures. For that purpose, the Court draws inspiration from the constitutional traditions common to the Member States and from the guidelines supplied by international instruments for the protection of human rights on which the Member States have collaborated or to which they are signatories. In that regard, the ECHR [European Convention on Human Rights] has special significance" (Joined cases C-402/05 and C-415/05, *Kadi and Al Barakaat International Foundation v. Council and Commission*, ECLI:EU:C:2008:461 at paragraph 283).

As part of its role in defending human rights, the CJEU is cognizant of and to some extent has been influenced by decisions and interpretations of the European Convention on Human Rights by the **European Court of Human Rights (ECtHR**, see Box 4.7).

The influence of the CJEU in the evolution of the EU and its legal order is evident from the fact that, after the CJEU created its general principles, the member states agreed to revise the treaties to expressly include them in the

**Box 4.7**  The Court of Justice of the EU and the European Court of Human Rights

Students often wonder what the difference is between two important European courts: the Court of Justice of the European Union (CJEU) in Luxembourg and the European Court of Human Rights (ECtHR) in Strasbourg. The former is an EU institution and rules on EU matters. The European Court of Human Rights (ECtHR) is a specialized European court of international human rights, set up in 1959. It rules on individual or state applications alleging violations of the civil and political rights set out in the European Convention on Human Rights (ECHR). The ECtHR is not an EU institution; rather, it is governed by the **Council of Europe**. The Council of Europe currently has 47 members: all EU member states are part of the Council of Europe, but the EU as an institution is not. Canada is an observer state (together with five other states).

"constitution" of the EU. Moreover, in connection with the negotiation of the Treaty of Nice in 2000, the EU institutions reached a political agreement on a Charter of Fundamental Rights for the EU. The Charter became legally enforceable by the CJEU and member state courts with the entry into force of the Treaty of Lisbon in 2009.

## Debate: Incremental Legal Integration, Direct Effect, and Supremacy

From the short (and therefore incomplete) description of the legal and judicial system in this chapter, it might be imagined that EU legal integration has been fully achieved. However, the evolution of EU law is incremental and non-linear, and there are always new cases to test existing principles and lead to further refinements.

It was therefore not inevitable that the two most fundamental judicially created principles, direct effect and supremacy, would become as firmly entrenched in EU law as they now are. Why did member states generally accept these principles, which so radically reduce their own **sovereignty**? How did the courts of the member states react to rulings from the CJEU? Some answers to these questions have been put forward by scholars of EU law and are offered here for debate.

The Court first enunciated these two fundamental principles in cases that were of little interest to anyone other than the private parties who initiated them. At the time, few lawyers were very familiar with the Court or the nature of EU law, and the Common Market project was limited in scope and impact. By the time more sensitive cases of interest to the public came before the Court, direct effect and primacy of EU law were well established. The Court of Justice has acted strategically and tempered its language in sensitive cases to test the acceptance of its decisions. In the exercise of its jurisdiction to give preliminary rulings, the Court has characterized its relationship with the national courts of the member states as one of cooperation. It often limits its preliminary rulings to narrow statements of the correct interpretation of the law, and then draws back to leave the final outcome of a case to the national court to decide.

From the other side, national courts may decline to make references for preliminary rulings if they believe they do not need the assistance of the Court of Justice. Rates of references from different member states vary greatly. It is also questionable whether national courts always correctly apply the preliminary rulings. The very different legal and judicial traditions of the member states, particularly since the 2004 **enlargement**, means that uniform, simultaneous application of EU law throughout the EU is still an aspiration rather than a fact. This makes it easier for member states to continue to support EU membership while not fully implementing EU law.

Finally, it can be argued that member states had no real choice but to accept the principles of direct effect and supremacy. There is no appeal from a judgment of the Court of Justice; if member states want to over-rule a decision by the Court, they must change the treaty. As this requires unanimity of the member states, it is a very difficult task, and one that has become ever more difficult with each enlargement of the EU. Most, if not all, rulings of the Court of Justice are acceptable to at least a few member states, so that finding **consensus** to amend the treaties simply to over-rule one "unacceptable" judgment is virtually impossible. The alternative is for those member states that cannot accept a judgment to withdraw from the EU. And it may be remarked that applicants for EU membership have not been deterred by the transfer of sovereignty that direct effect and supremacy entail. However, the British decision to leave the EU has been taken on the basis of arguments that a return to national sovereignty and control of national law, and escape from the jurisdiction of the CJEU, is in the interests of the British people.

## Conclusion

There are still many examples of imperfect integration, failures to imple-ment EU law that are not challenged by either Commission or private par-ties, and different interpretations of EU law that have not been resolved. The so-called activism of the Court also ebbs and flows at different times in its 60-year history. However, the legal integration of the EU is undeniably fur-ther advanced than either its political or economic integration, largely due to the fundamental principles laid down at an early stage by the CJEU and their reaffirmation since.

## References and Further Reading

Alter, K. 2003. *Establishing the supremacy of European law: The making of an international rule of law in Europe.* Oxford: Oxford University Press. https://doi.org/10.1093/acprof:oso/9780199260997.001.0001.

Barnard, C., and S. Peers, eds. 2014. *European Union law.* Oxford: Oxford University Press. https://doi.org/10.1093/he/9780199686117.001.0001.

Cichowski, R.A. 2007. *The European court and civil society: Litigation, mobilization and governance.* Cambridge: Cambridge University Press. https://doi.org/10.1017/CBO9780511491924.

Conant, L. 2013. *Justice contained: Law and politics in the European Union.* Ithaca, NY: Cornell University Press.

Craig, P.P., and G. De Búrca. 2011. *The evolution of EU law.* 2nd ed. Oxford: Oxford University Press.

Craig, P.P., and G. De Búrca. 2015. *EU law.* 6th ed. Oxford: Oxford University Press.

Dawson, M., B. de Witte, and E. Muir. *Judicial activism at the European Court of Justice.* Cheltenham, UK: Edward Elgar. https://doi.org/10.4337/9780857939401.

De Búrca, G., and J.H. Weiler. 2001. *The European Court of Justice.* Oxford: Oxford University Press.

De Mestral, A., and J. Winter. 2001. "Mobility rights in the European Union and Canada." *McGill Law Journal/Revue de Droit de McGill* 46: 979–1009.

Garrett, G. 1995. "The politics of legal integration in the European Union." *International Organization* 49 (1s): 171–81. https://doi.org/10.1017/S0020818300001612.

Hartley, T. 2014. *The foundations of European Union law.* 8th ed. Oxford: Oxford University Press. https://doi.org/10.1093/he/9780199681457.001.0001.

Piris, J. 2010. *The Lisbon Treaty: A legal and political analysis.* Cambridge: Cambridge University Press. https://doi.org/10.1017/CBO9780511762529.

Poiares Maduro, M. 1998. *We the court.* Portland, OR: Hart Publishing.

Schmidt, S., and D. Kelemen. 2012. *The power of the European Court of Justice.* New York: Routledge.

Shaw, J. *Law of the European Union.* 3rd ed. Basingstoke, UK: Palgrave MacMillan, 2000.

Tsebelis, G., and G. Garrett. 2000. "Legislative politics in the European Union." *European Union Politics* 1 (1): 9–36. https://doi.org/10.1177/1465116500001001002.

Weiler, J.H.H. 1991. "The Transformation of Europe." *Yale Law Journal* 100 (8): 2403–83. https://doi.org/10.2307/796898.

## Review Questions

1. What is the difference between a regulation and a directive?
2. Where did the CJEU find a basis for recognizing fundamental rights as part of the EU legal system?
3. What is an example of a purposive interpretation of the treaties?
4. What is transposition? Which EU institution(s) ensure(s) correct transposition?

## Exercises

1. Compare and contrast the Charter of Fundamental Rights of the EU with the Canadian Charter of Rights and Freedoms.
2. Do some research on the roles and responsibilities of other supreme or constitutional courts in federal countries (e.g., Canada, the United States, Germany, Switzerland, etc.). What are the major differences between these supreme courts and the CJEU? Are there parallels to direct effect and supremacy of federal law in the case-law of other supreme or constitutional courts? Are there differences in monitoring and compliance of laws? What does this tell you about the level of integration in the EU?

# 5

# Policy-Making and Governance in the European Union's Multilevel System

INGEBORG TÖMMEL

## Reader's Guide

This chapter highlights how policy-making of the EU evolved in the course of **European integration** and how appropriate **governance modes** and institutional structures emerged during this process. It points to the inherent constraints that the Union as a **multilevel system** faces compared to true federations like Canada. Whereas federations clearly allocate competences and also tax-raising powers to the different levels of government, the EU is constrained by the member states, which retain far-reaching powers for themselves. This constellation has resulted in the development of governance modes that allow for flexibility in balancing the interests of the Union against those of the member states.

## Introduction

The European Union (EU) has evolved mainly through an incremental process of establishing and expanding policies, accompanied by institution-building to make these policies work. The process started in the 1950s with the foundation of the three original Communities—the **European Coal and Steel Community (ECSC)**, the **European Economic Community (EEC)**, and the **European Atomic Energy Community (Euratom)**—which served to integrate certain economic sectors and to create a **Common Market**. Over the following decades, the three original Communities were merged and transformed into what is now the EU; at the same time, the scope of EU policies has steadily been expanded. At present, the EU policy portfolio encompasses nearly all areas that typically characterize the policy spectrum at the national level.

However, in spite of this enormous expansion of the scope of EU policy-making, the range of *governance tools* at the EU's disposal—in other words, the mechanisms and procedures that it can use to shape developments in the member states—has not been expanded correspondingly. The union is not allowed to raise taxes; its budget is rather limited and, hence, its capacity to achieve political effects through financial allocations remains constrained.

The spectrum of exclusive EU legislative competences has also remained limited. Responding to these limitations, the EU has developed a set of unique governance modes—that is, procedures for structuring policy processes that are used to achieve desired policy effects—which complement the EU's limited exercise of hierarchical, top-down control with mechanisms that seek to indirectly influence or coordinate policies that are fully or partially under member state control.

Decision-making in the EU thus usually involves both the European and national government levels and in certain cases even regions within the member states. For this reason, the EU has been characterized as a multilevel system. Policy-making in a multilevel system requires lengthy and complex processes of defining common ground and building **consensus**. In light of the multilevel nature of the EU, this chapter seeks to answer two basic questions: first, why is there a mismatch between the scope of EU policy-making and the governance tools available at the EU level? Second, what are the consequences of this mismatch for EU governance?

In the search for answers to these questions, this chapter is organized as follows. It starts by briefly sketching the fundamental constraints on EU policy-making. It then provides an overview of the evolution of EU policy-making from an initially limited set of policies to a highly diversified policy portfolio. It proceeds with analyzing the various governance modes developed during this process and highlights their characteristics. Furthermore, the chapter elaborates on the institutional structures underlying EU governance and the institutional innovations serving to improve governance processes. Finally, it discusses the effectiveness of EU governance. The conclusion provides answers to the questions raised above and explains the specific features and constraints of EU governance as a consequence of the EU's multilevel structure.

## The Fundamental Constraints on EU Policy-Making

The EU evolved as a political system that was superimposed on sovereign nation-states in order to tackle common policy problems. However, the resulting multilevel system did not evolve into a full-fledged federal state (Theme 2 of this book); for instance, the EU never acquired full **sovereignty** in order to legislate according to its own will or to raise taxes for its own needs. Instead, member states retained the authority to determine the EU's competences (through their control over the treaty-making process), to influence and possibly veto legislation at the European level (through their representation in the **Council**), and to set the parameters of the EU budget (through their decisions on what financial transfers go to the EU). Since legislation and financial allocations are the classical governance tools that political systems employ to achieve political objectives, national governments thus imposed strong constraints on the EU as a policymaker.

Why is European law-making so constrained and the budget of the EU so limited? Law-making in the European Union, as described in Chapter 3, is a process that involves primarily three players: the **European Commission**, which proposes a legal text; the **European Parliament (EP)**, which may amend, reject, or adopt the Commission proposal; and the **Council of the EU** as the representative of national governments, which also amends, rejects, or adopts the proposal. It may seem that the Parliament and the Council are more or less on an equal footing in the process of legislation, but this is not the case. In practice, the Council is much more powerful. Its decisions are taken by qualified majority and in some cases even by **unanimity**; this gives "blocking minorities" of states—and in the case of unanimity even individual states—a veto power. The EP has a veto power as well, but only if a majority of its 751 members support a veto. Since such a majority is much more difficult to achieve, the EP is more willing than the Council to compromise. By contrast, national governments that see their interests in danger do not hesitate to cast a veto and thus to stall the process of legislation, or else to bargain until the proposal is adapted to their preferences. These internal voting dynamics in the Council and in the EP explain why European law-making is often a stop-and-go process, characterized by delayed and suboptimal decisions, or even non-decisions. As a consequence, EU policy-making has evolved only through a step-by-step process and in an incomplete or asymmetric manner.

The budget of the EU is limited, as it consists mainly of transfers from the member states to the European level. This stands in stark contrast to both unitary and federal states, where the (central) government is sovereign in raising taxes according to its will and needs. Even worse, budgetary transfers to the EU are not fixed once and for all, but are determined by decisions of the **European Council** at seven-year intervals. These decisions on the so-called **Multiannual Financial Framework (MFF)** are characterized by tough bargains among the member states. In these negotiations, they fix the amount of the financial transfers to the EU as a certain percentage of the gross national income (GNI) of the member states. The most recent decision on the MFF in 2014 set the contribution of the member states to the EU budget at 1 per cent of their GNI; this is the lowest percentage in the history of the EU. Besides these transfers, the Union has a small amount of other resources at its disposal, called the Traditional Own Resources (TOR), which consist mainly of customs duties on imports from third countries.

Furthermore, the Union may levy 0.3 per cent on the harmonized Value Added Tax (VAT) base of each member state. The MFF sets the ceilings for the EU's annual budget. With €144 billion per year currently, this budget is comparatively small in light of the many tasks the EU has to fulfill and also in comparison to its member states (see Table 5.1). For instance, in 2014 the federal level in Germany had a tax income of €282 billion (German Ministry of Finance, 2016). The limited budget of the EU does not offer much room for manoeuvring in terms of distributive policies (e.g., investment in infrastructure and services that benefit the population), let alone for redistributing wealth or income among member states.

Summing up, the European Union is heavily constrained in its policy-making, as it has only limited formal competences and financial means at its disposal. Moreover, in both legislation and financial allocations, it is dependent on the will of the member states. As the history of EU policy-making shows, national governments have been more willing to establish policies based merely on legislation than policies relying on financial allocations. In the first case (regulation without financial allocations), the distributive impacts were unclear or hidden, whereas in the second case (financial allocations), such impacts were obvious, with clear winners and losers, which made it difficult to find a consensus.

**Table 5.1**   The EU's revenues

| Source of revenues | Definition | Revenues 2016 | Share of revenues |
| --- | --- | --- | --- |
| Traditional own resources (TOR) | Mainly customs duties from imports from outside the EU and sugar levies | €18,590 million | 12.9% |
| Own resources based on VAT | A uniform rate of 0.3% is levied on the harmonized VAT base of each member state | €18,813 million | 13.1% |
| Own resources based on GNI | Each member state transfers a standard percentage of its GNI to the EU (currently 1%) | €104,866 million | 72.9% |
| Other resources | Includes taxes on EU staff remuneration, payments from non-EU countries for certain programs, and surplus from the previous budget | €1,617 million | 1.1% |
| Total | | €143,885 million | 100% |

Source: Adopted budget for 2016, *Official Journal of the European Union*, L 48, 24 February 2016. 14

## The Evolution of EU Policy-Making

EU policy-making began in the postwar period when the initial six member states founded the three European Communities and embarked on a few joint activities. Yet after these first steps, the policy spectrum expanded rapidly, together with the transformation of the Communities into the EU. The process evolved in four phases, with the first and third phases characterized by policy expansion, and the second and fourth phases focused on policy experiments and procedural innovations respectively.

The *first phase* started in 1951 with the limited endeavour of **supranational** cooperation in two economic sectors, coal and steel. Yet the foundation of a European Coal and Steel Community (ECSC) was not as modest an undertaking as it might seem from our present perspective. In the 1950s, coal and steel were important primary industries, which provided raw materials to a broad spectrum of manufacturing industries. Moreover, in most of the six original member states, these sectors were state owned or run under far-reaching state control. Putting them under a supranational European umbrella was a first step in regulating these sectors with the objective of creating a common, transnational market. Subsequently, the original six member states proceeded in 1957 to establish the European Economic Community (EEC) as an institution to integrate their national markets. Furthermore, they established the European Atomic Energy Community (Euratom) to jointly regulate another primary sector, which they projected would form the energy source of the future. At the same time, though, member states realized that the agricultural sector would not fare well under a free market. They therefore agreed to also regulate this sector at the European level and thus to counteract possible market failure. Thus from the very beginning, the EU undertook both an ambitious project of market-making as well as a limited approach to market-correcting policies (Theme 1 of this book).

For the first 10 years, the EU was engaged in setting up the regulatory and institutional framework to make these policies work. In the case of the Common Market, the projected steps were smoothly realized, as they were based on a consensus among the member states. In contrast, the **Common Agricultural Policy (CAP)** was highly contested among national governments, and the ensuing conflicts were difficult to resolve. This situation highlighted a weakness in EU policy-making. Market-making policies, as far as they referred to the removal of barriers to free trade and thus constituted a form of **negative integration**, were comparatively easily established. By contrast, market-correcting policies, which would lead to **positive integration**, required interventions into the bestowed rights and regulations of member states and often resulted in unequal distributional impacts. They therefore were much more difficult to establish (for more about negative and positive integration, see the Introduction to Part II).

By the end of the 1960s, the *second phase* had set in. Despite major conflicts among the member states, a common understanding had emerged that the EU should proceed on its path of integrating more policy areas. In the following years, many such steps were discussed and projected, but implementation rarely followed. This lack of follow-through, among other things, was due to significant economic disparities between the member states. These disparities were further increased by the first **enlargement** (1973) to include the United Kingdom, Denmark, and Ireland. Under these conditions, political dissent between member states increased and the room for embarking on new policies diminished. Nevertheless, selected policies were established that either aimed at compensating for the disparities among the member states (the **regional policy**, later renamed **cohesion policy**; see Chapter 13) or sought to improve the EU's international competitiveness (technology policy). Furthermore, some market-correcting regulations were adopted under the guise of preventing distortions of fair competition, in particular social and environmental policy regulations (see Chapters 10 and 12). Finally, a monetary system including fixed as well as floating exchange rates was created as a first experiment on the way toward a full-fledged **Economic and Monetary Union (EMU)**. It led to the euro (see Chapter 7).

In the mid-1980s, the *third phase* began when national and particularly EU-level political leaders forcefully advocated for closer integration. After years of economic stagnation and major disagreement between the member states—not least aggravated by two rounds of Southern enlargement (with Greece joining in 1981, and Portugal and Spain in 1986)—they rediscovered the EU as the most suitable arena for tackling the declining competitiveness of Europe in the world. Consequently, they opted for further engaging in joint policy-making (with more opportunities for passing legislation through qualified majority vote rather than unanimity). What followed was the strongest boost to the expansion and enhancement of EU policies in the history of integration. The most outstanding project of the time was the completion of the **Single Market** by 1992, embracing more than 300 regulations for making the Common Market work and eliminating **non-tariff barriers** (see Chapter 7). Besides, policies established earlier were more forcefully implemented now (e.g., **competition policy**) or significantly strengthened (e.g., regional, social, and environmental policies). The latter served mainly to smooth conflicts among the member states. Indeed, poorer states claimed regional and social policies as compensation for their weaker competitive position in the Single Market; the richer states aimed at safeguarding their higher environmental standards under such conditions.

Thus, even though market-making policy was the first and foremost priority, some policy activity also focused on market correction.

After these successes, the next logical step was to embark on even more ambitious policy projects aimed primarily at further bolstering the functioning of the Single Market or, to a lesser degree, at compensating for market failures. Consequently, EMU was established during the 1990s, accompanied by various approaches to coordinating a broad spectrum of national policies, such as trans-European networks, energy, tourism, and education. Furthermore, the EU expanded its policy spectrum to areas that were hitherto the *domaine réservée* of the member states: a **Common Foreign and Security Policy (CFSP)**, as well as a set of activities in **Justice and Home Affairs (JHA)** (see Chapters 8 and 9). Thus, within a period of approximately 10 years, the EU expanded in size, made it easier to pass legislation, and fundamentally changed in appearance by embracing a broad spectrum of additional policies.

Around the mid-1990s, this massive expansion of policy-making came to a stall, and the *fourth phase* set in. It was now mainly external pressures that induced further changes. The end of the **Cold War** and the transformation of Central and Eastern European states into market economies and democratic political systems posed an enormous challenge to the Union. The Eastern neighbours knocked vigorously at the EU's doors, aspiring to full membership. In this situation, an expansion of policy-making was no longer a pressing issue; instead, stabilizing or restructuring the existing policy spectrum and preparing for enlargement prevailed. Within the Union, procedures of decision-making were streamlined and generous support measures for weaker economies curtailed in order to create room for accommodating the economically much weaker Eastern states. In addition, procedures for coordinating national policies were developed, aimed at inducing reforms within the member states (see the next section). Externally, the Union fostered convergence of the accession states with its own regulatory framework and policy model. To achieve this goal, it transferred its policies to the neighbours through applying strict **conditionality** in exchange for the benefit of membership. Conditionality in this context means that the EU set a series of conditions referring to various kinds of economic and political reforms that the **candidate states** had to fulfill before accession to the Union. Among others, it required that the candidate states implement the so-called *acquis communautaire*—the entire body of EU law (all treaties, legislation, court decisions, and the like) (see Chapter 15). Consequently, in order to enable joint policy-making under conditions of a rapidly increased membership, all attention shifted from new policy initiatives to procedural questions.

Procedural questions also dominated the agenda when, starting in 2008, clouds on the horizon announced what would soon unfold to become a serious financial crisis, a **sovereign debt crisis**, and finally a crisis of the euro (see Chapter 7). While the Union initially did not react at all, it later established tighter rules and stricter surveillance mechanisms for inducing compliance of the member states with the norms and rules of the Stability and Growth Pact (SGP). In addition, it subjected debtor states, in particular Greece, to a harsh regime of conditionality in exchange for huge loans, first from the European Financial Stability Facility (EFSF) and later the **European Stability Mechanism (ESM)**. It also compelled the debtor states to embark on economic and social "reforms," which essentially entailed adaptations to European norms of free markets, such as the liberalization of highly regulated businesses and welfare state institutions and the privatization of public goods (railways, seaports, power companies, hospitals, etc.). Overall, during the fourth phase policy-making expanded in the area of financial supervision, banking, and macroeconomic coordination; furthermore, procedural innovations for reinforcing EU policies and transferring them to both member and third states were of major concern.

Drawing conclusions on the evolution of EU policy-making, we see a process of rapid expansion of the policy portfolio. Yet the process did not evolve consistently. Phases of expansion (1 and 3) alternated with phases of relative stagnation (2 and 4). The latter have been characterized by path-breaking experiments (phase 2) or far-reaching improvements of policy processes (phase 4). Second, even though the policy portfolio encompasses both market-making and market-correcting policies, the former clearly prevail. Thus while the spectrum of EU policy-making resembles that of the member states, the significance of individual policy areas within this spectrum clearly differs. The EU continues to display a clear bias toward economic policies and market integration, while the correction of market failures is limited to the most pressing cases. As is stated in Theme 1 of this book, this balancing act between market-making and market correcting has been central to European integration developments since the very outset.

Looking for explanations, we can first state that EU policy-making expanded in reaction to both internal and external challenges. The problems resulting from increasing interdependences among European states, but also worldwide, created pressures to act in common, as even the larger states in Europe cannot solve such problems on their own. The asymmetry between market-making and market-correcting policies resulted from conflicts within the EU. Generally, member states expected benefits from market integration, so that they could easily agree to forceful steps in this direction. By contrast, market correction with its incalculable and unequal impacts remained contested. It therefore was pushed further to the back of the EU policy agenda.

In the next section, we turn to how these conflicts and asymmetries translated into widely varying and often unusual governance approaches.

## The Evolution of EU Governance Modes

Corresponding to the four phases of the evolution of EU policy-making, the specific "toolkit" of EU governance has also evolved as a phased process. This process was marked by ups and downs, various experiments, and finally a clear direction in developing and establishing governance modes suited for and adapted to the conditions of the EU's multilevel system. Yet the process was not one of rationally searching for the best governance modes at the EU level. Instead, it was framed, from the very beginning, by the particular features of the European Union as a multilevel system. As discussed above, the member states hold the decisive decision-making powers in this system, while the institutions of the EU, in particular the Commission, act as a motor of integration. In general, the Commission pushes for an expanded scope of EU policy-making, and for refining EU governance modes according to functional needs or economic and political pressures. By contrast, national governments tend to constrain any autonomous action at the EU level and to retain for themselves a maximum of control in EU governance. Hence EU governance evolves, to a large extent, through mechanisms that seek to influence policy in indirect ways and allow member states a high degree of autonomy.

Turning to the concrete course of setting up and exercising EU governance, we see a *first phase* marked by predominantly hierarchical rule and even features of state interventionism. In the early years of integration, political leaders envisaged creating a European federation, a sort of United States of Europe (see Chapter 2). Consequently, they opted for transferring clear competences to the European level. They set rules and regulations for creating a Common Market and established certain interventions to flank its functioning. For example, the European Union could intervene in cases of overproduction in the steel sector, falling market prices for agricultural products or, more generally, the distortion of fair competition. Most of these interventions, however, were never implemented. As far as they were put into practice, as in the case of CAP, they remained highly contested. Thus, in spite of the transfer of far-reaching powers to the European level, these hierarchical modes of governance did not work, because the member states did not accept them.

The *second phase* set in with tentative experiments in more flexible forms of governance. A prime example is the setting of industrial norms for the Common Market. National governments could not find a consensus on the definition of appropriate norms. In the end, they defined only a few framework parameters at the European level; specifying concrete norms was devolved to private umbrella organizations of the respective industries. Similarly, in other sectors and issue areas, if regulations or guidelines were adopted at all, they defined only basic objectives, leaving national governments much discretion. Regional policy as well as the European Monetary System (EMS), set up during these years, constitute prime examples for this approach. In both cases, the EU set certain procedural or substantive norms, while member states designed, implemented, or adapted their policies within this framework. Thus, during this phase, EU governance was conceived as a multilevel process that provided room for balancing the interests and preferences of the European and national government levels. Yet policy implementation during this phase of first experiments in multilevel governance was characterized by manifold implementation deficits, since member states often failed or refused to duly observe EU norms.

The *third phase* brought about decisive changes and also significant variations in EU governance. By this time, member states had agreed to improve market-making policies. Accordingly, a host of hierarchical rules in the form of regulations was adopted in order to "complete" the Single Market. In other policy areas, those that served to support or to correct the functioning of the market, national governments could not agree on transferring additional competences to the EU. Therefore, in these areas, the **Maastricht Treaty** (in force since 1993) set only general rules for coordinating national policies under European objectives. Furthermore, with the Maastricht Treaty, new policies were established at the EU level yet ruled exclusively by the **intergovernmental** bodies. I refer here to the CFSP, JHA, and EMU (see Chapters 7, 8, and 9). All these policies were subject to decisions and actions of the Council and the European Council, while the supranational institutions, the Commission, and the Parliament, played hardly any role in proposing legislation or action (Commission) or in deciding on such proposals (EP). Scholars termed this governance approach, which strengthened the role of member states in European integration, "new intergovernmentalism" (Puetter, 2012; Bickerton, Hodson, & Puetter, 2015; see also Chapter 6). In the case of EMU, binding decisions regarding monetary policy were devolved to an independent supranational institution: the **European Central Bank (ECB)**. Overall, the third phase, although at first glance characterized by the expansion of hierarchical rule, opened up two additional tracks for exercising governance: one where the member states act jointly at the European level ("new intergovernmentalism"), and another where the individual member states are the masters of policy-making, though guided to a certain extent by EU-wide objectives. Yet these approaches did not work as projected; accordingly, implementation rarely succeeded.

Unsurprisingly, therefore, the *fourth phase* was characterized by significant improvements in the procedural dimension of EU governance, particularly in those cases where the EU lacked clearly defined competences. Thus an organized procedure was set up for coordinating national policies. The procedure, named **Open Method of Coordination (OMC)**, was first defined in the Employment Title of the Amsterdam Treaty (which came into force in 1997; see also Chapter 10). In 2000, the Lisbon European Council adopted the procedure as the appropriate governance mode for inducing a broad set of economic and social reforms in the member states. The procedure entails a four-step process, whereby the EU level defines policy guidelines and targets, while member states formulate and implement their policies within this framework. Finally, the Council of the EU, in its various formations, examines national policy implementation and redefines or adapts the guidelines and targets for the next **coordination** cycle.

Furthermore, the sovereign debt crisis and the measures taken to resolve it gave rise to governance modes that sought to influence national policies without transferring many new competences to the EU level. In this case, strict conditionality was applied in order to trigger adaptations at national level in exchange for benefits provided by the EU. The debtor states received generous credits and loans, but only if they accepted "reforms" in line with EU standards and norms. In addition, stricter surveillance mechanisms were established in order to safeguard compliance with the rules of the Stability and Growth Pact (SGP).

Finally, during this phase certain powers in two policy domains—agricultural and competition policy—which previously had been fully controlled by the EU, were decentralized back to the national level. In both cases, national authorities now received broad leeway to adapt policies more flexibly to local circumstances.

Altogether, during the fourth phase, EU governance evolved to include new mechanisms, which reflect the multilevel structure of the EU polity. Examples are not only the OMC, where national policies are coordinated by the Union, but also previously highly centralized policies, which have been partially decentralized. The respective procedural innovations created room for balancing EU policy objectives with those of the member states. Even in face of the sovereign debt crisis, the Union did not extend its own competences by much but mainly established conditionality and surveillance mechanisms, which were meant to trigger adaptations in the member states, but did not directly enforce them in a hierarchical, top-down fashion. This is reflected in the EU budget, which continues to include only two big-ticket

**Table 5.2**  The EU's expenditures

| Budget category | Expenditures 2016 (payments, euro billions) | Share of expenditures |
|---|---|---|
| 1. Smart and inclusive growth | | |
| 1a. Competitiveness for growth and jobs | €17,418 million | 12.1% |
| 1b. Economic, social, and territorial cohesion | €48,844 million | 34.0% |
| 2. Sustainable growth: Natural resources (primarily CAP) | €55,121 million | 38.3% |
| 3. Security and citizenship | €3,022 million | 2.1% |
| 4. Global Europe | €10,156 million | 7.1% |
| 5. Administration | €8,935 million | 6.2% |
| Other expenditures | €389 million | 0.3% |
| Total | €143,885 million | 100% |

Source: Adopted budget for 2016, *Official Journal of the European Union*, L 48, 24 February 2016: 13.

spending items—the CAP and the cohesion policy, consuming together more than 70 per cent of the EU budget—while other budget items are relatively small, as most policy implementation occurs at the member state level (see Table 5.2).

Summing up the evolution of EU governance, we see a process initially based on hierarchical rule yet successively complemented with other governance approaches. These additional approaches range from (1) the shaping of national policies through EU framework regulations, (2) **joint actions** decided upon by the intergovernmental bodies of the EU, to (3) the coordination of national policies through firmly organized procedures (see Table 5.3).

EU governance is underpinned by three types of allocating competences to the EU and member state level, as defined by the treaties: one where the EU level holds exclusive competences, another one where competences are shared to varying degrees between various levels of government, and finally, a third one where member states retain all formal competences. In practice, most EU governance is exercised as a multilevel process of complex deliberations, negotiations, and actions, though with varying involvement of the various levels. Even in cases in which the Union has exclusive competences at its disposal, as in the Single Market or certain competition policy issues, there are many ways to involve national governments in the decision-making.

The evolution of EU governance to its present forms and varieties can be explained first of all by the reluctance of member states to transfer competences definitively to the EU level. Depending on the policy area at stake

**Table 5.3**  Phases of EU policy-making and associated governance modes

| Phase | Policies established | Competences | Governance mode | Function |
|---|---|---|---|---|
| 1 (1950–1965) | Coal and Steel | European level | Hierarchical rule | Market creation |
| | Common market | European level | Hierarchical rule | Market creation |
| | Competition policy | European level | Hierarchical rule | Market creation |
| | Agricultural policy | European level | Hierarchical rule | Market correction |
| 2 (1965–1985) | Regional policy | European/ national level | Framework regulation | Market correction |
| | Social policy | European/ national level | Framework regulation | Market correction |
| | Environmental policy | European/ national level | Framework regulation | Market correction |
| | Technology policy | European/ national level | Framework regulation | Market creation |
| | European Monetary System | National level | Coordination of national policies | Market creation |
| 3 (1985–1995) | Single Market completion | European level | Hierarchical rule | Market creation |
| | Economic and Monetary Union | European/ national level | Hierarchical rule/framework regulation | Market creation |
| | Foreign and Security Policy | European/ national level | Intergovernmental decision | Enhancing role of EU |
| | Justice and Home Affairs | European/ national level | Intergovernmental decision | Market correction |
| | Various policies (trans-European networks, energy, education, etc.) | National level | Coordination of national policies | Market correction |
| 4 (1995–present) | European Employment Strategy | National level | Coordination of national policies | Market correction |
| | **Lisbon Strategy** | National level | Coordination of national policies | Market creation/ correction |
| | **Europe 2020** Strategy | National level | Coordination of national policies | Market-creation/ correction |

Source: Compilation by author

and the existence of a consensus for EU-wide action, member states have either accepted hierarchical rule and binding decisions or retained control in various forms. Where the latter has been the case, EU governance has been further shaped and fine-tuned in reaction to frequent stalemates in decision-making, deadlocks in the policy process, or even obstruction by the member states of interference from "above." Thus, in the longer run, EU governance modes evolved as they adapted to the multilevel structure of the system and to two opposite objectives underlying EU policy-making: the need to act at the EU level, and the determination of member states to safeguard, as much as possible, national sovereignty.

## The Institutional Structure of EU Governance

Governance is not only exercised as a process but also has a structural dimension. Governance processes have to be underpinned with appropriate institutional structures so that they can work effectively. The structural dimension of EU governance is first and foremost formed by the basic institutions of the European level responsible for policy-making. Furthermore, the institutions of the national government level and, in some cases, also those of the regions as well as non-governmental organizations, form equally important underpinnings for EU governance. Finally, a variety of additional institutions have been created for facilitating EU governance as a multilevel process.

The basic institutional structure of the EU consists of four institutions that decide on all steps in policy-making (see Chapter 3). The European Commission acts as the motor of integration by proposing legislation and other projects, but it does not take binding decisions. The Council of the EU (formerly the Council of Ministers) is the institution that takes binding decisions on legislative proposals, in most cases together with the European Parliament (EP). The European Council acts as the supreme authority of the Union. It defines the overall direction of European integration and in certain cases decides, together with the Council, on the policies that pertain to intergovernmental control.

The four institutions responsible for EU policy-making differ fundamentally from each other in various ways. The Commission and the EP are supranational institutions, whereas the Council and the European Council are intergovernmental institutions. Somewhat generalizing, we can assume that the latter mainly represent the national interests of the individual member states, while the European Commission and the EP primarily represent the common interests of the Union as a whole. The EP represents not simply European interests in general but the collective interests of EU citizens, mediated by party politics. These interests may differ from, say, the common interests of the European business community. In any event, European decision-making inherently entails the balancing of—or mediating between—common European interests and specific interests of the member states. When the Commission, the Council, and the EP jointly legislate in policies that are based on a far-reaching consensus among the member states (all measures regarding the Single Market and specific aspects of environmental and social policies), they will balance various interests. By contrast, when the European Council takes decisions on its own, national interests, or in specific cases those of the most powerful states, prevail. This situation applies mainly to policies that have been recently established and are much more contested (CFSP, JHA, EMU).

Altogether, the institutional constellation at the EU level provides the "lower" level—the governments of the member states—an enormous and, in some cases, decisive say in EU policy-making. This EU institutional structure clearly differs from that of a federal state (such as Canada), where the federal level has its own competences and can override, at least in some domains, the state or provincial level (see Table 5.4).

**Table 5.4**   Institutional structure of governance: Comparison EU–Canada

|  | EU | Canada |
|---|---|---|
| Political system | Multilevel System | Federation |
| Sovereignty | National level | Shared between federal level and provinces |
| Competences | Limited competences at European level, often shared competences | Clear distinction between federal and provincial level |
| Finances | National level raises taxes, transfers from national to European level | Federal and provincial levels raise taxes, some transfers from federal to provincial level |
| Policies European/federal level | Dominance of market-making policies | Broad spectrum, market-making, market correcting, and **foreign policy** |
| Policies national/ provincial level | Full spectrum, including foreign policy | Mainly market-correcting policies |
| Governance modes European/federal level | Limited hierarchical rule, mix of framework regulation, intergovernmental decision, and policy coordination | Hierarchical rule within federal realm of competences |

Source: Compilation by author

The vertical institutional set-up of EU governance further confirms the strong role of the national level. In the multilevel structure of the EU, the member states and their governments have to fulfill a multitude of governance functions. The only exception is when European legislation is directly binding for all, as is the case in many Single Market matters. In this case, member states have no further tasks to perform. However, in all other cases, the EU sets a legislative framework of basic objectives and norms (**directives**) that member states have to transpose into national legislation, which leaves them ample room for discretion (see Chapter 4 for a discussion of EU legislative acts). Where the EU level provides subsidies to the member states for achieving certain objectives, as in cohesion policy (see Chapter 13), the latter formulate and implement their policies within this framework. In policies that are only coordinated at the EU level, the discretion of national governments to pursue their own objectives and preferences is even greater. Thus overall, the multilevel structure of the EU allows national governments to act in many ways as decisive policymakers, whereas EU-level actors can only urge them to follow a supranational path.

It is this institutional constellation of the EU multilevel system that has triggered the establishment of additional institutions, so that EU governance can better achieve its objectives. Below, I present two examples that structure the vertical relationships between the EU and the national, as well as partly the regional government levels, and, to a certain extent, also the horizontal relationships among the member states.

The first example refers to the so-called *system of partnership* in cohesion policy, the EU policy designed to provide support to disadvantaged regions in the member states (see Chapter 13). In this policy, the EU level used to set certain basic objectives, while the member states designed and implemented their policies within this framework. Yet in many instances, member states did not respect the EU objectives. These were not hierarchically superimposed on national governments and, hence, could not be effectively enforced. Then the reform of cohesion policy in 1989 introduced a partnership system. This system implied an institutional arrangement for sequenced negotiations among all three levels of government (European, national, and regional) regarding the elaboration, adoption, and implementation of assistance programs for less favoured regions. It thus enabled the government levels to discuss jointly and elaborate the substantial and procedural dimensions of cohesion policy and to mediate between EU policy objectives and those of the national and sometimes regional government levels. In these negotiations, the European Commission as the representative of the EU persuades national governments to accept European objectives. At the same time, regional authorities are empowered to bring in their own objectives.

Consequently, the system of partnership tends to weaken the gatekeeper position of national governments. Altogether, the system of partnership created a *vertical nexus* between the formally disconnected government levels and compensated for the lack of hierarchical relationships between them.

The second example refers to the *transnational networks* that are established in Competition Policy, the EU policy that seeks to safeguard a level playing field between economic actors in the Single Market. Initially, decisions regarding the distortion of fair competition were the exclusive competence of the Commission. Yet such decisions were often not welcomed or were even thwarted by the member states. In 2003, a major reform decentralized competences in minor competition cases to the member states, and each state had to establish a competition authority in the form of an independent agency. At the same time, transnational networks were created where delegates of these agencies cooperate under the guidance of the Commission. The members of the networks discuss problems of unfair competition, exchange experiences, and give advice to colleagues who deal with difficult cases. In addition, they elaborate proposals for further EU policy initiatives or for common strategies at the national level. Thanks to these networks, national actors get involved in EU competition policy, while the Commission enhances its ability to transfer EU policy objectives and governance practices directly to the member states. Overall, transnational networks in competition policy, even though linked to a step toward decentralization of competences from the European to the national government level, allow for more effective diffusion of European policy strategies throughout the Union,

Both the institutional innovations discussed above were established to compensate for specific weaknesses in the institutional structure of the EU. In the case of *partnerships* in cohesion policy, the lack of hierarchical relationships between government levels was addressed by a system of structured negotiations among all parties involved. In the case of *transnational networks* in competition policy, the excessive centralization of the policy in the hands of the Commission was alleviated by giving national authorities a greater say in decisions, while orienting them more vigorously on European objectives. Furthermore, the networks also serve to harmonize diverging national policy approaches. In both cases, a solution was found that enhances the authority of the EU level vis-à-vis the member states without expanding its formal powers. Unsurprisingly, therefore, similar institutional innovations were soon also applied in other policy areas and domains, for example in justice and home affairs (see Chapter 8) or in energy policy (see Chapter 12).

Thus, the institutional structure underpinning EU governance mirrors the properties and challenges of a multilevel system, based on sovereign states. The governments of these states are unwilling to allocate powers and competences indefinitely to the EU level. This reluctance is reflected in the basic institutional structure of the EU polity, but also in those institutional innovations that were created at a later stage. These innovations provided stability to a system in which national governments (and in some cases regions) claimed decisive influence, while at the same time joint European action was functionally required and politically desired. In other words, these institutional innovations served to square the circle.

## Debate: Is EU Governance Effective?

Does EU governance work effectively? In view of (1) the EU's incomplete powers, (2) the limited EU budget, (3) an institutional arrangement that privileges national governments in decision-making, and (4) governance modes that make relatively little use of hierarchical rule, one has to ask how effective EU governance is. Various answers to this question are possible.

By and large, scholars agree that the rules and regulations governing the Single Market do work effectively (Scharpf, 1999). The success of the Single Market is due in large part to the nature of these rules: they are directly binding on member states and private businesses, and they are reinforced by market mechanisms because they unleash competitive pressures. By contrast, when EU governance occurs through framework legislation that must be transposed into national law, it is much less effective (Falkner et al., 2005; König & Mäder, 2013). National governments use many ways to evade, circumvent, or delay due transposition. Of course, the European level has certain means at its disposal to counteract sluggish transposition, but these are time consuming, costly, and therefore only selectively applied. Scholarly research on legislative compliance hence points to mixed results with respect to these rules.

Strikingly, however, when the EU level has had the power to take binding decisions, these decisions may well have just as little effect. In many cases, such decisions, delegated to the Commission, were either not taken or were delayed. The Commission in these cases was hesitant, as it felt that a deliberate consensus among the member states was not given. Thus, overly centralized policies and governance processes are often ineffective and, therefore, tacitly replaced by multilevel approaches (Akman & Kassim, 2010).

Furthermore, the effectiveness of governance processes in policy areas where the European Council or the Council of the EU make intergovernmental decisions on their own—with the member states often acting as executives—is also highly questionable. Particularly the SGP in EMU has been defied by many member states. In the early 2000s, France and Germany could do this without incurring any sanctions, whereas today, debtor states, such as Greece, are compelled to adopt European norms and implement the suggested "reforms." This obvious inequality further undermines compliance with EU norms. The recent **refugee crisis** brought the disregard of Council decisions more clearly to the fore, with some member states explicitly refusing to adhere to the decisions on the distribution of refugees among member states, and others doing the same, but silently (Knodt & Tews, 2016; see also Chapter 8).

Finally, the effectiveness of governance processes coordinated by the EU through the OMC is also an issue of much contestation (see Chapter 10). Some scholars argue that it is only with hierarchy, or at least a strong "shadow of hierarchy" (in other words, the ability of the EU to directly intervene as a measure of last resort), that these modes of governance are effective (Börzel, 2010). Others, by contrast, claim that effectiveness should not be assessed by the achievement of the concrete objectives and targets set at EU level but rather by longer-term changes in problem perceptions and strategies of national actors and elites. In this view, it is not decisive whether the substantial aspects of a policy are successfully transferred to member states, but rather whether member states are willing to engage in the governance approaches of the EU level (Weishaupt & Lack, 2011).

In the end, EU governance processes have a mixed record with regards to their effectiveness. (1) Hierarchical rule as a governance model is effective, but only in the case of regulation by law, whereas binding decisions prove to be rather ineffective. (2) Framework **regulations** at the European level appear to be a less effective way of directing member states' policies. (3) Council and European Council decisions are only partially respected, or only under imposition of conditionality, which is pertinent when member states are in need of specific benefits. (4) Finally, the coordination of national policies is effective only in the long term and because it might transform the policy approaches of national governments.

At this point, it might seem that European governance, with the exception of the regulation of the Single Market, is in general ineffective. Such a judgment, however, would be misplaced. Rather we should say that the effectiveness of EU governance is not guaranteed but depends upon a host of factors: for example, the governance approach(es) used, the problems at hand and the pressure to find solutions, as well as external circumstances. However, the most decisive factor for the success or failure of EU governance is whether national governments and political elites acknowledge EU policy objectives and processes as appropriate and legitimate, or beneficial to their country.

## Conclusion

In this chapter we have seen that EU policy-making evolved through a process of rapid expansion of the policy portfolio and increasing diversification of governance modes. In this process, the transfer of formal competences to the EU level remained limited; accordingly, mechanisms of hierarchical governance could be used for only a limited set of policies. In all other policy areas, the EU developed varying governance modes that sought to influence national policies indirectly by passing EU framework legislation or establishing common targets, give member states a decisive say in EU decision-making, or allow the EU to coordinate member state policy. These variations in governance modes are a consequence of two contradictory objectives of national governments: on the one hand, the desire to further European integration in response to functional and political pressures; on the other hand, the reluctance to transfer the corresponding powers and financial means to the EU. The contradictions between these objectives, and the ways in which political leaders have responded to them, have resulted in the EU's specific governance modes. These have evolved in adaptation to the multilevel structure of the EU, instead of transforming the system into a more hierarchically organized polity or even a federal state. In spite of procedural and institutional innovations, EU governance modes have not reached a satisfactory degree of effectiveness, so that further reforms and experiments are likely to occur in the future.

## References and Further Reading

Akman, P., and H. Kassim. 2010. "Myths and myth-making in the European Union: The institutionalization and interpretation of EU Competition Policy." *Journal of Common Market Studies* 48 (1): 111–32. https://doi.org/10.1111/j.1468-5965.2009.02044.x.

Bickerton, C.J., D. Hodson, and U. Puetter, eds. 2015. *The new intergovernmentalism: States and supranational actors in the post-Maastricht era.* Oxford: Oxford University Press. https://doi.org/10.1093/acprof:oso/9780198703617.001.0001.

Börzel, T.A. 2010. "European governance? Negotiation and competition in the shadow of hierarchy." *Journal of Common Market Studies* 45 (2): 231–52.

Buonanno, L., and N. Nugent. 2013. *Policies and policy processes of the European Union.* Basingstoke, UK: Palgrave Macmillan.

Fabbrini, S. 2013. "Intergovernmentalism and its limits: Assessing the European Union's answer to the euro crisis." *Comparative Political Studies* 20 (10): 1–27.

Falkner, G., O. Treib, M. Hartlapp, and S. Leiber. 2005. *Complying with Europe: EU harmonisation and soft law in the member states.* Cambridge: Cambridge University Press. https://doi.org/10.1017/CBO9780511491931.

German Ministry of Finance. 2016. Kassenmäßige Steuereinnahmen nach Gebietskörperschaften 2011–2015. http://www.bundesfinanzministerium.de/Content/DE/Standardartikel/Themen/Steuern/Steuerschaetzungen_und_Steuereinnahmen/2016-05-24-kassenmaessige-steuereinnahmen-nach-gebietskoerperschaften-2011-2015.pdf?__blob=publicationFile&v=2).

Knodt, M., and A. Tews. 2016. Boundaries of European solidarity – Lessons from migration and energy policy. *CEDI Working Paper 5*.

König, T., and L. Mäder. 2013. "Non-conformable, partial and conformable transposition: A competing risk analysis of the transposition process of directives in the EU 15." *European Union Politics* 14 (1): 46–69. https://doi.org/10.1177/1465116512447703.

Puetter, U. 2012. "Europe's deliberative intergovernmentalism: The role of the Council and European Council in EU economic governance." *Journal of European Public Policy* 19 (2): 161–78. https://doi.org/10.1080/13501763.2011.609743.

Richardson, J., ed. 2012. *Constructing a policy-making state? Policy dynamics in the EU*. Oxford: Oxford University Press https://doi.org/10.1093/acprof:oso/9780199604104.001.0001.

Richardson, J., and S. Mazey, eds. 2015. *European Union: Power and policy-making*. 4th ed. London: Routledge.

Sabel, C., and J. Zeitlin, eds. 2010. *Experimentalist governance in the European Union: Towards a new architecture*. Oxford: Oxford University Press.

Scharpf, F.W. 1999. *Governing in Europe: Effective and democratic?* Oxford: Oxford University Press. https://doi.org/10.1093/acprof:oso/9780198295457.001.0001.

Tömmel, I. 2014. *The European Union: What it is and how it works*. Basingstoke, UK: Palgrave Macmillan.

Tömmel, I., and A.Verdun, eds. 2009. *Innovative governance in the European Union: The politics of multilevel policymaking*. Boulder, CO: Lynne Rienner.

Wallace, H., M.A. Pollack, and A. Young, eds. 2015. *Policy-making in the European Union*. 7th ed. Oxford: Oxford University Press.

Weishaupt, J.T., and K. Lack. 2011. "The European employment strategy: Assessing the status quo." *German Policy Studies* 7 (1): 9–44.

## Review Questions

1. Why is there an asymmetry between market-making and market-correcting policies in the EU?

2. What are the core characteristics of the four phases of EU-policy-making and governance, and what triggered the changes between them?

3. Why are certain policies decided upon jointly by intergovernmental and supranational bodies and others exclusively by the intergovernmental bodies of the EU?

4. Why did the EU establish the system of partnership (in cohesion policy) and transnational networks (in competition policy)?

5. Does the OMC procedure improve or weaken the effectiveness of EU governance?

## Exercises

1.  Consider the role of direct taxation in governance. What does the absence of tax collection at the EU level tell us about the EU's multilevel system of governance? How does tax collection compare to the Canadian federal system?

2.  Select one of the major EU policy areas (e.g., agriculture, energy, Single Market, transport, etc.) and investigate the specific system of policy-making within. What role is there for national sovereignty? How has this policy area evolved over time?

# 6
# Theories of European Integration and Governance

AMY VERDUN

## Reader's Guide

This chapter looks at **European integration** theories from a historical perspective and explains how they have helped us understand the EU's formation and operation. The goal is to provide students with various theoretical approaches used in European integration studies so that they can analyze policies and developments in the EU from competing theoretical perspectives. Drawing on the three main themes of this book, this chapter covers theories and approaches that seek to explain European integration as well as theoretical debates about the EU's democratic credentials, the EU as a global actor, and European disintegration.

## Introduction

European integration theories emerged as researchers sought to explain why countries in Europe collaborated. The European Union (EU) was created out of the ashes of World War II with the goal of not having another war among the participating states (Theme 1 of this book). Thus, academics initially drew on international relations (IR) theories because that field had explanations about the conditions under which sovereign states would collaborate. Already during the war, in 1943, David Mitrany had published *A Working Peace System*, which offered the building blocks of his functional theory. His student Ernst B. Haas later would build on it to produce his leading works on **neofunctionalism** in the late 1950s and early 1960s. The form that the EU took on was much coloured by the fact that its early policies were created during the **Cold War** era. The European way was a mixed system (an economy that is neither state controlled nor left to an unconstrained market); rather it was social-democratic (Theme 1 of this book). Its regulations and policies aimed at market correction and social inclusion. The spirit of functional cooperation within this context was prominent in the early years. Yet as power politics started to dominate developments in the 1960s, realist approaches, notably the work of Stanley Hoffmann (**intergovernmentalism**), won terrain.

Another theme of this book is that the EU is more than an international organization but less than a federation (Theme 2). In fact, one might be forgiven for thinking that the founding fathers were interested in building a "United States of Europe" (see Chapter 2). Numerous federalists, such as Jean Monnet and Altiero Spinelli, provided the inspiration for embarking on the process of European integration. Yet at no time was there an actual grand plan for setting up a European federation. Indeed, there have been developments that make the EU a **supranational** entity in many aspects, not least its consistent output of legislation that is binding on its member states, but it still falls short of a full-fledged federal state, with member state **sovereignty** retained in core areas such as direct taxation. Yet over time the EU became such an advanced polity (an organized society having a particular form of government) that scholars started to look at the EU as an entity in itself rather than explaining why member states choose to join it or their level of integration among themselves (which had been the original interest of integration scholars). With that change in perspective, more typical political science approaches, such as governance approaches and institutionalism, were applied to the EU.

The third theme of this book is that the EU construction is built on the postwar assumption that by integrating gradually in technocratic and economic areas, the rest of integration will automatically follow. Indeed, early theories of European integration concentrated on technocratic issues, born from functional principles. Over time, critics examined the integration process and concluded that the EU had become a distinct political entity. Not only was the division between market/economic integration versus defence/foreign affairs perhaps not as stark, the citizens wanted more say in the creation of this supranational entity that was increasingly both a generator of as well as a response to globalization. These insights spawned theoretical contributions about how to understand the EU from a democratic theory perspective as well as the ways in which the EU is a player within and formed by globalization.

This chapter provides an overview of different integration theories as well as institutional and governance approaches developed in EU studies. The review follows a mostly chronological approach by looking at the theoretical questions EU scholars engaged with during the various phases of the EU's development, while also following to some extent the three themes of this book.

## Federalism, Neofunctionalism, and Intergovernmentalism

### Federalism

The idea to create a "United States of Europe" lay at the heart of federalist thinking about European integration, which dates back to well before World

War II (see Chapter 2). Although there have been various strands of federalist thought, **federalism** refers to the distribution of power in an organization (as a government) between a central (federal) authority and its lower level units (e.g., states or provinces). A federal state would be the opposite of a unitary state; in the latter, state authority remains at the central level. Another definition of federalism is a political ideology advocating for a move toward achieving such an arrangement, be it a confederation or a federation (federal state). These two forms of political system are different from each other in two important ways: a confederation is a union of sovereign states that does not constitute a new state. Furthermore, states retain the right to leave. A federation, by contrast, is a state recognized in the international state system, whereby the constituent states are partially self-governing. The constituent states are not recognized in the international state system, and they do not automatically have the right to leave (see Box 6.1).

**Box 6.1**   Federalism in Canada and the EU

Canada was named a "Confederation" when it was created in 1867. This name refers to the process whereby provinces joined; however, Canada was governed as a federation. The constituent states do not have legal status in the international system. The EU was created out of the ashes of World War II, initially in 1950 with the foundation of the Coal and Steel Community. From that point onward, the EU has expanded in both its membership and the scope of policy that it is involved with. The EU maintains some policy areas at the level of member states (e.g., tax policy, primary and secondary education, and health policy), while other areas are predominantly EU-level policies (trade policy, monetary policy). The Canadian federation also started with fewer provinces and eventually expanded with respect to its members as well as the policies dealt with at the federal level. In the Canadian system, most sectors, such as foreign affairs, security, and monetary policy, are under federal jurisdiction. Other sectors, such as property, civil rights, labour relations, health care, and education, are under provincial jurisdiction (even though the **welfare system** was, in part, built on payments from the federal government to the provinces). Some sectors, such as taxation and unemployment, are under joint jurisdiction (in the latter sector, activation policy is a provincial and unemployment insurance a federal responsibility). For more details, see Verdun (2016).

One of the early federalist thinkers was the Italian Altiero Spinelli, who wrote the so-called *Ventotene Manifesto* in 1941 calling for European integration. In a speech delivered in Zürich, Switzerland, in 1946, British Prime Minister Winston Churchill called for a United States of Europe, which led to the creation of the **Council of Europe** in 1949 (see Chapter 2). Yet there was no agreement on whether federalism was the way forward. The approach that became more successful in the early years of integration was neofunctionalism (see below). The federalist approach to European integration has experienced something of a comeback in recent years. Scholars such as Michael Burgess have spent their whole academic careers studying federalism and federal states with a view to learning from those types of political systems. He and others, such as Dan Kelemen and Joseph H. Weiler, have argued that the EU has moved away from being a pure confederation and has started to meet some parts of the definition of a federation, effectively creating its own version of federation. Especially when the EU was going through the process of creating a Treaty establishing a Constitution for Europe in the early 2000s, many were wondering whether they were witnessing the birth of the European federation. Although the Constitutional Treaty was not ratified, the **Lisbon Treaty** maintained a few aspects of deeper integration that have paved the way for some level of federation in the EU Treaty: the EU now has legal personality in the international system and it has acquired new policy-making power in various areas that are typical in federations, including **foreign policy**, security, defence, and monetary policy. Yet the EU does not have exclusive competence over most of these fields. Moreover, its member states are still legal states in the international state system. These developments that have made the EU move beyond a confederation, but not quite become a federation, is a reason why the EU has often been referred to as a *sui generis* (one-of-a-kind) political system. Former Commission President Jacques Delors characterized the EU as an "unidentified political object."

## Neofunctionalism

One of the first influential studies of the European integration process was by Ernst B. Haas who, in 1958, published a book called *The Uniting of Europe*, which focused on the **European Coal and Steel Community (ECSC)**. His key concept was that of **spillover**, which Leon N. Lindberg later used in his 1963 book to examine the **European Economic Community (EEC)** and Haas developed further in his book *Beyond the Nation-State* (1964). While this approach was intended to be relevant to a wider scope than merely European integration (such as integration in other parts of the world, for example, Latin America), the theories have since been mostly applied to European integration and only to a much lesser extent in the rest of the world.

Inspired by the functional approach of liberal international relations scholar David Mitrany, Haas referred to his own work as "neofunctionalism." Haas focused on the *process* of integration, one in which political actors would shift their loyalties to the supranational level, thereby creating a new political community at that level. To get there, the main mechanism is technocratic decision-making, incremental change and learning among elites. The main actors included supranational institutions but also organized interest groups. Haas and Lindberg saw the process of integration as an incremental one, with the concept of spillover at its core. Spillover means that once a particular sector becomes integrated, the need arises to integrate other, connected sectors (functional spillover); an example of this would be the integration of the coal and steel sectors necessitating the integration of the transport sector. European integration would occur as countries went through this process. Countries would witness a gradual but automatic shift from economic to political integration, whereby political loyalty would be transferred to the supranational level. The important actors in this process would be elites—mostly peak associations (interest groups) and supranational authorities—while member states would gradually lose exclusive control over the integration process that they had initiated.

Neofunctionalism was able to explain the process for a few years, but by mid-1960s Stanley Hoffmann, a scholar of French politics, put forward his intergovernmentalist critique. Hoffmann (1966) responded to a change in the developments on the ground. The French president, Charles de Gaulle, was less supportive of European integration, and his opposition to supranationalism became clear with the Empty Chair Crisis, when the French boycotted **Council** meetings in 1965–66. Hoffmann argued that one should be open to conceptualizing "spillback" (the reversal of integration) due to the re-emergence of nationalism and the continuity of national identity in the context of a lack of a European identity. By 1968, when the second edition of *The Uniting of Europe* was published. Haas included a prologue in which he admitted that Hoffmann had a point and agreed with him that there was a difference between what Hoffmann had labelled "high" and **"low" politics** (the former being the policies that were central to state sovereignty, such as defence and foreign policy), whereas he still believed that more technocratic policies (economic policies) would fit the predictions of neofunctionalist theory. In the 1970s, other neofunctionalist scholars, such as Philippe Schmitter, a student of Haas, further developed neofunctionalism to include conceptual acceptance that neofunctionalism could also incorporate "spillback" or "spillaround" (intergovernmental cooperation outside of the EU framework). However, by 1975 even Haas himself declared that his theory was unable to explain the process of integration.

Subsequently, neofunctionalism was not much referred to by scholars, especially as the integration process seemed to stall in the 1970s. However, by the late 1980s, the integration process had picked up again, and neofunctionalism experienced a bit of a revival. Scholars like David Mutimer (1989) and Jeppe Tranholm-Mikkelsen (1991) jumpstarted the debate; before long, more scholarly volumes were published, further developing and reanalyzing neofunctionalism and taking on board new insights based on developments in the 1990s (Sandholtz & Stone Sweet, 1998). With the passing of Ernst B. Haas, a volume dedicated to his work appeared (Börzel, 2006), spelling out how the theoretical approach was still valuable in explaining the integration process, even if the claim was no longer being made that this approach could explain all of it. Scholars recognized that it served well as a **mid-range theory**, that is, one with a more limited scope than a **grand theory**, which is much broader in scope. Mid-range theories seek to integrate empirical insights with more modest theoretical understanding. Grand theory, as advanced by scholars such as the sociologist C. Wright Mills in the 1960s, would aim at a higher level of understanding about the nature of the political system but would not concern itself too much with the details of the empirics. The scholarship of European integration sought to differentiate between theories that would explain in an elegant way the entirety of European integration and mid-range theories that might be better suited to explaining some parts of the empirics by adopting a particular theoretical approach. In recent years, the work of Arne Niemann has applied neofunctionalism to explain EU decision-making, for example, during the euro crisis. Niemann and other present-day neofunctionalists use the approach more as a mid-range theory, their claim being that it is helpful in shedding light on a part of the process.

### Intergovernmentalism

Hoffmann's intergovernmental critique of the 1960s drew on realist international relations theory, as it focused on nation-states' power and was triggered by the renewed rise in nationalism in various Western European member states. Rather than concentrating on the mechanisms that neofunctionalists identified, it offered an alternative—state-centric—analysis of the integration process. The main actors in intergovernmentalism are states (national governments). According to the state-centric view, states would be unlikely to give up sovereignty in favour of deeper integration.

When integration did occur, automaticity would not be assumed; cooperation could be the result only if it was in the interests of the member states. Thus, intergovernmentalism assumed that cooperation would occur from time to time and on a case-by-case basis, but did not see any leadership role for supranational actors, as neofunctionalism had. Instead, according to intergovernmentalists, actors such as the **European Commission, European Parliament**, or the **Court of Justice of the EU (CJEU)** operate as agents of the member states, who are tasked with brokering deals, based on instructions and guidance received from the member states. Intergovernmentalists look at European integration initiatives as a form of cooperation for which there are costs and benefits. They weigh them against each other before deciding if they are in their interests. Paul Taylor, in a book published in 1983, further developed this approach, examining the limits of neofunctionalism and pointing to the importance of states. At this time, the integration process had seemed to move very slowly indeed, a period during which European integration was referred to as "eurosclerosis" (economic stagnation and apparent slow process of European integration). In recent years, research has shown that the courts kept moving the European integration process forward during this time, even if politicians on the whole showed less leadership in this regard.

In the 1990s, when the integration process picked up steam again, scholars such as Alan Milward and Andrew Moravcsik further developed this school of thought (see also Chapter 2). Both emphasized the crucial role of the nation-state in the integration process. Moravcsik developed a theory by adopting elements of liberal international relations theory, examining the domestic reasons that could explain national interests. This attracted a lot of attention, as it was an approach with clear theoretical foundations and precise testable hypotheses. It was attractive in its simplicity and worked well in some arenas, notably when applied to Council decisions. Moravcsik's theory consists of three components. First there is a liberal theory of national state preferences. It means that state preferences are shaped by societal interests at the domestic level (demand side) and that the sum of those preferences is what makes up the "state" preference. The second component is interstate bargaining. States are now seen as unitary actors. The larger states, with greater influence and bargaining power, have more say in this process. The final component is institutional delegation, whereby EU institutions function to improve the efficiency of interstate bargaining. According to this view, supranational institutions, such as the Commission, are not seen as actors that independently influence and advance the integration process, but rather as agents of the member states. Nation-states create supranational institutions as a way to commit each other to their agreements, for instance, by creating mechanisms in which the Commission and the Court of Justice ensure that all states adequately transpose and implement EU **directives**.

Recently, scholars such as Bickerton, Hodson, and Puetter (2015) have emphasized how the integration process since the financial crisis has led to the paradoxical situation whereby EU activity has increased but the constitutional features of the EU have stayed roughly the same. They call this form of integration without increased supranationalism "new intergovernmentalism." This approach is not without criticism. Scholars like Frank Schimmelfennig (2015) point out that the EU in its entirety has not necessarily become more intergovernmental. He points to the responses to the financial crisis: the strengthening of existing institutions such as the **European Central Bank**, and the creation of new supranational institutional structures such as the **Banking Union** and the **Capital Markets Union** (see Chapter 7). In fact, studies of the role of the European Commission since the **sovereign debt crisis** suggest that the Commission has obtained a larger role in macroeconomic governance even in steering the member states (Bauer & Becker, 2014; Savage & Verdun, 2015; Becker et al., 2016). What people have noticed in recent years, however, is the increasing influence of certain national leaders, such as the German chancellor, which seems in line with a more intergovernmental interpretation. Some of the reason for the rise of Germany is the decline of the economic and political power of France in recent years, following many years of a strong Franco-German tandem as an important locus of EU leadership.

## Multilevel Governance, Governance, Europeanization, and Institutionalism

As integration experienced a revival in the EU in the 1990s, new approaches came on the scene to study European integration. Simon Hix (1994) pointed out that the approaches derived from the field of international relations were suitable for studying the phenomenon of European integration, while those from comparative politics would be better suited for studying the internal politics of the EU. They examine the EU as its own "polity"—looking at internal politics. With the growth of the scope of European integration, scholars were also examining how the EU compared to other political systems.

The **multilevel governance** approach superseded the international relations–based assumptions of earlier theories that sought to understand why states collaborate in the international system. Liesbet Hooghe and Gary Marks (2009) formulated their multilevel governance perspective, by concentrating on the activities that occurred in the EU at various levels: the EU level, the national level, and the sub-state level (provincial or regional level). An important innovation in their theoretical contribution was to focus not only at the EU- and the nation-state–level but also at sub-state levels. Their study of **regional policy** showed how regional actors were able to move integration forward, sometimes even circumventing national state actors. Hooghe and Marks's, as well as other, governance approaches more generally, were able to show that the central claim of liberal intergovernmentalism—namely that state preferences are determined in national settings, and the nation-state government is the advocate for national interests—does not work in every policy arena. Policy studies showed that different modes of governance could influence the process of integration. For instance, in a collection of case studies published in 2009, Tömmel and Verdun identify four different, innovative modes of governance that are used in the EU: hierarchy, negotiation, competition, and cooperation. Each mode has a different influence on the integration process, and sometimes these modes are even used together (see also Chapter 5). One form of cooperation that has received much attention is the **Open Method of Coordination (OMC)** used in social policy (see Chapter 10). The actors involved in the OMC include both public and private actors, and they often represent different dimensions of the policy domain. Their aim is to improve the policy or to set goals that others seek to achieve. Governance approaches serve to spell out how integration can occur outside the classic domain in which the national government negotiates in an intergovernmental setting to advance national interests at the EU level.

Another concept that emerged in the 1990s was **Europeanization**. It was at first loosely used by a range of scholars without a clear uniform definition—sometimes even with considerably different applications. Over time, this concept has been widely understood to refer to two dimensions. The first is top-down Europeanization. When used this way, this term defines how the EU impacts the member states. Top-down Europeanization research focuses on how the EU shapes institutions, processes, and policies in the member states and even in countries outside the EU (in particular, accession countries and countries in the EU neighbourhood). By contrast, bottom-up Europeanization refers to how member states and other domestic actors shape the EU and its policies. Here the focus is on how the member states and other actors can "upload" their interest, experiences, and practices to the EU level. The Europeanization research seeks to understand how to identify how the EU has changed policies and politics in the member states but also outside the EU. Finally, there is one more group of research questions that adopt the concept of Europeanization, namely those that examine how the governance of the EU as a whole impacts other regional organizations, such as the African Union or the Association of Southeast Asian Nations (ASEAN). For example, recent work of Tanja Börzel and Thomas Risse (2012) has explored the extent to which these and similar regional organizations emulate the EU's institutional features or its policies.

Other theoretical approaches that gained attention in the 1990s were those that could be derived from political science research that studied political systems. Borrowing from the more general political science toolkit of theories, these approaches became popular in European integration studies the moment one could conceptualize the EU as a more typical political system. Recall that the early integration theories were born from international relations with a view to understanding why separate countries might wish to cooperate or integrate. With a gradual appreciation that the EU was starting to resemble more a regular political system, even if a so-called *sui generis* one the focus changed as to what had to be theorized. Rather than wondering why separate nations were collaborating, the focus now was on the actual system, how this system was functioning the way it did, and what policy outcomes could be expected, given the nature of the system. Markus Jachtenfuchs (2001) has pointed out this change in the object of study by differentiating between a classical phase of integration theory when the so-called EU polity was the *dependent variable* (the outcome to be explained) to the contemporary phase in which the EU polity is the *independent variable* (a factor that explains other outcomes).

With this change in the object of study, a whole range of general political science approaches became accessible to scholars. In fact, with the EU gaining some institutional features—such as developed executive, legislative, judicial, and bureaucratic bodies—it was possible to view the developments in the EU as a political system with these features. As a result, the insights from institutionalism became of interest. An institutionalist approach assumes that the nature of the institutions shapes the outcome of politics and policies. In the 1990s, there was a revival of institutionalism, labelled "**new institutionalism**" both to mark the difference between it and classical institutionalism and to signal the renewed interest in focusing on institutions against the behavioural backdrop of the earlier decades. Three main approaches of institutionalisms were developed during this time: historical institutionalism, rational choice institutionalism, and sociological institutionalism. Historical institutionalism defines institutions as formal or informal procedures, routines, norms, and conventions that are embedded in the structure of a polity. It conceptualizes the relationships between institutions and individual behaviour in broad terms and adopts the concepts of "path dependence," "unintended consequences," but also the "role of ideas" to highlight some of the dynamics of the developments of institutions.

Rational choice institutionalism examines how institutions may lower the transaction costs of making deals (passing legislative proposals). This branch of new institutionalism sees institutions as a way to solve all kinds of collective action problems that legislatures often face. Finally, sociological institutionalism argues that many of the institutional forms and procedures of organization are not adopted because they are the most efficient way to do so, but rather they are culturally specific practices and thus must be explained as such. Sociological institutionalism resembles "constructivism," as used in international relations literature, which also became very popular in EU research from the late 1990s onwards. Though there is not really one single "constructivism," the umbrella term brings together various approaches that themselves draw from institutionalism and interpretivism and aim to be a mid-range theory of integration. In the late 1990s, Thomas Christiansen, Knud Erik Jørgensen, and Antje Wiener brought together a collection of essays examining how one might make sense of European integration using constructivist approaches. Constructivism examines the role of norms, ideas, and identity in shaping international political outcomes. Scholars that fall under this rubric could range from more positivist and rational to more critical and radical ones.

## Theories of Democracy, Legitimacy, and the EU as a Global Player

Toward the end of the twentieth century, a body of literature emerged that concentrated on questions around the democratic nature of the EU. It considered the EU as a polity—a form of organized society with a political organization rather than merely a collection of nation-states. In this view, theorizing about the EU needed to include an analysis of its democratic features. The *trias politica* (separation between the legislation, administration, and jurisdiction as advocated by Greek democratic principles and French enlightenment philosophers such as Montesquieu) works reasonably well in the EU. As the EU's judiciary, the Court of Justice is independent and separate from the other two branches (see Chapter 4). The European Commission acts as an independent executive (administration) and is appointed by the Council (approved by the EP). The European Commission also has a role in the legislative process as it initiates legislative proposals. Proposals are approved by a combination of the Council and the EP (see Chapter 3). The legislative power has traditionally been seen to have the weakest democratic checks and balances. Compared to a usual "bicameral parliamentary democracy" or "representative democracy," the EU does not have as much of a vocal opposition. For instance, its popular opposition (located in the

European Parliament) was a bit weaker because for the longest time the EP had only a minor role as co-legislator and its "government" (Commission) was appointed rather than chosen through parliamentary elections. Thus, the system of checks and balances between the branches is weaker than in the ideal typical model of a liberal democracy. ·

A wide range of studies has been dedicated to the study of the EU's democratic credentials (see also Chapter 17). Some of these were more *normative* in orientation, asking what the EU ought to look like. Others were more *positive*, meaning that they were focused on explaining why the EU looked the way it did, without necessarily including a judgment about whether the EU was therefore "good" or "bad" or how it must change to improve. From these studies, it became clear that although it was attractive to think that the **democratic deficit** would disappear if only the EU looked more like a regular parliamentary democracy, such a change could not easily be made in the EU. These studies pointed out that precisely because the EU was not a full-fledged federal state, and given that its citizens did not fully identify with the EU, it was not (yet) possible to reproduce the standard political features of a parliamentary democracy at the EU level, as it would take away from the legitimate authority of the lower levels: the member states. Citizens felt better represented at the member state level than at the EU level. Thus, to increase the democratic credentials of the EU, the emphasis turned to increasing the role of participation in the EU and finding gradual increases in the power of the European Parliament. To increase participation meant finding ways to have citizens connect to the EU. But it also meant encouraging interest groups, experts, and national, transnational and European civil society groups to have access to and participate in the various stages of policy-making in the EU. This approach was often referred to as "participatory democracy." Various scholars emphasized the importance of deliberation and enabling various groups to give their views on draft policies and legislative proposals. Finally, the concern was that the EU did not have a single *demos*—a "people" with a shared identity or values that could be represented in one single body (see also Chapter 17). Even though the concept of a European citizenship emerged with the **Maastricht Treaty**, it did not right away contain the features needed for all to share a common identity. The new citizenship did give rise to numerous studies, theoretical and empirical, on understanding citizenship in the EU context.

Closely related to the concept of democratic deficit was the concept of "legitimacy." To what extent was the EU producing legitimate input or output? Input legitimacy means that the European people or peoples find the political system legitimate because they accept the process whereby the elected parliamentary and government officials have been selected, even if the outcomes of their decisions are not what they would have liked. Output legitimacy, by contrast, means that people find a political system legitimate because they find the results it produces satisfactory. Such outputs could be increased well-being and also the quality of governance—with transparent and coherent deliverables and adherence to principles of good governance. Making sure that there are improved opportunities for actors and stakeholders to be part of the policy-making process would also increase the likelihood that policy outputs would be in line with what the citizens and other stakeholders were hoping for.

Finally, as the EU became a more coherent actor, there were increasingly theories that started to look at how to theorize the EU as a global actor. One might think that such a research topic would bring the theories of integration full circle, back to the realm of international relations. And to some extent it is true. Hedley Bull famously said of the EU in 1982 that it was mainly a "civilian power" and not likely to become a main actor in international affairs. A lot has happened since 1982, so Bull can be forgiven for not having had a crystal ball. But the EU still remains an awkward actor in the global system (see Chapters 9, 14, and 18). It lacks very clear actorship, as EU leadership is often weak compared to the leadership of nations such as the United States or China. Also, the EU is a strong player in the global system in some policy areas (for instance trade, international development, human rights, and climate policies) but less so on others (such as foreign policy and defence), mainly because its constituent parts may have diverging policies and ambitions in those areas. The EU is obviously by definition weaker if the EU has joint competence with the member states and is required to check back in with member states before it can act in the international arena.

The EU, therefore, has often been characterized as an economic giant but a political dwarf. However, with the entering into force of the Lisbon Treaty it has the potential to become a more coherent foreign-policy actor as time goes by because some of its leadership roles have become more empowered. In the past it already capitalized on its relative strengths by using instruments, such as norms, that have been labelled by Joseph Nye as having **soft power** (persuasion)—rather than focusing on "hard power" (coercion) using, for instance, military capacity. Ian Manners (2002) has also spelled out a conception of "Normative Power Europe," arguing that the role of the EU in global affairs is first and foremost normative, rather than economic or military.

As mentioned above, when discussing the external component of Europeanization, scholars have recently also started to examine the role of the EU as a global actor in inter-regionalism. Here the focus is not only on how the EU serves as a model for other regions of the globe but also to what extent these regional organizations across the globe are becoming "actors" in global politics and what influence they have in world order and global govern-ance. Many of these regional organizations suffer from internal conflict, as does the EU. But remarkably, perhaps, these organizations are increasingly prominent on the global stage. Furthermore, the EU is the most coherent, advanced polity of all regional organizations, and although falling short of a full-fledged federal system, still often quite able to speak with one voice on international affairs. As such, it has become a leading player in world politics. As is discussed in more detail in Chapters 9, 14, and 18, various aspects of EU external relations must be distinguished in order to analyze the true impact of the EU on the global stage.

## Debate: Why Use Theories in European Integration Studies?

So far this chapter has pointed to the development in integration theo-ries from the very early days to the present time. In the first four decades, approaches based on international relations theories sought to put all of the activities in European integration under one umbrella. Both neofunctional-ism and intergovernmentalism at first sought to explain the entire integra-tion process through a single lens (grand theory). Over time, it became clear that European integration was too complex and that a single theory was unable to do justice to all the types of developments that occur throughout the European integration process. Furthermore, as was discussed above, with the turn toward considering the EU as a polity in its own right, schol-ars have increasingly considered more usual political science, comparative politics, and public administration approaches to studying the politics of and policy-making in the EU as well as the impact of the EU in member states. The purpose of why to use theory has also changed. Rather than focusing mostly on the question of why integration happens, the subject of study has become more concentrated on understanding how developments occur in the EU polity. Furthermore, scholars have increasingly become concerned with normative questions as to how the EU ought to function and what it might need to look like.

Until now this chapter has not yet provided an assessment of the useful-ness of the various approaches. In fact, in EU studies the ongoing and unre-solved salient debates, when it comes to using theory in the study of the EU, are today perhaps less passionate than in the early years, when there were fervent grand-theory debates about whether European integration could be characterized as more intergovernmental or more supranational. Today the richness of theories that can be deployed, together with the level of detail, onto whatever the researcher might want to study, has led to the existence of a large toolkit of theories and approaches at the disposal of a researcher.

**Table 6.1**   A schematic simple taxonomy of theories used in European integration studies

| Dominant actors and mechanisms in advancing European integration | Theoretical approach |
|---|---|
| *1. Dominant actors:* | |
| Supranational actors | Neofunctionalism, governance approaches |
| National actors | Intergovernmentalism, governance approaches |
| Regional actors | Multilevel governance |
| Transnational interest groups | Neofunctionalism, governance approaches |
| Organized stakeholders; civil society | Participatory democracy |
| *2. Dominant mechanisms in advancing European integration:* | |
| Spillover | Neofunctionalism |
| Bargaining | Intergovernmentalism |
| Unintended consequences and path dependence | Historical institutionalism |
| Uploading and downloading | Europeanization |
| Modes of governance | Governance approaches |
| Norms, ideas, and beliefs | Normative power Europe, constructivism |
| Cultural adaptation and socialization | Sociological institutionalism, constructivism |
| Citizen engagement in the policy-making process | Participatory democracy |
| *3. Theoretical objective:* | |
| Explaining European integration | Neofunctionalism, intergovernmentalism |
| Understanding European integration | Federalism, multilevel governance, Europeanization, institutionalism, constructivism |
| Evaluating the normative quality of the EU | Normative power Europe, participatory democracy, constructivism |

Source: Adapted from Verdun (2002a; 2002b)

Table 6.1 offers a taxonomy of the theories and approaches discussed in this chapter so far.

The taxonomy should be used only as a heuristic device. It should be clear that many of the approaches also place some value on other actors, mechanisms, or theoretical purposes than the ones listed in the table. Also, this chapter has not discussed every possible theoretical framework used by scholars of European integration. Thus, the taxonomy provided here is merely intended to sort the approaches and to summarize the above over-view. What it does make clear, however, is that the locus of attention is different in the various approaches. When researchers seek to develop their research questions and reflect on what theoretical frameworks would be best able to address their question, they may do well to consider each of their traditions and what their prime actors and mechanisms as well as research objectives have been.

Before closing, let us turn to an important related issue that the EU is confronted with at the present time: European disintegration. Hans Vollaard (2014) has argued convincingly that there have been many more instances in world history of political disintegration than of integration. Examples of disintegration include, for instance, the breaking up into two nations of Czechoslovakia as well as the collapse of the Soviet Union and Yugoslavia. Furthermore, there are current pressures in existing nation-states that have given rise to increased autonomy within the confines of the state, by giving more power to sub-national units in existing federations (such as the Flemish and Walloons in Belgium, the Quebeckers in Canada, and the Catalans in Spain). Examples of the integration of nations to create a union are fewer and include the unification of Germany, Vietnam, and Yemen. Thus one would need to be aware that disintegration is always a possibility.

In the EU today such a prospect of limited disintegration is emerging for the first time, given the decision by a majority of voters in a United Kingdom referendum to "leave" the EU (for more on the **Brexit** referendum, see Chapter 7). Although Greenland (part of Denmark) broke away from the EU in 1985, the departure of the United Kingdom is a more pertinent example of disintegration, even though the prospect of its departure is not currently anticipated to cause the disintegration of the EU in its entirety. Furthermore, the increase in seats won by Euroskeptic parties in the 2014 European Parliament elections is another indicator, as is the rise in nationalist and anti-European political parties in various EU member states. Hans Vollaard (2014) is quick to point out that, except for the concept of "spillback" of neofunctionalism, very few theories leave open conceptual theoretical space for disintegration. He convincingly argues that disintegration is not merely the opposite of integration. He argues that in disintegration it may not be as simple as giving powers back to nation-states. Instead powers could be handed back to sub-national regions, or, theoretically, the EU could become part of a more loosely organized global world. Thus Vollaard warns against a state-bias in our understanding of disintegration. Instead, he argues that one needs to study the way dissatisfaction with the EU is given voice to and in what ways one may want to address discontent. One also needs to think more creatively about how both the EU and the national level can find ways to allow groups to have partial **opt-outs**. Another major issue facing the EU today is finding ways to compensate for inequalities that arise due to European integration. Vollaard argues that failing to address these issues may lead to a faster disintegration of the EU. Of course, any increase in EU spending or expansion of EU powers would need to go hand in hand with an increase in the democratic powers of the EU—which would enhance its legitimacy (see Chapter 17).

## Conclusion

This chapter aimed to review the various theories that are adopted in European integration studies. Starting with the classic theories of neofunctionalism and intergovernmentalism that were dominant in the early decades, the chapter reviewed newer theoretical frameworks, such as governance approaches, Europeanization, and institutionalism. The chapter also reviewed some of the theoretical debates that centre on themes such as democracy and legitimacy in the EU, the questions around the EU as a global actor, and issues related to the possible disintegration of the EU. This chapter makes clear that the time of grand theorization has passed, but that the remnants of those approaches still penetrate contemporary EU studies. Contemporary research draws much more on general scholarly literature in the field of political science, public administration, and adjacent disciplines. The purpose of theory in European integration studies is to build on the insights of the past so as to inform our current research questions. Whether the scope of the research is smaller or wider, or whether it contributes to a smaller or larger part of the insight on European integration, is left to the choice of individual academic researchers.

## References and Further Reading

Bauer, M., and S. Becker. 2014. "The unexpected winner of the crisis: The European Commission's strengthened role in economic governance." *Journal of European Integration* 36 (3): 213–29. https://doi.org/10.1080/07036337.2014.885750.

Becker, S., M.W. Bauer, S. Connolly, and H. Kassim. 2016. "The Commission: Boxed in and constrained but still an engine of integration." *West European Politics* 39 (5): 1011–31. https://doi.org/10.1080/01402382.2016.1181870.

Bellamy, R., D. Castiglione, and J. Shaw, eds. 2006. *Making European citizens: Civic inclusion in a transnational context*. Basingstoke, UK: Palgrave Macmillan. https://doi.org/10.1057/9780230627475.

Bickerton, C.J., D. Hodson, and U. Puetter, eds. 2015. *The new intergovernmentalism. States and supranational actors in the post-Maastricht era*. Oxford: Oxford University Press. https://doi.org/10.1093/acprof:oso/9780198703617.001.0001.

Börzel, T., ed. 2006. *The disparity of European integration: Revisiting neofunctionalism in honour of Ernst B. Haas*. London: Routledge.

Börzel, T.A., and T. Risse. 2012. "From Europeanisation to diffusion: Introduction." *West European Politics* 35 (1): 1–19. https://doi.org/10.1080/01402382.2012.631310.

Christiansen, T., K.E. Jørgensen, and A. Wiener. 2001. *The social construction of Europe.* London: Sage.

Ericksen, E.O., and J.E. Fossum, eds. 2000. *Democracy in the European Union: Integration through deliberation?* London: Routledge.

Genschel, P., and M. Jachtenfuchs, eds. 2014. *Beyond the regulatory polity? The European integration of core state powers.* Oxford: Oxford University Press.

Haas, E.B. 1958. *The uniting of Europe: Political, social, and economical forces, 1950–1957.* London: Stevens.

Hix, S. 1994. "The study of the European Community: The challenge to comparative politics." *West European Politics* 17 (1): 1–30. https://doi.org/10.1080/01402389408424999.

Hoffmann, S. 1966. "Obstinate or obsolete? The fate of the nation-state and the case of Western Europe." *Daedalus* 95 (3): 862–915.

Hooghe, L., and G. Marks. 2009. "A postfunctionalist theory of European integration: From permissive consensus to constraining dissensus." *British Journal of Political Science* 39 (1): 1–23. https://doi.org/10.1017/S0007123408000409.

Hueglin, T.O., and A. Fenna. 2005. *Comparative federalism: A systematic inquiry.* 2nd ed. Toronto: University of Toronto Press.

Jachtenfuchs, M. 2001. "The governance approach to European integration." *JCMS: Journal of Common Market Studies* 39 (2): 245–64.

Kohler-Koch, B., and B. Rittberger. 2006. "Review article: The 'Governance Turn' in EU studies." *Journal of Common Market Studies* 44 (s1): 27–49. https://doi.org/10.1111/j.1468-5965.2006.00642.x.

Leuffen, D., B. Rittberger, and F. Schimmelfennig. 2013. *Differentiated integration: Explaining variation in the European Union.* Basingstoke, UK: Palgrave Macmillan.

Long, D., and L.M. Ashworth. 1999. "Working for peace: The functional approach, functionalism and beyond." In *New perspectives on international functionalism,* edited by L.M. Ashworth and D. Long, 1–26. Basingstoke, UK: Palgrave Macmillan. https://doi.org/10.1007/978-1-349-27055-2_1.

Marks, G., L. Hooghe, and K. Blank. 1996. "European integration from the 1980s: State-centric v. multilevel governance." *Journal of Common Market Studies* 34 (3): 341–78. https://doi.org/10.1111/j.1468-5965.1996.tb00577.x.

Manners, I. 2002. "Normative power Europe: A contradiction in terms?" *Journal of Common Market Studies* 40 (2): 235–58. https://doi.org/10.1111/1468-5965.00353.

Moravcsik, A. 1998. *The choice for Europe: Social purpose and state power from Messina to Maastricht.* Ithaca, NY: Cornell University Press.

Mutimer, D. 1989. "1992 and the political integration of Europe: Neofunctionalism reconsidered." *Journal of European Integration* 13 (1): 75–101.

Niemann, A., and D. Ioannou. 2015. "European economic integration in times of crisis: A case of neofunctionalism?" *Journal of European Public Policy* 22 (2): 196–218. https://doi.org/10.1080/13501763.2014.994021.

Pentland, C. 1973. *International theory and European integration.* London: Faber.

Pollack, M.A. 2002. *The engines of European integration: Delegation, agency and agenda setting in the European Union.* Oxford: Oxford University Press.

Rosamond, B. 2000. *Theories of European integration*. Basingstoke, UK: Palgrave Macmillan.

Sandholtz, W., and A. Stone Sweet, eds. 1998. *European integration and supranational governance*. Oxford: Oxford University Press.

Savage, J.D., and A. Verdun. 2015. "Strengthening the European Commission's budgetary and economic surveillance capacity since Greece and the euro crisis: A study of five Directorates-General." *Journal of European Public Policy* 23 (1): 101–18. https://doi.org/10.1080/13501763.2015.1041417.

Schimmelfennig, F. 2015. "What's the news in 'new intergovernmentalism'? A critique of Bickerton, Hodson and Puetter." *Journal of Common Market Studies* 53 (4): 723–30. https://doi.org/10.1111/jcms.12234.

Söderbaum, F., and L. Van Langenhove. 2005. "Introduction: The EU as a global actor and the role of interregionalism." *Journal of European Integration* 27 (3): 249–62. https://doi.org/10.1080/07036330500190073.

Taylor, P. 1983. *The limits of European integration*. London: Croom Helm.

Tömmel, I., and A. Verdun. 2009. *Innovative governance in the European Union*. Boulder, CO: Lynne Rienner.

Tranholm-Mikkelsen, J. 1991. "Neo-functionalism: Obstinate or obsolete? A reappraisal in the light of the new dynamism of the EC." *Millennium. Journal of International Studies* 20 (1): 1–22.

Vollaard, H. 2014. "Explaining European disintegration." *Journal of Common Market Studies* 52 (5): 1142–59. https://doi.org/10.1111/jcms.12132.

Verdun, A., ed. 2002a. *The euro: European integration theory and Economic and Monetary Union*. Lanham, MD: Rowman and Littlefield.

Verdun, A. 2002b. "Why EMU happened: A survey of theoretical explanations." In *Before and beyond EMU–View from across the Atlantic*, edited by P. Crowley, 71–98. London: Routledge. https://doi.org/10.4324/9780203463390.pt2.

Verdun, A. 2015. "A historical institutionalist explanation of the EU's responses to the euro area financial crisis." *Journal of European Public Policy* 22 (2): 219–37. https://doi.org/10.1080/13501763.2014.994023.

Verdun, A. 2016. "The federal features of the EU: Lessons from Canada." *Politics and Governance* 4 (3): 100–10. https://doi.org/10.17645/pag.v4i3.598.

Wiener, A., and T. Diez. 2011. *European integration theory*. 3rd ed. Oxford: Oxford University Press.

Wood, D., and A. Verdun. 2011. "Canada and the European Union: A review of the literature from 1982 to 2010." *International Journal* 66 (1s): 9–21. https://doi.org/10.1177/002070201106600102.

## Review Questions

1. Are theories of federalism helpful in explaining developments in the EU?

2. Why were neofunctionalism and intergovernmentalism the dominant approaches in the early years of European integration? Why did both of them witness a revival in the 1990s?

3. Why have approaches from political science and public administration emerged in more and more studies that cover developments in the European Union?

4.  How has widening, deepening, and differentiation affected European integration theories?

5.  How have concerns over the EU's democratic credentials influenced the use of theory in EU studies?

6.  Why did international relations theories lose their attraction for studying the EU and why they are more frequently used again today?

## Exercises

1.  When studying the EU comparatively, when is it appropriate to compare the EU to other federal countries, and when is it appropriate to compare the EU to other international organizations? What theoretical approaches are used in each tactic?

2.  Consider the history and trajectory of the EU alongside the two major theories of European integration—neofunctionalism and liberal intergovernmentalism. What major events support and challenge each theory?

# PART II

# Policies

## Introduction to Part II

A S WE HAVE SEEN IN PART I OF THIS BOOK, the EU is neither a "normal" state, nor an international organization. Part II introduces readers to the large range of policies that bring the member states together into a union; it also provides details on how each policy has evolved. Each one of the following 10 chapters shows the gradual development of the mixed system that has reduced economic barriers between the member states while seeking to implement solidarity. This development is the result of the creation of the **Single Market** as well as the **Europeanization** of policy domains such as agriculture; energy and the environment; regional and social affairs; foreign and defence policy; and justice, freedom, and security policies; but also policies on external trade, EU **enlargement**, and relationships with neighbouring states.

Initially, European integration focused on the flagship project of completing the single European market, defined by four freedoms—the free movement of goods, services, labour, and capital across all member states. Two approaches were used to achieve this objective. First, existing barriers inhibiting free movement between the member states—such as customs duties or employment rules discriminating against people from other member states—were abolished. This approach was called **negative integration**. Second, common policies were created insofar as it was necessary to regulate economic transactions in the Single Market and to offset possible negative economic and social side effects. This approach was called **positive integration**. Positive integration was necessary, given that the EU represented a mixed economy, which aims at achieving important social objectives (Theme 1 of this book). In the early years of the EU, the stability of the food supply was a particularly pressing goal, addressed with positive integration measures; later product safety, the protection of workers, and more recently gender equality and environmental sustainability emerged as priorities. Since the late 1970s, a particular form of negative integration, namely **mutual recognition**, has become salient. Mutual recognition means that member states are expected to respect each other's regulatory systems. This allows for quicker economic integration than if each and every law throughout the EU had to be harmonized. Positive integration strategies continue to be used but only in cases where mutual recognition falls short, and thus common EU-wide rules are considered necessary.

As an entity that seeks to not only establish but also shape the operation of a single, EU-wide market, the EU possesses the ability to pass *EU-wide legislation*. It also has its own *budget*, funded by contributions from the member states. However, this budget is very small; it amounts to only about *1 per cent* of the EU's gross domestic product (GDP). By comparison, public spending in the member states ranges from about 30 per cent of GDP in Ireland to nearly 60 per cent of GDP in Finland. Given the small size of its budget, the EU does not engage extensively in *redistributive* policies, that is, policy measures that consist of the transfer of funds benefiting specific groups of the population. There are, however, two exceptions that have a specific redistributive character and take up a considerable part of the EU budget: (1) the EU's **Common Agricultural Policy**, which supports farmers, and (2) the **regional** or **cohesion policy**, which provides public investment to support people and regions with social and economic development funds. Apart from these two areas, most of the EU's activities focus on *regulation*, that is, the establishment of standards for how economic and social actors may or may not behave. In fact, the EU is best known for its regulatory capacity. It has been a leading actor, globally, for setting standards in numerous global arenas, including health and safety in the workplace, banking regulation, or environmental protection.

In brief, Part II is about the policies EU member states have developed together as a union. In introducing EU policies in various fields, we examine in the chapters that follow which integration strategies, policy types, and legislative mechanisms the EU has employed. We also include some details about the budgetary resources that the EU has devoted to each policy and offer a brief comparison to Canada's activities in the same policy areas.

# 7

# The Single Market and Economic and Monetary Integration

PAUL SCHURE AND AMY VERDUN[1]

## Reader's Guide

This chapter discusses the **Single Market** and **Economic and Monetary Union (EMU)**. It places these cornerstones of **European integration** in historical and current context. Our discussion of the historical context includes the stages of economic integration the EU went through before arriving at the Single Market and economic and monetary union. We take the 2008 **global financial crisis** as the starting point for our discussion of the current context, which also includes the 2010 **sovereign debt crisis** in the EU. As we explain, the current situation of increased macroeconomic and fiscal **coordination** between EU member states, the **Banking Union**, and the current proposal for a **Capital Markets Union** can be understood only in relation to these two crises. We conclude by briefly discussing **Brexit**.

## Introduction

Since the very early days of European integration, from the 1951 **European Coal and Steel Community (ECSC)** and the 1957 **European Economic Community (EEC)**, European integration has centred on taking steps toward deeper economic integration. The philosophy of the EU's founding fathers, Jean Monnet and Robert Schuman, was to integrate sectors of the economies of the member states, starting with coal and steel, so that a war between the member states would become unthinkable (Theme 1 of this book; see also Chapter 2). This chapter discusses the developments in European economic integration that have taken place since World War II. The chapter is arranged in chronological order, with close attention to the challenges that the EU faced in the integration process and the institutions that were created to address these challenges.

The history of European integration is one of two competing integration initiatives. While seven European countries formed the **European Free Trade Association (EFTA)** in 1960 (Austria, Denmark, Norway, Portugal,

Sweden, Switzerland, and the United Kingdom), six member states formed the European Economic Community (EEC) in 1958 (Belgium, France, Italy, Luxembourg, the Netherlands, and West Germany). The EFTA was meant to be, and still is, a free-trade agreement, while the EEC was more ambitious, as it aimed to reach a deeper form of integration from the outset.[2] The first major step in economic integration of the six EEC members was the completion of a **customs union**, which it managed to achieve in July 1968. The next step was the completion of a **Common Market**, but that ended up being considerably more difficult than envisaged. It is still a work in progress, even after getting another boost through a detailed plan, the Single Market Programme (1985), to complete the "Single Market" by a deadline of December 31, 1992.

The next important plan was to create an Economic and Monetary Union (EMU), and this proved to be difficult as well. When EMU—with the euro as its single currency—was ultimately created in 1999, it was put in place without many of the policies and institutions that would be necessary to maintain the stability of the **Euro Area** in case of a financial crisis. As this chapter shows, the shortcomings of EMU became abundantly clear during the so-called sovereign debt crisis, the period in 2010–12 of acute financial distress of the governments of Greece and some other Euro Area member states, as well as the banking sectors in several member states. The **European Central Bank (ECB)** emerged as a leading institution in this period, embarking on policy activism that arguably challenged the limits of its mandate.

During and after the sovereign debt crisis, new policies and institutions were created to impose fiscal discipline on member state governments and deal with possible financial market crises. Two notable EU initiatives are the measures collectively known as the Banking Union and the 2015 action plan for building a Capital Markets Union, intended to result in a true free movement of capital flows in the EU. Also, Commission President Jean-Claude Juncker with four other EU presidents—the presidents of the ECB, the Eurogroup, the **European Council**, and the **European Parliament (EP)**—launched the next steps to complete EMU, as spelled out in the **Five Presidents' Report**.

## From the Common Market to the Single Market

In 1961 Bela Balassa wrote one of the first books on European economic integration in which he famously identified economic integration as both a process and a state of affairs (Balassa, 1961, p. 1). He also identified four stages ("degrees") of economic integration, namely, in order of increased degree of integration: Free Trade Area (FTA), Customs Union, Common Market, and Economic Union (see Box 7.1 below). Balassa's term "Common Market," which was standard in the 1960s and 1970s, was replaced by "Single Market" in the 1980s, while his "Economic Union" is known nowadays as "Economic and Monetary Union" (EMU).

From its creation in 1957, the European Economic Community (EEC) had as its goal the creation of a Common Market based on the so-called **four freedoms**, namely the freedom of movement of goods, services, persons, and capital. Barriers to the free movement of goods included **tariffs** and quotas (in the EU context, quotas are often referred to as "quantitative restrictions"), subsidies, preferential **public procurement**, and several **non-tariff barriers**, such as, for example, cumbersome border procedures or unnecessary national product regulations.

The envisaged first step toward the Common Market was a Customs Union, which was completed in July 1968 (see Box 7.1). Next was the elimination of non-tariff barriers. The issue of differing product standards across the Union was initially addressed though **positive integration** (see the introduction to Part II of this book), specifically harmonization efforts initiated by the Commission. Harmonization proved to be very challenging, however, in part because the adoption of a product standard often has distributional

**Box 7.1**   Stages of economic integration

| Stage | Defining features |
| --- | --- |
| Free Trade Agreement (FTA) | Zero tariffs between member countries and reduced non-tariff barriers |
| Customs Union (CU) | FTA + common trade relationships (common external tariff and trade agreements, if any) with countries outside the CU) |
| Common Market (CM); from 1985 referred to as "Internal Market" or "Single Market" | CU + free movement of capital and labour (together with freedom of movement of goods and services, called the "four freedoms") and some policy harmonization |
| Economic and Monetary Union (EMU) | CM + common economic and monetary policies and institutions |

Source: Adapted from Balassa (1961)

effects: the product standard may result in a competitive advantage for the firms in some countries over firms in other countries. However, a landmark ruling of the European Court of Justice (now **Court of Justice of the EU [CJEU]**) switched the focus to challenging barriers to trade based on appeals to the Court and **negative integration** (see the introduction to Part II and Glossary), specifically **mutual recognition** of each other's product standards.

In the **Cassis de Dijon** case (Case 120/78 *Rewe-Zentral AG v. Bundesmonopolverwaltung für Branntwein* [1979] ECR 649), the Court rejected a German ban on the sale of Cassis de Dijon (a French blackcurrant liqueur containing 15–20 per cent alcohol) as a liqueur in Germany. The German regulator had argued Cassis did not conform to the product standard regarding liqueurs in Germany. (German liqueur standards stipulated a minimum of 25 per cent alcohol on fruit liqueur. Cassis had a dangerously low alcohol percentage!) The Court ruled that the Cassis sales ban was equivalent to a quantitative restriction and hence should be lifted. It suggested that the difference in French and German liqueur standards could be dealt with through clear labelling. Again, the bottom line was that this ruling of the Court established the principle of mutual recognition: if a product can be legally marketed in one member state then it should normally be legally marketable in other member states as well. Mutual recognition (of other countries' regulatory bodies and their regulations) made positive integration through harmonization unnecessary in many cases.

Despite the Court's success cases, there were still abundant barriers to the free movement by the beginning of the 1980s. In January 1985, Jacques Delors, the president of the **European Commission**, declared that he wanted to push forward the main objective of the EEC, namely completion of the Single Market. The Commission prepared a white book (a planning document) "Completing the Internal Market" (COM/85/0310), and the European Council of Milan in June 1985 agreed to call an **intergovernmental** conference to amend the EEC Treaty. The resulting treaty, the Single European Act of 1986, introduced important changes to the Community legislative procedure. One important change was that legislative acts with regard to the Single Market would be taken by **qualified majority vote (QMV)** (see Chapter 3), while previously individual member states could insist the decision be taken by **unanimity**—effectively enabling a single member state to block legislative acts on Single Market–related decisions. The Single European Act gave new momentum to the process of completing the Single Market. While it was not yet as such "complete," considerable progress in market integration had been made by the end of 1992.

An important common policy to make sure the Single Market functions well is **competition policy**. Similar to the Competition Bureau in Canada, the **Directorate-General (DG)** Competition of the European Commission tries to prevent anti-competitive behaviour of companies, including price agreements, market-sharing agreements, or abuse of a dominant position a firm may possibly have in a market. On occasion it imposes hefty fines on companies found to have engaged in such practices. DG Competition also reviews proposed mergers between companies ("mergers" broadly speaking, so including all cases in which a company proposes to take over another company). DG Competition can block mergers between companies if the merged company would achieve a dominant position in certain markets. Finally, DG Competition can act only if the anti-competitive practice or potential merger has a cross-border dimension. In addition, DG Competition can disallow "state aid," i.e., subsidies to companies by national, provincial, or municipal governments. All these pillars of competition policy aim to promote a "level playing field" between firms across the EU. Besides implementing an active competition policy, DG Competition has also actively promoted the development of competitive markets in areas such as energy, postal services, telecommunications, and transportation. Until the mid-1980s, many of these sectors had been run by state-owned monopolies. In the process of market liberalization, several state monopolies were privatized, and one goal was obviously to ensure that the newly privatized companies would not become monopolies that would abuse their power.

In the beginning of the current millennium it became clear that, although the EU had been successful in promoting the free movement of goods, it had made much less progress on the free movement of services. The Services **Directive** (Directive 2006/123/EC) (colloquially called the "Bolkestein Directive," after the commissioner for the internal market at the time, Frits Bolkestein) aimed to make it easier for services to be "traded" across borders. This **directive** initially met with heavy criticism. Many questioned if such a directive might lead to a "race to the bottom" in social and labour provisions, which generated comments about "Polish plumbers" (mythical Eastern European tradespersons who represented the threat of cheaper rates in more expensive Western European markets due to his or her presumed inferior social insurance and wage). The interesting fact about the Services Directive was that there was nothing new in it that had not already been mentioned in the EU Treaties and reinforced by the Court in relevant case law. But, by making it explicit, the directive drew attention to the effect of the four freedoms on the delivery and trade of services across borders. Critics were worried that temporary workers from EU member states with lower wages and inferior social security would undermine the so-called **European Social Model** (see Chapter 10). They demanded that member-state labour laws would apply to temporary workers and service providers as well.

After numerous changes of the proposed directive, in part as a response to demands by the EP, the Services Directive was accepted in December 2006. This episode shows that it has not been easy to guarantee the free movement of services. Some obstacles also remain regarding the free movement of persons (see Chapter 8) and capital (see below; for a comparison with Canada, see Box 7.2).

## Creating Europe's Single Currency

The idea to create an EMU in the EEC was first agreed to in 1969 by the heads of government and state at the summit in The Hague. In 1970, a Committee chaired by Luxembourg's prime minister and finance minister, Pierre Werner, presented a possible blueprint (the **Werner Plan**). It foresaw the setting up of two **supranational** bodies: a Community System for the Central Banks (monetary policy) and a Centre of Decision for Economic Policy (to coordinate macroeconomic policies including some tax policies) by 1980. Most of the recommendations of the Werner Plan were adopted, yet no action was taken to achieve the end goal of creating the EMU by 1980 (see Chapter 2).

The reasons for this failure of EMU in the 1970s are twofold. First, member states differed in their views on how to get to EMU—whether to first integrate more in the economic realm and unify monetary policies later, or vice versa. Second, in the early 1970s, the international economic and monetary situation changed dramatically (Verdun, 2000). Following the collapse of the Bretton Woods system of fixed exchange rates, currencies started to float, there was a major oil crisis and accompanying recession, and opinions on how to tackle the crisis differed wildly. To keep the exchange rates of their national currencies stable during this time, five of the six original EEC countries, as well as some non-EEC countries, participated in their own system (called the "snake in the tunnel") of pegging exchange rates, with some flexibility. The West German mark became central to this system, while the French franc did not manage to stay in. In 1979, the system was reformed and the European Monetary System (EMS) was created in which all EEC countries participated. At the heart was the **European Rate Mechanism (ERM)**, which featured the currencies of all EEC member states except the United Kingdom. The UK's pound sterling was, however, part of the calculation of the European Currency Unit (ECU)—the unit of account at the heart of the EMS. The British non-participation in the ERM underscores that the United Kingdom had an ambivalent relationship with Europe's monetary integration project from the outset. Note that the UK eventually joined the ERM in 1990.

**Box 7.2**    The Canadian Single Market

The European Union has a Single Market and an Economic and Monetary Union. Following the sovereign debt crisis it has introduced further supranational oversight of the banking sector and is considering steps toward deeper budgetary and fiscal integration.

Canada is a federal state that since its creation in 1867 has had free movement of commerce across the country, at least on paper. However, contrary to what one might expect given those formal rules, Canada is not at all a fully integrated Single Market. An article in the influential weekly *The Economist* ("Canada's internal trade," 2016) asked why oil and mining firms in the province of Alberta were buying heavy equipment from Asia and having it transported to Alberta through the United States. The argument was that Canada's Single Market was bogged down in bureaucracy, rules that effectively favour local producers.

In 2016 the Senate Committee on Banking estimated the cost of the incomplete Single Market in Canada at $130 billion a year. In 1994, following the signing of the North American Free Trade Agreement (NAFTA) an attempt was made to eliminate specific trade barriers in Canada through the Agreement on Internal Trade (AIT), but it did not manage to remove all the barriers to trade. For example, there are still provincial regulations that protect the butter market in various provinces. There are also differences across the country in licensing requirements for professions and other forms of regulations.

In Canada, removing internal trade barriers is a political matter, while in the EU this outcome has often been achieved through the judicial system. Although some provinces have sought to reduce barriers between them, there is not even the principle of mutual recognition internal to Canada, because the various provincial jurisdictions do not necessarily recognize regulations created and administered by other jurisdictions when they vary from their own regulations.

The Canadian Single Market is now subject to pressure for removal of interior trade obstacles, as the trade agreement between Canada and the European Union (CETA) makes amply clear that the EU is more integrated than Canada in internal trade freedom. Or as Laura Dawson, director of the Canada Institute at the Woodrow Wilson Center in Washington, has said, "Without action to remove internal trade barriers, Canadians will again find themselves in the position of granting better market access to non-Canadians than to themselves" (Cayo, 2015).

Sources: *The Economist* 2016; Cayo, 2015; Government of Canada: https://www.ic.gc.ca/eic/site/081.nsf/eng/h_00007.html

The first four years of the ERM were characterized by several exchange-rate realignments, but there were none from 1987 until the summer of 1992. In fact, by 1992 the ERM had become an important symbol of successful European integration. Informally, the German mark was the "anchor currency," and other monetary authorities often followed the decisions of the German central bank (the *Bundesbank*). The success of the EMS helped create an environment conducive to deeper monetary integration. EMU also featured in the above-mentioned 1986 Single European Act that aimed at completing the Single Market. On September 12, 1987, the EMS was further strengthened at the Basel/Nyborg accord. On June 24, 1988, the Commission approved a directive that provided for full capital liberalization by July 1, 1990. On June 28, 1988, the Hanover European Council asked Commission President Jacques Delors to produce a blueprint for EMU. With the help of central bank presidents and a few other experts, the committee eventually presented its report the following April.

The **Delors Report** proposed a road to EMU in three stages. It also envisaged the creation of a **European System of Central Banks** (**ESCB**) with a new supranational European Central Bank that would work together with the national central banks of the member states. Contrary to what had been proposed in the Werner Plan of 1970, no supranational authority was foreseen for budgetary and fiscal policies.[3] In that area, the Delors Report merely suggested working with rules by placing maximum limits on national budgetary deficits and national public debt. EMU was to create an integrated area with full freedoms of movement of goods, services, capital, and labour, and fixed exchange rates among the currencies of the member states that met the criteria, or, ideally, a single currency. At the June 1989 European Council meeting in Madrid, the EMU blueprint was adopted as a basis for further discussion in an intergovernmental conference that would discuss the next concrete steps, which would eventually be included in the **Treaty on European Union** (often referred to as the **Maastricht Treaty**). Article 104 TEC (now Article 126 TFEU), stipulated the so-called **convergence criteria** that countries needed to meet in order to join EMU: upper limits on budgetary deficits, public debt, inflation rates, and low long-term interest rates; successful participation in the ERM for two years (i.e., not having its currency deviate by more than 15 per cent from the central parity); and an independent central bank (see Box 7.3).

The first stage of EMU lasted from July 1, 1990, until January 1, 1994, after which time capital markets were considered liberalized. In stage two (1994–98), the European Monetary Institute, the predecessor of the European Central Bank, was set up in Frankfurt. Its main task was to create the operational framework of its successor, the ESCB. The mandate of the ECB was defined as maintaining price stability. Without "prejudice to that primary mandate," the ECB would also support the "general economic policies" and "objectives" of the Union (such as full employment and balanced economic growth). Both the ECB and the national central banks were to be politically and operationally independent. During the course of the 1990s, it turned out to be difficult for the majority of the countries to meet the EMU convergence criteria required for them to join the third and final stage of EMU. Public debt levels rose, and countries also found it challenging to satisfy the 3 per cent budgetary deficit criterion. Despite some missing criteria, 11 member states joined the third and final stage toward EMU, which started with the irrevocable fixing of the exchange rates on January 1, 1999. A year later, Greece joined the third stage as well. EMU was fully completed on January 1, 2002, when euro banknotes and coins were circulated in 12 member states—a much larger number than had been anticipated during the signing of the Maastricht Treaty in 1992.

## The First Ten Years of EMU

Initially the introduction of the euro met with some skepticism due to the fact that citizens felt inflation had increased. They associated the price increases with the introduction of the euro. However, interestingly, this feeling among citizens of high inflation was not borne out by unusually high official inflation figures. Prices in some industries had indeed gone up sharply, including the food and beverage services industry, catering services, hairdressers, and recreational services (Sturm et al., 2009). Another source of initial popular skepticism was the fact that the exchange rate of the euro against the US dollar fell swiftly by about 30 per cent after its introduction.

However, EMU had a few other, quite striking initial effects. A liquid corporate bond market developed very rapidly in the Euro Area. Before euro adoption it had arguably been hard for firms to issue corporate bonds in their local currencies. It frequently happened that such firms borrowed in British pounds, Swiss francs, or US dollars. Also, the cost of borrowing for firms and governments dropped dramatically, most notably in several of the southern member states and in Finland and Ireland. As a result, investment levels went up, again particularly strongly in the South. Finally, and relatedly, long-term interest rates in the euro zone revealed remarkable levels of convergence, as Figure 7.1 shows.

In 2004, 10 new member states joined the European Union, namely eight Central and Eastern European countries and two Mediterranean islands (see Chapter 15). Of these 10, seven have also joined EMU: Slovenia (2007), Cyprus and Malta (2008), Slovakia (2009), Estonia (2011), Latvia (2014), and

**Box 7.3**   Convergence criteria for EMU membership as in the Maastricht Treaty

(1)  The ratio of government deficit to gross domestic product must not exceed 3 per cent.

(2)  The ratio of government debt to gross domestic product must not exceed 60 per cent or has "sufficiently diminished" and now approaches 60 per cent at a "satisfactory pace."

(3)  There must be a sustainable degree of price stability and an average inflation rate, observed over a period of one year before the examination, which does not exceed by more than one and a half percentage points that of the three best-performing member states in terms of price stability.

(4)  There must be a long-term nominal interest rate, which does not exceed by more than two percentage points that of the three best-performing member states in terms of price stability.

(5)  The normal fluctuation margins provided for by the exchange-rate mechanism in the European Monetary System must have been respected without severe tensions for at least the last two years before the examination.

To join the Euro Area, a member state must also have central bank laws in place that ensure that its national central bank is independent, that is, that it can make decisions without having to resist influence or pressure from the country's government or parliament. In EMU, monetary financing of governments by central banks would also not be permitted.

In 1995 the so-called Stability and Growth Pact (SGP) was created to ensure that after member states joined EMU, they would maintain their budgetary and fiscal discipline. They would need to adhere to the same criteria, especially the budgetary deficit criterion of no more than 3 per cent deficit or potentially face sanctions.

Source: Adapted from Art. 126, Art. 140 TFEU and protocols

Lithuania (2015). Some other countries that are not members of the EU also use the euro as their official currency, namely the Principality of Monaco, the Republic of San Marino, the Vatican City State, and the Principality of Andorra. Finally, there are countries, such as Kosovo and Montenegro, which use the euro as their currency without having made any agreements

**Figure 7.1** Yields ("interest rates") on 10-year government bonds of select member states

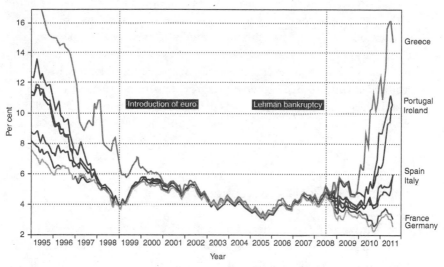

Differences in yields may reflect a variety of things, including the time-value of money, default premiums, and consequences of a potentially fractured bond market. The large yield differences before the introduction of the euro is usually interpreted as reflecting a fractured bond market (notably differences in inflation expectations in the bond market segments). The small differences before 2008 underscore both the absence of frictions as well as the absence of default premiums.

Source: *Spiegel Online*, August 15, 2011

with the EU to do so (they used the German mark before it was replaced by the euro).

In 2007–08 the world was rocked by what is now called the 2008–09 global financial crisis (henceforth "global financial crisis"). For most observers the collapse of the US investment bank Lehman Brothers marked the start of the worst period of the global financial crisis. Several other financial institutions went bankrupt, and there was an imminent danger that the entire financial system would collapse. Low interest rates and weak financial regulation had led to a bloated financial sector and excessive risk-taking on the part of banks and other financial institutions. Rajan (2010) explains that these problems in the financial system were themselves a consequence of deeper underlying fault lines, including global macroeconomic imbalances and rising income inequality in the United States. While the crisis erupted in the US, it spread globally and hit several European countries particularly hard.

The initial perception during the global financial crisis was that EMU protected the Euro Area countries against the most negative effects of the crisis. Many recalled that previous crises had often included strong currency fluctuations, with drastic central bank interventions and capital controls as a result. Currency fluctuations were obviously no longer possible between the EMU countries, but the euro kept up its value well vis-à-vis other currencies (for good or bad). The euro was initially viewed as a "stable ship" that made it easy for countries to navigate the crisis well. However, the crisis hit the financial sectors of several countries in the Single Market (inside and outside EMU), and a need emerged to provide national support to destitute banks. Indeed, the financial crisis was particularly severe in the US and most Western European countries. By contrast, the financial sectors in Canada and some other European countries, such as Italy, were not affected as much in 2007–08.

## From Financial Crisis to Sovereign Debt Crisis

In the first years of the financial crisis, most EU governments chose to run higher budgetary deficits (trying to soften the ensuing recession). Public finances were particularly strained by government guarantees, capital injections, and other measures to buttress banks. About two years later, the global financial crisis had turned into a sovereign debt crisis in the Euro Area: interest rates on the government debt of some of the EMU countries rose to unsustainably high levels. As Figure 7.1 shows, interest rates on public debt were about equal across the Euro Area between 2003 and 2007. This reflected that investors essentially deemed all government debt in the Euro Area to be safe. This radically changed between 2008 and 2010. Particularly alarming was the case of Greece.

By fall 2009 the newly elected Greek government announced that its budgetary deficit was much higher than what the previous Greek government had reported. The result was a wave of downgrades of Greek government bonds. Would EU institutions or other member states bail out the Greek government if it had to default on its bond payments? A first consideration was the so-called no-bailout clause in Article 125(1) of the **Treaty on the Functioning of the European Union (TFEU)**. However, was the no-bailout clause in line with the preferences of member states? If Greece were left to its own devices, it would likely have to default on its public debt. Besides severe troubles in Greece, a default would mean that Greek public debt held by banks in Greece and elsewhere would then turn into bad loans, putting already strained banks in further jeopardy, and hence potentially trigger a second EU-wide banking crisis. It was, however, also argued that a bailout of the Greek government would discourage the governments of other countries from behaving in a fiscally sound manner.

To complicate matters further, it was clear that a bailout, if any, would need to be funded through a new financial commitment from the member states, given that the EU budget is only 1 per cent of GDP (about €143.9 billion in 2016 for all of its expenses—see Box 7.4 below).

In May 2010 Greece was no longer able to refinance its public debt and therefore faced imminent default (see Box 7.5 below). It was then decided that a member state in need was one that had to be supported. The EU member states made ad hoc funds available through an impromptu arrangement called the Greek Loan Facility (see Table 7.1 below). In the next few months and years they would have to do the same a few more times, and also to provide financial support to Portugal, Ireland, Spain, and Cyprus. The EU needed to either give up EMU, or keep it but deal with some of its design flaws through new institutions.

## Crisis Responses: New Institutions for the Single Currency

After the Greek Loan Facility, the next institution that was created was a fund that was called the European Financial Stability Facility (EFSF) (see Table 7.1). It was a temporary intergovernmental arrangement put into place in August 2010 by the Euro Area member states. The idea was to provide assistance in case a government was unable to refinance its sovereign debt.

**Box 7.4**  Budget of the Single Market and economic and monetary integration

The 2016 EU budget was €143.9 billion (less than 1 per cent of the 2016 estimated GDP of €16.5 trillion). Under line item 1, "economic and financial affairs," the total spending is €2.5 billion, or 1.76 per cent of the EU budget. Another item discussed in this chapter is the Single Market. The budget for the Single Market includes line item 2, "internal market, industry, entrepreneurship, and SMEs," with €2.3 billion, or 1.6 per cent of the EU budget. The budget for line item 12, "financial stability, financial services, and capital markets union," is €85 million, or 0.06 per cent; and the budget for line item 14, "administrative expenditure of the Taxation and Customs Union," is €166 million, or 0.12 per cent.

Source: Adopted 2016 budget, *Official Journal of the European Union*, L 48, February 24, 2016

**Box 7.5**    The Greek sovereign debt crisis

Greece joined the Euro Area in 2000 after having had difficulties meeting the convergence criteria. When it did eventually submit its macroeconomic and fiscal performance data, there was already a doubt as to
whether those figures were solid. However, the Commission and the
EU member states did not question the numbers the Greek authorities
put forward.

Before the onset of the financial crisis, during the first seven years
of EMU, Greece did remarkably well. Economic growth was high,
and for citizens, firms, and governments alike, the cost of borrowing
money came down dramatically (see Figure 7.1). The Greek economy
boomed, growing by more than 25 per cent (on a per capita basis)
during the first seven years in EMU and coming very close to the EU
average. Youth unemployment in Greece before 2000 stood at 25 per
cent; it had come down eight percentage points by 2007. However, in
the same period, unit labour costs went up quickly, outpacing productivity growth and making Greece less competitive internationally. As
a result, Greece was importing much more than it exported, thereby
running an increasingly large deficit on its current account.

During the good years, the government was not very prudent,
and the country's public debt kept rising. When the financial crisis
struck Europe, Greece was particularly hard hit in two of its main
industries: shipping and tourism. More importantly, in autumn 2009,
after parliamentary elections, the new government announced that its
budgetary deficit was much higher (about three times as high) than
the previous government had announced (because deficits caused by
defence spending had not been recorded) and was almost four times
as high as the permitted maximum according to the EU budgetary
rules. Not only did the Greek government effectively admit to having
flouted the rules of the so-called Stability and Growth Pact (which
also would mean that the Greek government could face sanctions),
it also reinforced a prejudice that bureaucratic mismanagement, corruption, and tax evasion were rampant in Greece. The result was a
gradual reduction in the credit rating of Greek sovereign debt, which
made refinancing of public debt extremely expensive. (The term "sovereign debt" is typically used for central government debt denoted in a
reserve currency, or in this case a joint currency over which the Greek
government has no control.) Faced with the astronomically high cost

of refinancing, there was no doubt that Greece needed assistance from other member states or it would default on its loans.

The problem was that the EU Treaty contains a so-called no-bailout clause that does not permit the EU to assist when another member state has difficulties with its public debt—a provision that the Germans had bargained hard to obtain in the 1990s. To turn around and make money easily available to Greece, under the above circumstances, seemed difficult for domestic voters in Germany to accept. Thus, when German Chancellor Angela Merkel announced that it was possible that Greece might have to leave the Euro Area, the crisis was complete. The problem was, however, that a default on the part of Greece would mean that many loans would not be paid back. Those loans provided to Greece also came from lenders in other EU member states, including German and French banks. It was unclear whether a Greek default would be as problematic as the Lehman Brothers collapse had been at the outset of the financial crisis. Eventually the EU member states agreed to make funds available to Greece numerous times between 2010 and 2016.

Despite the support Greece received, the cost of the crisis has been very high for Greece and has meant economic contraction and record high unemployment, with its youth unemployment the second-highest in the world. In addition, the Greek government has had to promise to cut various government programs (including pensions), increase its tax collection, and reform its bureaucracy. Greek citizens have heavily opposed these "austerity programs," as unemployment was rampant, people lacked resources, and the country experienced a seven-year long recession. In fact, these cutbacks made it difficult to return to growth quickly. Even with the bailouts and debt relief, Greece's debt-to-GDP ratio is still very high (179 per cent of GDP in 2016).

The **European Stability Mechanism (ESM)** subsequently replaced the EFSF. The ESM is a permanent institutional structure that provides loans to member state governments, as well as equity investments for banks in need. It is set up as an international organization, which is eventually to be incorporated into the EU Treaty. The ESM has a €500 billion lending capacity and is based in Luxembourg. The so-called troika of the European Commission, the IMF, and the European Central Bank, and the EU member state national finance ministers, which were all involved in the ESM's design, required that recipient countries receiving loans from the mechanism make major administrative reforms, cut back on government spending (so-called austerity measures), increase their tax base, and restructure their economies. The imposed austerity measures were not at all popular among the citizens of the member states that received funding through the ESM or its predecessor, the EFSF (see Table 7.1). The member state governments who signed the international treaty stipulated the reforms that were needed in order to receive these emergency funds from the ESM. These conditions on loans led to occasional violent protests as unemployment (especially youth unemployment) was very high and the populations of the recipient countries felt further cuts were unreasonable. Of all the Euro Area member states, Greece has been hit the hardest by the sovereign debt crisis. Its GDP per capita stood at US$30,000 in 2007; by 2015 this had dropped to US$22,500.

During the global financial crisis and sovereign debt crisis, it was difficult for the EU member states to decide what path to choose. During these trying times, the European Central Bank acted as a leader, when few other EU institutions felt they had the legitimacy or ability to do so (Verdun, 2017). The ECB took the lead despite the permanent challenge to set its monetary policy for an area consisting of 19 individual member states that often have diverse needs in terms of monetary policy. Without a supranational authority that could offset some of the imbalances created by a single monetary policy, having a one-size-fits-all policy was inevitably going to be difficult. In fact, at the start of the crisis, the ECB was criticized for being too much focused on its mandate of price stability, even as inflation was coming down fast. However, as the crisis unfolded the ECB came up with unprecedented and unconventional monetary policy responses that touched (some say even pushed) the limits of its mandate (Högenauer and Howarth, 2016).[4] At the same time it was trying to keep to its mandate of maintaining low inflation, defined at 2 per cent over the medium term. During the height of the crisis, through newly developed programs called the "enhanced credit support" and the "securities markets programme," the ECB flooded financial institutions with "cheap money" in an attempt to ensure that funding remained available to businesses and households. Despite the ECB's very loose monetary policy in recent years, Euro Area inflation has been below the 2 per cent target since 2012.

## Banking Union and Capital Markets Union

On January 1, 1993, the Second Banking Directive (Council Directive 89/646/EEC) came into effect. Its most important provisions were harmonized rules for obtaining a banking licence, bank regulation, and the freedom for banks to establish branches outside their home member state.

**Table 7.1**  Institutions for policy coordination and financial support since the 2010 sovereign debt crisis

| Institutions | Dates | Main content |
|---|---|---|
| Greek Loan Facility (formally Loan Facility Agreement between the euro member states and Greece) | Eurogroup agrees on May 2, 2010; agreement signed on May 7, 2010; entered into force May 11, 2010. | Provide loans to Euro Area member state in need (in first instance, Greece). Commission coordinates and disburses the bilateral loans (provided by member states). International Monetary Fund (IMF) also contributes. Lending capacity of €80 billion (member states; later lowered to €52.9 billion); IMF contribution: €30 billion. |
| European Financial Stability Facility (EFSF) | Agreed to on May 9, 2010; operational August 4, 2010. | Safeguards financial stability in the EU by providing financial assistance to Euro Area countries. No new loans since July 2013. Ireland, Portugal, and Greece benefited from the loans issued by this temporary facility. |
| European Systemic Risk Board (ESRB) | Agreed to on November 24, 2010; entered into force on December 16, 2010. | The European Systemic Risk Board is responsible for the macro-prudential oversight of the financial system. This means that it tries to reduce the risk of a crisis in the financial system by gauging the spillovers and interconnectedness between financial institutions, markets, regulators, and government policy. |
| European Semester | Agreed to on September 7, 2010; introduced from 2011. | The European Semester is the EU's annual cycle of economic policy guidance and surveillance. Its goal is to coordinate economic policy to ensure member states meet objectives. An abridged synopsis of the process is as follows: The European Commission adopts the Annual Growth Survey; the European Council provides policy orientations; member states submit their economic plans; the Commission makes detailed analysis and recommendations of EU member states' economic programs; and the Council adopts the country-specific recommendations. |
| European Stability Mechanism (ESM) | Agreed to at the European Council of December 16–17, 2010; inaugurated on October 8, 2012. | The ESM is a permanent facility and the direct successor to the EFSF. This financial emergency loan fund provides loans to Euro Area countries in financial difficulty. Its own resources and credit guarantees add up to €500 billion. The IMF has guaranteed another €250 billion. Total: €750 billion. |

*(continued)*

**Table 7.1** (Continued)

| Institutions | Dates | Main content |
|---|---|---|
| Six Pack | Agreed to on October 4, 2011; entered into force December 13, 2011. | Agreed to by the member states of the EU; some more detailed rules for **Euro Area** member states. Strengthens the Stability and Growth Pact (SGP) (stricter application of the fiscal rules). Five **regulations** and a directive (EU Secondary Law). Defines deviation from the Medium Term Objectives; focuses more on the debt than the earlier SGP. Financial sanctions more gradual. Reverse qualified majority vote is introduced. It means that an RQMV is needed for the **Council** to reverse a Commission recommendation or proposal; otherwise it is adopted. |
| Fiscal compact (formally, Treaty on Stability, Coordination and Governance in Economic and Monetary Union) | Signed March 2, 2012; entered into force January 1, 2013. | An agreement of the Euro Area member states and eight other EU member states. It is formally an international treaty but there is a commitment to transfer its content into the EU Treaty within five years of signing. |
| Two Pack | November 23, 2011. | The two pack, based on Article 136 of the TFEU, improves Euro Area budgetary coordination by introducing a common budgetary timeline and rules for Euro Area member states. It integrates into EU law some components of the fiscal compact and requires the establishment of independent national fiscal councils by October 2013. |
| Banking Union | From 2012 to present. | Stronger prudential requirements for banks, a single rulebook, a Single Supervisory Mechanism (SSM), a Single Resolution Mechanism (SRM) for banks, a Single Resolution Fund (SRF), as well as a European Deposit Insurance Scheme (EDIS). |
| Capital Markets Union | From September 2015 to present. | Enhance capital market integration with a view to facilitating cross-border funding and investments flows, effectively creating a true Single Market for capital. |

Source: Adapted from Verdun (2015)

With the Second Banking Directive, the feeling was that the EU had a solid foundation for a Single Market for banking services.[5] The market for banking services relied heavily on mutual recognition in the sense that banks were regulated in their home country but could offer banking services in all member states. This arrangement appeared to work well for many years, during which several EU banks became multinationals offering services in multiple EU countries.

We explained earlier that the euro looked like a reasonably "stable ship" during the global financial crisis. However, we also saw that the stable currency did not insulate EU countries from a banking crisis. Indeed, mutual recognition, in combination with free capital flows, turned out to be a recipe for easy contagion of the financial crisis across national borders, ironically particularly in the Euro Area, due to the absence of exchange-rate risk (Engineer, Schure, & Gillis, 2013; Schure, 2013). Free capital flows in the EU resulted in a situation that small differences (or even just small *perceived* differences) between EU countries in terms of deposit insurance, bank supervision, or banking sector stability, could generate quite large cross-border capital flows and destabilize the national banking sectors of the potential "outflow countries." The bank rescue measures that were adopted in the crisis were intended first of all to rescue banks, but arguably also to avoid and stem such potentially destabilizing capital flows. However, these bank rescues came at a very high political cost at both the national and EU levels. It became painfully clear that EMU had certain design flaws, which needed to be remedied in order to make the project ultimately a success. Banking Union was the answer: harmonized rules across the EU regarding bank supervision, deposit insurance, a safety net for banks, and a resolution mechanism for failed banks. The term "Banking Union" did not exist as such before the sovereign debt crisis. It was invented and put forward by Commission President Barroso to indicate that the EU had insufficient integration in the area of banking and to capture various aspects of an improved framework for financial governance.

The Banking Union proposal attempts to subject banks to the same rules. These rules apply to Euro Area banks as well as banks in non-Euro Area countries that have decided to opt in. The rules aim to ensure that banks take measured risks and that banks do not force possible losses on taxpayers and can yet be rescued, if need be, or declared bankrupt at minimal damage to the economy. The Banking Union is incomplete as yet, and there have been considerable delays and hesitations in adopting legislation toward achieving its three pillars, i.e., the Single Supervisory Mechanism, the Single Deposit Guarantee Scheme, and the Single Resolution Mechanism (see Figure 7.2 Banking Union).

**Figure 7.2** Banking Union and its three pillars

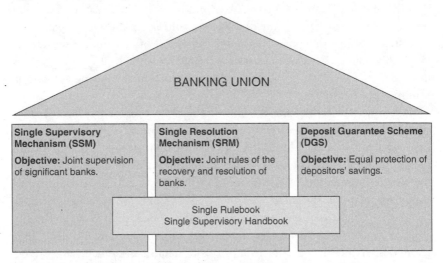

Source: Authors' design, adapted from Central Bank of Austria

The European Council of June 2009 recommended establishing a single rulebook for all financial institutions in the Single Market. Three new European supervisory authorities were created in the area of banking, securities markets, and insurance and occupational pensions. The European Commission also put forward plans for a Bank Recovery and Resolution Directive (BRRD). By the end of 2012, European member states had mobilized just under €600 billion (or 4.6 per cent of the 2012 GDP of the EU) in public funds to support their banks, and the DG Competition of the European Commission stated that it had approved even larger amounts to financial institutions between October 2008 and 2011. The Commission proposed the BRRD to ensure that EU member states could intervene to manage banks in difficulties, while still trying to preserve, as much as possible, a level playing field.

Another important move toward the Banking Union was increased harmonization in terms of national deposit insurance schemes across the Union. Since 2009, EU legislation requires that all EU deposit insurance schemes guarantee deposit accounts for €100,000; prior to that, a minimum of €20,000 had been required, but by 2009 this higher, unified level had been set. The Banking Union is still a work in progress at the time of writing. For example, although standardization of the coverage of Deposit Guarantee Schemes was a major step, a further step would be a **European Deposit Insurance Scheme (EDIS)**. Thus, by June 2015, the Five Presidents' Report, among others, called for EDIS.

The Commission put forward a legislative proposal to this effect in November 2015.

The Capital Markets Union (CMU) is a more recent initiative. EU law has prohibited all restrictions on capital movements and payments across borders since 1994. The government bond markets are essentially fully integrated. Furthermore, as discussed, a liquid corporate bond market developed rapidly after EMU was realized. In summary: for governments, large businesses, and financial institutions there are no significant barriers to the free movement of capital. However, the same is not true for small and medium-sized enterprises and consumers. In 2016 Commission President Jean-Claude Juncker announced the creation of a CMU by 2019. It will try to create a true single capital market, with "capital" broadly defined. For example, the rules regarding crowd-funding for individuals, charities, or small businesses would be the same in a true CMU. The overarching purpose is to remove any remaining barriers to cross-border borrowing and investing. The idea is to expand the variety of funding options for market players as well as individuals, diversifying the financial system and thereby hopefully making it more resilient.

## Debate: Fiscal Federalism, Vicious Circle, and Brexit

The sections above have made abundantly clear that EMU had been introduced without sufficient checks and balances to deal with situations involving a major financial crisis. The cost of not having had these measures in place has been high; it came in the form of a major increase in unemployment, extended periods of negative GDP growth in several countries, and even a collapse of GDP in Greece. The political cost to the EU has been high. It came in the form of loss of support among its citizens many of whom blamed the EU for the sovereign debt crisis, putting popular support for the EU in doubt, because of its deemed inability to deliver (Theme 3 of this book). One could argue that EMU was designed as a "fair weather arrangement." Drastic measures have been taken in the decade following the financial crisis, although possibly further measures are needed to keep the Union together from an economic perspective. When seen through a neo-functionalist lens (see Chapter 6), the main challenge for the EU is, however, to increase its overall political support by the people—its democratic legitimacy (see also Chapter 17).

A recent initiative for further deepening of EMU and the economic market is the Five Presidents' Report. This report suggests that the next steps are to take the EU to a deeper level of integration and deepen EMU in three phases: first (2015–17), deepen current instruments, complete the financial union, and improve democratic accountability; second, complete EMU through agreed benchmarks and possibly a Euro Area minister of finance; and by stage three (2025 at the latest), all the steps would be fully in place (Juncker, 2015, p. 5). At that point EMU would consist of a deeper economic union, a financial union, a fiscal union, and a political union.

This ambitious plan of the Five Presidents' Report has been considered by the national parliaments. Its success is subject to support from the member states. The fundamental question it raises about the EU is whether to move in the direction of a federal state (Theme 2 of this book). Euro-enthusiasts and Euroskeptics alike have argued that the structure of a federal state is necessary because one cannot have a monetary union without deeper economic, fiscal, and thus more political integration. If this claim is true, then the choice is between either dismantling EMU (as some skeptics might argue) or creating a full-fledged federal state with expanded economic and fiscal competences at least in the Euro Area.

However, an (unanswered) important question is whether the suggested next steps toward deeper integration (the **fiscal federalism** of the Five Presidents' Report) are in fact necessary if one wants to keep the euro. Fiscal federalism is usually associated with the following key components:

(1) The sharing of critical functions between the different levels of government, namely the supply of public goods and services, redistribution of income, and macroeconomic stabilization.

(2) The identification of welfare gains for the different parts of that "fiscal federation."

(3) Taxation at the level of government that provides the function. For example, economic stabilization and income redistribution could be done at the federal (supranational) level whereas other allocation of resources could be done at lower levels.

(4) The use of instruments of fiscal policy (tax and spend) also for the purpose of redistribution at both federal (supranational) and lower levels of government (national and sub-national) levels.

In the EU, the last two components of fiscal federalism would be very controversial, as there appears to be as yet only limited solidarity between citizens across the EU. Whether there might be another model, some kind of "European in-between" that might do the trick, remains to be seen. What is clear is that EMU governance is no longer the same, and presumably more resilient, now that the Banking Union is under way. A more deeply integrated "labour market union" (to coin a new term), while not turning the EU into a federal state, would also make a very substantial difference. Indeed, what is in our view the essential feature of a sustainable architecture for EMU is that it builds in sufficiently many "automatic stabilizers."

Another challenge that the EU faces is one that that can be described as its "perennial vicious circle," which is probably best described by providing an example. As we explained above, EMU contributed to an abundance of cheap funding, during the early years, particularly in the "periphery" of the Euro Area. Cheap funding boosted investments and economic growth in the pre–financial crisis environment. But there were no clear rules on macroeconomic imbalances, good fiscal governance, or banking regulation. These imperfections appear to have contributed to the buildup of the financial crisis, and the EU did not have instruments to manage the crisis either. A logical next step was therefore to introduce EU-level rules to reduce the probability of a crisis as well as to manage it. However, this next step required convincing the citizens and their leaders that deeper integration was necessary. This was very hard, because in the eyes of the citizens the EU fell short. In this case, the perennial vicious circle was avoided through impressive crisis measures as well as moves toward deeper economic integration. Figure 7.3 presents the challenge of the "perennial vicious circle."

A final major challenge that we would like to briefly discuss is that one of its member states, the United Kingdom, has voted in a referendum to leave the European Union. The so-called Brexit decision (or, more precisely, "UK-exit") was the result of a referendum held on June 23, 2016, in which 48 per cent of the voters chose to remain, and 52 per cent elected to leave the EU. This outcome shocked observers within the country and abroad. The period since that referendum has been very rocky for the UK, as various political leaders have resigned and few, if any, politicians and observers fully understand the implications of Brexit. Furthermore, although a majority voted to leave, it remained unclear for the longest time what the relationship between the United Kingdom and the EU would look like after Brexit—in the jargon, whether it would be "hard" or "soft" Brexit. In this context "soft Brexit" meant an arrangement such as the one that Norway has with the EU, namely to be part of the Single Market and, as such, abide by the four freedoms, like any EU member state. (The EU made clear that picking and choosing among the four freedoms would not be an option.) By March 2017, when UK Prime Minister Theresa May formally notified the European Union that her country wanted to leave the EU, it was apparent she was aiming for hard Brexit: the UK would no longer be either part of the Single Market, subjected to rulings of the Court of Justice of the EU, or obliged to accept the free movement of labour (i.e., the UK would regain control over its migration policy). But the hard Brexit choice also makes it

**Figure 7.3** (Potential) vicious circle of European integration

Source: Authors' design

unclear under what conditions the UK and the rest of the EU will trade in goods and services.

Brexit is at any rate going to be very complex. The Treaty of Lisbon includes an article (Article 50 TEU) that states the applicable rules if member states decide to leave the European Union. It prescribes that the process be completed within two years. In the case of the UK, should that period end, and no new arrangements be made with the EU, EU-UK trade relations would revert back to the rules of the **World Trade Organization**. Brexit may also trigger a constitutional crisis of the United Kingdom of Great Britain and Northern Ireland (and Gibraltar), as the voters in Scotland (62 per cent), Northern Ireland (56 per cent), and Gibraltar (96 per cent) voted to remain in the EU. Furthermore, Brexit may also affect the political situation in other countries. To date no other country has subsequently had a political party in power that advocates leaving the EU, but political parties that support this policy have received some votes in numerous EU countries.

## Conclusion

European economic integration has had a chequered past with many ups and downs. Still, European economic and monetary integration has progressed immensely since the early days of European integration. Important milestones on the way to the Single Market were the Customs Union, which was completed in 1968, and the Single European Act (1986), which imposed qualified majority vote to complete the Single Market by the end of 1992. Between these two milestones, several Court of Justice rulings furthered the process through negative integration. These rulings paved the way for a focus on mutual recognition, as reflected in the Single European Act.

The path to monetary integration also went through a few blueprints and various setbacks before currencies were irrevocably fixed in 1999, according to the Maastricht Treaty provisions, with banknotes and coins eventually introduced in 12 member states from 2001 and in circulation in 19 member states today. The first years of EMU were successful, but the financial and economic crisis and the sovereign debt crisis revealed that EMU was vulnerable and incomplete. The first years of the financial crisis were littered with bank guarantees and bank rescues by governments.

As public resources reached their limit in several member states, the global financial crisis turned into a sovereign debt crisis. Whether or not to bail out member states in financial distress posed a real dilemma for EU member states. However, with the prospect of a possible Euro Area collapse, member states created lending facilities for member states in distress, albeit under the condition of far-reaching fiscal reform in recipient countries. Other EU institutions, notably under the condition of the European Central Bank, also stepped up to the plate by adopting a range of unorthodox measures.

The global financial crisis and the ensuing sovereign debt crisis revealed severe issues associated with the mutual-recognition approach to creating a Single Market for banking and EMU; further deepening of integration in the areas of financial regulation and supervision was needed. Specifically, the Single Market for banking was in need of harmonization in terms of bank supervision, recovery and resolution rules and mechanisms, deposit insurance, and bank safety nets, i.e., Banking Union. For EMU to function well, more supranational oversight in areas of budgetary, fiscal policies appeared to be required. Some other new institutions and prospective plans have been created in response to the financial, economic, and sovereign debt crisis, including a capital market union.

Not all citizens in EU member states are equally excited about the prospect of deeper economic integration. A striking example is the UK, where in a June 2016 referendum its citizens voted to leave the EU, a scenario colloquially referred to as Brexit.

With **Euroskepticism** in several member states and the rise of populism, the challenge for the EU is to convince its citizens that it is beneficial to growth and prosperity. There are also challenges in the domain of EU democracy and legitimacy: deeper integration may require more political integration and representation.

## References and Further Reading

Balassa, B. 1961. *The theory of economic integration.* London: George Allen and Unwin.
Baldwin, R., and C. Wyplosz. 2015. *The economics of European integration.* 5th ed. London: McGraw-Hill.
"Canada's internal trade: The great provincial obstacle course." 2016, July 23. *The Economist* (American ed.).
Cayo, D. 2015, November 26. "Canada's internal market disjointed by trade barriers." *Vancouver Sun.* http://www.vancouversun.com/business/cayo+canada+internal+market+disjointed+trade+barriers/11545665/story.html.
Closa, C., and A. Maatsch. 2014. "In a spirit of solidarity? Justifying the European financial stability facility (EFSF) in national parliamentary debates." *Journal of Common Market Studies* 52 (4): 826–42. https://doi.org/10.1111/jcms.12119.
De Grauwe, P. 2016. *Economics of Monetary Union.* 11th ed. Oxford: Oxford University Press.
Dyson, K., and K. Featherstone. 1999. *The road to Maastricht: Negotiating economic and monetary union.* Oxford: Oxford University Press. https://doi.org/10.1093/019829638X.001.0001.
Egan, M.P. 2015. *Single markets: Economic integration in Europe and in the United States.* Oxford: Oxford University Press. https://doi.org/10.1093/acprof:oso/9780199280506.001.0001.
Engineer, M.H., P. Schure, and M. Gillis. 2013. "A positive analysis of deposit insurance provision: Regulatory competition among European Union countries." *Journal of Financial Stability* 9 (4): 530–44. https://doi.org/10.1016/j.jfs.2013.10.001.
European Commission. 2016, September 14. "State of the Union 2016: Completing the Capital Markets Union—Commission accelerates reform." Press release. Strasbourg: European Commission. http://europa.eu/rapid/press-release_IP-16-3001_en.htm.
European Parliament. 2016. *Banking Union.* Fact sheet. http://www.europarl.europa.eu/atyourservice/en/displayFtu.html?ftuId=FTU_4.2.4.html.
Featherstone, K. 2011. "The Greek sovereign debt crisis and EMU: A failing state in a skewed regime." *Journal of Common Market Studies* 49 (2): 193–217. https://doi.org/10.1111/j.1468-5965.2010.02139.x.
Heipertz, M., and A. Verdun. 2010. *Ruling Europe: The politics of the stability and growth pact.* Cambridge: Cambridge University Press. https://doi.org/10.1017/CBO9780511750380.
Hodson, D. 2011. *Governing the euro area in good times and in bad.* Oxford: Oxford University Press. https://doi.org/10.1093/acprof:oso/9780199572502.001.0001.
Högenauer, A.L., and D. Howarth. 2016. "Unconventional monetary policies and the European Central Bank's problematic democratic legitimacy." *Journal of Public Law / Zeitschrift für öffentliches Recht* 71(2): 425–48.
Howarth, D., and L. Quaglia. 2016. *The political economy of European banking union.* Oxford: Oxford University Press. https://doi.org/10.1093/acprof:oso/9780198727927.001.0001.
Juncker, J.C. 2015. *Completing Europe's Economic and Monetary Union (Five President's Report).* Brussels: European Commission.
Katsanidou, A., and S. Otjes. 2016. "How the European debt crisis reshaped national political space: The case of Greece." *European Union Politics* 17 (2): 262–84. https://doi.org/10.1177/1465116515616196.

O'Leary, B. 2016. "The Dalriada document: Towards a multinational compromise that respects democratic diversity in the United Kingdom." *Political Quarterly* 87 (4): 518–33. https://doi.org/10.1111/1467-923X.12312.

Pelkmans, J. 2013. "The economics of Single Market regulation." In *Mapping European economic integration*, edited by A. Verdun and A. Tovias, 79–104. Basingstoke, UK: Palgrave Macmillan. https://doi.org/10.1057/9781137317360_5.

Rajan, R.G. 2010. *Fault lines. How hidden fractures still threaten the world economy.* Princeton, NJ: Princeton University Press.

Sadeh, T., and A. Verdun. 2009. "Explaining Europe's monetary union: A survey of the literature." *International Studies Review* 11 (2): 277–301. https://doi.org/10.1111/j.1468-2486.2009.00849.x.

Schure, P. 2013. "European financial market integration." In *Mapping European economic integration*, edited by A. Verdun and A. Tovias, 105–24. Basingstoke, UK: Palgrave Macmillan. https://doi.org/10.1057/9781137317360_6.

Schmidt, S., ed. 2008. *Mutual recognition as a new mode of governance.* London: Taylor and Francis.

Sturm, J.E., U. Fritsche, M. Graff, M. Lamla, S. Lein, V. Nitsch, D. Liechti, and D. Triet. 2009, June. "The euro and prices: Changeover-related inflation and price convergence in the euro area." *European Economy, Economic Papers 381.* Brussels: European Commission.

Verdun, A. 1996. "An 'asymmetrical' Economic and Monetary Union in the EU: Perceptions of monetary authorities and social partners." *Journal of European Integration* 20 (1): 59–81. https://doi.org/10.1080/07036339608429045.

Verdun, A. 2000. *European responses to globalization and financial market integration: Perceptions of Economic and Monetary Union in Britain, France and Germany.* Basingstoke, UK: Palgrave Macmillan.

Verdun, A. 2015. "A historical institutionalist explanation of the EU's responses to the euro area financial crisis." *Journal of European Public Policy* 22 (2): 219–37. https://doi.org/10.1080/13501763.2014.994023.

Verdun, A. 2017. "Political leadership of the European Central Bank." *Journal of European Integration* 39 (2): 207–21.

Verdun, A., and A. Tovias, eds. 2013. *Mapping European economic integration.* Basingstoke, UK: Palgrave Macmillan. https://doi.org/10.1057/9781137317360.

## Review Questions

1. Why was mutual recognition not only a way to advance the Single Market but also at the heart of the banking crisis?

2. Economic and Monetary Union, introduced in 1999–2002, had a supranational monetary authority but no supranational budgetary and fiscal authority. What EU institution is the *supranational monetary authority*? What are the differences between EMU today and that of 2002? Can you explain how these differences came about?

3. What were the pros and cons of providing Greece with financial support during the sovereign debt crisis? What was the main reason that Greece ended up receiving support from the so-called troika?

4.  Which are the main features advanced in the Five Presidents' Report? To what institutions do the "Five Presidents" belong, and why was it important that the president of the European Parliament be among them?
5.  What is meant by "hard Brexit" and "soft Brexit"? Explain the difficulties associated with Brexit.

## Exercises

1.  Divide students into two groups. Have one group argue the position "The EU Single Market is a form of globalization." Have the other group argue the converse: "The EU Single Market is a protective shield from the forces of globalization." Discuss together as a single group after the debate.
2.  Undertake an examination of fiscal federalism in Canada or in another federal country. How is a province of Canada (or a US state, a German *Land*, etc.) protected from financial crisis, as compared to Greece within the Euro Area post-2008?

## Notes

1    The authors thank Rachel Epstein, David Howarth, Erik Jones, Patrick Leblond, and Lucia Quaglia for comments on an earlier version of this chapter. The usual disclaimer applies.

2    In 1994, the EFTA countries and the EU formed the **European Economic Area (EEA)**, which gives them access to the Single Market. All EFTA countries, except for Switzerland, joined the EEA. Switzerland has made bilateral agreements that effectively give that country full access to the Single Market.

3    The choice to agree on monetary, but not on fiscal, integration is often called "asymmetrical EMU" (Verdun, 1996). At the outset pundits foresaw problems for EMU due to this asymmetry.

4    Unconventional monetary policy means using a non-standard monetary policy instrument, for example buying up government bonds with newly issued money.

5    Together with several other important directives, namely the Money Laundering Directive (91/308/EEC), the Own Funds Directive (89/299/EEC), the Solvency Ratio Directive (89/647/EEC), the Consolidated Supervision Directive (92/30/EEC), the Deposit-Guarantee Directive (94/19/EC), the Large Exposures Directive (92/121/EEC), the Capital Adequacy Directive (93/6/EEC), and the Investment Services Directive (93/22/EEC).

# 8

# Justice, Freedom, and Security

OLIVER SCHMIDTKE

## Reader's Guide

The European Union's (EU) **Area of Freedom, Security, and Justice
(AFSJ)** covers policies related to justice, security, migration, and borders. It
was first introduced as **Justice and Home Affairs (JHA)** in the **Maastricht Treaty**. Challenges related to the implications of increased cross-
border mobility and border security (through irregular migration, organized
crime, or terrorism) have led to a rapid expansion of the policy area. The
governance of migration, asylum, and borders raises politically controversial
issues about state **sovereignty** and **supranational** rule. The recent refugee
crisis and fight against terrorism have lent urgency to questions about the
EU's ability to deal with pressing policy challenges.

## Introduction

This chapter traces the origins of the Area of Freedom, Security, and Justice
(AFSJ) from its modest beginnings as part of Justice and Home Affairs (JHA)
and Pillar III established under the 1992 Maastricht Treaty to its central role in
addressing migration, crime, and the threat of terrorism in the second decade
of the twenty-first century. This field of European Union (EU) policy-making
is relevant to each of the three themes of this textbook, as discussed in the
introductory chapter: the development of the AFSJ is driven by the necessity to address the effects of creating a **Single Market** (Theme 1), as well as
external shocks like terrorist attacks or the refugee crisis, which challenge the
viability of the EU's border and migration regime. Since the EU is not a state
(Theme 2), the AFSJ has emerged as the outcome of difficult negotiations
between the member states, which realize the benefits of cooperation but seek
to protect their sovereignty. Finally, the AFSJ has also been used as a vehicle
to address the challenges that the EU faces in terms of its popular legitimacy and support (Theme 3). Protecting fundamental rights and introducing
elements of an emerging EU citizenship status gives substance to how **European
integration** can significantly shape the daily lives of EU citizens.

As one of the fundamental **four freedoms** guaranteed by EU Law (freedom of movement of goods, people, services, and capital across borders), the

principle of **freedom of movement** ensures every EU citizen the right to move freely, to stay and to work in another member state. Yet the increasingly uninhibited cross-border mobility, first for goods and services within the European Single Market, then also for people in the so-called **Schengen Area** (see Box 8.1 and Table 8.1), has created a set of new challenges. If EU citizens can move from one member state to another without being restricted by visa requirements or work permits, what should their legal status be? For instance, should EU citizens, once they reside in an EU member state of which they do not hold the national citizenship, enjoy social and political rights equivalent to citizens of that country?

Similarly, organized crime and terrorism are no longer primarily a national phenomenon but largely European, if not global, in scale. Recent terrorist attacks are a stark reminder that fighting crime and terrorism is a task that transcends national borders and needs to be tackled by a coordinated European response. Over the past 25 years, the EU has been trying to address the implications of cross-border mobility, one of the EU's most fundamental freedoms. The AFSJ has hence developed into a prolific EU policy area in terms of both cooperation and legislative output. The growing relevance of this policy area in the process of European integration is reflected in the swift move toward an expanding AFSJ agenda, driven by a community logic.

## Justice, Freedom, and Security: From Humble Beginnings to a Key EU Policy Field

The AFSJ constitutes a policy field that is notably different from others in two ways. First, EU competences in this field started modestly and were

**Box 8.1**    The Schengen Area

- The Schengen Agreement came into being in 1985, committing France, Germany, and the Benelux countries to remove controls at their internal borders.
- Until now, 22 EU member states and 4 non-EU states have joined the Schengen Area.
- In the aftermath of the Paris terrorist attacks in late 2015 and of the refugee crisis in 2015–16, some Schengen countries have temporarily reintroduced border controls.

**Table 8.1** Member states of the Schengen Area

| EU member states part of Schengen | Non-EU member states part of Schengen | Schengen candidate countries | EU member states not part of Schengen |
| --- | --- | --- | --- |
| Austria | Iceland | Bulgaria | Ireland |
| Belgium | Liechtenstein | Croatia | United Kingdom |
| Czech Republic | Norway | Cyprus | |
| Germany | Switzerland | Romania | |
| Denmark | | | |
| Estonia | | | |
| Finland | | | |
| France | | | |
| Greece | | | |
| Hungary | | | |
| Italy | | | |
| Latvia | | | |
| Lithuania | | | |
| Luxembourg | | | |
| Malta | | | |
| Netherlands | | | |
| Poland | | | |
| Portugal | | | |
| Slovakia | | | |
| Slovenia | | | |
| Spain | | | |
| Sweden | | | |

somewhat fragmented in its first iterations in the form of anti-terrorism cooperation in the 1970s under the umbrella of the TREVI agreement and then more formalized with the Maastricht Treaty in 1993. As Lavenex and Wallace (2005) put it, the policy area has traditionally been characterized by a distinct "disjointed incrementalism." Yet since its inception in the Maastricht Treaty (or **Treaty of the European Union, TEU**), signed in 1992 and entered into force in 1993, it morphed quickly into an area of policy-making in which, particularly after the 1997 Amsterdam Treaty, the EU developed considerable collective decision-making capacity and institutional independence. Second, AFSJ describes a complex and somewhat disconnected field of policies that range from border control to cooperation in the field of law enforcement. Still, what provides a certain degree of coherence to AFSJ as a policy field is the reference to cross-border mobility as a catalyst for seeking solutions that traditionally were defined by national approaches to security, mobility, and fundamental rights.

AFSJ received formal recognition, under the label of JHA, as Pillar III of the TEU. The TEU identified the need to develop collective initiatives primarily in the form of—loose—**intergovernmental** cooperation addressing the consequences of cross-border mobility. Markedly, cross-border cooperation now extended from the realm of goods and services to people (see the key stipulations of the Schengen Agreement in Box 8.1). At the same time, the issues addressed in JHA also reflected the ambitious agenda of the TEU to establish the EU as a political union, in particular with regard to border management, migration, and judicial cooperation (Table 8.2 provides an overview of the policy fields in AFSJ).

The intergovernmental mode of decision-making meant that initially the JHA policies were marginal to EU institutions and subject to **unanimity** voting in the **Council of the EU**, which means that every member state has to agree to it and either vote in favour or abstain. This constraining procedure to make decisions in this policy area increasingly became a problem in the 1990s when the EU sought to improve its status with citizens and address the practical challenges related to the Schengen principle of removing border controls. As a result, this period witnessed a gradual communitarization, in particular of EU asylum and immigration policies. In 1999, as the Amsterdam Treaty entered into force, JHA was reformed and the **European Commission**, the **European Parliament (EP)**, and, most importantly, the **Court of Justice of the EU (CJEU)** received a more robust role in this policy domain. The **ordinary legislative procedure (OLP)** applies to most AFSJ policies since the **Lisbon Treaty**. Monar (2012) describes JHA as one of the most momentous innovations of the Maastricht Treaty. For him, this treaty was a significant "intergovernmental gate opener" for the

**Table 8.2**  Policy areas in the AFSJ

| Home affairs | Justice |
| --- | --- |
| Immigration | Fundamental rights |
| Common European Asylum System | EU citizenship |
| Borders and visas (Schengen) | Justice |
| Organized crime and human trafficking | Gender equality |
| Terrorism | Fight against discrimination |
| Police and law enforcement | Cross-border judicial cooperation |

AFSJ, one whose operational dynamic would lead to regularized institutional cooperation among member states and, as a result, the emergence of a common perception of shared policy challenges. Monar (2015) calls this a "culture of co-operation" on a European scale. Most notably, the 2007 Lisbon Treaty pushed for an ambitious set of policies under community authority in the AFSJ domain. Article 3(2) of the TEU now reads as follows: "The Union shall offer its citizens an area of freedom, security and justice without internal frontiers, in which the free movement of persons is ensured in conjunction with appropriate measures with respect to external border controls, asylum, immigration and the prevention and combating of crime." With this agenda, AFSJ has become one of the key driving forces behind what defines the EU as a political union.

### Migration and Asylum

Migration has transformed European societies profoundly. This trend will likely continue, considering the far-reaching demographic changes (aging populations and a declining birth rate) that these societies face. Without newcomers to these societies, these challenges are anticipated to produce labour shortages and considerable pressure on social security systems. Most European countries have been trying to increase their birth rates, to no avail. Thus, most European countries know that they should encourage the arrival of newcomers in order to tackle these demographic challenges. Yet boosting regular immigration is a highly contested issue in domestic politics.

Figure 8.1 below refers to the two dimensions of migration in the EU. First, there is cross-border mobility within the EU—a trend that the recent economic crisis has further accentuated. At the same time, the segment of EU citizens that chooses to reside in another member state is still relatively small, in spite of the widespread fears about unmanageable mass migration that most rounds of enlarging the EU have provoked in public discourse (most recently the Eastern **enlargement** in 2004/2007). The overall proportion of EU citizens residing in a country in which they were not born makes up a small, albeit increasing, segment of EU member states. According to Eurostat (the statistical office of the EU) data for 2015, 15.3 million EU citizens live in an EU member state other than their country of citizenship (roughly 3 per cent of the EU's total population).

Second, Europe has persistently attracted migrants and refugees from around the world. The so-called **third country nationals (TCNs)** make up a fast-growing demographic group. In 2015, 35.1 million people born outside of the EU-28 lived in one of the EU member states. Although these numbers are still smaller than in traditional immigrant societies, such as Canada,

**Figure 8.1** Foreign and foreign-born population in EU-28 (as of January 1, 2015)

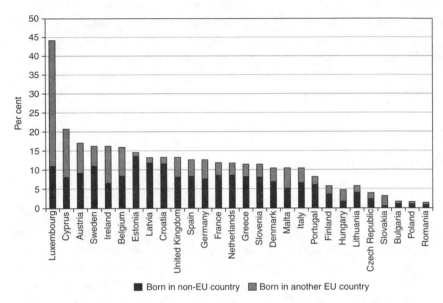

Source: Eurostat (http://emn.ie/index.jsp?p=128&n=229)

EU member states are increasingly resembling immigrant societies in certain ways, with amplified cultural and religious diversity[1] (see Box 8.6). This change in population composition has resulted in a new set of policy challenges regarding the recruitment, settlement, and long-term integration of migrants. The EU responses fall within the AFSJ domain. Most prominently, in 2009 the EU introduced a five-year plan (the so-called Stockholm Program, 2010 to 2015) with goals related to, among others, the protection of fundamental rights, border management, minority rights, and EU citizenship.

Individual member states still determine the procedures through which migrants can settle in their countries and gain access to national citizenship. However, with the AFSJ, the EU has started to pursue a coordinated European migration and asylum policy that has various components:

1) *Common framework for legal immigration*: Responding to the fact that only a relatively small number of highly skilled migrants settle in the EU as compared to North America,[2] the EU has taken first steps toward setting the framework for legal immigration. The regulations at the EU level concern the conditions of entry and residence for certain categories of migrants, such as highly qualified workers, students, and researchers. Most notably, in 2009

the EU Blue Card Initiative has introduced an EU-wide work permit allowing highly skilled non-EU citizens to work and live in any country within
the EU (with the exception of Denmark, Ireland, and the UK). This scheme
of recruiting skilled labour works in parallel to national immigration laws
and is designed to position the EU as an important player in the increasingly
globalized labour market for highly skilled workers. The Canadian immigration regime, with its focus on recruiting skilled labour, has served as a
blueprint for EU initiatives in this policy field.

2) *Supporting integration*: In the 1997 Amsterdam Treaty, the EU committed to the "fair treatment of third country nationals" targeting the long-term
integration of migrants as a genuine field of EU policy-making. Between 2014
and 2020, the EU has committed €3,137 billion mandating the Asylum, Migration and Integration Fund (AMIF) to coordinate the efficient management of
immigration flows (including initiatives such as language and civic education
courses, and intercultural training) and to allow for fair burden sharing across
the EU. The support for the societal integration of TCNs also refers to the
anti-discrimination rules that were developed in form of the Employment
Equality **Directive** and the Race Equality Directive in 2000, and then more
recently fully adopted into national law. The EU's policies to fight racism and
xenophobia are promoted by a dedicated agency, the European Union Agency
for Fundamental Rights (set up in 2007 with a mandate inherited from the
European Monitoring Centre on Racism and Xenophobia), which monitors
developments throughout the EU and has established legal recourse in particular for Europe's migrant and minority population (Ippolito, 2015).

The task of integrating migrants into society highlights the tensions between intergovernmental and supranational cooperation. As most of the initiatives in this field are still under the sole jurisdiction of the member states,
this dimension of EU's migration policies is still in its infancy. While the EU
set an ambitious agenda in the Hague Program (2004) with the **European
Council**'s commitment to enhancing the equal treatment of long-term
residents, regardless of their place of origin, it has not yet developed the
institutional capacity to follow up fully on this promise. In this respect, "Eu-
ropeanizing" the task of migrant integration is complicated by the variety of
approaches adopted to deal with this task throughout Europe. The EU faces
a similar picture when it comes to legal immigration. While the principle of
free movement of EU citizens is one of the four freedoms on which the EU
was founded in 1957, immigration related to TCNs is still handled primarily
on an intergovernmental basis. Member states have been determined to hold
on to this key element of state sovereignty—control of immigration and
access to citizenship—a fact that has complicated the European response to
the recent refugee crisis enormously (on this point, see more details below).

3) *Asylum*: Europe has become the main destination for hundreds of thousands of refugees from around the world. In its Charter of Fundamental Rights (see also below) the EU commits to protecting those fleeing political persecution in their home countries and has established one of the world's most successful and attractive asylum policies. The Common European Asylum System (CEAS) was introduced in 1999 in order to harmonize asylum processes, guarantee similar standards for protecting and treating refugees, and establish a common system that would allow for cooperation between member states. In an attempt to avoid asylum seekers moving from one country to another ("asylum shopping") the EU established a single system. The so-called Dublin Agreement stipulates that refugees need to register, be fingerprinted (all EU member states participate in the database Eurodac storing data on this group), and claim asylum in the first EU member state they land in. However, since 2015, as a consequence of the overwhelming number of refugees arriving in the EU and the fact that they typically arrive in peripheral EU member states much more than in other central and northern states, the Dublin Agreement is no longer being enforced (see also the section on the refugee crisis below).

4) *Irregular migration*: Migrants who come to the EU irregularly or who overstay their visa are a far bigger challenge in the EU than in Canada. In particular, since the end of the **Cold War**, Europe has become relatively easy for migrants to access. Enforcing internal mobility law in this area has posed real challenges to supranational coordination. Yet one initiative that the EU has developed, and that is of critical importance, is fighting human trafficking. In line with the EU's commitment to human rights (see next section), this initiative addresses primarily issues of sexual and labour exploitation (e.g., October 20 is the EU Anti-Trafficking Day, signalling the importance that the EU attributes to this challenge). As part of the Schengen legislative framework, the EU has also introduced a Return Directive (2008) that sets EU-wide standards and procedures for returning illegal TCNs to their home countries.

5) *Cooperation with non-EU countries*: During the recent refugee crisis, cooperation with countries outside of the EU has become a significant strategy to address the global migration phenomenon. Since 2005, the EU's Global Approach to Migration and Mobility (GAMM) has developed the external dimension of its migration and asylum policy. It promotes cooperation in governance in the field of migration and asylum across the EU's external borders (including development cooperation). This aspect of the EU's external relations became particularly important during the years of the Arab Spring and the subsequent socio-political unrest it created in the EU's extended southern neighbourhood.

## Justice, Fundamental Rights, and Citizenship

At first glance, it might be surprising to find justice as a cornerstone of the EU's public policies. Yet its prominent role in EU policy-making becomes apparent when one considers that the rule of law and the legislative process are constitutive of the European integration process in two ways. First, the mandate and nature of the EU has changed since its inception in the 1950s. Over time, following a procedure of **mutual recognition** and harmonization, a standardization of legal provisions throughout all member states has taken place. The so-called *acquis communautaire* constitutes the accumulated body of EU law (EU legislation, legal acts, court decisions, treaties, and fundamental rights provisions) that, given the **supremacy** of EU law over national law, member states need to adopt as part of their own national laws (see Chapter 4). It is with this body of law—and the Court of Justice of the EU to enforce it—that the EU has defined its authority and policy prerogative vis-à-vis its member states. The respect for the rule of law, fundamental rights, and the independence of the judiciary are essential principles of the EU, which prove their effectiveness particularly in the process of enlarging the EU and reforming (potential) new member states (see Chapter 15).

Second, rights and legal entitlements are a pivotal instrument for the EU to make itself relevant in the daily lives of its citizens. The introduction of EU citizenship status was also an attempt to address the legitimacy issue facing the EU. By empowering EU citizens through a set of legal standards and entitlements established at the EU level, its leaders tried to make the benefits of European integration more tangible and meaningful.

In 1993, with the entering into force of Maastricht Treaty, the status of EU citizenship was first introduced. The 1997 Amsterdam Treaty gave more substance to what it means to be a citizen of the EU and declared at the same time the limitation of this legal status by asserting that the "Citizenship of the Union shall complement and not replace national citizenship." Similarly, it is worth noting that EU citizenship is a derivative of national citizenship and that the EU does not have the authority to make someone its citizen. Box 8.2 summarizes some of the key elements of what this status entails. Again, the principle of free movement constitutes the essence of what it means to be a citizen of the EU. Another key issue tackled by EU citizenship is political representation: EU citizens have the right to vote and stand as candidates in local and European Parliament elections in the country in which they reside regardless of their country of origin. While Canada is regularly portrayed as the country with the most accomplished record of immigrant integration, its permanent residents are not able to vote in any

**Box 8.2**    Key elements of an emerging EU citizenship regime

- Right of free movement of persons.
- Right to vote and stand in local government and European Parliament elections in the country of residence.
- Right of petition to the European Parliament and appeal to the European Ombudsman.
- **Non-discrimination** principle by reason of nationality.
- Right to organize or support a citizens' initiative to call for new EU legislation.
- Protection of fundamental civic, political, and social rights (under the Charter of Fundamental Rights of the European Union).

election. Thus, the EU has broken new grounds in terms of decoupling some fundamental rights (such as the right to vote) from a nationally defined citizenship status.[3]

The project of building a "European area of justice" has additional components that focus on the scope and enforceability of EU law in the EU member states. The harmonization of legal rules and procedures throughout the EU means that individuals as well as businesses have proper access to legal recourse. Currently the EU has two programs (Justice Program; and Rights, Equality and Citizenship) designed to build an effective pan-European legal infrastructure and procedural safeguards for citizens (including initiatives such as privacy and data protection, guarantees for bioethics, or a Consumer Rights Directive).

One key institutional component of this infrastructure is the European Convention on Human Rights—a document drawn up by **Council of Europe** in the early 1950s that all EU member states have signed. Building on this commitment the EU introduced more recently the EU Charter of Fundamental Rights[4] that became a legally binding component of EU law with the Lisbon Treaty, entering into force in 2009. Under six titles (Dignity, Freedoms, Equality, Solidarity, Citizens' Rights, and Justice) the Charter brings together the fundamental rights protected in the EU in one single document. EU citizens have an additional legal recourse beyond national courts if they consider their fundamental rights violated. In practice, political advocates can use the Charter at the national and European level in their fight for human rights, gender equality, and non-discrimination.

## Borders and Security

With the removal of its internal border controls, the EU's Schengen Area has faced the task of addressing the issue of border control and internal security (most prominently irregular migration, crime, and terrorism). One immediate functional requirement related to an unrestricted cross-border mobility zone was a common European visa policy. Canadian passport holders, for instance, have to apply for a visa for the EU ("Schengen visa") and not individual member states when they intend to stay in the Schengen Area beyond the three months allowed for tourism. In addition, the Schengen Information System data on non-EU visitors is shared among the authorities in the participating member states.

EU-wide information systems and an agency on the ground are tasked with the management of the EU's external borders. The central role falls to **Frontex**, the European Border and Coast Guard Agency, which came into being in October 2016 (before that, from 2004, it was known as the Agency for the Management of Operational Cooperation at the External Borders of the Member States of the European Union). Based in Warsaw, Frontex supports the border surveillance resources of the EU member states with the objective of monitoring and controlling their external borders (see Box 8.3). This border-management system under EU leadership has come under particular stress during the recent refugee crisis. In 2015–16, NATO forces had to step in and assist in the protection of the Mediterranean coastline.

Under the auspices of the EU Internal Security Strategy, a whole set of operative institutions cover different dimensions of guarding the internal security of the EU by fighting crime, protecting borders, and policing. With its headquarters in The Hague, **Europol**, the European Union Agency for Law Enforcement Cooperation, plays a front-line role in coordinating Europe's fight against terrorism and cross-border crime (most importantly, in the fields of illicit drugs, human trafficking, irregular migration, cybercrime,

**Box 8.3**    Key tasks of Frontex

- Cooperation between member states in external border management; control and surveillance of external borders.
- Technical and operational assistance at external borders.
- Training of national border guards; carrying out risk analyses.
- Support for member states in organizing joint return operations.

money laundering, organized crime, and terrorism). Becoming operational in 1999, as the EU's law enforcement organization, Europol coordinates the sharing of intelligence among national police forces and their collaboration on a European scale. Similarly, the European Union's Judicial Cooperation Unit (Eurojust) coordinates judicial action by facilitating cooperation between investigating and prosecuting agencies and by exchanging data and judicial information. Again, the justification for these EU organizations is that the challenges at hand, in this case organized crime, trafficking, and terrorism, are European—if not global—in scale, and they need a policy response that is more effective when coordinated among member states. The terrorist attacks in Paris, Brussels, London, Nice, Berlin, and Stockholm from 2015 to 2017 underlined the urgency of coordinated and forceful action at the supranational level. Some of the attackers could rely on a support structure of fundamentalist groups spanning several EU member states. Complementing its police-based counterterrorism and law-enforcement strategy, the EU has also developed initiatives designed at prevention by targeting radicalization and recruitment, in particular of Europe's Muslim youth.

Beyond the immediate task of fighting terrorism, the EU has embarked on an ambitious agenda to create what it labels a "European Area of Justice." At the core of an enhanced cooperation in this area across all member states is the mutual recognition of judicial decisions—regardless of the diversity of judicial systems throughout the EU. This cooperation also extends to law enforcement. Driven by the international anti-terror efforts after the 9/11 attacks in New York and Washington in 2001, the EU launched the **European Arrest Warrant (EAW)** in 2004 that commits member states to surrender to another EU member state their citizens if they are wanted in relation to significant crimes or to serve a prison sentence for an existing conviction. The extradition mechanism under the EAW has greatly increased in significance, with numbers of issued EWAs expanding from 7,100 in 2005 to over 15,000 in 2009. In practice, the harmonization of extradition rules means that criminals can be investigated and also prosecuted across EU member states. The EAW has put an end to lengthy extradition procedures within the EU's territorial jurisdiction and replaced it with a system of simplified and effective judicial cooperation across national borders. In particular within the Schengen Area, the close collaboration of law-enforcement agencies has led to transnational networks of police and judicial authorities that are of critical importance for the implementation of AFSJ policies.

However, the widespread recognition that a community approach to security challenges is warranted comes with vocal public criticism regarding how the EU balances security policies and those designed to protect the fundamental rights and liberties of its citizens. One critical assessment of

EU action points to a general conundrum that is shaping this policy field in countries around the world, including Canada. In a post-9/11 environment and faced with a series of terrorist attacks (also on European soil), liberal democracies are confronted with a politically contested policy challenge. How should state authorities strike an appropriate balance between security and surveillance on the one hand and civil liberties on the other? While the EU seeks to promote a more tolerant and inclusive society as part of its AFSJ domain, it nonetheless remains a major player in fortifying its external borders, supporting a comprehensive surveillance system, and portraying migrants from outside the member states as a veritable security risk. In the scholarly debate, this issue has been discussed in terms of securitizing the EU's governance of borders and migration (Bigo, 2014; Huysmans, 2006).

The second argument focuses more closely on the tension and interplay between national and European responses to security challenges. With respect to managing migrants and refugees under the AFSJ domain, it proves to be considerably easier to find **consensus** among member states on EU initiatives targeted at (external) border control and policing. In contrast, the EU mandate to protect human and civil rights and to promote societal integration of non-EU nationals is regularly perceived as a more challenging infringement on sovereign prerogatives of nation-states. This is also reflected in the EU budget (see Box 8.4). The 2015–16 **refugee crisis** has highlighted how the need for security and border control can come at the expense of some of the EU's basic liberties and commitments to human rights. The inability of the EU to address effectively the suffering of the refugees on their treacherous voyage to Europe has provoked harsh criticism from human rights advocates. The long-standing debate on "fortress Europe" reflects, among other concerns, the worry of those who consider the EU's border regime to be driven by a strong emphasis on security and militarized border control at the expense of the EU's humanitarian commitments.

In a similar vein, the refugee crisis has triggered a political development that challenges the EU's capacity for collective action at its core and that has emboldened political actors critical, if not outright hostile, to the very project of European integration (see the debate section for a discussion of the rise of the populist right in Europe). The **Brexit** vote in 2016 is a case in point: the response to the refugee crisis and migration more broadly were key themes driving popular sentiments directed at the idea of sovereign nation-states losing control of their borders. Similarly, one of the central issues in the UK and the EU negotiating the terms of Brexit (and the British request to remain part of the Single Market) is the principle of freedom of movement. In this regard, cross-border mobility has been a driving force in nurturing a sense of Europeanness over the past decades while

**Box 8.4**   Budget allocation to the AFSJ

In the 2016 budget, the EU allocated a total of €2,323 million (1.6 per cent of the total budget) to "migration and home affairs" and €239 million (0.2 per cent) to "justice and consumers"; these figures include administrative expenditures. The main spending items were "internal and border security" with €849 million (including €239 million for Frontex, almost twice the agency's 2015 budget) and "asylum and migration" with €1,147 million (including an investment of €785 million in the CEAS). By contrast, only relatively small sums were allocated to "fostering European citizenship" (€22 million) and projects in the areas of "rights, equality and citizenship" and "justice" (€84 million each).

Source: Adopted budget for 2016, *Official Journal of the European Union*, L 48, February 24, 2016, 1194–1251; 1616–50

simultaneously being at the centre of a nationalist backlash against the scope and nature of European rule.

## Debate: Governing Migration and Borders: The Refugee Crisis and Its Impact on the EU

While policies related to justice, freedom and security[5] are located in an area of public policy-making that itself has come under increased community oversight, this field also reflects the tensions between intergovernmental and supranational rule in the EU. Issues of border control, security, citizenship, and migration are central to the very principle of state sovereignty in the tradition of the modern nation-state. For instance, the governance of borders and migration has become a critical test case for the ability of EU member states to establish an effective pan-European policy response and to pool resources that traditionally were the prerogative of sovereign nation-states. In a similar vein, AFSJ is a field of public policy through which the EU envisions itself as a political community balancing the need for security in a post-9/11 world, and the commitment to citizens' freedom and fundamental rights across national borders.

The refugee crisis of 2015–16 clearly illustrates how politically contested and sensitive an EU-led approach to governing borders and migration can be. In the wake of the Arab Spring that started in late 2010, Europe experienced an enormous influx of irregular migrants travelling across the

Mediterranean Sea or overland through Southeast Europe. Driven largely by the civil war in Syria, these numbers peaked in 2015. During that year, according to UNHCR figures, 1.3 million migrants reached the shores of Europe, while almost 4,000 migrants are feared to have lost their lives primarily during their treacherous voyage by sea. For some countries in the EU, accommodating such large numbers of migrants meant massive logistical challenges; in Germany, authorities had to register, house, and process the refugee claims of close to one million newcomers in 2015.

As mentioned above, under the rules of the Dublin Agreement, refugees need to register and file their asylum claim in the EU member state in which they first land. The **Dublin Regulation** assigns clear responsibility (see Box 8.5). Yet it could not be kept in place in light of the sheer numbers of refugees crossing the external borders of the EU. In particular, the front-line member states claimed that their administrative capacity had rapidly reached its limits, with thousands of refugees arriving daily from northern Africa. To complicate the situation further, the reality of a borderless Europe in the Schengen Area meant that, once inside the EU, refugees could avoid registration and easily move onwards to the member state of their choice, defying the logic of the Dublin Agreement and its rule for asylum seekers to claim asylum in the country of landing.

Manifestly, the issue of external border control and asylum has proven to be one that could not be tackled by individual member states and thus demanded a pan-European solution (for a comparison to border-control and migration-policy issues in Canada, see Box 8.6). Partly due to key elements of the project of European integration, most notably the Single Market and cross-border mobility, the EU had to address challenges that exceeded the regulative capacity of individual member states (scholars also call this a "functional **spillover**" from the Single Market project; see Chapter 6).

**Box 8.5**   Dublin Regulation (in force since 1997)

- Establishes which EU member state is responsible for processing applications by asylum seekers.
- Its principal aim is to prevent asylum seekers from submitting applications in multiple member states.
- As part of the Dublin system, the EU has established the EURO-DAC Regulation, a Europe-wide fingerprinting database for unauthorized entrants to the EU.
- All EU member states except Denmark have signed the **regulation**.

**Box 8.6**   Border control and migration policy: Comparison EU–Canada

In order to consider the scale and nature of the policy challenges posed by governing Europe's border regime and its cross-border mobility, it is important to ponder Europe's geography. Different from Canada, which is protected by large oceans and a long border with a friendly neighbour to the south, the EU's external borders are subject to large-scale irregular migration and organized crime. It is a matter of geographic proximity to Eastern Europe and the African side of the Mediterranean coast and key geopolitical developments in the region (i.e., the collapse of communism and the Arab Spring) that have made EU member states far more exposed to their immediate neighbourhood. Hence, security risks related to cross-border mobility and the urgency of addressing them in policy terms are more pronounced in the European than in the Canadian context. From a transatlantic perspective, it is also worth noting the degree to which national borders have changed their nature as part of the European integration process. Before 2001, the Canada–US border used to be much more open than inner-European borders. Since then, the US–Canada border has become far more securitized, while the EU has moved toward eradicating border controls inside the Schengen Area.

The other dimension of AFSJ policies relates to how EU member states respond to migrants and refugees with respect to the long-term task of societal integration. While this dimension of Canada's migration regime is strongly shaped by multiculturalism as an ethical norm and state policy, public policies in the field of cultural diversity and integration are highly diverse and politically contested in EU member states (for instance, recently many high-ranking politicians in Europe have declared multiculturalism to be inadequate for European societies). Comprehensive integration policies directed at the long-term inclusion of newcomers are often still in their infancy in individual countries and the EU itself.

It has been one of the defining features of the Canadian immigration and integration regime that it provides new residents with fast and straightforward access to citizenship. As a result, Canada has one of the highest naturalization rates among recently settled immigrants worldwide. According to Citizenship and Immigration Canada, 85 per cent of all eligible immigrants had opted for naturalization in 2011. These rates are considerably lower for European countries (with Germany and France at around 40 per cent and the United Kingdom and the Netherlands at around 60 per cent).

The relative success of Canada to facilitate the societal inclusion of its immigrants also has a security dimension. Like Europe, Canada has to face the challenge of terrorism and global political radicalism. Yet the social environment in which, for instance, the terrorists of the attacks in urban centres across Europe were radicalized and received support, in neighbourhoods with large proportions of disaffected Muslim youth, seems to be less virulent in major Canadian cities.

However, in the case of the refugee crisis, a coherent and effective response by the EU proved to be difficult. The proposal of an EU distribution scheme for refugees across all member states was vigorously opposed, in particular by countries in Central and Eastern Europe. A series of EU summits on the refugee issue demonstrated how divided heads of state and government were. It also showed how sensitive the policy domain of borders and migration was, particularly with a view to domestic electoral politics. In the end, a series of emergency summits led to a compromise that was too limited in scope to provide a sufficient answer to the challenge. Instead, individual member states adopted their own policies that were directed primarily at border control. The principle of a borderless Europe was compromised—at least temporarily.

Beyond the difficulty of developing an effective EU approach to governing asylum during the recent refugee crisis, two more general features of policies in the JHA domain have become manifest. First, when it came to confronting the refugee crisis, most EU member states resorted to what they perceived to be in their "national interest" and resisted the burden-sharing approach put forward by the European Commission. Essentially, most EU member states perceived the responsibility for the refugees not as a collective one but one that lay within the jurisdiction and sphere of responsibility of individual member states. With the Lisbon Treaty and the introduction of the AFSJ, asylum has come under community jurisdiction. Politically this communitarization is as of yet contested.

Second, throughout the EU, issues such as controlling borders, fighting terrorism, or controlling migration are prone to divisive domestic debates and mobilizing efforts of the anti-immigrant populist right. While pursuing migration or asylum policies through JHA could be interpreted as an attempt to circumvent domestic opposition against such plans (a strategy of vertical policy-making that Virginie Guiraudon [2000] conceptualized as "venue shopping" in Europe's system of **multilevel governance**), the objective to come up with an EU approach to the refugee challenge has developed into a veritable crisis for the EU. The populist backlash against refugees has sparked a renationalization and a great degree of skepticism with respect to the very project of European integration. Particularly in the former communist member states of the EU (most prominently Hungary and Poland), the issue of migration has taken centre stage in popularizing anti-EU sentiments and in pushing for a nationalist agenda. The EU could have hardly been more divided than when responding to the refugee challenge. On the one end of the spectrum was the German chancellor, Angela Merkel, advocating a compassionate response to the suffering of the refugees and a pan-European policy response. On the other end, the Hungarian prime minister, Viktor Orbán, opted for the fortification of borders and the categorical rejection of any collective European policy response to governing migration.

While politically contested, the policies subsumed under AFSJ go to the very heart of what the EU stands for as a political union. As European Council President Donald Tusk stated with respect to the refugee crisis, mutual support and the readiness to stand by Greece (where the greatest number of refugees had arrived) should be seen as "a test of our Europeanness." He referred to both an effective burden sharing across the member states in the collective response to the refugee crisis as well as the political values that the EU claims to stand for in terms of its commitment to human rights and liberties. At the time of writing, the refugee crisis has not yet been dealt with effectively (in spite of an agreement between the EU and Turkey designed to curb the number of irregular migrants crossing the Aegean Sea). Time will tell what the effect will be of the attempts to respond with a unified EU approach versus national approaches.

The complexity of AFSJ poses two fundamental challenges to the development of coherent public policies at the EU level. First, AFSJ shows an inherent tension between some of its key policy initiatives. The drive to prop up security and external border control directed at threats emanating from irregular migration, terrorism, or organized crime is prone to come into conflict with the EU's constitutive commitment to fundamental civic and human rights. The securitization literature has drawn considerable attention to the socio-political implications of the EU's external border control or at times its normatively questionable treatment of refugees. Second, while the very nature of the open-border regime within the EU pushes for community solutions for issues related to the governance of borders and migration, JHA tests the resolve of member states to agree to supranational rule. If we have witnessed a restrengthening of intergovernmental cooperation in the EU over the past decade, this trend has most poignantly been articulated in a policy area that touches on security and migration. As the recent refugee crisis has exemplified, there is increasing domestic pressure to "claw back sovereignty" and to challenge the policy prerogative of the EU, in particular in governing migration.

## Conclusion

The development of policies under the AFSJ was a major leap forward in bringing JHA under community rule. It assigned a greater degree of competence to EU institutions to shape this policy domain. When JHA was introduced in 1993, a European approach to justice and security was in its infancy. Today, the way in which member states address the challenge of organized crime and terrorism is almost impossible to imagine without the pivotal role that EU agencies such as Frontex or Europol play in Europe's security framework.

The substantial expansion of the JHA's mandate, scope of policy initiatives, and organizational resources was driven by two closely interconnected factors. First, the creation of a Single Market and an unprecedented degree of cross-border mobility has made issues such as standardizing the EU legal framework, managing borders and migration, and fighting crime functional prerogatives of the most recent phase of European integration. Second, external shocks such as recent terrorist attacks or the massive influx of refugees during the second decade of the twenty-first century have lent a new sense of urgency to the AFSJ policy agenda. Even if some of the ambitious plans concerning EU migration and asylum policy have not fully materialized yet and the Dublin Agreement needs to be fundamentally redesigned, other policy fields—most notably cross-border judicial, police, and security cooperation—have gradually become "Europeanized" with a remarkable degree of convergence and policy coordination across the EU member states.

## References and Further Reading

Acosta Arcarazo, D., and A. Geddes. 2013. "The development, application and implications of an EU rule of law in the area of migration policy." *Journal of Common Market Studies* 51 (2): 179–93. https://doi.org/10.1111/j.1468-5965.2012.02296.x.

Bigo, D. 2014. "The (in)securitization practices of the three universes of EU border control: Military/navy, border guards/police, database analysts." *Security Dialogue* 45 (3): 209–25. https://doi.org/10.1177/0967010614530459.

Boswell, C. 2010. "Justice and home affairs." In *Research agendas in the European Union: Stalking in the elephant*, edited by M. Egan, N. Nugent, and W. Paterson, 278–304. Basingstoke, UK: Palgrave Macmillan.

Busuioc, M. 2013. *European agencies: Law and practices of accountability.* Oxford: Oxford University Press. https://doi.org/10.1093/acprof:oso/9780199699292. 001.0001.

De Waele, H. 2010. "The role of the European Court of Justice in the integration process: A contemporary and normative assessment." *Murdoch University Electronic Journal of Law* 6 (1): 3–26.

Guiraudon, V. 2000. "European integration and migration policy: Vertical policy-making as venue shopping." *Journal of Common Market Studies* 38 (2): 251–71. https://doi.org/10.1111/1468-5965.00219.

Guild, E., C. Costello, M. Garlick, and V. Moreno-Lax. 2015. *Enhancing the common European asylum system and alternatives to Dublin.* Brussels: Centre for European Policy Studies, LIBE Committee.

Hix, S., and B. Høyland. 2011. "Judicial politics." In *The political system of the European Union*, 3rd ed., edited by S. Hix and B. Hoyland, 75–101. New York: Palgrave Macmillan.

Huysmans, J. 2006. *The politics of insecurity: Fear, migration and asylum in the European Union.* London: Routledge.

Ippolito, F. 2015. "Migration and asylum cases before the Court of Justice of the European Union: Putting the EU Charter of Fundamental Rights to test?" *European Journal of Migration and Law* 17 (1): 1–38. https://doi.org/10.1163/15718166-12342070.

Lavenex, S., and W. Wallace. 2005. "Justice and home affairs." In *Policy making in the EU*, edited by H. Wallace., W. Wallace., and M. Pollack, 457–80. Oxford: Oxford University Press.

Maas, W. 2013. *Democratic citizenship and the free movement of people.* Leiden: Martinus Nijhoff Publishers. https://doi.org/10.1163/9789004243286.

Marsh, S., and W. Rees. 2012. *The European Union in the security of Europe: From Cold War to terror war.* New York: Routledge.

Monar, J. 2012. "Justice and home affairs: The Treaty of Maastricht as a decisive intergovernmental gate opener." *European Integration* 34 (7): 717–34. https://doi.org/10.1080/07036337.2012.726011.

Monar, J. 2015. "Justice and home affairs." *Journal of Common Market Studies* 53 (S1): 128–43. https://doi.org/10.1111/jcms.12261.

Nohl, A., K. Schittenhelm, O. Schmidtke, and A. Weiss. 2014. *Work in transition: Cultural capital and highly skilled migrants' passages into the labour market.* Toronto: University of Toronto Press.

Rosamond, B. 2005. "The uniting of Europe and the foundation of EU studies: Revisiting the neofunctionalism of Ernst B. Haas." *Journal of European Public Policy* 12 (2): 237–54. https://doi.org/10.1080/13501760500043928.

Trauner, F., and A. Ripoll Servent. 2015. *Policy change in the area of freedom, security and justice: How EU institutions matter.* New York: Routledge.

Schain, M. 2009. "The state strikes back: Immigration policy in the European Union." *European Journal of International Law* 20 (1): 93–109. https://doi.org/10.1093/ejil/chp001.

Walker, N., ed. 2004. *Europe's area of freedom, security and justice.* Oxford: Oxford University Press. https://doi.org/10.1093/acprof:oso/9780199274659.001.0001.

## Review Questions

1. What are the key challenges to which the introduction of JHA in 1993 was a response?
2. What are the constitutive elements of the European citizenship status, and why are they important?
3. Why are many of the policies in the AFSJ domain so contested among the EU member states?
4. Why has there been consistent resistance to bringing AFSJ policies under supranational, European rule?

## Exercises

1. Consider the specific reactions of EU member states and Schengen Area countries to the EU's 2015 proposal for a quota system for refugees. Which countries opposed the quota system, and what were their reasons? Which countries supported the proposal, and why? How do these reasons for and against the quota proposal dovetail with arguments for and against the need for European integration?
2. Research the rules of the Schengen Agreement. What allowances are there for temporary reinstatement of border controls? What measures exist to monitor compliance?

## Notes

1. Further information can be found through the European Migration Network: https://ec.europa.eu/home-affairs/what-we-do/networks/european_migration_network_en.
2. In 2007, then Commission Vice-President Franco Frattini gave urgency to an EU approach to legal immigration by declaring that "85% of unskilled labour goes to the EU and only 5% to the USA, whereas 55% of skilled labour goes to the USA and only 5% to the EU." http://europa.eu/rapid/press-release_SPEECH-07-526_en.htm
3. For more details, see the 2013 EU Citizenship Report (available at: http://ec.europa.eu/justice/citizen/files/com_2013_269_en.pdf).
4. For more details, see http://ec.europa.eu/justice/fundamental-rights/charter/index_en.htm.
5. Since it was introduced in the Maastricht Treaty in 1993, the title Justice and Home Affairs has changed several times; currently the EU describes this policy field as Justice, Freedom, and Security.

# 9

# Foreign, Security, and Defence Policies

FRÉDÉRIC MÉRAND AND ANTOINE RAYROUX

## Reader's Guide

Issues of **"high politics"**—foreign affairs, **diplomacy**, security, and military affairs—have long been the sole preserve of member states in the European Union (EU). The emergence of a **Common Foreign and Security Policy (CFSP)** and a **Common Security and Defence Policy (CSDP)** in the late twentieth and early twenty-first centuries is a unique achievement and the result of a slow and contested process. The resulting decision-making system is a hybrid of **intergovernmental** and community institutions designed to promote **consensus** between member states. However, diverging interests between smaller and larger European powers, or among the latter, and the absence of a coherent strategic vision remain major hurdles for turning the EU into a full-fledged global actor.

## Introduction

In the modern international system that emerged from the 1648 Treaty of Westphalia, **foreign policy**, diplomacy, security, and defence belonged to the core of **sovereignty**, along with the administration of justice and the issuing of currency. While the latter two have been Europeanized to a large extent, the former two had remained under the sole control of member states until the 1990s. Since the enactment of a Common Foreign and Security Policy (CFSP) after the **Maastricht Treaty** entered into force in 1993, followed by a European Security and Defence Policy (ESDP, later CSDP) after the Treaty of Nice entered into force in 2003, things have changed. These evolutions have pushed the reflection over the political "finality" of the European Union (EU) a step further: Is the EU meant to become a federation, with its foreign policy governed by a European minister for foreign affairs? Should the EU think of itself as a power willing to balance the United States (US) or the large emerging economies known as the **BRICS** countries? Or does it merely aim to build a large and strong economic bloc exercising **soft power** through trade and international norms?

As we will see in the first section of this chapter, the fact that the EU was conceived of as a peace project (Theme 1 of this book) from the start influenced Europeans' early attempts at creating a common structure where hard security (the military) would be integrated supranationally. After this early attempt failed, the EU focused most of its common foreign policy efforts on soft foreign policy issues, in particular trade and development policies. Nowadays, the institutional foreign policy system of the EU still lives with this tension between **supranational** integration on soft issues and the preservation of national interests when it comes to hard issues related to security. This hybrid system—reflecting the character of the EU as less than a state, but more than an international organization (Theme 2 of this book)—is the focus of our second section. In a final section, we highlight some of the main debates that EU foreign policy is confronted with today. This way, we hope to help readers make sense of why the EU is able—or unable—to speak with a single voice on such issues as diverse as conducting diplomatic negotiations with Iran over its nuclear program; implementing military intervention in the Balkans, Iraq, Libya, or the Sahel; or negotiating a sanctions regime against Russia.

## A Short History of EU Foreign Policy

In the current world system, the EU foreign policy is an anomaly for two reasons. Historically, no other international organization to date has been endowed with a common foreign policy; legally, the Westphalian international system recognizes no actor other than the nation-state. How did this new and hybrid form of international actor come about?

While **European integration** has largely proceeded according to the economic logic of **Common Market** building, high politics came into play early. (In international relations, high politics pertain to state survival— foreign affairs, security, and defence—as opposed to "**low politics**" such as health, trade, or education.) The post–World War II settlement between Western Allies, Germany, and Italy against the Soviet Bloc was at the origin of attempts to foster West European defence cooperation. Following the creation of the **European Coal and Steel Community (ECSC)** in 1951, and under strong pressures from Washington, the French head of government René Pleven launched a project for a **European Defence Community (EDC)**. In the midst of the **Cold War**, the project was meant to allow for rearming Germany in the supranational framework of a European army composed of troops from the six founding countries of the ECSC, under a central command. However, the EDC treaty failed to be ratified by the French parliament in 1954, when it was opposed by an alliance of nationalist Gaullists and communists who refused both German rearmament and the alliance with the US (see also Chapter 2). Following this first moment of crisis in the history of European integration, high politics disappeared from the agenda for several decades, and the issue was not revived until after the Cold War ended.

The fact that the European Community nevertheless developed a key trade and development role in the following decades (see Chapter 14) created controversies concerning the international role and legal personality of the Commission. On April 26, 1977, the **Court of Justice of the EU (CJEU)** gave an opinion stating that "whenever community law has created for the institutions of the Community powers within its internal system for the purpose of attaining a specific objective, the Community has authority to enter into the international commitments necessary for the attainment of that objective even in the absence of an express provision in that connection" (Koutrakos, 2015, p. 90). This case law allowed the Commission to gain a seat at the Food and Agriculture Organization (FAO) for issues pertaining to the **Common Agricultural Policy (CAP),** whereas in other organizations, such as the International Civil Aviation Organization (ICAO), it failed to do so.

In contrast to this movement toward narrow, but supranational Community competences over development and trade, EU member states retained strict control over security issues. It was not until 1970 that a common foreign policy initiative was launched—the European Political Cooperation (EPC)—albeit with a very limited agenda. The EPC was an intergovernmental forum designed to foster foreign policy cooperation and **coordination** among member states, including the United Kingdom (UK), which joined the Community in 1973. It acted as a non-constraining and informal mechanism, whose powers were declaratory. Its realizations remained modest, apart from a few well-known cases such as the achievement of a common European diplomatic position on the Israel-Palestine conflict (viz. the principle of a peaceful coexistence between two independent states) or the imposition of economic sanctions against the South African apartheid regime in the 1980s.

Over the years, member states, in particular France and the UK, wary of losing their sovereignty over diplomacy and foreign policy, remained cautious toward the EPC. Several barriers were erected to safeguard the strictly intergovernmental nature and limited role of EPC: diplomats and EPC working groups were authorized to discuss only the *political* aspects of security issues, the **European Commission** was systematically sidelined, and there was no permanent EPC secretariat until the Single European Act entered into force in 1987 and created one. Despite these limitations, however, the EPC contributed to initiating a sense of shared European diplomatic practice through the diffusion of common norms, rules, and information among national foreign services, and thanks to the socialization among European diplomats (Davis Cross, 2007). The voting behaviour of EU states at the United Nations (UN) offers an oft-cited illustration of the progressive emergence of such diplomatic coordination. While the nine **European Economic Community (EEC)** members converged on a common position on only 40 per cent of UN General Assembly resolutions in the 1970s, the figure has climbed to 90 per cent in the early twenty-first century. EU member states have internalized the habit of organizing daily preparatory coordination meetings in New York or Geneva in order to speak with one voice at the UN General Assembly.

In the early 1990s, several events gave a new impetus to the EU foreign policy: the end of the Cold War, German reunification, and the road to political union in the context of the Maastricht Treaty negotiations. The three main EU foreign policy and diplomatic powers—France, Germany, and the UK—held competing agendas. The French favoured a strong European independence, whereas the British and the Germans preferred close relations with the US; the Germans were open to a stronger executive, decision-making role for the Commission, while the British and the French were attached to the status quo. Nonetheless, all three agreed to create Pillar II of the Union, called the Common Foreign and Security Policy (CFSP). A compromise was struck, whereby EPC instruments and personnel were integrated into the Secretariat General of the **Council of the EU** (to guarantee the intergovernmental nature of CFSP, as demanded by France, the UK, or, for example, Denmark or Ireland), while EPC working groups merged with those of the Commission (to please supranationalists such as Germany or the Benelux countries, i.e., Belgium, the Netherlands, and Luxembourg).

The CFSP came about in a time of great optimism, characterized by George H.W. Bush's "new world order"—the idea that the post–Cold War order marked the victory of the model of free-market liberal democracies, the advent of **multilateralism**, and a renewed role for Europe as a global political actor. However, hopes were quickly thwarted by the erupting wars in Yugoslavia, which revealed Europe's weaknesses, and what Christopher Hill famously described as the "capabilities-expectations gap" (Hill, 1993). Europeans launched numerous diplomatic initiatives to prevent the escalation of the conflict in Bosnia, but the EU failed to be more than a weak civilian power when the time came to envision a military involvement. When Bosnians and Serbs went to war against each other, the North Atlantic Treaty Organization (NATO) and the US had to intervene. When peace agreements were signed in Dayton in 1995, it was under US rather than European leadership.

The postwar settlement in Bosnia and then the war in Kosovo in 1999 demonstrated that the EU was poorly equipped to deal with the military management of crises. The European Security and Defence Policy (ESDP), which came as a result of this Yugoslavian failure and the increasing reluctance of the US to act as the fireman on the European continent, attempted to address this shortfall. The ESDP (which was subsequently renamed the Common Security and Defence Policy, or CSDP, when the **Lisbon Treaty** came into force in 2009) mostly came about as a result of then UK Prime Minister Tony Blair's decision to drop the traditionally minimalist UK view on CFSP and to drive the European ambition further (Hofmann, 2011). In 1998, Blair met with then French President Jacques Chirac in Saint-Malo for a bilateral summit that established the main guiding principles of this new EU policy. France had long been a staunch advocate of a strong defence component to the CFSP—what French officials refer to as *Europe puissance*, meaning "military power Europe"—but it needed the support of the other significant military powers of the continent. The first politico-military decision-making structures were set up with the Treaty of Nice.

Between 2003 and 2015, the EU undertook 32 civilian and/or military operations, from the Balkans to Indonesia, and from the African Great Lakes region to Afghanistan (see Table 9.1). It is crucial to note that according to Article 43 of the **Treaty on European Union (TEU)**, CSDP operations are dealing with **crisis management**. Possible tasks include joint disarmament operations, humanitarian and rescue tasks, military advice and assistance tasks, conflict prevention and peacekeeping tasks, and tasks of combat forces in crisis management, including peace-making and post-conflict stabilization. Defence in the classical sense, i.e., the defence of the European territory, remains the prerogative of NATO. While the most ambitious EU military operations—up to 7,500 soldiers in Bosnia in 2007 and 3,500 in Chad and the Central African Republic in 2008–09—remain far below NATO standards and capabilities, the EU emphasizes that it should not be seen as a competitor to the Atlantic Alliance. Rather, it claims that its added value to international crisis management lies in its ability to mobilize both military and civilian instruments, as well as its soft policy instruments—humanitarian policy, development cooperation, and economic partnerships—inherited from the former Community Pillar.

Given that in 2016, 24 of the EU member states were also members of NATO, it should come as no surprise that the CSDP focuses on medium- to long-term conflict prevention policies, in order to avoid duplicating the Atlantic Alliance's mandate and tools, which are more focused on short-term military crisis management. However, the CSDP's political finality remains ambiguous. The Treaty of Lisbon adopted a new article (Article 42) in 2009, which is relatively similar to NATO's mutual defence clause (Article V of the North Atlantic Treaty). The EU article calls for a mutual assistance

**Table 9.1** Ongoing CSDP operations, 2016

| Operation name and host country | Start date | Type and main objectives | Manpower (incl. local staff) | Number of contributing member states (plus non-member states) |
|---|---|---|---|---|
| ALTHEA Bosnia–Herzegovina | 2004 | Military: Training and capacity-building of armed forces, deterrence | 600 | 16 (plus 5 non-EU) |
| EUBAM Moldova and Ukraine | 2005 | Civilian: Support to border control, customs, and trade norms | 200 (120 local) | 13 |
| EUBAM Rafah (Palestinian Territories) | 2005 | Civilian: Monitor Gaza Strip border crossing point | 14 (7 local) | N/A |
| EUPOL COPPS Palestinian Territories | 2006 | Civilian: Support to police and law enforcement capacities | 115 (45 local) | 21 (plus 3 non-EU) |
| EUPOL Afghanistan | 2007 | Civilian: Support to capacity-building of police forces | 270 (140 local) | 22 |
| EUNAVFOR Somalia | 2008 | Military: Protection of World Food Program and AMISOM vessels, deterrence (piracy) | 1,200. 5 ships, 2 air assets | N/A |
| EULEX Kosovo | 2008 | Civilian: Support to rule of law institutions, delivery of rule of law | N/A | N/A |
| EUMM Georgia | 2008 | Civilian: Monitor peace agreement between Georgia, Abkhazia, and South Ossetia | 200 | 22 |
| EUTM Somalia | 2010 | Military: Training and capacity-building of armed forces, strategic advice | 195 | 11 (plus 1 non-EU) |
| EUCAP Nestor (Horn of Africa, based in Somalia) | 2012 | Civilian: Support to capacity-building in maritime security (counter-piracy) | 180 (40 local) | 17 |

(continued)

**Table 9.1** (Continued)

| Operation name and host country | Start date | Type and main objectives | Manpower (incl. local staff) | Number of contributing member states (plus non-member states) |
|---|---|---|---|---|
| EUCAP Sahel Niger | 2012 | Civilian: Support to capacity-building of security forces (terrorism, organized crime) | 135 (50 local) | 11 |
| EUTM Mali | 2013 | Military: Training and capacity-building of armed forces, strategic advice | 580 | 23 (plus 4 non-EU) |
| EUBAM Libya | 2013 | Civilian: Support to border management and security | 17 | N/A |
| EUAM Ukraine | 2014 | Civilian: Strategic advice for civilian security sector reform (law enforcement and rule of law) | 200 (majority of which local) | N/A |
| EUCAP Sahel Mali | 2014 | Civilian: Support to capacity-building of internal security forces (police, gendarmerie, garde nationale) | 100 (40 local) | 13 |
| EUNAVFOR Med (Mediterranean) | 2015 | Military: Identify and capture vessels of migrant traffickers, training of Libyan coastguard and navy | Manpower N/A. 5 ships, 3 helicopters, 3 air assets | 24 |
| EUTM Central African Republic | 2016 | Military: Training and capacity-building of armed forces, security sector reform | N/A | N/A |

Source: European External Action Service (EEAS), https://eeas.europa.eu/topics/military-and-civilian-missions-and-operations/430/military-and-civilian-missions-and-operations_en

commitment and states that "if a Member State is the victim of armed aggression on its territory, the other Member States shall have towards it an obligation of aid and assistance by all the means in their power, in accordance with Article 51 of the United Nations Charter. This shall not prejudice the specific character of the security and defence policy of certain Member States." The last sentence is a safeguard for the four non-NATO members of the EU (Austria, Finland, Ireland, and Sweden), which to date remain neutral or non-allied. As for the rest of the treaty clause, it is less constraining than the NATO mutual defence commitment, since it does not explicitly refer to the use of military assets to assist an EU member under attack. Even though this Article 42 represents a considerable move toward an EU common defence, which had until then been advocated by France but been regarded by the UK as an unnecessary duplication of NATO, it remains very unclear under what conditions such a clause could be called on in the future. France was the first member state to rely on it following the Paris terrorist attacks of 2015, without much immediate effect.

Apart from these institutional evolutions, the EU has tried to formalize its so-called **comprehensive approach** to security, characterized by the mix of military and civilian instruments. It initially did so in its first European Security Strategy, published in 2003, which was presented as the EU's way of tackling the major threats it was confronted with at that time: terrorism, the proliferation of weapons of mass destruction, regional conflicts, state failure, and organized crime (Biscop & Coelmont, 2013). More than a decade after this initial strategic effort, the comprehensive approach remains the dominant narrative of the EU security policy. However, the initial strategy has proven ill-suited to several international events that the EU has been faced with since then. First, the EU member states were not able to anticipate the wave of democratic protests that erupted in Arab countries in 2011, as they had bet on the stability of the authoritarian regimes that, for the most part, had been in place for several decades. Second, the EU failed to envision that its soft-power strategies of negotiating economic association agreements with its Eastern neighbours could have some real hard-power backfiring. In late 2013, the pro-Russia Ukrainian government refused to ratify such an association agreement, which led to a wave of protests in the Western parts of the country and a toppling of the government in favour of a pro-Europe coalition. With the Russian involvement in the conflict starting in 2014, the EU was drawn into a crisis that brought back memories of the Cold War (see Chapter 18). Third, EU member states have also struggled to prevent the spread of radical Islam in the Sahel and the Middle East, and the EU's border and migration policies have suffered a blow in the wake of devastating civil wars in Iraq, Libya, and Syria that have left millions of people fleeing their war-torn countries.

These unforeseen events have forced the EU into rethinking its strategic discourse. In June 2016, the **European External Action Service (EEAS)** released its new Global Strategy on Foreign and Security Policy. While this new strategy's main ambition remains to devise concrete guidelines to implement the EU's comprehensive approach to security, it is noteworthy that the tone, scope, and priorities have changed. Whereas the 2003 document mostly focused on global threats far away from the European continent, the 2016 one puts a much stronger emphasis on internal security (see Chapter 8) and on Europe's immediate neighbours to the east and south.

## A Hybrid Foreign Policy System

As demonstrated at great length in this textbook, the EU is more than a traditional international organization, but it is less than a federal state (Theme 2 of this book). It is a particular kind of actor, whose powers ultimately depend on the member states' goodwill, and this general observation also applies to the case of the EU foreign, security, and defence policies. A European foreign policy entails three overlapping realities: the foreign policy of individual EU member states, the external relations portfolios of what used to be known as the Community pillar until 2009 (mainly trade, development, and humanitarian aid), and the foreign policy of the Union as such (White, 2001). The foreign policy system of the EU is the result of confrontations and compromises between these different realities and between the supranational and national levels. This context explains many of the differences between foreign policy-making in the EU and in a sovereign state like Canada (see Box 9.1).

Potentially, there are several actors in the EU foreign policy system. To begin with, there are, of course, member states and their representatives, who sometimes consider that national interests are best defended strictly through unilateral or bilateral channels, whereas in other cases a common EU approach will be more efficient. For example, when a security crisis erupted in Mali in early 2013, France took the unilateral decision to intervene militarily to prevent a *coup d'état* with potentially far-reaching regional consequences; only then did the EU get involved with a military operation to train a new Malian army (operation EU Training Mission [EUTM] Mali). In Brussels, member states do not meet only at the level of the Foreign Affairs Council, the monthly meeting of foreign affairs, defence, and development ministers; most of their concerns are voiced through their permanent representation, which acts as both a transmission belt for member states in Brussels and as a consensus-seeking machine. In matters of foreign and security policy, these national ambassadors meet weekly in the Political and

**Box 9.1**    Foreign policy making: Comparison EU–Canada

In contrast to the EU's hybrid foreign policy system, Canada appears to have a centralized diplomacy, like that of other sovereign states. The federal government enjoys Crown prerogative, which enables it to conduct diplomatic relations unencumbered by the provinces or, for that matter, genuine parliamentary oversight. This is in line with the Westphalian tradition whereby sovereign states are the only legitimate actors in the international system, allowed to sign treaties, declare war, and become full members of the United Nations. As the queen's representative, the governor general is the commander-in-chief of the armed forces and, although they are collectively responsible before the federal Parliament, the prime minister, the foreign minister, and the defence minister have much greater decision-making autonomy than the **European Council** president, the European Commission president, or the EU High Representative.

Still, there are interesting parallels between the EU and Canada (see Box 9.2). While EU members were beginning to delegate a number of external competences to Brussels in the 1960s and 1970s, the Canadian federation was devolving some external competences to the provinces. This is particularly the case for Quebec, which since the late 1960s conducts its own international relations and has developed a kind of a "paradiplomacy" (Paquin, 2010). The province has its own international relations minister and 11 delegations abroad, one of which has full diplomatic status (in Paris). Quebec is a full member in La Francophonie (along with New Brunswick) and has a formally distinct status inside the Canadian delegation to UNESCO. Like the EU, Quebec claims that "all its internal competences are also external competences," according to the so-called Gérin-Lajoie Doctrine, named after the province's education minister who stated its basic principles in 1965. This includes immigration, education, economic development, culture, health, and the environment. Other Canadian provinces also appoint agents in foreign capitals and have opened trade promotion and immigration bureaus abroad.

The powers of the provinces remain residual: they cannot sign foreign treaties, cannot raise an army, and operate an external policy only in the narrow fields delineated by the federal level. By contrast, European member states must approve treaties signed by the EU and can always decide to revoke the powers they have delegated to Brussels. An area where the EU seems to have greater power than the Canadian

*(continued)*

**Box 9.1**    (Continued)

federal government, however, is in the enforcement of international treaties: while the European Commission can take member states to court if they fail to comply, there is little the federal government can do to force provinces to act in their area of competence, even when an international treaty has been signed.

On many issues, these differences between the EU's hybrid system and Canada's federal system may not matter so much. If you take development aid, trade, or the fight against climate change, both the EU and its member states and Canada's federal government and the provinces must work hand in hand to shape global governance. In these areas, the EU, despite its "constitutional" limitations, is a much bigger actor than Canada when it coordinates Europe's actions and resources. This suggests that the formal division of powers does not explain everything: remember that Canada became a foreign policy actor, independent from the British Crown, only in 1931, with the Statute of Westminster!

Security Committee (PSC), which is the heir of the old European Political Cooperation forum. In addition, national civil servants prepare PSC and Council meetings in more than 30 thematic or geographic working groups dealing with foreign affairs.

In the EU's institutional system, most foreign policy working groups and preparatory committees are spearheaded by the EEAS, which was created by the 2009 Lisbon Treaty (Spence & Bátora, 2015). The EEAS is the EU's diplomatic service, with headquarters in Brussels and a worldwide diplomatic presence in 140 states. It is worth noting that only two member states—France and Germany—have more embassies abroad than the EU. The EEAS was created to increase consistency in the EU foreign policy system by bringing together the Council working groups and the European Commission committees dealing with external relations. For example, the Commission's former **Directorate-General (DG)** External Relations (Relex) has disappeared, and its structures have been merged with those of the Council within the EEAS. Only a Service for Foreign Policy Instruments remains as a stand-alone Commission body, but it is co-located in the EEAS building. Interestingly, the EEAS works as an autonomous body, not under the control of either the Council or the Commission, but with a "corporate board" made up of secretary generals, deputy generals, director generals, etc.

The EEAS is headed by a High Representative (HR) of the Union for Foreign Affairs and Security Policy, who is nominated by the European Council, i.e., the member states' heads of state or government. The position of the HR is probably the most telling illustration of the hybrid nature of the EU foreign policy. Its portfolio is very broad: the HR acts as the EU chief diplomat in charge of overseeing certain nominations (EU Special Representatives) and the work of EU Delegations; represents the EU in international organizations and negotiations; chairs the intergovernmental Foreign Affairs Council; coordinates the Commission's services dealing with external relations; and heads a series of additional EU agencies. Needless to say, the multiplicity of tasks implies that the HR has to share the responsibilities with other key figures whose influence and autonomy in the system is significant, such as the secretary general of the EEAS or the commissioners responsible for trade (DG TRADE), neighbourhood and **enlargement** negotiations (DG NEAR), or development cooperation (DG DEVCO). Also, the nature of the position itself is tricky: being a Commission member, the HR is bound by the rule of collegiality, while being de facto a *primus inter pares* when it comes to issues of foreign affairs, and at the same time acting as a mediator of national foreign policy views at the Foreign Affairs Council, while speaking in the name of the EU at the UN or in other international forums.

Not all institutions with a foreign policy responsibility have been moved under the umbrella of the EEAS, however. Both the Commission and the member states have refused to hand over some of their foreign policy competencies to the new service. At one end of the spectrum, several former community competences such as trade and development still have their own departments and structures. At the other end, security and military affairs working groups and structures remain under the exclusive control of the Council, i.e., the member states. Below the PSC level, a series of intergovernmental crisis management structures have been created to deal with CSDP operations. These include the EU Military Committee (EUMC)—made up of representatives of national chiefs of staff—the Committee for Civilian Aspects of Crisis Management (CIVCOM), the EU Military Staff (EUMS), the Crisis Management and Planning Directorate (CMPD), the Civilian Planning and Conduct Capability (CPCC) and its military equivalent, the Military Planning and Conduct Capability (MPCC). They all support the PSC, which exercises political control and strategic direction of crisis management operations, under the responsibility of the Council and the HR.

Certainly, the EU foreign policy system has made progress toward greater consistency, but it has not solved the debate about which institution should ultimately be responsible for EU foreign policy. In the fields of development or partnerships with third countries, foreign policy issues work in a way similar to other EU policies. This means "open political competition" (Haroche, 2009) characterized by the participation of all of the three main EU institutions (Council, Commission, Parliament), the existence of controversial debates between political parties, the involvement of interest groups and public opinion, etc.

In contrast to this logic of open competition, decision-making in the areas of diplomacy, security, and defence can be described as a "regime of closed negotiation," where the Council of the EU, deciding by **unanimity**, plays the central role (Haroche, 2009). The Commission and the Parliament play only a modest role, and civil society is largely excluded. Since the Lisbon Treaty, the CFSP/CSDP remains the only strictly intergovernmental EU policy, making security and defence the preserve of traditional diplomacy and national interests. Even though the pillar structure of the Union has been abolished with the Lisbon Treaty, treaty provisions have created a specific title for CFSP (Title V), separated from other areas of EU external action. Also, Declarations 13 and 14 annexed to the treaty reaffirm that the CFSP does not affect the power of member states to conduct their foreign policy, and that the powers of the Commission and Parliament in security issues remain mostly unchanged (Wouters, Coppens, & De Meester, 2008).

Under the treaty provisions of this Title V, it is up to the European Council— the meeting of heads of state or government—to decide by unanimity on the general guidelines and directions of the CFSP. Once these unanimous decisions have been taken, the Foreign Affairs Council may decide on **common positions** or **joint actions**, some of which may be taken by qualified majority vote. A common position is taken by member states on a foreign policy issue, and it must in principle be followed and implemented at the national level. There are around 200 common positions adopted each year, and examples include joint voting on United Nations resolutions, condemnation of human rights violations, statements on transversal issues (such as gender or non-proliferation), positions on crisis situations, etc. A joint action is more ambitious, since it is not limited to a statement, but mobilizes joint resources (financial, human, etc.) in support of a foreign policy decision. Joint actions give concrete guidelines and define or prorogate mandates of EU foreign policy decisions, in particular CSDP operations. Concrete examples of joint actions include the arms embargoes against the Democratic Republic of Congo and Liberia, travel bans against political leaders from Belarus, economic sanctions against Zimbabwe, the nomination of EU special representatives in the Balkans or in the Great Lakes region in Africa, etc. There are around 25 joint actions taken each year. If a member state disagrees with a joint position or action, it may rely on the procedure of "constructive abstention," which consists of not blocking a decision but not participating in its implementation either.

The description of the CFSP/CSDP decision-making machinery demonstrates that although national permanent representations and civil servants play a central role, the system also depends on a modest yet fundamental EU bureaucracy, in particular the 4,000 individuals working for the EEAS in Brussels and abroad. For these reasons, Jolyon Howorth (2012) argues that even CFSP/CSDP is more than purely intergovernmental and that it may best be described as a unique kind of "supranational intergovernmentalism," by which he means that the institutional logic of intergovernmental cooperation has come closer to the traditional culture of supranational integration and collective decision-making.

## Debates in EU Foreign Policy

Today, the EU has acquired the potential to be a significant international actor, with a voice that carries beyond the continent. External action and CFSP institutions have solidified over time, and they have generated a set of rules, norms, and practices that have become internalized by civil servants, diplomats, and military officers working in Brussels. However, it would be a mistake to view this evolution as an inevitable road to success. Several important debates remain, four of which we highlight in this section.

A first debate concerns the *influence of big member states vis-à-vis smaller ones*. This debate has taken centre stage in the context of the UK negotiating its departure from the EU after the **Brexit** vote of June 2016. Leadership is a key question in foreign and defence affairs. While EU coordination at the UN has made much progress, France and the UK have retained their permanent seats on the UN Security Council, where they are required only to inform the EU. In terms of military capabilities, France and the UK alone make up 50 per cent of the EU's total spending, which is a strong sign of the EU's dependence on a few countries (see Box 9.2). France, being a strong supporter of CSDP, has contributed roughly half the total troops deployed in the 11 EU military interventions launched between 2003 and 2016. Germany has been more reluctant to contribute, in particular when it comes to operations that are deployed in Africa, often in former French colonies and under the pressure of the French diplomacy. However, the Germans have provided a significant effort in various EU civilian and military operations in the Balkans (such as EUFOR Althea Bosnia-Herzegovina or EULEX Kosovo). The UK's contribution has been much smaller on average, outperformed by other European states such as Italy, Spain, and Poland, which are also strong supporters of the CSDP.

The level of ambition of the EU's foreign and defence policy depends on the level of cooperation between large and small member states. On the one hand, it depends on whether its most powerful states—France and Germany, followed by

**Box 9.2**    The EU's budget for foreign, security, and defence policy

The EU budget under heading "Global Europe" amounted to €10.156 billion in 2016, roughly 7 per cent of the EU's total budget. This amount included €2.079 billion for support to (potential) candidate countries (countries in the Balkans, Turkey, etc.), €2.329 billion for the **European Neighbourhood Policy**, €2.729 billion for development cooperation, and €1.471 billion for humanitarian aid. Only a relatively small amount was allocated to the CFSP (€299 million) and related instruments for conflict prevention and peace-building (€316 million) as well as democracy promotion and human rights (€181 million).

With a staff of around 4,000 people, the EEAS had an annual budget of €633 million in 2016, which is less than half the budget of the French or the German foreign ministry. Most CSDP military expenses are borne by the member states themselves and are not included in the EU's budget. This situation results from the "costs-lie-where-they-fall" rule, which stipulates that every state pays for its own contribution to an operation. In addition, the EU spends €30,000 million between 2014 and 2020 for development projects in Asian, Caribbean, and Pacific (ACP) countries through the European Development Fund, which is separate from the EU budget.

Source: Adopted budget for 2016, *Official Journal of the European Union*, L 48, February 24, 2016

Italy, Spain, and Poland (if one excludes the UK)—are willing to cooperate with one another in Brussels and to reach more than the "lowest common denominator" that the unanimity decision-making rules tend to imply. On the other hand, smaller member states have often suspected that the larger ones use the EU for their own national interests. When their national interests collide, the EU is damaged, and this is often at the expense of the smaller European states, whose diplomatic influence relies more heavily on the EU. For example, one of the first major foreign policy crises experienced in the framework of the CFSP was the sharp divide over the war in Iraq in 2003, when France and Germany refused to endorse the US military intervention, while the UK government immediately joined the coalition, accompanied by others. This situation created a strong diplomatic breach among European diplomats, which prevented the EU from adopting a clear foreign policy stance during the crisis. Another example was provided a few years later, as the Europeans were caught off-guard by the Arab Spring (see Chapter 16). When the time came to envision a military intervention to stop Muammar Gaddafi's violent repression of protest movements in Libya in 2011, Germany's reluctance proved detrimental to a common EU operation, thus leaving France and the UK acting unilaterally, with US logistical support.

The future direction of this first debate is uncertain. Some experts fear that the UK's departure from the EU will be the last nail in the coffin of an ambitious EU endowed with real military capabilities. However, others point to the fact that the UK has acted as the main obstacle preventing the EU from becoming a more capable actor, by opposing the creation of a permanent military command structure or by limiting the budget of the European Defence Agency, which is in charge of promoting a common European defence procurement market. As it turns out, in November 2017, 23 EU member states signed a commitment to strengthen European defence under the framework of a Permanent Structured Cooperation (PESCO) to move forward with capability development and operational readiness.

A second debate precisely concerns *whether all member states have to participate in EU actions*. In terms of decision-making and implementation, a member state can always refuse to endorse a common position or a joint action. Also, the Council of the EU sometimes decides on new CSDP operations before making sure that member states will actually offer sufficient contributions in human resources and material capabilities. In the CSDP system, there is no permanent EU army or EU battalions, despite occasional calls from EU officials in that direction.[1] Member states are always free to refuse to take part in an EU operation, even when they have voted in favour. There is only a small joint budget that covers expenses related to headquarters. Other than that, costs lie where they fall, which means that every contributing state to an operation has to fund its own deployment.

While **opt-outs** and the mechanism of constructive abstention are useful to allow the EU to move forward despite the reluctance of a few member states, these provisions have created a culture of free-riding (Adler-Nissen, 2014). A few member states are expected to shoulder the EU's foreign and defence policies while others stand on the side. This inequity diminishes the EU's impact and creates a problem of fairness. For example, several EU military operations—in the Democratic Republic of Congo, in Chad, and in the Central African Republic—have experienced significant delays because of the lack of actual commitments. In Chad in 2008, it was only when Russia offered to contribute to the operation with key strategic airlift assets that the operation was able to move ahead.

A third debate is whether the EU should *focus on soft power or develop into a stronger military actor*. Soft power is the idea that the EU's power and global influence rely mostly on its role as a creator and promoter of global norms in areas such as the protection of human rights, the fight against climate change, or the definition of ambitious development cooperation programs. There are several reasons why the EU has not developed into a full-fledged military actor. One reason is that most EU members are also part of NATO, the military alliance that benefits from US leadership. Another reason is that some member states are either neutral, like Ireland, or reluctant to engage in military action, like Germany. For some observers, the fact that it is not perceived as a military actor helps the EU promote a normative agenda.

But for others, "the silent 'D' in CSDP" (Pomorska & Vanhoonacker, 2015, p. 222), i.e., the generalized lack of enthusiasm for the security and military aspects of the EU foreign policy, is troublesome for the future. The main reason why this is seen as worrying is that the EU has so far proven unable to provide a satisfactory answer to the changing strategic attitude of the US, characterized by an increasing reluctance to provide for the continent's security needs. With the election of Donald Trump as US president, there is a possibility that the US retreat from the European continent will become a more pressing issue. While he pulled back from his original statement that NATO was "obsolete," President Trump has reaffirmed Washington's position that the Europeans need to increase defence spending.

Back in 1999 in Helsinki, the EU had set an ambitious military goal for itself, as it had signed a capability commitment according to which it should be able to deploy 60,000 soldiers in three simultaneous operations. This target was never achieved, and it was progressively replaced by less ambitious strategic concepts, in particular the EU Battle Group concept, namely the capability to deploy multinational battle groups of 1,500 soldiers within 15 days. Even this modest target has been more and more difficult to achieve, in the context of shrinking defence budgets and increasing difficulties in actually deploying forces abroad. While the pooling and sharing of military resources and investments has been constantly highlighted as the solution to capability gaps and shrinking national budgets, there still seems to be a long way to go (Hagman, 2013).

Finally, a fourth debate concerns the *democratic dimension of CFSP and CSDP*. There are very few checks and balances in issues of high politics (diplomacy, security, and defence). Given that a small number of member states provide the bulk of the military resources, decisions remain at the national level. Furthermore, member states differ in how much parliamentary control is involved in these policies. While some member states grant their parliaments significant say over foreign and defence policy, others entrust almost all powers to the executive. In the EU context there is little parliamentary oversight: although there is a foreign affairs committee where MEPs can ask questions to the HR, the **European Parliament (EP)** has very little oversight or budgetary power over CFSP, and obviously none over the member states' national decisions on defence spending or deployment. For some observers,

CSDP operations in particular suffer from a lack of democratic control (Wagner, 2006). For others, because foreign and defence policy will always be a sensitive area, it would be foolhardy to instil too much democracy before CFSP and CSDP have reached a substantial degree of maturity.

## Conclusion

Given the challenges facing the EU at the present time, it is tempting to look at the half-empty glass when it comes to assessing the state of European foreign and diplomatic integration. The EU's foreign, security, and defence policies are probably areas that help us avoid exaggerated pessimism. Certainly, these policies have numerous limitations, mostly when it comes to mobilizing the political energy and material resources needed to address some of the major international crises the world is faced with. That being said, these foreign and security policies have also been characterized by a remarkable set of achievements. With the notable exception of the UN Security Council, EU coordination is now routine at the UN and in several other international organizations. Also, only a decade ago, no one would have believed that the EU would possess one of the largest diplomatic networks in the world. These evolutions are experiments in supranational integration not seen since the emergence of the Westphalian state system. The EU definitely deserves credit for these achievements, despite all the ambiguity and the institutional consensus-seeking machinery needed for the implementation of these policies.

Naturally, as a result of such compromise-seeking logic, the political objectives that stand out at the EU level are often the most consensual ones: promotion of human rights, conflict prevention, and development policies, while controversial issues are left behind and show up only in times of international crisis. Put differently, some common norms and practices do exist among EU member states, but core national divergences do not seem to be fading fast. At the same time, EU member states have come a long way since the end of World War II, when the parties stood at opposite ends of a devastating war. The mere existence of a common EU defence policy is a testament to this peace achievement.

## References and Further Reading

Adler-Nissen, R. 2014. *Opting out of the European Union: Diplomacy, sovereignty and European integration*. Cambridge: Cambridge University Press. https://doi.org/10.1017/CBO9781107337916.

Biscop, S. 2015. *Peace without money, war without Americans: Can European strategy cope?* Farnham, UK: Ashgate.

Biscop, S., and J. Coelmont. 2013. *Europe, strategy and armed forces: The making of a distinctive power.* Abingdon, UK: Routledge.

Bretherton, C., and J. Vogler. 2006. *The European Union as a global actor.* Abingdon, UK: Routledge.

Davis Cross, M.K. 2007. *The European diplomatic corps: Diplomats and international cooperation from Westphalia to Maastricht.* Basingstoke, UK: Palgrave MacMillan.

Hagman, H.G. 2013. European crisis management and defence: The search for capabilities. *Adelphi Paper 353.* London: The International Institute for Strategic Studies.

Haroche, P. 2009. *L'Union européenne au milieu du gué. Entre compromis internationaux et quête de démocratie.* Paris: Economica.

Hill, C. 1993. "The capability-expectations gap, or conceptualizing Europe's international role." *Journal of Common Market Studies* 31 (3): 305–28. https://doi.org/10.1111/j.1468-5965.1993.tb00466.x.

Hofmann, S.C. 2011. *European security in NATO's shadow: Party ideologies and institution building.* Cambridge: Cambridge University Press.

Howorth, J. 2012. "Decision making in security and defence policy: Towards supranational intergovernmentalism?" *Cooperation and Conflict* 47 (4): 433–53. https://doi.org/10.1177/0010836712462770.

Howorth, J. 2014. *Security and defence policy in the European Union.* 2nd ed. Basingstoke, UK: Palgrave MacMillan.

Jones, S.G. 2007. *The rise of European security cooperation.* Cambridge: Cambridge University Press. https://doi.org/10.1017/CBO9780511491443.

Keukeleire, S., and T. Delreux. 2014. *The foreign policy of the European Union.* 2nd ed. Basingstoke, UK: Palgrave MacMillan.

Koutrakos, P. 2015. *EU international relations law.* 2nd ed. Oxford: Bloomsbury.

Manners, I. 2015. "Normative power Europe: A contradiction in terms?" *Journal of Common Market Studies* 40 (2): 235–58. https://doi.org/10.1111/1468-5965.00353.

Mérand, F. 2008. *European defence policy: Beyond the nation state.* New York: Oxford University Press. https://doi.org/10.1093/acprof:oso/9780199533244.001.0001.

Paquin, S. 2010. "Federalism and multi-level governance in foreign affairs: A comparison of Canada and Belgium." In *Is our house in order? Canada's implementation of international law,* edited by C. Carmody, 71–96. Montréal: McGill-Queen's University Press.

Pomorska, K., and S. Vanhoonacker. 2015. "Europe as a global actor: The (un)holy trinity of economy, diplomacy and security." *Journal of Common Market Studies* 53 (S1): 216–29. https://doi.org/10.1111/jcms.12272.

Spence, D., and J. Bátora, eds. 2015. *The European external action service: European diplomacy post-Westphalia.* Basingstoke, UK: Palgrave MacMillan. https://doi.org/10.1057/9781137383037.

Wagner, W. 2006. "The democratic control of military power Europe." *Journal of European Public Policy* 13 (2): 200–16. https://doi.org/10.1080/13501760500451626.

White, B. 2001. *Understanding European foreign policy.* Basingstoke, UK: Palgrave MacMillan. https://doi.org/10.1007/978-0-333-98561-8.

Wouters, J., D. Coppens, and B. De Meester. 2008. "The European Union's external relations after the Lisbon treaty." In *The Lisbon treaty: EU constitutionalism without a constitutional treaty?* edited by S. Griller and J. Ziller, 143–203. Wien: Springer Verlag. https://doi.org/10.1007/978-3-211-09429-7_7.

## Review Questions

1. Why did it take more than 30 years before there was a successful attempt at integrating issues of "high politics" in the EU?
2. Why do supranational institutions such as the Commission or the European Parliament have so little power in issues of security and defence?
3. How might the UK leaving the EU affect the latter's foreign and security policies?

## Exercises

1. Take one case of a recent international crisis (possible examples include, but are not limited to, the war in Libya in 2011, the Russia-Ukraine conflict in 2014, and the Syrian civil war starting in 2011). Looking at the foreign policy positions taken by France, Germany, and the United Kingdom during the selected crisis, how can you explain the weakness of the EU in addressing the crisis? Is it because of diverging national interests, or something else?
2. What conditions limit the possibility of an EU-level military? To make this exercise more specific, examine the structure and governance of the Canadian Armed Forces to illustrate the challenges of EU supranational authority. Is it fair to compare the CFSP to examples of national security and defence?

## Note

1   For example, in his 2016 State of the Union speech, European Commission President Jean-Claude Juncker called for the establishment of an EU army with a permanent headquarters.

# 10

# The Social Dimension of the European Union

HEATHER MACRAE AND DONNA E. WOOD

## Reader's Guide

Overall, social policy competencies remain at the national level. However, as this chapter shows, there have been some important developments at the EU level. The chapter views EU social policy as an example of the neofunctionalist logic of **spillover**, where steps toward increased integration in one area trigger increased cooperation in related areas. This leads to EU-level guidelines and minimum standards, which complement member state social policy. In recent years, we have also seen a trend toward voluntary policy **coordination** under the so-called **Open Method of Coordination**. This cooperation, however, may be jeopardized by the crises currently facing the EU, including the **Euro Area financial crisis** and the **refugee crisis**, which place extraordinary pressure on national **welfare systems**. It is an open question whether the response to this pressure will be "more Europe" or "less Europe" in the social policy domain.

## Introduction

Social policy occupies a rather unusual place in the European Union (EU). On the one hand, the market-building projects of the early days of integration have been balanced, to some extent, by market-correcting measures such as the **European Social Fund**, the **Common Agricultural Policy (CAP)** and related initiatives in labour-market and employment matters. Nonetheless, social policy has remained one of the weakest and most controversial parts of the integration project, with primary competencies still allocated to the national level.

In the introduction, the editors set out three themes that run through this textbook. These three themes are especially useful in drawing out some of the key ideas and challenges around the evolution of European social policy. Recall that the EU was born out of a desire to build a peaceful and stable Europe through economic integration and social inclusion (Theme 1). Clearly, employment and social stability needed to be at the core of that project. However, social welfare always has been, and remains, the prerogative of the state. This inherent conflict between the national and the **supranational** has demarcated the projection of social policy since the 1950s. This conflict is also illustrative of Theme 2: that the EU is more than an international organization, though less than a federal state. The conflict between the national and the European around social policy reflects the fact that the European institutions do not have the resources or jurisdiction to develop an EU-level welfare state. However, free movement of people and services requires at least basic coordination of social policies. Thus, as the EU's mandate has gradually expanded, it has become necessary to coordinate and even harmonize some aspects of the welfare state. Finally, social policy sits at the nexus of so many of Europe's contemporary challenges. As the EU struggles to address economic, demographic, and legitimacy challenges (Theme 3), social policy becomes implicated as both part of the problem and part of the solution. Although it is not the main part of the European project, some form of social policy needs be connected to a market-building and market-correcting EU.

In this chapter, we begin by asking what social policy is and how it has been positioned within the overall project of **European integration** during the past decades. We then ask what tools the EU has developed in order to facilitate and implement social policies. Finally, we close with some questions about how social policy is currently under challenge from the various crises facing the EU and its member states. Overall, we argue that although social policy is an important part of the European project, its future is open to debate.

## The Evolution of EU Social Policy

Taken broadly, social policy refers to those areas that influence citizens' well-being. Hartley Dean, professor of social policy at the London School of Economics, defines social policy as being "about the many and various things that affect the kinds of life that you and I and everyone can live" (2012, p. 1). In a state, this generally involves redistributive policies and government payment schemes, such as unemployment insurance, pensions, housing allowances, child benefits, social assistance, and similar schemes. These are commonly referred to as the welfare system. However, the welfare of individuals is also influenced by policies, which do not involve **direct payments**, such as the availability of public education, childcare, and health care. These are also part of social policy, broadly defined. Finally, social policy can also include legislation, **regulations**, and guidelines governing areas as diverse as workers' health and safety, gender equality and **non-discrimination**, and even marriage and reproduction.

Taken together, these policy areas fall under the rubric of social policy. While the welfare part of social policy is frequently associated with the redistribution of resources (money) within a society, other aspects of social policy are regulatory. That is to say, enacting regulations and legislation influences citizens' well-being. It is this type of social policy that we see most frequently at the European level. Specifically, the most developed aspects of social policy are in the realm of employment, the health and safety of workers, and non-discrimination policies. In these areas, the EU generally sets out a common policy framework and encourages each state to work toward the jointly agreed-upon goals and outcomes from within their own nationally defined welfare systems. Member states need conform only to the minimum standards that the member states collectively agree on. As such, a great deal of variation in national policies remain among the member states.

## The Early Years

Social policy has been part of the European integration project since the **Treaty of Rome** (EEC Treaty). As we know, European integration began as a political and economic project to secure peace and prosperity in postwar Europe. While "social progress" was recognized as one aim of the new Community (Article 2 of the Treaty Establishing the **European Economic Community**, or **EEC**-Treaty), the framers of the agreement generally believed that this would evolve naturally out of increased economic integration. Since social progress would be a by-product of economic policies, most political leaders felt that there was no need to take concrete steps at the European level. However, as member states retained control of social policy, it quickly became clear that different national standards could be construed as contributing to an uneven playing field and thus acting as a barrier to economic integration. For example, states with a lower-paid workforce might be advantaged over those with higher labour costs, a practice called "social dumping." As a result, the states and leaders recognized that some aspects of social policy required harmonization in order for a fair and level playing field to be maintained (Collins, 1975).

Social policy made its first appearance—albeit brief—in Articles 117 through 123 of the EEC-Treaty. These provisions were included in part as a means of securing this level playing field, and partly to appease organizations such as the labour unions and other actors who were hopeful that the European agreements would help to increase social protection at the national level (Hoskyns, 1996). The resulting treaty articles did not transfer competence for social policy to the European level, but rather outlined common commitments, which the member states agreed to pursue at the national level. The only competences granted to the **European Commission** were tools of oversight to coordinate some areas of social policy. Despite their limited scope, these formed an important base from which further claims to social harmonization would soon be made.

Article 119 (now Article 157 TFEU) was particularly important in advancing social policy at the European level. This article obliged member states to implement the principle of equal pay for equal work through national legislation. This was not a new or radical provision, but instead sought to ensure that no state could enjoy a competitive advantage by employing a lower-paid female workforce. It was, however, later appropriated for far more radical ends than the framers could have envisioned (McKeen, 1994; MacRae, 2010). The remaining articles in the social policy chapter (now Articles 151–161 TFEU) provided a minimum standard for paid holidays and established a fund—the European Social Fund—to be used to improve the prospects of those who faced the greatest obstacles in finding or retaining work. The member states did not intend for any of these minor and seemingly inconsequential EU instruments—legislation, policy coordination, and modest funding—to have real influence. But over time they have helped to bring about important minimum standards and legislation in a range of social policy areas.

## Bringing the Supranational into the National

By the late 1960s, the stage was set for a new era in EU social policy. A favourable institutional environment in the European institutions, increased civil activism across Europe, and international pressure all contributed to a new importance of the European level for social policy activism. Bolstered by a judgment of the European Court of Justice (now **Court of Justice of the EU**) that European laws have a **direct effect** on citizens of the member states (see Chapter 4), European equal-pay provisions were finally imposed on the member states. Through legal activism in the Court of Justice of the EU, social policy was underlined as an integral part of the project of integration. In a particularly forceful ruling in 1975, the Court stressed that Article 119 was "one of the foundations of the Community" (ECJ Case 43/75). With this ruling, social policy became a "European" concern.

This successful outcome for EU social policy sparked interest and support to pursue similar steps in other aspects of social policy. In the period from 1975 to 1978, four social policy **directives** were passed.[1] All of these were in the area of equal treatment for men and women in relation to their rights to employment and training. The Commission, anxious to increase its own position in the process of integration, also sought to deepen European cooperation in, and coordination of, social policy by implementing a series of action programs that outlined major goals and steps that the Community was endeavouring to achieve. For example, the first social policy action program, initiated in 1972, aimed to reduce unemployment, improve working conditions, and give increased voice to unions and labour in the decision-making process. These programs were not binding on member states, but as a result of these efforts, social policy remained on the political agenda of both the Commission and the member states.

It is interesting to note that European leaders have seldom pursued social policy at the European level as a good in its own right. Rather, it has often been seen as a necessary step in creating a level playing field for workers and employers across the member states, and facilitating the free movement of labour. For example, an individual's ability to work in different member states may be restricted in practice by barriers such as non-recognition of professional qualifications, non-transferability of pension entitlements, inability to access health care, or other social provisions. Thus, in order to really create a space in which workers (and capital, goods, and services) are able to move freely, these barriers must be removed. The provision of benefits remains in the hands of the individual member states, but European legislation now regulates the coordination of benefits if an individual moves within the EU. Social policy coordination has been one important aspect of the completion of the **Single Market**. The dynamic whereby policy coordination in one area necessitated increased coordination in a related area is an excellent example of what neofunctionalist theorists termed spillover (Falkner, 1998). We can see that the right to move and work throughout the EU has "spilled over" and necessitated cooperation in related areas, such as social security benefits.

As easily as the conditions of the 1970s moved in favour of social policy, the 1980s saw a rollback in social policy initiatives as conservative governments, including the Thatcher government in the UK, refused to take part in any form of social policy at the European level. However, after a brief pause, the project was restarted by Commission President Jacques Delors in the late 1980s when he endeavoured to make "Social Europe" a priority.

Delors served as president of the Commission from 1985 to 1995. Two of the key accomplishments of this period included the Social Charter (1989) and the Agreement on Social Policy (1992). In addition, in 1993, the Commission under Delors developed and published an influential white paper on growth, competitiveness, and employment. These documents highlighted the importance of social policy to the overarching project of integration. They constituted an exception to the tendency of pursuing social policy only as a "by-product" of economic integration. However, because they were largely non-binding, the impact of these initiatives was more symbolic and political than legal.

Over time, these various agreements and charters have been modified, revised, and repositioned within EU social policy legislation. Many of the provisions expressed in the Social Charter were included in the Agreement on Social Policy, which was annexed to the Protocol on Social Policy of the **Maastricht Treaty**. As such, they have moved from being simply **recommendations** to a legally binding set of provisions. However, the United Kingdom chose to remain outside of this policy. The agreement specified an **opt-out** for the UK in further social policy integration, thus effectively creating a "two-track" or "multi-speed" Europe. While all member states, including the UK, remained bound by the original social provisions of the Treaty of Rome and subsequent legislation, only the remaining 11 states agreed to new procedures laid down in the agreement. The UK neither participated in, nor was bound by, any decisions taken through the Social Policy Agreement. Following these new procedures, only 11 of the then 12 member states agreed to the directives on European works councils (1994), parental leave (1996), and part-time work (1997). Only in 1997, with the newly-elected Blair government, did the UK terminate the opt-out clause and agree to the Social Policy Protocol. This clause has since becoming binding on all states that have subsequently joined the European Union.

### New Policy-Making Tools

As the scope of EU social policy has gradually widened, so too have the tools that the EU has at its disposal. Initially the European states used directives (binding EU legislation) as the primary tool to level the playing field in a given area. However, by the 1990s, several other tools had been developed in order to facilitate cooperation in social policy among the member states and mitigate their diverse approaches. These tools both increased the scope of social policy and shifted the relationship between the national and the European level.

First, there was a move toward **qualified majority voting (QMV)** in some areas of social policy. The move to QMV means that legislation can be binding in a member state even if a state is opposed, provided there is sufficient support from the other member states. Normally, however, **Council** decisions are taken by **consensus**, even if there is a provision to vote by QMV. As a result, social policy has partially shifted away from the absolute control of the member states. Member state control was further watered down through the so-called Social Protocol established by the Maastricht Treaty. This process empowers the **social partners**, that is, the representatives of labour and management at the European level, to draft legislation on social policy. A draft proposal agreed on in this way can be only accepted or rejected, but not amended, by the member states. This provision was first put to the test in the mid-1990s as the Commission sought to revive a proposal on minimum provisions for parental leave. Despite several attempts, the Commission was unable to secure an agreement with the member states. However, when tasked with drafting legislation, the social partners were successful at reaching an agreement on a minimum level of policy coordination. This new provision further shifted social policy from a purely national to a slightly more European stage.

Even as the range of policy actors expanded to include players other than the member states, the primary tool for building an EU dimension to social policy was still legislation. However, as the UK opt-out demonstrated, there were limits to binding legislation, and member states were reluctant to give up control over welfare policies in this way. Moreover, as the national systems of the individual member states each continued to develop independently of the EU, variation among the national systems kept growing. This made coordination even more difficult. Although the Amsterdam Treaty (1997), expanded decision-making in the area of social policy to qualified majority voting rather than **unanimity**, this did little to overcome the stalemates. What was really required, particularly in light of the new economic challenges facing states, were new tools to coordinate social policy without taking away member state autonomy. These types of coordination mechanisms, which enabled cooperation through voluntary measures and individual national strategies, were developed in the late 1990s and early 2000s. This development marked the next step in the evolution of EU social policy.

In the area of employment, a major step forward was taken in 1997, when member states officially recognized employment policy to be a common European task. This took social policy onto a new route in the integration process. At the same time, it further entrenched the link between social policy and employment/labour market policies. The completion of the Single Market in the late 1990s coincided with a recession and rising unemployment in Europe. Stimulated by the Commission's white paper on growth, competitiveness, and employment, the European Employment Strategy (EES) began to take shape. In 1997, the objective of a high level of employment became a specific priority for the EU, and a separate employment chapter was included in the Amsterdam Treaty (now Articles 145–150 TFEU). The European-wide mobilization of social NGOs also contributed to the incorporation of a social inclusion competence in the treaty.

The next development was the launching of the so-called **Lisbon Strategy** (2000), which envisioned positive synergies between economic, labour-market, and social policies. Strongly influenced by the "social investment" paradigm, the Lisbon Strategy broadened the notion of social policy beyond its traditional focus on social protection so as to include social promotion and human capital development. As a result, there was a renewed emphasis on the "active welfare state" through public policies designed to help individuals, families, and societies adapt to various transformations, including a focus on children and fighting social exclusion (Jenson, 2010; Vandenbroucke, Hemerjick, & Palier, 2011).

The Open Method of Coordination (OMC), an important and innovative new tool for the governance of EU social policy, was developed as a means of supporting the Lisbon Strategy. The OMC is a highly institutionalized and cyclical process, managed by an **intergovernmental** body of ministers from all 28 member states who comprise the Employment,

Social Policy, Health, and Consumer Affairs Council (EPSCO) and who are supported by the European Commission and by officials working in an Employment Committee (EMCO) and a Social Protection Committee (SPC). The OMC is a mode of governance that involves both the European and the national levels in a process of setting guidelines and benchmarks, and identifying best practices to facilitate the gradual and voluntary coordination of policies. In the first stage, the heads of state or governments collectively agree on common objectives (political priorities). Each member state then translates these EU-wide actions into individual national social policy plans. Peer review (discussion among equals) takes place on the basis of National Reform Programmes (reports) prepared by each member state on their efforts to meet the EU objectives.

Rather than produce binding legislation, this process generates soft (voluntary) recommendations to member states from the Commission/Council. Progress toward the common objectives is measured through commonly agreed-upon indicators and targets. States, with the help of the Commission and some specialized agencies, are expected to learn from each other and develop best practices to reach common goals. Member states are offered some financial assistance in this endeavour through the European Social Fund, which supports initiatives to implement programs in line with the common objectives. Other EU institutions as well as civil society actors have clearly defined ways to influence the process. As Figure 10.1 indicates, the OMC is a cycle. Goals are identified, and policies implemented and then reviewed for effectiveness, generally leading to a further cycle of goal setting, policy-making, and review.

The OMC is meant to deliver change at the national level without relying on formal EU legislation. It is more intergovernmental in nature than the traditional Community method, as it leaves the member states to determine the type and scope of implementation. As it is a voluntary process, there is no penalty if states do not reach the agreed-upon targets or benchmarks. The aim is to reach voluntary coordination and adaptation of member state policy, and to stimulate learning from the experiences of others. The focus is on policy convergence—not harmonization—of objectives, performance, and to some extent policy approaches, but not means (institutions, rules, and concrete measures). As already noted, harmonization of social policies was considered not only a sensitive political matter but also one very difficult to put into practice, given the complexity of and differences in national welfare traditions and systems. Interestingly, several studies have shown that the enactment of binding legislation in the area of social policy has not declined with the implementation of the OMC (Anderson, 2015). Rather, the two processes work together to achieve increased EU cooperation in a wider number of areas, while leaving much of the control and primary decision-making with the member states.

**Figure 10.1** Open Method of Coordination (OMC)

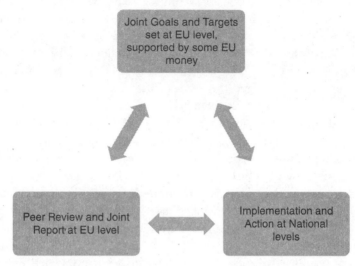

Source: Authors' design

The post–Lisbon strategy period also saw a major expansion in the recognition of new actors in the social policy realm to actors other than the social partners, member state governments, and the European Commission. The powers of the **European Parliament (EP)** were expanded, and a structured process for the Council and the Commission to consult regularly with the Economic and Social Committee and the Committee of the Regions[2] was solidified. Women's groups had already staked out a role in relation to the important directives on equal pay and equal treatment in the 1970s. Once social exclusion came to be identified as a major problem to be tackled at the EU level, participation and dialogue was expanded through a process called "civil dialogue" to include civil society organizations representing the excluded, the poor, and the socially marginalized. With the OMC's focus on social indicators to assess progress, statisticians who design indicators and experts who assess results also became engaged (Jenson 2010). This entire process was further reinforced by the 2001 white paper on European governance, which identified openness and participation as two of the five key principles of good governance for the EU.

### The Lisbon Treaty and Europe 2020

The EU member states signed the **Lisbon Treaty** on December 13, 2007, and it entered into force on December 1, 2009. The Lisbon Treaty amended the EU treaties, which are now named **Treaty on European Union (TEU)** and **Treaty on the Functioning of the European Union (TFEU**; see Table 4.1). The changes of the Lisbon Treaty enhanced the EU social dimension with regards to rights and objectives, as well as the content of policies and the means of decision-making. For example, the Charter of Fundamental Rights acquired a legal quality that guaranteed social rights by national and community judges. As outlined in Article 3 in the TEU, EU policies and activities must strive to promote a high level of employment, the guarantee of adequate social protection, the fight against social exclusion, and a high level of education, training, and protection of human health. Nonetheless, jurisdiction for most of these activities remains with the member states.

To implement these social policy commitments, the Commission is expected to facilitate the coordination of member state action in all social policy fields—notably employment; labour law and working conditions; basic and advanced vocational training; social security; prevention of occupational accidents and diseases; occupational hygiene; and the right of association and collective bargaining between employers and workers. The Lisbon Treaty also confirmed the OMC process of establishing guidelines and indicators, exchanging best practices, and monitoring and evaluation in order to achieve these objectives.

These objectives are furthered through **Europe 2020**—the successor to the Lisbon Strategy—which explicitly aims at "smart, sustainable and inclusive growth" through increased coordination of national and European policy. Europe 2020 has five headline targets to boost growth and employment in the EU; three of these targets relate to social policy:

1. Increase employment of the population aged 20–64 to 75 per cent.
2. Reduce the rates of early school leaving to below 10 per cent, and achieve at least 40 per cent of 30–34-year-olds completing university/ college education.
3. Lift at least 20 million people out of poverty and social exclusion.

In addition to funding from their own taxpayers, member states may also receive European funds to help them meet these EU-wide social policy objectives. These funds are allocated to governments or regions, not individuals. For example, the European Social Fund (ESF) promotes employment and labour mobility; invests in education, skills, and lifelong learning; promotes social inclusion and combats poverty; and enhances institutional capacity and efficient public administration. In various iterations, the ESF has been in place since the late 1950s. A related initiative, the Youth Employment Initiative, specifically targets young people who are not currently in education, employment, or training. Numerous other programs support nationally led action in health care, education, training, and employability. Box 10.1 identifies 2016 funding commitments to various social policy initiatives.

**Box 10.1**    Budget: EU spending on social policy

It is rather difficult to ascertain definitively what portion of the EU budget is allocated toward social policy. Part of this difficulty stems from the vagueness around the term "social policy" and what is really included under that heading. Some social goals may be indirectly supported through a variety of different projects, including the Common Agricultural Policy (see Chapter 11) and the **regional policy** (Chapter 13). Other "social" items in the EU budget are not explicitly defined as such, but rather are geared toward increasing the competitiveness of the EU and increasing employment across the Union. In 2016, the EU allocated a total of €13,031 million (about 9 per cent of total expenditures) to the Commission for the budget title Employment, Social Affairs and Inclusion. This allocation included the programs below.

| Initiative | Annual payment allocation |
|---|---|
| Administrative expenditure | €102 million |
| European Social Fund (including Youth Employment Initiative) | €12,164 million |
| Employment, Social Affairs, and Inclusion | €208 million |
| European Globalisation Adjustment Fund (EGF) | €30 million |
| Instrument for Pre-accession Assistance—Employment, Social Policies, and Human Resources Development | €65 million |
| European Aid to the Most Deprived (FEAD) | €461 million |
| Total spending on Employment, Social Affairs, and Inclusion | €13,031 million |
| Total EU spending 2016 | €143,885 million |

In contrast to the member states, the EU does not make use of large-scale financial resources to pursue social policy objectives. Whereas the states themselves can combat social exclusion, poverty, and other social problems through income transfer programs, the EU cannot.

Instead, the EU's main tool is to coordinate policy and to offer states some financial support to implement changes to facilitate policy convergence, however they see fit.

Source: Adopted budget for 2016, *Official Journal of the European Union*, L 48, February 24, 2016, 515–94

One of the main differences between the political system of a federal state and that of the EU is that in the area of social policy the primary task of the EU is one of coordinating, directing, and facilitating. This is reflected in the tiny amount of the EU budget (around 9 per cent) that is specifically earmarked for direct social policy spending by the EU. In fact, this coordinating role has not fundamentally changed since the Treaty of Rome. As such, social policy spending has barely expanded over the past six decades. In contrast, a (federal) state often coordinates and also finances social policy initiatives, even if these are then executed by the sub-national units (see Box 10.2).

**Box 10.2**   Social policy making: Canada-EU comparison

To understand social policy in the EU, it can be useful to think about how it compares to social policy in a federal state such as Canada. Both are complex **multilevel governance** systems in which authority is distributed among orders of government—local, regional, provincial, national, and supranational—as well as across spheres and sectors including markets, stakeholders and citizens. In both Canada and the EU, the constituent units—28 EU member states and 13 Canadian provinces and territories—have primary constitutional responsibility for most social policy matters. The welfare state in Canada developed concurrently with the Canadian federation and is embedded within it through largely similar provincial approaches. It is closely intertwined with the Canadian identity. In contrast, EU social policy has been added on to pre-existing national welfare states that vary widely. As national provisions remain central to citizens in each member state, EU-level initiatives can cluster only at the periphery of existing national programs.

The federal government in Canada possesses three distinct institutional advantages in social policy matters that the EU level lacks: exclusive constitutional jurisdiction in some key areas, access to its own source revenue through its capacity to tax citizens directly, and a Westminster system that gives majority federal governments free rein to make decisions. Unlike the EU, Canada's federal government does not require provincial approval to act and is constitutionally able to do this—even in areas of provincial competence—through the federal spending power.

The Government of Canada plays a large redistributive role in social programs (about 31 per cent of all federal spending in 2015) that touch citizens directly through money sent to the unemployed, the elderly, and children. Not only does this redistribution provide a

*(continued)*

**Box 10.2**    (Continued)

sense of pan-Canadian social citizenship, it reinforces the legitimacy of the federal government. In the EU it is the member states that provide these kinds of benefits and consequently are accorded citizen legitimacy. The federal government in Canada also plays a large role in financing core social programs—health care, postsecondary education, childcare, social assistance, and social services—through transfer payments to provinces and territories. Constituting about 18 per cent of all federal spending, most of these transfers are now unconditional. The European Social Fund and its complementary social policy funding play a somewhat similar role; however, there is much less money and many more conditions on receipt of the funding than in Canada.

While the EU level has a defined regulatory role in the workplace (e.g., occupational health and safety, employment standards), in Canada these responsibilities are under the jurisdiction of the provinces (except for federally regulated workplaces, which constitute 10 per cent of total workplaces). Harmonization efforts in Canada are minimal in this or any other area of social policy as provinces—just like member states in the EU—are reluctant to cede to a federal role in agenda-setting, even if they are quite content to take federal funding. For the past 20 years, Canada has been decentralizing or "provincializing" social policy.

By contrast, the EU level through the Commission has a large role in the overall coordination of member state social policy through the Open Method of Coordination (OMC). They can embark on coordination because the Commission has two important characteristics that the Government of Canada does not possess: the "right of initiative" and the guarantee of respect for the treaties. These two features give the Commission a defined role in facilitating pan-European dialogue and the sharing of information on best practices between governments, social partners, and civil society. In Canada, this kind of dialogue is much more limited.

Where the EU has a highly developed and institutionalized system of intergovernmental relations (IGR) to facilitate cooperation and coordination among member states, Canada's IGR are more ad hoc. Unlike the EU, where heads of state or government meet regularly to direct and energize the entire system, Canada's first ministers meet (or not) as decided by the prime minister. Federal-provincial activities at the sector level—for example in health care, social services, postsecondary education, pensions, labour market, and housing—vary from one policy area to another. In contrast, coordination in all areas of social policy in the EU is extensive.

## Debate: EU Social Policy in Challenging Times

Several interrelated crises are currently challenging the European Union and its ability to cooperate around questions of social and welfare policy. As states struggle to manage the refugee crisis, the financial crisis, the implications of the **Brexit** vote, and other ongoing challenges such as an aging population and declining birthrates, the tension between the national and the European levels of authority has become increasingly visible. As more than an international organization, but less than a state, the EU requires the European nations meet these challenges collectively. However, without the foundations and legitimacy of a state, this is increasingly difficult to navigate.

Many commentators have noted that the Euro Area financial crisis that started in 2008 has raised the salience of issues of social policy and social justice in the EU more than ever. Certainly, the high unemployment figures in various Southern European member states and the reforms imposed in response to the crisis have brought about changes and cutbacks to social and welfare services in many member states. They have also necessitated new forms of regulation and coordination from the EU level. As poverty and social inclusion rises in many EU states, it is clear that the targets set in Europe 2020 are unlikely to be met.

The ongoing refugee crisis has further strained the already tight resources of a number of states. It has, moreover, highlighted and increased the visibility of fissures between the member states. A number of analysts have also pointed out that the EU is currently suffering from an institutional crisis, or a crisis of democracy. A manifestation thereof has been a sharp increase in support for radical and Euroskeptic parties in recent years. The legitimacy of the EU to act, particularly in areas typically considered to be the purview of member states, has contributed to a reframing and retrenching of the EU's social project.

Finally, over the past decade or more, analysts have been warning that many of the EU member states find themselves in a severe demographic crisis, which is bound to pose fundamental challenges to these states' ability to support their welfare projects. As the working-age population decreases relative to the number of dependents (in particular, pensioners), EU member states are required to stretch fewer financial resources to a greater number of people. Many states were already struggling to address this demographic change even before the EU implemented structural reform measures to manage the financial crisis. When we consider all these issues, it is not surprising that there is little agreement on how the EU social dimension should evolve.

The financial crisis and the reforms in place to address it represent a fundamental threat to national welfare systems. High unemployment, more precarious work, reduced public services, and a growth in the gap between rich and poor have increased risks of poverty and social exclusion. As a result of the crisis, the unemployment rate in the EU increased from under 7 per cent in spring 2008 to 10.8 per cent in spring 2013. While by September 2015 it had declined somewhat to 9.3 per cent, there were still about 22.5 million people looking for work. The unemployment rate for young people was even worse, averaging 19.9 per cent in September 2015.

But these numbers disguise the disparity in the crisis among the member states. In some states, such as Greece and Spain, the youth unemployment rate remains at about 50 per cent of the active population. In contrast, in the "core" European states like Austria and Germany, unemployment rates have remained around 5 per cent, with youth unemployment only slightly higher. Thus, while all states have been affected by the financial crisis, its impact has varied widely from state to state. With variation among states increasing, it becomes even more difficult to coordinate social policy initiatives, and discord among the states increases.

Member states have implemented structural reform measures, including cuts to social expenditures, labour-market and pension reforms, and cutbacks to public-sector jobs and wages in conjunction with higher taxation, reductions in public spending on infrastructure projects, and the privatization of state-owned corporations. The differences in reaction and the degree of cuts in the member states have, according to some, divided member states into "two classes— creditors and debtors—with the creditors in charge" (Soros, cited in Crum, 2014, p. 161). However, if the financial crisis has pitted creditor against debtor and challenged the solidarity of the member states, it has also reinforced the interdependencies of the European economies and the need for cooperation and solidarity not only within but also among the member states. In this way, the financial crisis has demonstrated the limits of the European social project for some, and highlighted the importance of increased coordination for others.

In 2013, and partly in response to the economic and financial crisis, the European Commission introduced a policy framework to guide member states on how they might use their social budgets more efficiently and modernize their welfare systems. Monitoring progress on all matters related to **Economic and Monetary Union (EMU)** as well as employment and social policy matters was consolidated and recast as the "European Semester" (see Chapter 7). Each year, the Commission undertakes a detailed analysis of EU member states' plans of budgetary, macroeconomic, and structural reforms and provides them with recommendations for the next 12 to 18 months. If member states do not act on recommendations within the given time frame, the Commission can issue policy warnings. There is also the option of enforcement through incentives and sanctions in the case of excessive macroeconomic and budgetary imbalances.

Similar divisions in member state approaches are visible in the responses to the refugee crisis. Germany's initially welcoming response to the influx of refugees has been criticized by a number of other states as undesirable and unaffordable. With only a few of the member states taking direct responsibility for resettling refugees, there have been calls for a sharing of the financial burden across the Union. To date, it has not been possible to reach an agreement, which again highlights the difficulty that the EU member states have when faced with questions of social justice and welfare. Some suggest that the repercussions of the refugee crisis could bring about fundamental changes to the EU's open-border regime and even call into question some of the rules coordinating social benefits.

It remains to be seen how the EU's social project will emerge out of these crises. It may be that these crises prove too substantial to overcome and contribute to the disintegration of the EU or perhaps, less drastically, the move toward a multi-speed or multi-layered Europe or some other reconfiguration of the European project. Indeed, in the wake of the UK's referendum on membership (Brexit), it seems clear that reconfiguration of the transferability of social security benefits and health insurance will be necessary in the coming years. Alternately, the crises may reinforce the importance of European solutions to European problems and might lead to even closer entwining of the European economies. In other words, we may observe that the solution to the crises in Europe is, in fact, more and stronger coordination at the European level. It is possible, although perhaps not very likely, that in the coming years we will see the EU developing more of the characteristics of a state.

## Conclusion

Social policy at the EU level embodies the very nature of the EU as "more than an international organization, but less than a state." As the member states have retained control of most aspects of social and welfare policies, the EU's social policy role is one of coordination around a common, though vaguely defined, set of European goals. These goals include sustained economic growth, a high and rising standard of living, high levels of employment, high quality education, comprehensive welfare and social protection, low levels of inequality, and high levels of solidarity, as well as an important role for dialogue with social partners and civil society. Many use the term **"European Social Model"** to describe this common vision that binds the European states together.

The influence of the EU level varies from issue to issue within the scope of social policy. In some areas, such as legislation around non-discrimination, equal rights, and equality in the workplace, the EU has amassed a rather impressive set of provisions and legislation. As integration progressed beyond the basic goals of economic coordination, the effects of policy spillover led to more and deeper integration in social policy spheres. Thus, EU-level initiatives to activate more women in the labour market have encouraged states to make access to high-quality, regulated childcare a priority. In these areas, the EU level has played a much larger role than the member states originally anticipated.

However, this process of spillover has also been one of the main reasons that social policy in the EU continues to be generally linked to, and defined by, the labour market and employment. There are very few initiatives that go beyond this broad framework. In light of this, two things are clear: social policy is going to remain under the joint influence of the national and the EU levels; and, although the EU's involvement may increase slightly, employment and labour-market matters are likely to remain the primary frames for defining the extent of EU social policy.

## References and Further Reading

Anderson, K. 2015. *Social policy in the European Union.* New York: Palgrave MacMillan.
Collins, D. 1975. *The European communities: The social policy of the first phase.* London: M. Robertson.
Crum, B. 2014. "A multi-layered social Europe? Three emerging transnational social duties in the EU." In *Social policy and the Eurocrisis: Quo vadis social Europe?* edited by G. Menz and A. Crespy, 161–81. Basingstoke, UK: Palgrave MacMillan.
Dean, H. 2012. *Social policy.* 2nd ed. Cambridge: Polity Press.
European Commission. 2001. *European governance – A white paper.* http://eur-lex.europa.eu/legal-content/EN/TXT/?uri=celex:52001DC0428.
European Commission. 2012. *Social Europe guide – Volume 2 – Social dialogue.* http://ec.europa.eu/social/main.jsp?catId=738&langId=en&pubId=6352&furtherPubs=yes.
European Commission. 2016. *Employment and social developments in Europe 2015.* http://ec.europa.eu/social/main.jsp?catId=738&langId=en&pubId=7859&furtherPubs=yes.
Falkner, G. 1998. *EU social policy in the 1990s: Towards a corporatist policy community.* London: Routledge. https://doi.org/10.4324/9780203299074.
Finance Canada. 2015. *Strong leadership, a balanced budget, low-tax plan for jobs, growth and security.* http://www.budget.gc.ca/2015/docs/plan/budget2015-eng.pdf.
Hoskyns, C. 1996. *Integrating gender: Women, law and politics in the European Union.* London: Verso.
Jacobsson, K. 2004. "Soft regulation and the subtle transformation of states: The case of EU employment policy." *Journal of European Social Policy* 14 (4): 355–70. https://doi.org/10.1177/0958928704046878.
Jenson, J. 2010, April 30. Ideas and policy: The European Union considers social policy futures. Paper prepared for the European Studies Association – Canada ECSA-C 8th Biennial Conference, Victoria, BC, April 29–May 1, 2010.
Levrat, N. 2016. "The European Union: From international relations to intergovernmental relations." In *Intergovernmental relations in federal systems, comparative structures and dynamics,* edited by J. Poirier, C. Saunders, and J. Kincaid. Don Mills, ON: Oxford University Press.
MacRae, H. 2010. "The EU as a gender equal polity: Myths and realities." *Journal of Common Market Studies* 48 (1): 155–74. https://doi.org/10.1111/j.1468-5965.2009.02046.x.

McKeen, W. 1994. "The radical potential of the European community's equality legislation." *Studies in Political Economy* 43 (1): 117–36. https://doi.org/10.1080/19187033.1994.11675391.

Robert Schuman Foundation. 2009. *The Lisbon Treaty: 10 easy-to-read fact sheets.* https://www.robert-schuman.eu/en/dossiers-pedagogiques/traite-lisbonne/10fiches.pdf.

Vandenbroucke, F., A. Hemerjick, and B. Palier. 2011. The EU needs a social investment pact. *OSE Paper Series*, Opinion Paper No. 5.

Zartaloudis, S. 2014. "The impact of the fiscal crisis on Greek and Portuguese welfare states: Retrenchment before the catch-up?" *Social Policy and Administration* 48 (4): 430–49. https://doi.org/10.1111/spol.12069.

## Review Questions

1. Through legal activism in the Court of Justice of the EU, social policy has become more robust at the supranational level. However, a great deal of variation remains among the member states. What do you think accounts for the variation among the member states?
2. How has social policy coordination been an important aspect of the completion of the Single Market?
3. Do you think qualified majority voting (QMV) should be used in all areas of social policy? Why would most member states disagree to hypothetical change?
4. Do you think the targets set in Europe 2020 are realistic? Draw on the Euro Area financial crisis, the refugee crisis, and the demographic crisis to answer the question.

## Exercises

1. Select an area of social policy in Canada (possible examples include but are not limited to health care, childcare benefit, and unemployment insurance). What level of government has authority over this policy area, and how is the policy funded? How different is this process from the EU setting?
2. In considering "neofunctionalist spillover," what areas of domestic social policy in the future might come under Single Market pressure to become "Europeanized"?

## Notes

1 These are the 1975 Equal Pay Directive; the 1976 Equal Treatment Directive; the 1977 Directive on Action by the European Social Fund for Women; and, in December 1978, the Social Security Directive, which enshrined the principle of equal treatment for men and women in matters of social security.
2 These are separate EU-wide advisory bodies representing 1) employers, trade unions, farmers, consumers, and other interest groups that collectively make up "organized civil society"; and 2) representatives of regional and local authorities.

# 11
# Common Agricultural Policy

CRINA VIJU

## Reader's Guide

The **Common Agricultural Policy (CAP)** of the European Union (EU) was one of the first European policies introduced at a time when the events of World War II and its devastating consequences were still fresh in everyone's minds. This chapter analyzes the CAP's main objectives, instruments, and outcomes. It also examines its evolution over time. The discussion focuses on core issues related to the CAP, such as pressures for reform, reasons for resistance to change, and ongoing debates.

## Introduction

The main goals in the creation of the European Union (EU) were both political (to not have another war) and economic (to recover from the devastation of World War II). The means of achieving these goals were mainly economic, with the view that once the EU member states were economically integrated, another war would be almost impossible (see Theme 1 of this book). Economic integration trumped all up until the 1990s, when other non-economic issues started to gain importance for the EU political elites and citizens. Agriculture was one of the first policy areas where market integration was seen as highly important. The six founding member states of the **European Economic Community (EEC)** (Belgium, Luxembourg, France, Italy, the Netherlands, and West Germany) considered the Common Agricultural Policy (CAP) a necessity in order to cope with food shortages stemming from the aftermath of World War II, prevent at any cost such future shortages, and stabilize income for farmers. The CAP was an attempt to reach these objectives by creating a common agricultural market that would facilitate the movement of goods and factors of production among the European countries.

To achieve its original objectives, the CAP introduced several policy instruments, which had important domestic and international consequences and influenced the evolution of the CAP through the years. Over time, the EU has become larger, more diverse, increasingly focused on sustainable development, and competitive in a highly globalized world. Thus, the main question this chapter sets out to address is whether the objectives of the CAP have been altered in response to new domestic and international conditions. The chapter analyzes the impacts of the main agricultural policy instruments and whether the pressure for change was strong enough to result in policy that sustains an efficient and internationally competitive sector.

## Common Agricultural Policy: History, Instruments, and Reforms

### History

The CAP is one of the oldest **supranational** policies of the EU included in the **Treaty of Rome** (the EEC Treaty), which established the EEC in 1958. However, while the CAP's treaty foundations were established in the 1950s, the CAP came into existence as an EEC policy only in 1962. The need for a common policy arose because national intervention in agriculture was a characteristic of the original EEC member states. The differences in agricultural support systems between member states were an impediment to the freedom of movement of agricultural products, and hence to the **Common Market**[1] that the EEU was seeking to establish. In light of this, the EEC Treaty (Articles 38–47) defined the main objectives of the CAP as follows:

- to increase agricultural productivity by promoting technical progress and by ensuring the rational development of agricultural production and the optimum utilisation of factors of production, in particular labour;
- thus to ensure a fair standard of living for the agricultural community, in particular by increasing individual earnings of persons engaged in agriculture;
- to stabilise markets;
- to secure availability of supplies;
- to ensure that supplies reach consumers at reasonable prices. (Article 39, EEC Treaty)

The Stresa conference of 1958 established the fundamental principles of the CAP, which came into force in 1962. These were market unity, community preference, and financial solidarity. Market unity referred to the objective of common agricultural prices throughout the EEC as an outcome of the Common Market, while community preference signified that products of European origin were to be given preference over imported products. The financial solidarity principle defined the common responsibility of the

EEC member states with regards to the financial consequences of the CAP; on this basis, the European Agricultural Guidance and Guarantee Fund (EAGGF) was established to provide agricultural payments. From an institutional perspective, decisions regarding the CAP were to be taken by **qualified majority voting** in the Council of Ministers.

In 1965–66, a dispute between the **European Commission** and France over proposed reforms of the CAP led to the Empty Chair Crisis, in which France temporarily withdrew its representatives from the Council. The conflict was resolved through the Luxembourg Compromise, which stated that member states could exercise a veto over decisions that touched upon important national interests. The result was that the Council adopted qualified majority voting in various sectors, including agriculture. The **European Parliament (EP)** had no co-decision role in relation to agriculture until the entry into force of the **Lisbon Treaty**. This treaty brought the CAP under the **ordinary legislative procedure**, meaning that the EP is now able to propose amendments and veto proposed legislation. CAP is still one of the few policy areas that is under the main control of the EU, with member states having limited power. No other regional integration project across the globe has achieved the deep integration of the EU's agricultural markets.

### CAP Instruments and Their Outcomes

The CAP was focused on the development of a set of common policy instruments, including common prices. The institutional core of the CAP, as established in 1962, was a price-support mechanism, which defined target, threshold, and intervention prices. These were established on a yearly basis by the Council of Ministers (now called **Council of the EU**) for all major farm products such as grains, dairy products, beef, pork, poultry, fruits, and sugar. In the CAP system, the target price was the maximum price for agricultural goods that was deemed acceptable and was the basis for calculating all other common prices. The threshold price (set below the target price) was a minimum entry price for products imported from third parties, while the intervention price (set below the threshold price) represented the minimum price farmers would receive on their products.

Setting a threshold price shielded European farmers from low-cost competition from non-European producers; this was achieved by imposing variable import levies (**tariffs** that fluctuated according to changes in world prices) on imported goods from the rest of the world. Setting an intervention price secured a minimum price floor for agricultural goods; if market prices fell below this price, **intervention agencies** funded from the CAP budget would purchase the product in question to stabilize farmers' income. In addition, the CAP provided export subsidies or refunds to farmers selling their goods outside of the EEC; these support measures covered the difference between high European prices and lower world prices and thus made European agricultural products internationally competitive.

Between 1962 and 1968, the CAP was considered highly successful because it achieved its main goals. The price schemes resulted in higher and more stable incomes for farmers, while European food production was substantially increased, contributing to the decline in Europe's dependence on imported food products. However, the same set of policies proved to be economically damaging and unsustainable in the long run.

Indeed, faced with stable prices that were clearly higher than world market prices, farmers expanded their production rapidly to such a high level that the EU not only achieved self-sufficiency but, in the 1970s, also began to run large surpluses. The stockpiles of surpluses had to be purchased at intervention prices and stored by intervention agencies, and the EU became famous for its "butter mountains" or "wine lakes." The surplus stocks were either sold on world markets at subsidized prices (through export subsidies), provided as aid to less developed countries, or simply destroyed. The CAP was losing support, and its failure to produce the desired results made its high costs appear ever less justifiable (Theme 3 of this book).

As a result, at the beginning of 1970s the EU also became a large exporter of agricultural products. However, these subsidized exports depressed agricultural prices in the rest of the world and thus affected agricultural production outside the EU. The US, in turn, reacted by increasing its subsidies. Such further actions from other developed countries also hurt developing countries, which were not able to compete with subsidized European and US agricultural production.

Other negative effects of the CAP were that European consumers had to pay higher prices for their food products, while the prolonged use of chemical fertilizers and the destruction of wetlands were increasingly resulting in environmental damage. Also, because support was linked to prices, those engaged in large-scale farming benefited the most from the system, with approximately 80 per cent of the financial support from the EAGGF going to about 20 per cent of the farmers (Commission of the European Communities, 1984). Furthermore, Northern European farmers benefited much more from this system than Southern European farmers, mainly because of the higher support prices for dairy products. Another negative consequence of the price mechanism was a large increase in EU budget expenditures. As world prices were depressed, payments to farmers in the form of export subsidies and price interventions increased significantly, as did storage costs. In addition, reduced imports resulted in smaller tariff revenues on agricultural imports, which led to a decline in EU revenues.

Thus, the CAP can be described as a redistributive policy: first, between member states, by moving finances from less agricultural countries to ones with important agricultural sectors; and second, within member states, indirectly, from small to large farms and from producers of agricultural goods that receive less CAP support (such as fruits) to producers of highly supported goods (such as dairy).

## CAP Reforms

The reform of the CAP has proven to be a difficult task due mainly to the vested interests it created and its redistributive character. First, the benefits of the CAP permitted producers in low-cost countries to invest their profits in land, driving up the costs for new entrants. Reducing price support would have meant that a significant number of farmers might face financial hardship, which in turn could have endangered the stability of financial institutions that had lent them money. Second, for farmers in high-cost countries, who were able to continue their economic activity due to high prices and decreased competition from cheaper imports, a reduction of price support could have resulted in bankruptcy. Third, other vested interests were represented by agro-input and processing industries that expanded their activities to accommodate the production surplus (Gaisford, Kerr, & Perdikis, 2003). Thus, the agricultural lobby groups, in particular in countries that received the most support (such as France, Germany, Ireland, and Spain in the 1970s, 1980s, and 1990s), put strong pressure on national political elites to maintain the status quo on agriculture policy. The pressures were transferred to the EU level through the agricultural ministers in the Agricultural Council.[2] As the CAP is a redistributive policy, each minister of agriculture tried to bring home as much as they could from the EU budget. Thus, any proposal for a reduction of agricultural support or a change in the redistribution of finances was highly debated and would usually be rejected by the Agricultural Council (Fouilleux & Ansaloni, 2016).

Minor reforms were implemented in the 1980s; these were mainly triggered by a large increase in costs, as well as the EU accession of Greece, Spain, and Portugal in the 1980s. In 1984, milk quotas were introduced, as the dairy sector proved to be the most expensive. The main idea behind milk quotas was to limit production. Farmers were required to pay a fine if they produced more than their quota allocation. In 1988, stabilizers were introduced to set a maximum limit on quantities guaranteed to receive support. The 1988 package brought other important policy changes such as support for a set-aside of agricultural land from production, early retirement for farmers, reforestation, and more extensive production methods.

However, the main pressures for reform intensified over time and came from various sources (see Table 11.1). First, budget expenditures for agriculture were increasing year by year, even as a larger part of the Community budget was needed in other policy areas (**regional policy**, **Single Market**, monetary union, **enlargement**, etc.). There were also external pressures through multilateral trade negotiations, starting with the Uruguay Round. Finally, food safety concerns and environmental damage were becoming core issues among political elites and in public debates.

Before the 1986 Uruguay Round of international trade negotiations, when agriculture was brought under the umbrella of General Agreements on Tariffs and Trade (GATT), the sector was seen as exceptional, deserving special attention from national governments in all Western countries. However, this stance started to change in the late 1980s, first in the US, where the idea that agriculture is not that different from other economic sectors gained more and more support. The US pushed for its so-called zero-2000 option in the GATT negotiations, proposing a phasing out of all agricultural subsidies that affect trade directly and indirectly, as well as eliminating import barriers. Since then, through a series of farm bills, the US has tried to reduce programs that would incentivize farmers to produce more. Farm trade negotiations in the Uruguay Round were impacted by this switch in US farm policy. As the US and the EU were at the time by far the largest producers and exporters of agricultural commodities, a compromise between the two players was the only solution for successful negotiations.

As a result, the first substantial reform in the EU, the so-called **MacSharry reforms**, came into effect in 1992. The MacSharry reforms started to replace the guaranteed agricultural prices for cereals and beef with a new system of direct compensation payments to farmers, activated if prices fell below a certain level. **Direct payments** were "decoupled" from production, meaning that they were not directly related to how much a farmer produced; thus, the link between agricultural payments and production was removed. **Decoupled payments** implied less economic distortion than support pricing schemes or coupled payments, as they did not affect prices, only the income of farmers. Further, the MacSharry reforms implemented programs for the development of rural areas and made available additional funding in exchange for environmentally friendly agricultural practices.

In 1999, the CAP was further reformed under the Agenda 2000. These reforms came into effect as a result of the possibility of an eastern enlargement of the EU. Production subsidies continued to be replaced by a set of direct payments, which were increasingly made conditional on food safety,

**Table 11.1** CAP reforms

| Year | Policy | Triggers | Implemented Reforms | Achievements |
|------|--------|----------|---------------------|--------------|
| 1984 | Dairy reform | Surpluses of products, especially butter. | Introduction of quotas on dairy products. | Ability to reform a small part of the CAP after years of opposition. |
| 1992 | MacSharry reforms | GATT Rulings (Uruguay Round)—inclusion of agricultural negotiation. | Decrease of subsidies by 35 per cent for cereals and 15 per cent for beef. Introduction of "compensation payments" based on total cultivated area and historical yields of a product eligible for payments; total number of animals. Introduction of early retirement aid, reforestation of arable land, and the set-aside system (co-financed by the Community and member states). | The CAP becomes less market distorting. The budget is kept a little more under control. |
| 1999 | Agenda 2000 | Preparing for future enlargement to include the CEECs. | Introduction of the two pillars of the CAP. Pillar I includes market and income support. Pillar II focuses on rural development in preparation for the less-developed agricultural sector of CEECs. Direct payments are given to member states based on regional priorities and the fulfillment of specific environmental criteria. Compensation payments are reduced and a further decrease in subsidies by 15 per cent for dairy, 15 per cent for cereals, and 20 per cent for beef is introduced. | The introduction of Pillar II (i.e., rural development) makes the CAP a more multifunctional policy. |
| 2003 | Mid-term Review of Agenda 2000 (Fischler reform) | Enlargement to CEECs/Doha Round. | Further decreases in subsidies. Introduction of the **Single Farm Payment** scheme (narrows the imbalances between small- and large-scale farmers) and phase-out of income support. Gradual transfer of payments (modulation) to Pillar II, which were saved from the reduction of direct payments from Pillar I. Intervention mechanisms such as storage and export restitution are phased out and turned into safety nets. | Decoupling of payments and less market interventionism. |

**Table 11.1** (Continued)

| Year | Policy | Triggers | Implemented Reforms | Achievements |
|------|--------|----------|---------------------|--------------|
| 2008 | Health Check | | Preparing for the abolishment of milk quotas by 2015. Remaining interventionist measures are phased-out. The compulsory set-aside system is cancelled. Financial subsidies are switched to be all SFPs. Increased transfer of funds to Pillar II focusing on environmental **sustainability**. | Increased liberalization. |
| 2013 | Post-2013 Reform | 2008 economic crisis | Focus on organic farming and environmental stewardship. Mainstreaming of "greening" policy by including funding for large-scale organic farming in Pillar I rather than Pillar II. Devoting a small percentage of national envelopes to encourage young farmers. Creation of a crisis reserve fund and a mechanism of risk prevention. | Decrease of the total CAP budget. Encouraging environmentally conscious farming. |

Sources: Fouilleux (2013); Roederer-Rynning (2015)

animal rights, and environmental concerns. The Agenda 2000 introduced several new concepts that would define the reform process of the CAP from that point on. First, "multifunctionality" was introduced, which entailed that farmers should be seen not only as producers of agricultural goods but also as important players in rural development, environmental protection, the increased safety and quality of goods, and animal welfare promotion. Thus, the European model of agriculture was no longer defined mainly by economic considerations but also by social and environmental ones. Second, the Agenda 2000 introduced a "second pillar of the CAP," consisting of rural development policy, which was distinct from support payments to farmers, known as Pillar I of the agricultural policy. Pillar II includes payments for rural development, environmental protection, animal welfare, and higher food safety standards; these policies are co-funded by the EU member states. Policies under Pillar II are more flexible, as they allow member states to choose their national objectives from a list provided by the EU and to implement their own national programs. Third, a voluntary modulation scheme was introduced that allowed member states to choose to switch up to 20 per cent of their allocation of CAP funds in Pillar I (direct support) to Pillar II (rural development).

Another major CAP reform was the Mid-term Review of Agenda 2000 (Fischler reform) that came into effect in 2003 as a result of a new round of multilateral trade negotiations (Doha Round) and the imminent enlargement of the EU to include the first eight Central and Eastern European countries (CEECs). The newest and most innovative element of this reform was the introduction of the Single Farm Payment (SFP), which replaced a vast array of direct payment schemes. Under this system, any farmer would receive a single farm payment regardless of whether the land was used to produce something or not. This scheme was attached to cross-compliance, meaning that to be eligible for the SFP, farmers were asked to comply with the EU's environmental, food safety, animal welfare, and occupational safety standards and to keep the farmland in good agricultural and environmental condition. The Fischler reform also introduced compulsory modulation—a required annual transfer of funds from Pillar I to Pillar II of the CAP at the time. One of the important achievements of this reform was an even greater decoupling of agricultural support from production.

The main objective of the CAP Health Check of 2008 was the reinforcement of the Fischler reform package. The ambition was to transform all direct payments into decoupled payments and to increase the modulation rate. In addition, to prepare for the abolishment of milk quotas in 2015, an increase of quota sizes and rural development measures for areas heavily dependent on milk production were implemented.

The core of the post-2013 reform was a "greening" of the CAP. A new **green payment** was introduced, representing 30 per cent of the direct payments, which rewarded farmers for respecting practices such as the maintenance of permanent grassland and ecological focus areas, and crop diversification. Member states fought to introduce flexibility into the reform, and as a result, each country could use its own method of "greening" its farms, rather than having the Commission decide what an environmentally friendly farm should look like. The 2013 CAP reform replaced the SFP with a new instrument, the Basic Payment Scheme (BPS), which offered basic income to active farmers with the goal of achieving internal convergence.

Payments under the CAP's Pillar I will be reduced by 13 per cent by 2020 (compared to 2013), and only active farmers will be eligible for farm payments. In addition, young farmers entering the sector will benefit from additional financial support. Payments under Pillar II will be cut by 18 per cent by 2020 (compared to 2013); a minimum of 30 per cent of this spending must be done on environmentally friendly and organic projects (European Commission, 2013). Thus, the latest reform did not bring a radical change in instruments; however, it allowed for more flexibility for the member states and a stronger focus on environmentally friendly agricultural practices.

## Debate: Distributing the Budget, Farm Support, and Decentralization

Three issues are at the core of current debates in the EU regarding the CAP: (1) the distribution of the CAP budget among the member states (see Box 11.1), (2) the distribution of CAP support among different types of farms, and (3) the further decentralization of the CAP. In addition, the use of new policy instruments such as geographical indications (GIs) has been brought into the debate due to the Deep and Comprehensive Free Trade Agreements that the EU has been negotiating with various countries, including Canada, the US, and South Korea. For debates relating to the EU's Common Fisheries Policy, which is often compared to the CAP, see Box 11.2.

The cost of the CAP has been a highly debated issue ever since the policy came into existence (see Figure 11.1). The EU member states are divided into two groups regarding their preference on CAP spending. The large net contributors to the budget—such as Denmark, Germany, Sweden, and the UK—favour a further reduction of CAP spending, while the large beneficiaries of agricultural payments—such as France, Ireland, and Spain— are pressuring to maintain a significant CAP budget. When joining the EU in the 2000s, Eastern European countries lobbied for direct payments that would match the EU average level, thus siding with the second group.

**Box 11.1**  CAP budget

As the CAP was one of the first market-correcting policies of the EU, once it was implemented, it accounted for 90 per cent of the EU budget. Although the EU budget is relatively small, now representing only about 1 per cent of the EU gross national income (GNI), the distribution of the money between the EU policies/activities and among various instruments has always involved tough negotiations in the Council of the EU. The CAP expenditures decreased over time, with agriculture accounting for approximately half of the EU budget by 2006, and falling below 40 per cent in 2013 (Figure 11.1). Other policy areas, such as regional policy, started to gain importance during this period. However, the reforms of the 1990s and 2000s had only a limited effect on the spending on the CAP. In the 2016 budget, €42,212 million was allocated to spending on Pillar I of the CAP (direct payments and market support) and €11,746 million was allocated to Pillar II (rural development). Thus, the CAP still represented the largest spending item in the EU budget.

Source: Adopted budget for 2016, *Official Journal of the European Union*, L 48, February 24, 2016, 595–686

**Box 11.2**  Common fisheries policy

The Common Fisheries Policy (CFP) was established together with the CAP by Article 38 of the EEC Treaty. The CFP shares the main objectives of the CAP, including an increased emphasis over time on the conservation of fish stocks and environmental considerations. The main objectives of CFP were defined by the Council in 1992[3] as being the conservation of fish stocks, the protection of the marine environment, the economic viability of the fleet, and respect for consumers' interests.

State intervention in the fisheries sector is considered necessary due to the character of fish stocks as common goods, as the sea is a common property. Thus, without an intervention of governments in the market, overconsumption (overfishing) would be the result, with private producers and consumers ignoring the social costs.

Because not all EEC member states were interested in a CFP, the policy was not set up until 1970, after a long period of negotiation, and became fully operational only in 1983. The first two regulations gave free and equal access to all EU fishermen to all EU fishing grounds, with certain exceptions for sensitive coastal waters.

International debates under the United Nations Convention on the Law of the Sea as to how far fishers could go established a 200-nautical-mile limit, which was agreed upon by the EC in 1975. The 20-year agreement achieved by the EC in 1983 introduced national zones of access of up to 12 miles and exclusive EU zones of 200 miles.

In terms of market-support instruments, the CFP defined quotas or total allowable catches (TACs) for each member state for many fish species. In addition, it set prices for all species of fish caught within EU waters and provided compensation for fishermen who had to withdraw their catch from the market. Structural measures were focused on the reduction of overcapacity and the restructuring of the fishing industry, which would eventually make it more competitive and efficient. Conditions were set for member states to develop their fleet capacity.

Issues of overfishing have persisted for years, and, thus, the Commission has proposed reductions in total amounts of catch for certain species. In 1999, a new **regulation** was adopted encouraging fishermen to catch only what they could sell. This regulation was in response to concerns about the diminishing stocks of cod and other fish. However, well before the expiration of the 1983 agreement, it was clear that the agreement was not achieving its objectives. Thus, a reform agreed upon in 2002 changed several characteristics of the CFP by considering the environmental sustainability of the policy. One important reform focused on regulating the amount of fish that could be taken from the sea by imposing restrictions on catches of young, small fish; bans on the use of certain fishing techniques and gears; and the closure of certain fishing areas. Public payments for the modernization of national fleets were phased out, while minimum prices for fish that could not be sold were kept in place.

In 2014, a further reform of the CFP was implemented, with three important changes: a ban on the wasteful practice of discarding perfectly edible fish; a legally binding commitment to fishing at sustainable levels; and decentralized decision-making, allowing member states to take measures appropriate to their fisheries.

*(continued)*

**Box 11.2**    (Continued)

Originally, the CFP was funded from the same fund as the CAP, the European Agricultural Guidance and Guarantee Fund (EAGGF). In 1993 a separate fund was created, the Financial Instrument of Fisheries (FIFG), which was transformed into the European Fisheries Fund (EFF) in 2007. With the reformed CFP of 2014, the European Maritime and Fisheries Fund (EMFF) was introduced for the period 2014–20, with an allocated budget of €5.7 billion.

The CFP represented one of the important reasons for two Nordic countries, Norway and Iceland, not to become EU member states (see Chapter 15). In both countries, the fisheries sector is one of the top sectors of the economy. Despite that most of their fisheries exports are going to the EU, the majority of the population considers **sovereignty** over this sector important. Equal access, unlimited foreign investment in the processing industry, and the failure of the EU's CFP to limit overfishing are important contributors to the two countries' positions.

Overfishing was a subject of controversy between the EU and Canada as well. During the so-called Turbot War, which started in March 1995, the Canadian government accused vessels from Spain and Portugal of overfishing turbot in international waters outside Canada's 200-mile limit. The North Atlantic Fisheries Organization (NAFO) established the quotas of allowable catches. The relationship between Canada and Spain (and by implication the EU) became so tense that the Canadian government even arrested the captain and crew of a Spanish vessel. Also, a Canadian ship cut the nets of one Portuguese vessel and two Spanish vessels. In response, Spain sent a warship to protect its fishermen. The EU fisheries commissioner responded with severe criticism of the actions of the Canadian government. In April 1995, Spain, Canada, and the EU reached an agreement, which set new quotas and tougher conservation and enforcement rules to limit overfishing.

However, accession negotiations with the CEECs in agriculture overlapped with the CAP mid-term review. Accession countries had to go through a transition period of CAP direct payments and were then phased in over a period of nine years (Grant, 2005).

In addition, direct payments under CAP are higher for cattle and dairy products than for fruits, vegetables, and oils.[4] Thus, EU member states that specialize in the former set of products (Denmark, France, Germany, Italy, and Sweden) are the ones that attract the largest percentage of the CAP

**Figure 11.1** CAP expenditure in total EU expenditure (2011 constant prices)

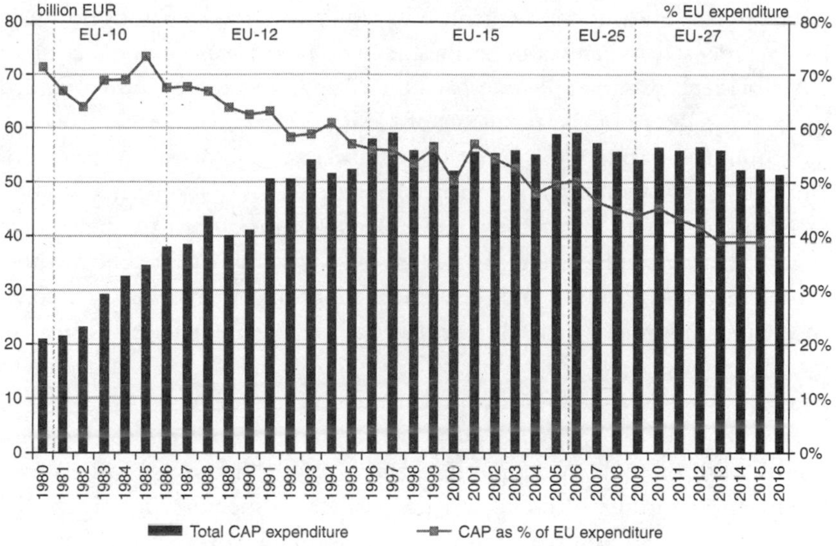

Source: https://ec.europa.eu/agriculture/sites/agriculture/files/cap-post-2013/graphs/graph1_en.pdf

payments. To a certain extent, the transfer of payments from Pillar I to Pillar II of CAP addresses the unbalanced distribution of payments among the EU member states.

A second debate is related to the unequal distribution of CAP payments between types of farms. The enlargement of the EU from six to 28 countries has resulted in a large variation between the member states in terms of not only natural and climatic conditions, farm size and structure, and productivity but also the importance of the agricultural sector for the respective domestic economy and the level of employment in agriculture. Indeed, 72 per cent of the farms in the new member states had a size of less than five hectares, compared to 47 per cent in the old member states (Gorton, Hubbard, & Hubbard, 2009). For example, in 2004, when the first eight CEECs joined the EU, on average 23 per cent of their population was employed in the agricultural sector, compared to 10 per cent in the old member states.

The EU market-based support rewards large, high-yield farms in the most favoured areas. Regardless of the method of calculation, either per hectare or per annual working unit, most payments are directed at the richer northern areas of the EU. Thus, farms in less-favoured regions and in the CEECs that have a fragmented farm sector are receiving less financial aid from the CAP. In 2004, when a list of CAP individual payments was made publicly available, it showed that most of the payments were going toward prosperous northern EU member states and to large agribusinesses. This unbalanced distribution of CAP payments was not fully transparent until 2007, when the Council agreed to a full disclosure of the recipients of CAP payments. In the 2013 reform, the Commission sought to correct these imbalances and defined the goals of "internal" convergence (among farmers) and "external" convergence (among member states). The 2013 reform includes various measures to achieve these goals, such as the replacement of payments based on historic references with a flat-rate national payment, and the adjustment of direct payments in accordance with a minimum national average direct payment per hectare across all member states (European Commission, 2013). A transition period of one to two years was established for the implementation of these reforms.

The third debate that takes place within the EU is related to the renationalization of the CAP. The enlargement of the EU has resulted in a heterogeneous group of member states, each with specific climatic conditions, agricultural infrastructure, institutional frameworks, and challenges. This has resulted in a greater divergence of preferences for different types of agricultural programs. The debate regarding decentralization has focused on two issues: decision-making and funding. The decision-making competence is divided between the EU and the member states in certain aspects of the CAP, such as the rural development policy (Pillar II of the CAP) and the Single Farm Payment, replaced in 2015 by the Basic Payment Scheme (the core of Pillar I of the CAP). In Pillar II of the CAP, the EU member states have an important role to play, as they are charged with choosing objectives, specifying targets, and defining measures to achieve them, while the EU's role is constrained to defining objectives, approving national plans, and co-financing. In Pillar I of the CAP, the EU member states have a more limited role, though they are charged with specifying targets for particular programs and implementing cross-compliance measures. The reform of 2013 has introduced more flexibility in Pillar I application. The shift of funds between the pillars thus has important implications for the degree of member state influence on the CAP. While past reforms have shifted funds from Pillar I to Pillar II, Pillar I spending is still about three times larger than Pillar II spending. The 2014–20 EU **Multiannual Financial Framework (MFF)** reduces the spending for Pillar I by 1.8 per cent and for Pillar II by 7.6 per cent (European Commission, 2013). It is the financial aspect of the CAP renationalization that is highly debated and faces major opposition from certain member states.

One of the ongoing debates at the international level is related to new policy instruments that affect the trade in food products. In the wake of CAP reforms during the 2000s that have reduced agricultural subsidies, the granting of geographical indication (GI) status has become an important facet of EU agricultural policy. GIs are a form of **intellectual property**; they require that a product with GI status may originate only from a certain place or region (e.g., champagne must be made of grapes grown in the Champagne region of France). GIs require protection from the state because they represent goods whose value is derived from *credence attributes*, those that consumers cannot identify even after the product is consumed. As agricultural policy has become more oriented toward GIs, the EU has become increasingly interested in garnering additional protection for their GIs in foreign markets. There are three contentious international issues pertaining to GIs: (1) a major global split in the mechanism used to protect this particular form of intellectual property (GIs and trademarks); (2) the treatment of some products that have been granted GI status in the EU as *generic* terms in some other countries—meaning that they are considered common terms and not identified with production being undertaken in a particular geographic location (e.g., feta cheese in Canada); and (3) garnering foreign protection for less well-known or new EU GI designations. For example, in the Canada-EU **Comprehensive Economic and Trade Agreement (CETA)** signed in 2016, Canada agreed to various levels of acceptance of the EU GIs for 179 foods and beers.

## Conclusion

The CAP is one of the EU's most ambitious policies; it is as comprehensive as national agricultural policies in states such as Canada (see Box 11.3). The CAP came into existence in a period of economic turbulence when food security was seen as one of the main goals of the EEC. It developed into a common, redistributive policy that received wide support from European citizens and political elites. The instruments that were implemented to achieve food security were initially considered legitimate regardless of the food price increases and inefficiencies that followed. In the following decades, however, the distortions of the price-support system became obvious, and various intra-European and international pressures made a reform of the CAP necessary. However, the CAP proved difficult to change, mainly due to the vested interests that the price-support system had created.

Pressures for CAP reform have included, at various points of time, (1) oversupply of agricultural products, (2) increased budgetary expenses, (3) international trade distortions, (4) the eastern enlargement of the EU, and

**Box 11.3**    Canada's agricultural policy

Like any other Western country, Canada has put in place a variety of agricultural programs, which are continuously evolving. One characteristic of the Canadian agricultural policy is that it is the responsibility of both federal and provincial governments. This **multilevel** structure is similar to the general framework of the CAP. As Canadian provinces have the power to implement their own programs, governments at both levels must overcome the challenge of coordinating their agricultural policies. Another outcome of the dual responsibility is that some provinces offer greater assistance to their farmers than others.

The main goal of Canada's agricultural programs, as in the EU, was income stabilization for farmers, achieved by offering price or gross/net return guarantees. The two major original stabilization programs were the Agricultural Stabilization Act (ASA), which was put in place in 1958, fully funded by the Canadian federal government, and the Western Grain Stabilization Act (WGSA), introduced in 1976 with the main goal of helping the prairie farmers to stabilize their crop incomes.

The Uruguay Round of negotiations of 1986 and the Free Trade Agreement signed with the US in 1987 (superseded by the North American Free Trade Agreement of 1994 including Mexico) has pushed Canada to revisit its agricultural programs and to reduce coupled farm payments. In the 2000s, food safety and environmental sustainability have become the centre of the debate related to reforms of agricultural policy. The Canadian Agricultural Income Stabilization Program (CAIS), introduced in 2003, emphasized risk management, innovation, food safety, and environmental responsibility. In 2007, the federal, provincial, and territorial governments decided to replace the CAIS with alternative business risk management programs that would follow a new market-driven vision for the Canadian agriculture (labelled Growing Forward; see Schmitz, 2008). The successor program (Growing Forward 2) for the period 2013–18 aims to generate market-based growth and manage farmers' business risk by focusing on innovation and market development.

The Canadian agricultural policy evolved from using price-based, commodity-specific instruments to generally available farm-based instruments, which have the benefit of being less production distorting. These reforms hence go in the same general direction as the reform strategy followed by the EU. Canada still has national supply management programs for dairy, poultry, and eggs, which were implemented in the early 1970s because of depressed market conditions. The national supply management program is a policy that regulates supply through quotas for domestic production and imports. In addition, farmers collectively negotiate the farm-gate prices for products covered by supply management.

(5) environmental and food safety concerns. Through several different reforms in the 1990s and the 2000s, the CAP has become a more efficient, less distorting, and better-targeted policy. The CAP reforms have returned some power to the member states by forming a second pillar focusing on rural development, which is co-financed by the member states. Compared to the agricultural policies of other Western countries (including Canada), the reformed CAP focuses on not only economic objectives but also social and environmental goals. However, as the CAP has food safety, animal and plant health, and environmental regulations higher on a list of priorities than other countries, it is still widely perceived as protectionist.

## References and Further Reading

Baldwin, R., and C. Wyplosz. 2012. *The economics of European integration*. 4th ed. Columbus, OH: McGraw-Hill Higher Education.

Burrell, A. 2009. "The CAP: Looking back, looking ahead." *Journal of European Integration* 31 (3): 271–89. https://doi.org/10.1080/07036330902782113.

Commission of the European Communities. 1984. *Commission Communication to the Council on the economic effects of the agri-monetary system.* https://ec.europa.eu/agriculture/cap-history/crisis-years-1980s/com84-95_en.pdf.

Commission of the European Communities. 1987. *The agricultural situation in the Community. 1986 Report.* http://aei.pitt.edu/31390/1/CB4686557ENC_002.pdf.

European Commission. 2013. *Overview of CAP reform 2014–2020*. Agricultural Policy Perspectives Brief No. 5. https://ec.europa.eu/agriculture/policy-perspectives/policy-briefs/05_en.pdf.

European Commission. 2017. *CAP post-2013: Key graphs & figures*. https://ec.europa.eu/agriculture/sites/agriculture/files/cap-post-2013/graphs/graph1_en.pdf.

European Union. 2016. EU by topic/budget. https://europa.eu/european-union/topics/budget_en.

Fouilleux, E. 2013. "The Common Agricultural Policy." In *European Union politics*, 4th ed., edited by M. Cini and N. Pérez-Solórzano Borragán, 309–24. Oxford: Oxford University Press.

Fouilleux, E., and M. Ansaloni. 2016. "The Common Agricultural Policy." In *European Union politics*, 5th ed., edited by M. Cini and N. Pérez-Solórzano Borragán, 308–22. Oxford: Oxford University Press.

Gaisford, J.D., W.A. Kerr, and N. Perdikis. 2003. *Economic analysis for EU accession negotiations: Agri-food issues in the EU's eastward expansion.* Cheltenham, UK: Edward Elgar Publishing.

Gorton, M., C. Hubbard, and L. Hubbard. 2009. "The folly of European Union policy transfer: Why the Common Agricultural Policy (CAP) does not fit central and Eastern Europe?" *Regional Studies* 43 (10): 1305–17. https://doi.org/10.1080/00343400802508802.

Grant, W. 2005. "The Common Agricultural Policy: Challenges in the wake of Eastern enlargement." In *The European Union in the wake of Eastern enlargement: Institutional and policy-making challenges,* edited by A. Verdun & O. Croci, 57–71. Manchester: Manchester University Press.

Kerr, W.A., and J.D. Gaisford, eds. 2007. *Handbook on international trade policy.* Cheltenham, UK: Edward Elgar. https://doi.org/10.4337/9781847205469.

Josling, T. 2006. "The war on terror: Geographic indications as a transatlantic trade conflict." *Journal of Agricultural Economics* 57 (3): 337–63. https://doi.org/10.1111/j.1477-9552.2006.00075.x.

Nello, S.S. 2013. *The European Union: Economics, policies & history.* 3rd ed. Columbus, OH: McGraw-Hill Higher Education.

OECD. 2015. *Agricultural policy monitoring and evaluation.* http://www.oecd-ilibrary.org/agriculture-and-food/agricultural-policy-monitoring-and-evaluation-2015_agr_pol-2015-en;jsessionid=37tncako10hrb.x-oecd-live-02.

Poon, K., and A. Weersink. 2014. "Growing forward with agricultural policy: Strengths and weaknesses of Canada's agricultural data sets." *Canadian Journal of Agricultural Economics/Revue Canadienne d'Agroeconomie* 62 (2): 191–218. https://doi.org/10.1111/cjag.12023.

Roederer-Rynning, C. 2015. "The Common Agricultural Policy: The fortress challenged." In *Policy-making in the European Union.* 7th ed., edited by H. Wallace, M. Pollack, and A. Young, 197–219. Oxford: Oxford University Press.

Rude, J., A. Eagle, and P. Boxall. 2015. "Agricultural support policy in Canada: What are the environmental consequences?" *Environmental Reviews.* https://tspace.library.utoronto.ca/bitstream/1807/70016/1/er-2015-0050.pdf.

Schmitz, A. 2008. "Canadian agricultural programs and policy in transition." *Canadian Journal of Agricultural Economics* 56 (4): 371–91.

Skogstad, G., and A. Verdun, eds. 2010. *The Common Agricultural Policy: Policy dynamics in a changing context.* London: Routledge.

Swinbank, A. 1989. "The Common Agricultural Policy and the politics of European decision making." *Journal of Common Market Studies* 27 (4): 303–22. https://doi.org/10.1111/j.1468-5965.1989.tb00347.x.

## Review Questions

1.  Why was the CAP introduced in the European Economic Community, and why has it always played a central role in the EU?

2.  Were the original objectives of the CAP achieved? Have the original objectives of the CAP changed over time, and if so, how?

3.  What instruments did the CAP introduce in the 1960s to achieve its objectives? What effects did they have?
4.  What were the main pressures for reform of the CAP, and how did they change over time?
5.  Why was the CAP resistant to reforms? Describe the main reforms of the CAP and their main mechanisms.
6.  What are the main ongoing debates related to the CAP? Explain.
7.  Compare the CAP of the EU with Canada's agricultural policy. What are the main commonalities? What about the main differences?

## Exercises

1.  Do some research on the CETA negotiations pertaining to agricultural products. What were the main areas of difficulty? How is the CAP related to some of the early Canadian objections?
2.  What is the significance of the CAP in the context of the tension between ideas of national security and **European integration?**

## Notes

1   Characteristics of a Common Market: no barriers to trade; free movement of goods, services, capital, and labour among countries participating in the Common Market; and a common tariff toward third parties (see Chapter 7).
2   For further information on the EU decision-making and CAP, see Swinbank (1989).
3   http://eur-lex.europa.eu/legal-content/EN/TXT/?uri=celex:52002PC0185.
4   Direct payments for beef, milk, sheep, and goat represent 73 per cent of total EU commodity-specific payments (OECD, 2015).

# 12
# Environmental and Energy Policy

G. CORNELIS VAN KOOTEN AND REBECCA H. WORTZMAN

## Reader's Guide

It took the European Union (EU) nearly half a century to establish coordinated environmental and energy policies. In the twenty-first century, the EU aspires to be a leader in the global fight against climate change and has established ambitious plans for an **Energy Union**. However, the member states continue to exercise power in these jurisdictions, which often makes it difficult for the EU to meet its own objectives. The stringent climate mitigation goals that the EU has set for itself could require significant economic restructuring, but they may also hit physical obstacles that limit the potential of generating energy from renewable sources. The EU's energy policy, meanwhile, needs to respond to issues of energy insecurity, which derive from Europe's dependency on Russia as principal supplier of petroleum and natural gas.

## Introduction

Environmental and energy policy are closely connected because energy consumption is one of the major sources of greenhouse gas emissions, which in turn contribute to climate change. In Europe, energy consumption increased significantly as the economies of European states began to grow rapidly after World War II. Large amounts of energy were and are needed to provide citizens with a high standard of material well-being. Between 1965 and 2006, total primary energy consumption in Europe climbed from just under 1,000 million tonnes of oil equivalent (Mtoe) to nearly 1,850 Mtoe, or at an annual rate of 1.5 per cent. This rise in energy consumption not only had adverse environmental impacts, it also increased Europe's need for energy imports, as domestic production could not keep up with demand. Partly as a result of greater environmental awareness, energy consumption began to fall after 2006. This development coincided with an increasing shift toward **renewable energy** sources.

What role have the policies of the European Union (EU) played in this context? At first sight, it might seem that energy has been quite important in the **European integration** process. After all, two of the three original European Communities founded in the 1950s—the **European Coal and Steel**

**Community (ECSC)** and the **European Atomic Energy Community (Euratom)**—related to matters of energy production. However, energy played a relatively minor role in the most important community created in the **Treaty of Rome**, the **European Economic Community (EEC)**, and an integrated approach to energy policy was not developed in the EU until the turn of the millennium. Even after 2000, progress on EU energy policy has been slow, as energy markets and energy policy are still fragmented, and member states maintain substantial control and competencies in this policy area.

In contrast to energy, the environment was not explicitly mentioned in the Treaty of Rome. Nevertheless, the first environmental legislation of the EU was developed in the 1970s, well before the EU began to define energy policy as a priority. In the absence of an explicit treaty base, the EU's first environmental law was passed in an effort to harmonize environmental standards in the **Common Market**, in line with the mixed-economy model (Theme 1 of this book), so as to ensure that states with strong environmental protection would not incur economic disadvantages. The Single European Act (SEA) of 1986 gave the EU formal treaty authority to act on environmental issues and established the aim of a "high level of protection" as core principle of EU environmental policy (now Article 191 TFEU). In recent years, the EU has been particularly active in developing policies that seek to combat climate change. Some hope that climate change policy can become a new "signature policy" of the EU in the twenty-first century, similar to the **Single Market** in the first 50 years of its existence. Commission President Jean-Claude Juncker, for instance, proclaimed in his State of the Union Speech in September 2016, "We Europeans are the world leaders on climate action." But has the EU really been a leader, and is it perceived as one?

This chapter examines how the EU came to acquire competences and develop policies in the fields of environmental and energy policy. It then assesses how innovative and successful the EU has been in dealing with the most important recent challenges in these two policy fields, namely climate change and **energy security**. Lastly, the chapter discusses the future potential of renewable energy sources in Europe, whose expansion could contribute to addressing both of these challenges.

## History of EU Environmental Policy

Activity in the environmental policy arena in the EU began in earnest in the 1970s, almost two decades prior to when it was officially included as a treaty objective in the SEA. Prior to 1987, more than 100 items of environmental legislation were implemented to address water and air quality and waste disposal. In 1972, the first United Nations (UN) Conference on the Human

Environment was held. It was during this time that scientists linked cross-border $SO_2$ emissions from power plants to acid rain, which caused declining fish stocks in Scandinavian lakes and forest dieback in Germany. Environmental issues were gaining political attention. In response, member states began to pass national environmental regulations. European policymakers viewed national regulations as potential **non-tariff barriers**. They pushed to harmonize standards and thereby further promote European economic integration. The EU adopted its first **Environmental Action Programme (EAP)** in November 1973. The 1973 EAP, and those that followed, outlined general environmental objectives and strategies for implementation. Specific measures were, and remain, the responsibility of individual member states. By the time environmental policy gained treaty status under the SEA, it merely formalized actions that were already under way in the EU.

Environmental legislation passed in this era was based on improving air and water quality, reducing other specific pollutants, and protecting nature. Regulatory needs were determined by researching the cause, nuisance, and impacts of pollution. This approach led to targeted, often industry-specific, **directives** to improve environmental quality through minimum standards (command) followed by strict monitoring and enforcement (control). **Command-and-control** is viewed as more interventionist and less flexible than market-based instruments, and regulations from this era amounted to a piecemeal, top-down approach. Prior to 1987, legislation had to be linked to the goals of the Common Market—the harmonization of administrations and the limiting of new non-tariff barriers. This approach made it difficult to implement more flexible and comprehensive policy instruments and contributed to the proliferation of regulatory legislation. Examples of these early directives included minimum standards on water quality through the imposition of individual directives on fishing and bathing waters in the 1970s and directives regulating pollutants from motor vehicles. Other examples include industry limits on $SO_2$ as well as other atmospheric pollutants.

The 1980s saw an increase in procedural legislation leading to more institutional support for EU environmental policy. This development was primarily a result of international efforts to improve the environment, efforts in which the EU played an important role. European legislation included the Environmental Impact Assessment Directive (1985), the creation of the **European Commission**'s Environment **Directorate-General (DG)**, and the establishment of the Coordination of Information on the Environment (CORINE) program. Much of the legislation focused on harmonizing the procedural and institutional basis for environmental intervention and built on early environmental directives. These initiatives set the stage for the eventual establishment of the European Environment Agency in 2011. The inclusion in the 1986 SEA of treaty objectives "to preserve, protect and improve the quality of the environment, to contribute toward protecting human health, and to ensure a prudent and rational utilization of natural resources" ensured the permanence of EU-level environmental policy.

Institutional and procedural changes intended to facilitate the completion of the Common Market also impacted environmental policy. The SEA introduced **qualified majority voting (QMV)** for establishing policies, rather than **unanimity** (as remains the case for taxation and fiscal decisions), and since the entry into force of the **Maastricht Treaty** in 1993, QMV is used for nearly all environmental policy decisions. As a result, policymakers have begun to utilize a wider range of instruments, introducing more flexible and **comprehensive approaches** to environmental issues. The surge in environmental legislation over the past several decades can be viewed as a by-product of the EU's economic integration process, though policies far exceeded the regulatory requirements for a harmonized market. Environmental legislation gained political salience as European citizens became more aware of environmental issues, particularly climate change. Member states opted for Europe-wide policies as the means to address transnational pollutants, not only as an important strategy to deal with pollution but also as a way to ensure a level playing field. Equal rules for all would ensure that domestic firms would not be unfairly disadvantaged by competitors operating in neighbouring countries with more lenient environmental standards. These motivations were compounded by internal dynamics as institutions gained additional power in the integration process. Not only institutions but also various member states, who were advocates for stringent environmental rules, were able to influence the policy agenda for stricter regulatory regimes.

The new millennium and the fifth Environmental Action Programme **(EAP)** marked the beginning of a new phase in environmental policy and **regulation**. In particular, regulation increasingly gave way to market incentives. The existence of differing national and regional contexts was acknowledged, and the possibility for burden sharing was introduced. This mechanism was subsequently used to meet the climate targets stipulated in the **Kyoto Protocol**. In addition, there was an explicit desire to integrate policies and set longer-term **sustainability** goals. For example, the framework directive for action in the field of water policy aimed to achieve a more unified approach to policy by consolidating previous directives and promoting the sustainable use of water resources. Also with the new millennium, the EU began to have a more visible presence as a global leader in international climate negotiations, particularly lobbying for stringent action to reduce $CO_2$ emissions. One of the EU's cornerstone policies for

**Box 12.1**    Carbon trading

The EU-ETS is a cap-and-trade system that sets a limit (cap) on total emissions of greenhouse gases (GHGs) in high-emitting industries by creating $CO_2$ emission permits (as $CO_2$ is the dominant GHG). These allow firms to buy and sell (trade) permits and find the least costly mechanism to reduce emissions. The EU-ETS is the largest international system for trading carbon emission allowances, accounting for three-quarters of international carbon trading. It currently covers more than 11,000 power stations and manufacturing facilities in 31 countries. The ETS is emblematic of the new era of flexible regulations, but has suffered from a surplus of allowances as a result of the inclusion of carbon offsets, the overreporting of emissions by companies (the number of emission permits issued exceeded actual emissions), and slow growth after the 2008 crisis. These caused the price of permits to drop below the level necessary to incentivize firms to reduce emissions. The price of carbon traded below €10/t$CO_2$ (tonne of $CO_2$) during 2015, compared to nearly €30/t$CO_2$ in 2008.

combating climate change is its **Emissions Trading System** (EU-**ETS**), which is discussed further in Box 12.1 and is emblematic of a **market-based style of environmental regulation**. The EU-ETS was implemented after EU ratification of the Kyoto Protocol in 2005 but underwent a significant revision in 2009.

The EU's approach to environmental policy is now dominated by its role as an international player in climate negotiations. Under the Paris Agreement reached at the 21st Conference of the Parties (COP21) to the UN Framework Convention on Climate Change in December 2015, the EU committed to reduce domestic greenhouse gas emissions at least 40 per cent from 1990 baseline emissions by 2030, with an aspiration to reduce its emissions 80–95 per cent by 2050 compared to 1990. Both are ambitious targets compared to the legally binding targets already in place: to reduce GHG emissions 20 per cent by 2020 compared to 1990. To do so, the EU is hoping to rely on renewable sources of energy. These goals are part of an integrated approach to environmental policy, and include the **Climate and Energy Packages** that address specific goals, and policy mechanisms to achieve them. Despite the fact that the United Kingdom was a major force behind EU climate policy, it is unlikely that EU policy will change with the UK leaving the Union (see Chapter 7).

The EU is currently operating under the seventh EAP, which prioritizes the need to meet the EU's climate objectives by 2020. It continues to maintain the EU's guiding environmental policy principles, which have been progressively introduced through EAPs and various treaties. The three main ones are as follows: (1) polluters should pay for damages they impose on the environment; (2) action to improve the environment should be taken at the local level to the greatest extent possible (this is known as the subsidiarity principle); and (3) precautions should be taken to prevent the undertaking of any activity or measure that threatens human health or the environment, even if some cause-and-effect relationships have not yet been fully established scientifically. However, given the priority attached to reducing $CO_2$ emissions, the European Commission and **European Parliament (EP)** have taken on a greater role as a result of the Paris Agreement. Previously under Kyoto, member states agreed to individual targets and means for meeting these targets so that the EU could achieve its overall target. Member states no longer have individualized targets; the decisions for meeting targets are now vested at the EU level.

Although the EU has been a strong advocate for strict environmental rules internationally, and has tried to be a norm-setter in this domain, it has not always been perceived as a successful actor. In the period following the failed 2009 United Nations climate change conference in Copenhagen, various scholars noted that the EU had not been taken seriously as a leader in environmental policies (Oberthür, 2011; Chaban, Knodt, & Verdun, 2017). However, the research on the successful COP21 climate summit in Paris in 2015 suggests that the EU has been a more influential leader in these negotiations, although it has had to share the stage with up-and-coming leaders such as China (Oberthür & Groen, 2017; Parker, Karlsson, & Hjerpe, 2017).

## History of EU Energy Policy

Energy policy in the EU is characterized by three primary goals: (1) ensuring secure supply, (2) integrating the internal energy market to ensure liberalization and competitive prices, and (3) minimizing the environmental impacts of energy consumption, primarily by reducing $CO_2$ emissions. Despite being fundamentally linked to early EU institutions through the ECSC and Euratom, energy policy did not initially garner the same attention as environmental policy. Unlike environmental policy, energy policy falls under the jurisdiction of the member states, who have near total discretion in the choice of their energy mix and how they exploit their natural resources. Member states can and do enter into bilateral energy trade agreements, which reinforce an already fragmented internal energy market, while efforts to create a common energy policy have been resisted. This plethora of bilateral agreements leads to disunity and frustration at EU-level energy negotiations because national positions can override a unified EU position. With the Treaty of Lisbon (2009), energy policy became a shared competence area, giving rise to the possibility of Europe-wide energy policy **coordination**; energy security became a specific EU objective. In 2015, the EU launched the Energy Union Framework Strategy, the latest step toward achieving integrated energy policy goals.

The need for an EU-level energy policy became apparent through a variety of internal and external factors—the provision of energy in an integrated market clearly requires an integrated solution. Three factors that persistently characterized the EU energy scene eventually led to an integrated energy policy. First, the EU became the world's largest energy importer. In the 2000s, domestic energy production began to slow, and the EU expanded to include Central and Eastern European countries (CEECs), which gave rise to new security concerns because many of these countries' energy supplies are not diversified. Second, energy policy was being shaped by recent efforts to create more competitive energy markets. In 2005, the European Commission launched an inquiry into energy markets to identify barriers to competition triggered by the lack of cross-border trade and high market concentration, particularly in the gas and electricity sectors. High market concentration and accompanying high electricity prices relative to those in the US has spurred concerns about the competitiveness of EU industry. The completion of infrastructure projects in the electricity sector to support an influx of renewable energy sources, and efforts to ensure more diverse origins of supply across the EU, became a central focus of EU energy policy after 2005. Third, it became clear that, to achieve ambitious climate goals, an integrated approach to energy and environmental policy would be required, because energy accounts for 80 per cent of the EU's GHG emissions.

The EU sought to take an integrated approach to policy through new legislation. In 2007, the Commission adopted new structural rules for the gas and electricity sectors; these included the unbundling of ownership, as well as a system of regulatory bodies and networks to promote cross-border interconnections and other infrastructure projects. The EU has identified and invested in projects of common interest in an effort to accelerate infrastructure projects necessary for meeting energy objects and completing the internal energy market. The EU budget allocated to energy policy is now almost four times as large as the budget for environmental policy (see Box 12.2).

In 2008 the EU began to integrate climate and energy policy through **recommendations** that fed into the 2020 Climate and Energy Package—a legal framework for implementing emission targets. The package became administered by a newly created DG Climate Action, which is now also responsible for the **Paris Treaty**'s 2030 emission-reduction targets and the Roadmap to a Competitive Low Carbon Economy in 2050. Further, in 2015

**Box 12.2**    Budget allocations for environmental and energy policy

In the EU budget for 2016, the EU allocated €397 million for environmental policy and €82 million for climate action (including administration); the combined allocation amounts to about 3.3 per cent of total expenditures. The EU's environmental and climate policy is relatively inexpensive, since it primarily sets standards and targets that have to be implemented at the member state level. By contrast, the EU invests more heavily in energy policy. The total budget allocation for this policy field in 2016 was €1,524 million (10.6 per cent of total expenditures), which included €375 million for conventional and renewable energy (including investments in energy infrastructure), €175 million in nuclear energy, €427 million in energy-related research through the Horizon 2020 program, and €465 million support for the ITER fusion device that is being constructed in Southern France.

Source: Adopted budget for 2016, *Official Journal of the European Union*, L 48, February 24, 2016, 738–69; 1567–1609; 1652–62

the Commission created the so-called Energy Union: a framework strategy to address energy security, competition, liberalization of energy markets, and climate targets. Finally, the Commission announced that by 2017 it would present a strategy, in the form of a new Renewable Energy Directive, for achieving at least 27 per cent renewable energy in the EU's energy mix by 2030. The directive would also include a bioenergy sustainability policy.

## Current Challenges for EU Environmental and Energy Policy

The EU has defined climate change as one of its core priorities for the twenty-first century, and this objective relates to both environmental and energy policy. At the Paris climate summit, the EU committed to reduce domestic GHG emissions, principally $CO_2$, by at least 40 per cent by 2030 compared to 1990. Earlier, the 2009 Renewable Energy Directive adopted an aggressive "20-20-20" target to be met by 2020—a minimum 20 per cent reduction in $CO_2$ emissions from 1990 levels, a minimum 20 per cent share of renewables in energy production, and a 20 per cent improvement in energy efficiency. Under the more ambitious target for 2030, renewable energy is expected to account for 27 per cent of the EU's total energy production. Given that renewables accounted for only 7.4 per cent of total primary energy consumption in 2014 (Figure 12.2), the targets pose a tremendous challenge for policymakers.

There are five ways to reduce $CO_2$ emissions:

1.  Dramatically reduce population;
2.  Drastically reduce the gross domestic product (GDP);
3.  Generate the same or a higher level of GDP with less energy;
4.  Generate energy with lower $CO_2$ emissions; or
5.  Some combination of the first four factors.

Drastically reducing population or GDP is not politically feasible. With an aging population and recent influx of refugees into Europe, population decline is unlikely to be the main road to reduced $CO_2$ emissions. Likewise, citizens are unlikely to accept reductions in their standard of living. Thus, the burden of reducing $CO_2$ emissions will rest with efforts to reduce the energy required to produce output (better energy intensity) and to decarbonize energy (improve the carbon intensity of energy). The latter options can be combined into a "technology option" that simply considers the ratio of $CO_2$ emissions to GDP, or carbon emissions intensity (EI).

The carbon EI varies greatly across countries, depending on their energy sources, level of development, economy, and geography. The EI for the EU as a whole, the largest EU countries, and the US and China are provided in Figure 12.1. In 2011, France had an EI of 0.14 kg of $CO_2$ per US\$ of GDP,

**Figure 12.1** Emissions intensity (kg $CO_2$/\$ of GDP) EU and selected countries, 1990–2011

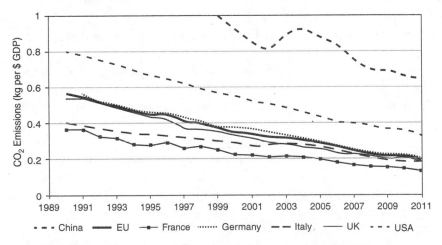

Source: Authors' calculations, using data from European Environment Agency (EEA) and Eurostat (2016)

**Table 12.1**  Emissions intensity ratios, selected regions and countries, 2011

| Region or Country | % rate of decline in emissions intensity, 1990–2011 | Region or Country | % rate of decline in emissions intensity, 1990–2011 |
|---|---|---|---|
| European Union | 5.0% | OECD | 4.1% |
| • Denmark | 5.5% | • US | 4.2% |
| • UK | 5.0% | • Canada | 4.0% |
| • Germany | 4.8% | • Japan | 2.5% |
| • France | 4.7% | China | 6.0% |
| • Spain | 4.0% | Sub-Saharan Africa | 3.6% |
| • Italy | 3.2% | India | 3.2% |
| Russian Federation | 7.0% | Brazil | 1.7% |
| Norway | 5.0% | Indonesia | 0.4% |

Source: Authors' calculations, based on the World Bank's development indicators

which is the lowest among developed countries. Only a few city states and many poor countries have lower EIs. Global carbon EI fell from 0.78 kg of $CO_2$ per $ of GDP in 1990 to 0.38 kg in 2011.

The average rate of decline in EI also varies considerably from one country to another (see Table 12.1). Since 1990 many rich countries have shifted manufacturing to developing countries, or replaced coal-fired generating capacity with gas plants (UK and US) or nuclear power (France). In the 1990s, after reunification, Germany replaced inefficient power plants and manufacturing facilities in the east with less-polluting facilities or simply decommissioned assets. Spain and Denmark invested heavily in wind power, while Russia was impacted by recession following the collapse of the Soviet empire. Likewise, the recession that followed the 2008 financial crisis led to a reduction in carbon emissions.

The EI data raise three concerns about efforts to mitigate global warming. First, many poor countries have lower EIs than those of France; indeed, $CO_2$ emissions per dollar of GDP are almost negligible in countries such as Chad (0.02) and Mali (0.05). Before many of the poorest countries can even reach middle-income status, not only will GDP need to increase significantly, those countries' EIs will also increase. Therefore, if poor countries are given the opportunity to grow, policymakers should anticipate an increase in global $CO_2$ emissions. Recognizing this, EU countries feel obligated to reduce emissions to a greater extent than they otherwise would.

The second issue is more directly applicable to EU energy policy. The UK likely has the most draconian climate legislation in the EU: climate legislation passed in December 2008 requires the UK to reduce GHG emissions by 34 per cent by 2022. The UK already has one of the lowest EIs in the world (0.22 in 2010); among EU countries, France has the lowest carbon intensity index at 0.15. The reasons for the low rates in both Britain and France include the 2007–10 recession, the decommissioning of coal plants, success in moving manufacturing offshore, and, in the case of France, heavy reliance on nuclear energy. To meet its climate policy targets, the UK would need to get to the French EI level in less than one-third the time it took France to make that improvement. Achieving these targets would likely require the use of nuclear power.

The third issue relates to economic incentives. Because of cheap natural gas from shale plays, the US invested in gas plants that led to the elimination of inefficient coal plants. In Europe however, natural gas prices have remained high. Thus, EU countries have mainly invested in coal rather than gas plants for producing reliable power. Yet a variety of incentives have been implemented by EU countries to increase investment in renewables.

These measures have had some degree of success. Figure 12.2 shows that, since 2005, except for renewables, in the EU consumption of all energy sources has fallen. Today renewables account for about one-quarter of the energy consumed in the EU. As Figure 12.3 shows, the largest share of

**Figure 12.2** EU primary energy consumption by source, 1965–2014

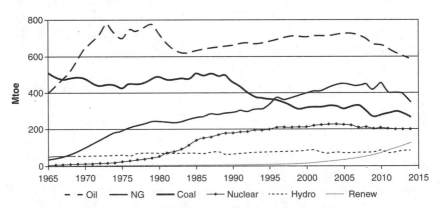

Note: 1 tonne of oil equivalent (toe) = 11.63 megawatt hours (MWh) of electricity.
Source: Authors' calculations using data from BP Statistical Review of World Energy 2015, http://www.bp.com/en/global/corporate/energy-economics/statistical-review-of-world-energy.html.

**Figure 12.3** Production of primary energy, EU-28, 2013 (based on Mtoe)

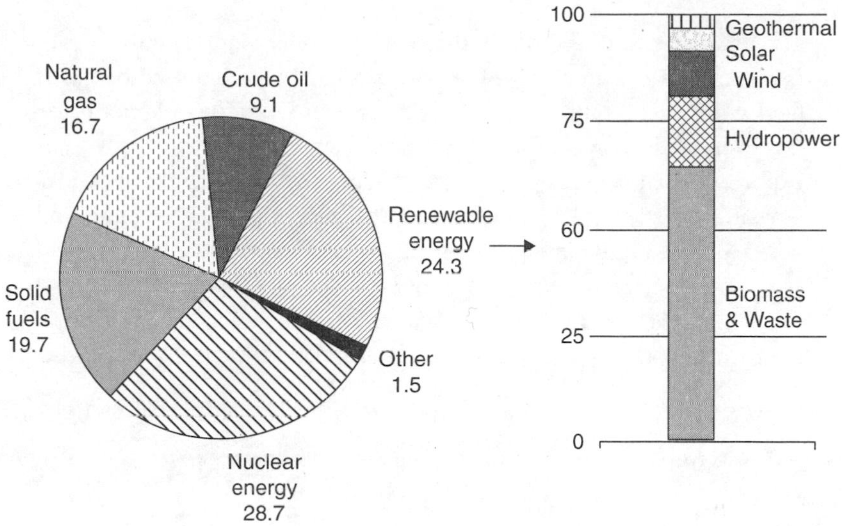

Source: Eurostat (online data codes: nrg_100a and nrg_107a)

renewables is accounted for by biomass and waste as well as hydropower. Due to increased efficiency and conservation, energy use per person and total energy consumption have also been on a downward trajectory since 2006.

As was previously mentioned, one of the core institutions that the EU has developed for reducing $CO_2$ emissions is a carbon market, the EU-ETS, which now covers about 45 per cent of total EU $CO_2$ emissions. It is considered crucial to achieving the EU's target of 40 per cent emissions reductions below base year (1990) by 2030. Previously the EU-ETS was plagued by insufficient oversight (private and public sector agents overstating their emissions), with the price of emission permits collapsing entirely at one point. However, under phase III (2013–20), this seems to have been corrected. The emissions cap will be reduced by 1.74 per cent annually and an increasing proportion of permits will be sold at auction, with 40 per cent already sold that way in 2013; after 2020, the cap will be reduced by 2 per cent per annum. This should raise the cost of emitting $CO_2$, thereby incentivizing conservation, the use of non-carbon sources of energy, and research and development into alternative energy sources.

While the fight against climate change is a global priority shared with many other countries, including Canada (see Box 12.3), the second crucial challenge

**Box 12.3**   Canadian environmental and energy policy: Summary and comparison

Canada is similar to the EU in the sense that jurisdictional power over the environment and energy resides primarily with provinces, as it does with EU member states. Canada differs in two important aspects, however: (1) Energy security is not a concern because Canada is a net exporter of oil, natural gas, coal, and electricity; (2) Canadian GHG emissions are among the highest in the world on a per-capita and per-dollar-of-GDP basis. This is seen in the following table. Canadian $CO_2$ emissions are high because energy is needed to produce energy for export, particularly crude oil from oil sands, which account for 60 per cent of national oil production and 8.5 per cent of $CO_2$ emissions.

| Item | Units | Canada | EU |
|---|---|---|---|
| Crude oil production | ($\times 10^6$ bbl*/day) | 4.29 | 1.41 |
| Crude oil consumption | ($\times 10^6$ bbl/day) | 2.37 | 12.53 |
| Natural gas production | ($\times 10^9$ m³**) | 162.0 | 132.3 |
| Natural gas consumption | ($\times 10^9$ m³) | 104.2 | 386.9 |
| Coal production | ($\times 10^6$ tonnes) | 68.8 | 537.6 |
| Coal production | (Mtoe) | 36.6 | 151.4 |
| Coal consumption | (Mtoe) | 21.2 | 269.8 |
| Electricity production | ($\times 10^6$ MWh = TWh) | 615.4 | 3,010.5 |
| Net electricity exports | (TWh) | 57.6 | −11.1 |
| GHG emissions total | ($\times 10^6$ t$CO_2$) | 620.5 | 3,705.0 |
| GHG emissions per person | (t$CO_2$/person) | 16.2 | 7.7 |
| GHG emissions intensity | (kg $CO_2$/\$ GDP) | 0.34 | 0.20 |

* bbl: barrel
** m³: cubic metres

In 2015, Canada committed to reduce GHG emissions by 30 per cent below 2005 levels by 2030. It intends to do this by preventing the construction of new coal-fired power plants and either phasing out existing plants or converting them to co-fire with biomass; implementing regulations on vehicle fuel standards; requiring 5 per cent renewables in gasoline and 2 per cent in diesel fuel; and relying on forestry activities. There are two problems with the plan: (1) While $CO_2$ emissions fell and the economy grew between 2005 and 2013, this resulted in only limited annual emission reductions despite the fact that economic growth was below expectations; and (2) the burden of emissions reduction will fall on individual provinces, and they may not have the appetite for imposing costs on citizens.

for the EU in the environmental and energy domain—the protection of energy security—is more urgent for the EU. The EU is highly dependent on foreign energy sources, particularly from Russia. As shown in Figure 12.4, over 70 per cent of petroleum and nearly half of the natural gas used in the EU are imported, primarily via pipelines from Russia and often transiting through Ukraine. European import reliance leading up to the first Climate and Energy Package was of great concern due to rising energy prices and repeated Russo-Ukraine gas crises (as in 2006 and 2009), which in part prompted energy policy to be included as an EU-level competence in the Treaty of Lisbon (in force since 2009). Although security of supply is a key objective of energy security, little has been done to integrate the **Common Foreign and Security Policy** (CFSP; a policy arena dominated by national autonomy; see Chapter 9) and energy security concerns, or to improve the market position of the community by delegating more control over energy policy to the EU level. As member states still enter into bilateral agreements with external suppliers, some members enjoy better terms of trade than others. For example, the Nord Stream gas pipeline (completed 2011) runs 1,222 km under the Baltic Sea from Russia to Germany, thus bypassing countries of Eastern Europe. Although a unified energy policy may curtail security concerns by allowing the community to leverage its role as a large energy importer, it is resisted by some member states that are reluctant to forgo their current market standing.

The EU is dependent on Russia for more than one-third of its primary energy imports. In 2013, more than 45 per cent of oil imports into the EU came from Russia and Norway, followed by the Middle East and other OPEC sources. Together with Russia (39 per cent), Norway and Algeria account for 81 per cent of natural gas imports, with the remainder from the Middle East. Nearly three-quarters of imported coal comes from Russia (29 per cent), Colombia, and the United States, with South Africa and Australia accounting for much of the remainder. As the US shuts down its coal plants in response to new supplies of unconventional oil and gas, the EU can be expected to import more coal from the US, which has only recently become a major source of EU coal. The US is also a primary source of wood bioenergy.

Overall, some 20 per cent of the energy consumed in the EU comes from imports. To reduce the risk of being dependent on one source or one primary supplier, the EU is increasingly seeking to diversify its energy portfolio, acquire fossil fuel imports from less precarious sources, and reduce the energy employed per unit of GDP. It has also launched a number of other initiatives to diversify and secure energy supplies, while attempting to decrease reliance on carbon imports (e.g., importing biomass for energy from North America). These initiatives include diplomatic efforts to provide greater access to the internal energy market for key suppliers and neighbours, such as the

**Figure 12.4** Fossil fuel import dependency, EU, 1980–2013

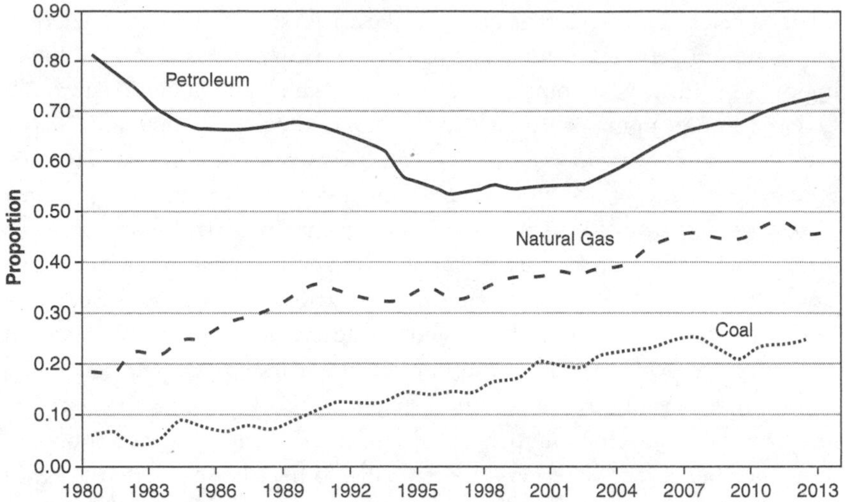

Source: Authors' calculations, using data from EuroStat (2016) (online data code: tsdcc310)

**European Neighbourhood Policy (ENP)**, initiated in 2006 (see Chapter 16). The ENP seeks to improve foreign relations with countries to the east and south of the Union. The EU has also tried to include Russia in the International Energy Charter, which was originally signed as a measure to bridge the East-West divide after the **Cold War**. Including Russia as a signatory would provide the EU with a legally binding framework to enhance cooperation and mitigate energy security risks, but the agreement is largely seen to be more favourable to energy importers than suppliers.

As one means to reduce reliance on Russia, the EU has promoted greater competition in the natural gas market. Russia is keen on supplying natural gas to the EU, but it has resisted efforts to change the structure of EU energy markets (see also Chapter 18). By presenting a united front in purchasing natural gas from Russia, the EU could counter Russian monopoly power, as the largest EU member state, Germany, was able to do by collaborating with Russia in the development of Nord Stream, getting lower prices than those available to other countries. Russia has in turn opposed any new EU legislation and international energy agreements that could adversely affect its market position. For example, it has resisted new structural rules governing natural gas and electricity infrastructure, going as far as to file a dispute against the EU with the **World Trade Organization (WTO)** over requirements to grant third-party operators access to Gazprom pipelines. However, these structural rules are in line with the EU's efforts to ensure secure supply and create more competitive internal energy markets by diversifying supply and improving infrastructure to allow for increased flows within its borders.

In the market for coal, almost 25 per cent of the EU's consumption is now imported (compared to 6 per cent in 1980), despite vast reserves of domestic coal, because imported coal is of a higher quality with lower $CO_2$ emissions than domestic coal. Nonetheless, 44 per cent of coal-generating capacity in the EU continues to rely on lignite coal that is low-energy with high $CO_2$ emissions; surprisingly, some of the largest lignite coal plants in the EU began operations only in 2011–12. The EU requires reliable electricity, which can be generated only from nuclear, coal, or natural gas plants, because wind and solar power are too variable and electricity cannot currently be stored on a large scale. Nuclear power is no longer considered an option in some EU countries (most notably Germany), natural gas prices are extremely high, and natural gas and high-quality coal need to be imported. As a result, some EU countries have turned to domestically mined lignite coal as the only realistic alternative for reliable power—in spite of its unfavourable emissions rating.

## Debate: $CO_2$ Reduction and the Role of the EU in Sustainable Energy Development

The evidence linking access to cheap, reliable energy to economic prosperity and the realization of social objectives is strong and well documented. Currently, as shown in Figure 12.5, coal, oil, and natural gas account for 45 per cent of electricity generation; when nuclear power and hydro are taken into account, 84 per cent of electricity is generated by non-renewable sources. The remainder includes geothermal, wind, solar, tidal, wave, biomass, and heat energy. While this "renewable" fuel share has increased tremendously in recent decades to nearly 16 per cent today, the share remains small. More importantly, if we compare installed renewable capacity (21 per cent) against actual production (16 per cent), questions remain regarding the reliability and cost of renewables. Clearly, greatly reducing reliance on fossil fuels presents a tremendous challenge for the EU.

Only two realistic strategies for reducing $CO_2$ emissions are currently on the policy table: (1) wind and solar energy, and (2) biomass. The remaining renewable energy options are expected to make only minor contributions to future electricity supply because of high costs or, in the case of new large hydroelectric dams, adverse environmental impacts.

Globally, wind farms have the potential to generate almost 17 per cent of total future expected electricity demand, but this assumes that wind turbines would operate at or near full capacity all the time. A British study found that UK wind turbines could operate at 90 per cent of rated capacity for merely

**Figure 12.5** Generating capacity and production by energy source, EU, 2013

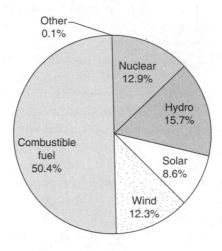

(a) Capacity: Total = 956,416 MW

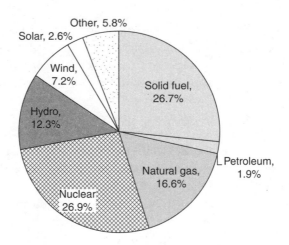

(b) Generation: Total = 3,261,537 GWh

Source: Authors' calculations, using data from EuroStat (2016) and *BP Statistical Review of World Energy 2015*

17 hours per year, with deliverable power below 20 per cent of rated capacity for almost 40 per cent of the time. Similar or worse results were found for other EU countries. Fossil fuel power plants of equal capacity often had to be operated alongside wind turbines to mitigate deficiencies. Intermittency begets additional costs, as it requires fast-responding backup generating capacity and increases network instability.

The EU will clearly be a dominant player in the development of wind and solar energy into the future. However, this will require the continuation and expansion of policies that support renewables, including subsidies to producers of clean fuels, publicly funded R&D, and contracts to reduce risks. Alternatively, carbon taxes or carbon emission–trading schemes can be used to drive up fossil fuel prices, thereby inducing consumers to switch to alternative clean energy sources. Existing policies that incentivize investing in wind and solar power in the EU include carbon offset credits eligible for sale in the mandatory EU-ETS market (or in a voluntary carbon market), feed-in **tariffs** that guarantee producers a price irrespective of the market price (or even the existence of a buyer), production and capital investment subsidies, and carbon taxes. These policy instruments are implemented on the premise that, because renewables potentially displace emission-intensive electricity, the social benefits of increasing wind capacity will exceed the social costs. Studies indicate that this is not always the case. Wind power does not always replace electricity produced from coal; often it replaces electricity produced from natural gas, making wind subsidies less effective.

An alternative to unpredictable wind and solar is wood biomass, which already accounts for about half of all renewable energy. Although reliable, wood biomass suffers from limitations related to a shortage in global supply. The EU's latest goal to produce 27 per cent of all energy from renewable sources by 2030 implies a projected demand for biomass of 752 million cubic metres ($m^3$) annually. This far exceeds the total Canadian biomass harvest of around 170 million $m^3$. Given that other countries are looking to increase their reliance on bioenergy, and biomass is used in making paper and engineered wood products, competition for wood biomass could greatly increase the cost of wood fibre. The use of biomass to reduce emissions raises other concerns, because legislation treats biomass as carbon neutral despite the fact that biomass does not reduce $CO_2$ emissions from fossil fuels one-for-one. If commercial timber is used as bioenergy, the $CO_2$ deficit may be worse than using coal, because the carbon in biomass would otherwise have been stored for long periods in wood products such as lumber. It can take from 10 to 60 or more years to recover the $CO_2$ released at the time of biomass burning by sequestering carbon in trees. The shortest times to recover the $CO_2$ released by using wood biomass occur when residues from logging are used, as these combustible materials would otherwise decay in the forest. Yet their decay provides essential nutrients for regrowth, so their use may not be a sustainable forestry practice. Overall, there seem to be economic and physical limits to a country's ability to absorb great amounts of wind and solar sources of energy and expand the use of wood biomass.

## Conclusion

EU environmental and energy policy faces two main challenges: (1) achieving the EU's GHG reduction targets and (2) protecting security of supply. Solutions to these issues pose challenges to physical infrastructure and to economic and political institutions. Although renewable energy holds much promise, it also presents considerable challenges and costs. The best prospects for renewable energy are solar, wind, and biomass, but these are encumbered by physical limitations and expanding production costs, although technological advances could improve some of their prospects. Securing energy supply will require diversifying sources of imports and the mix of energy types used to meet demand. Implementing these policies without further fragmenting the internal energy market will require political coordination, and increased coordination of infrastructure projects to integrate new energy sources into existing electricity grids, across national borders. Despite these challenges, environmental policy in the EU can be viewed as one of the greatest successes of the integration project. The shape and future of the EU may be uncertain, but environmental policy has served to reinvigorate support for integration and enhance the Union's legitimacy on the international stage. Although much work still remains to be done, the EU's record as a leader in climate change mitigation and environmental regulation is likely to continue because of its leadership, not only domestically through high standards but also internationally, especially since the successful completion of the UN Framework Convention on Climate Change, signed in Paris in 2016.

## References and Further Reading

Chaban, N., M. Knodt, and A. Verdun. 2017. "'Talking with' not 'talking at'? Perceptions of the EU as a global normative energy actor in the eyes of BRICS and EU 'Big 3.'" *Comparative European Politics* 15 (1): 1–22. https://doi.org/10.1057/cep.2016.11.

Covert, T., M. Greenstone, and C.R. Knittel. 2016. "Will we ever stop using fossil fuels?" *Journal of Economic Perspectives* 30 (1): 117–38. https://doi.org/10.1257/jep.30.1.117.

Darwall, R. 2015. *Central planning with market features. How renewable subsidies destroyed the UK electricity market.* Surrey, UK: Centre for Policy Studies.

Dreger, J. 2014. *The European Commission's energy and climate policy: A climate for expertise?* Basingstoke, UK: Palgrave Macmillan. https://doi.org/10.1057/9781137380265.

European Commission. 2013, September 20. *A new EU forest strategy: Forests and the forest-based sector.* Communication from the Commission to the European Parliament, the Council, the European Economic and Social Committee and the Committee of the Regions, COM(2013) 659 Final. Brussels: European Commission.

European Commission. 2014, January 22. *A policy framework for climate and energy in the period from 2020 to 2030.* Communication from the Commission to the European Parliament, the Council, the European Economic and Social Committee and the Committee of the Regions, COM(2014) 015 Final. Brussels: European Commission.

European Commission. 2014. *EU energy, transport and GHG emissions trends to 2050: Reference scenario 2013.* Luxembourg: Publications Office of the European Union. https://ec.europa.eu/transport/sites/transport/files/media/publications/doc/trends-to-2050-update-2013.pdf.

Eurostat. 2016. *Statistics explained.* http://ec.europa.eu/eurostat/statistics-explained/index.php/Main_Page.

Global Wind Energy Council (GWEC). 2015. *Global wind report. Annual market update 2014.* http://www.gwec.net/publications/global-wind-report-2/.

International Energy Agency (IEA). 2015. *World energy outlook 2015.* http://www.worldenergyoutlook.org/weo2015.

Jordan, A., and C. Adelle, eds. 2013. *Environmental policy in the EU: Actors, institutions and processes.* Abingdon, UK: Routledge.

Kaya, Y., and K. Yokobori. 1997. *Environment, energy and economy: Strategies for sustainability.* Tokyo: United Nations University Press.

Lacal Arántegui, R., and J. Serrano-González. 2015. *2014 JRC wind status report.* Joint Research Centre of the European Commission, Scientific and Policy Report. Luxembourg: Publications Office of the European Union, http://publications. jrc.ec.europa.eu/repository/bitstream/JRC96184/reqno_jrc96184_2014%20 jrc%20wind%20status%20report%20-%20online%20version.pdf.

Mann, C.C. 2013, May. "What if we never run out of oil?" *The Atlantic.* http://www.theatlantic.com/magazine/archive/2013/05/what-if-we-never-run-out-of-oil/309294/.

Oberthur, S. 2011. "The European Union's performance in the international climate change regime." *Journal of European Integration* 33 (6): 667–82. https://doi.org/10.1080/07036337.2011.606690.

Oberthür, S., and L. Groen. 2017. "The European Union and the Paris Agreement: Leader, mediator, or bystander?" *WIREs Climate Change* 8 (1): e445. https://doi.org/10.1002/wcc.445.

Parker, C.F., C. Karlsson, and M. Hjerpe. 2017. "Assessing the European Union's global climate change leadership: From Copenhagen to the Paris Agreement." *Journal of European Integration* 39 (2): 239–52. https://doi.org/10.1080/0703633 7.2016.1275608.

Smil, V. 2003. *Energy at the crossroads. Global perspectives and uncertainties.* Cambridge, MA: MIT Press.

Tosun, J., S. Biesenbender, and K. Schulze, eds. 2015. *Energy policy making in the EU.* London: Springer. https://doi.org/10.1007/978-1-4471-6645-0.

U.S. Energy Information Administration (EIA). 2014. *Annual energy outlook 2015 with projections to 2040.* https://www.eia.gov/outlooks/archive/aeo15/pdf/0383(2015).pdf.

van Kooten, G.C. 2013. *Climate change, climate science and economics. Prospects for an alternative energy future.* Dordrecht: Springer. https://doi.org/10.1007/978-94-007-4988-7.

van Kooten, G.C., and C.M.T. Johnston. 2016. "The economics of forest carbon offsets." *Annual Review of Resource Economics* 8 (1): 227–46. https://doi.org/10.1146/annurev-resource-100815-095548.

Vogler, J. 2013. "Changing conceptions of climate and energy security in Europe." *Environmental Politics* 22 (4): 627–45. https://doi.org/10.1080/09644016.2013.806634.

## Review Questions

1. The long-term objective to 2050 is that the EU will reduce GHG emissions by 80 per cent compared to what they were in 1990. Given the discussion in this chapter, do you think it is realistic for the EU to eliminate almost all reliance on fossil fuels?

2. Germany and other EU countries have recently invested in new coal plants to back up unreliable wind power, and some coal plants in the US have been producing electricity for nearly 100 years. Should these plants be closed in the next decade?

3. The share of renewable energy in EU consumption has grown steadily over the past two decades, but it still remains small. However, to meet biomass energy targets, the EU will need to import massive amounts of wood biomass from non-EU regions such as Canada. There is concern that this will lead to unsustainable forestry and even ecological destruction in these regions. Is the trade-off between energy needs and possible ecological damage to forests acceptable? Under what circumstances might the EU rely on biomass energy?

## Exercises

1. What legal tools are used to design and protect EU environmental policies? What does this indicate about the depth of European integration and its potential?

2. Research the position of (the governments of) various EU member states on climate change. Which member states would you characterize as leaders in the fight against climate change? Which ones emerge as laggards?

# 13
# Regional Policy

EMMANUEL BRUNET-JAILLY

## Reader's Guide

This chapter examines how the European Union (EU) implements **regional policy**. The EU's regional policy today is characterized by solidarity and partnerships between the member states, their lower-level governments (regions, cities, and other local governments) and the **European Commission**. These partnerships are called **multilevel governance**. The EU's regional policy provides transfers of funds to the poorest regions, representing about 30 per cent of the EU annual budget. This chapter reviews how the regional policy that emerged in the 1970s was reformed in 1988, 1993, and 1999, and changed again in 2008. It also discusses ongoing criticism of the policy in terms of its redistributive effectiveness.

## Introduction

This chapter reviews the regional policy of the European Union (EU): its origin and development over the last 60 years; why the first six EU member states (Belgium, France, Italy, Luxembourg, the Netherlands, and West Germany) agreed to a policy imposing forms of solidarity and financial redistribution of wealth across their regions in the 1950s; and how this policy evolved to become what it is today. The chapter discusses (1) how successive **enlargements** impacted regional policy and (2) why despite criticisms and doubts, the **Lisbon Treaty** (post-2009) confirmed its importance. The last section of the chapter looks at the reason for changes that occurred after 2006, when the policy was refocused on **smart, sustainable, and inclusive growth**.

Our goal is to understand and assess two of the themes that organize this book and run throughout the discussion. First, regional policy is a core component of the post–World War II era. There was an understanding that the European economy should be mixed (neither state-controlled nor left to an unconstrained market) and that it should comprise mechanisms of social inclusion and market correction (Theme 1 of this book). Second, regional policy is also of crucial importance for the question on how well economic legitimacy and integration work as fundamental mechanisms of **European integration** (Theme 3 of this book).

At their inception, the EU's regional programs basically reimbursed member states for existing national projects. In 1988, however, regional policy was renamed and refocused. The new name, **cohesion policy**, represents a policy that brings together member states to partner with each other, with European regions and cities, with other local governments, and the with the European Commission in the development of a coherent all-inclusive regional policy.

Finally, during the late 1990s, critics repeatedly pointed toward the increasingly uneven development of the EU's regions. Indeed, a few of the richest and most populated regions are creating wealth much faster than all the other ones put together. The Lisbon Treaty nevertheless reasserted the EU's regional policy, which continues to receive more than 30 per cent of the total EU budget (see Box 13.1). Today, when compared to any state or international organization, it is one of the largest redistributive policies in the world.

## The Origins and Development of the EU's Regional Policy

The European Community found its way into regional economic development, and regional policy, because the 1957 **Treaty of Rome** stated, in Article 2 of

**Box 13.1**    Budget allocation to regional policy

Regional policy is one of the two main spending items in the EU budget, the other being the **Common Agricultural Policy (CAP)** (see Chapter 11). Because of its large share of the budget, policy priorities for regional policy are often set when the EU's **Multiannual Financial Framework (MFF)**—the EU's seven-year budget plan—is being negotiated. The 2014–2020 MFF allocates €366,791 million to the budget heading "economic, social and territorial cohesion"; this amount represents 33.9 per cent of the total seven-year budget.

In the yearly EU budget for 2016, the payment allocation to "economic, social and territorial cohesion" is €48,844 million, which also represents 33.9 per cent of the budget. This sum includes budget allocations of €29,056 million to the ERDF, €6,637 million to the Cohesion Fund, and €12,164 to the ESF. The first two of these funds are administered by the Commission DG Regional Policy; the ESF is administered by the DG Employment, Social Affairs and Inclusion (see also Chapter 10).

Source: Adopted budget for 2016, *Official Journal of the European Union*, L 48, February 24, 2016

the Treaty Establishing the European Economic Community (TEEC), that the EU, at the time called **European Economic Community (EEC)**, "shall have as its task, by establishing a **Common Market** and progressively approximating the economic policies of member states, to promote throughout the community a harmonious development of economic activities, a continuous and balanced expansion, an increase in stability, an accelerated raising of the standard of living and closer relations between the states belonging to it."

In other words, Article 2 suggested that economic integration should be harmonious, continuous, and balanced, while increasing standards of living across member states. This objective pointed to policies of cohesion and solidarity. Article 3 TEEC then described a number of important **inter-governmental** tools of public policy: the elimination of custom duties, the Common Agriculture Policy (CAP), the **competition policy**, the **European Social Fund (ESF)**, and the European Investment Bank (EIB). Through the creation of these mechanisms, the treaty enhanced the role of the Commission regarding the economic and social cohesion of the EU. It underscored three redistributive instruments: the ESF, the EIB, and the European Agricultural Guidance and Guarantee Fund (EAGGF; see also Chapter 11). These instruments were designed to help member states adjust to enhanced competition and economic integration, and to work out cohesion and solidarity policies based on limited forms of redistribution.

Initially, regional concerns were raised in the EU context only as part of competition policy. Indeed, the Treaty of Rome attempted to limit and regulate competition. It states that "state aids" in particular are acceptable only to the extent that they are part of market adjustments and integration. The treaty encourages economic and social cohesion across the EU (Allen, 1996); at the time the assumption was that limiting competition would lead to a reduction of the influence of market forces on states and regional markets. Articles 92 and 93 TEEC are about competition policy; they restrict financial intervention of member states targeting "mobile private sector investment to a particular location through the use of public subsidies" (European Parliament, 1991, p. 3). Hence, in line with the goals set by the Treaty of Rome, the Commission set clear guidelines to limit bidding wars between regions and states to attract foreign investors. The rationale was that financial incentives, in the form of regional or state aids, distort competition among regions across the EU. The goal was to limit competition and to reduce the ability of richer regions (or states) to offer larger amounts of subsidies than poorer regions (see Chapter 7). Articles 92(3)a and 92(3)c TEEC provided a basis for the limitation of state aids focusing on unemployment in regions facing industrial decline, as the Commission established aid ceilings and criteria to limit subsidies in richer regions.

Although the member states that concluded the Treaty of Rome made specific references to economic and social imbalances, including the redistributive policy instruments mentioned above, it was not until 1965 that the Commission adopted a communication regarding regional policy for the first time. The **Directorate-General (DG)** for Regional Policy was set up in 1968, and in 1972 the member states agreed that a regional policy was an essential factor in strengthening the European Union. From 1967 to 1973, and really until 1988, successful enforcement of European policy gained momentum.

### From Six to Twelve: The European Regional Development Fund (1967–1988)

During the years until 1988, the Commission realized that it was nearly impossible to provide a level playing field in competition policy. First, it recognized that to gain traction, such a policy would need to focus on areas where public authorities (governments) already had some influence, such as the quality of public administration, infrastructure, telecommunications, or energy policies, and also public subsidies. In this context, adequate regulation might be an important tool. Second, the Commission realized that, thanks to the Treaty of Rome (Article 92, Section 3 TEEC), it managed a budget that only marginally increased its influence in matters of cohesion in the EU, in particular regarding structural adjustments to the **Single Market**. At the time the EU budget represented 1.27 per cent of the member states' gross national income (GNI), which amounts to €97.5 billion in today's currency. Third, financial issues developed regarding states' contributions to the EU. For example, before the United Kingdom even joined, it became clear that it would be a so-called net contributor to the EU budget (contributing more money to the budget than it drew from it). Indeed, planning the expansion of the EU from six to nine members (with the accession of Denmark, Ireland, and the United Kingdom) raised the issue of the redistribution of EU funds to the UK in form of EU programs, because its economy imported from outside the EU and was in little need of subsidies from the CAP. Hence, the redistribution of EU funds through the CAP was seen as inadequate for this new member state. However, the UK was facing the transformation of its textile, coal, and steel industrial regions. In this situation, the regional policy was identified as an alternative to the CAP, as a form of side payment to the UK (and other member states) and as a redistributive mechanism. This ended up being the breakthrough that led to the creation of the **European Regional Development Fund (ERDF)**, a substitute system favouring regional industrial redevelopment and modernization. At the time, it was of great interest to the UK and Italy in particular, but also to Belgium, France, West Germany, and Luxembourg.

The creation of the ERDF also led to the implementation of two important principles of EU fund management: the *partnership and additionality principles*, which state that state funds can leverage EU funds (in other words, a project must be co-funded by the member state in question) and that such mechanisms should take place within a member state–Commission partnership. All these changes were relevant to ongoing conflicts about who should control regional policy: the member states or the Commission. Indeed, partnership and additionality were the answer: the allocation of funds by the ERDF relied on a quota system. Concentrating on regions suffering from late development and declining industrial regions, it funded infrastructure and productive investments. The first ERDF was set up in 1975 with a tri-annual budget of €1.3 billion, and with the overall goal of correcting regional imbalances that were the result of structural changes in agriculture, industry, and employment. At its inception, the ERDF's eligibility criteria included the requirement of 50 per cent co-funding by EU member states, and the program targeted small and medium-sized enterprises that created at least 10 new jobs. The fund also focused on major infrastructure developments, such as roads and bridges, and investments in mountainous areas.

It was at this time that regional policy had its first exclusively dedicated commissioners in the person of George Thomson (1973–77), a British journalist and politician, and then Italian politician Antonio Giolitti (1977–85), because their countries (the UK and Italy) were the primary beneficiaries of the emerging policy. Earlier portfolios held by competition policy commissioners such as Hans von der Groeben (1967–70) and Albert Borschette (1970–73) combined both competition and regional policy responsibilities. Even after the institutional separation, however, the competition portfolio remained relevant to regional policy. In the late 1970s and 1980s, competition commissioners Borschette (until 1976), Raymond Vouel (1976–81), Frans Andriessen (1981–85), and Peter Sutherland (1985–89) implemented a systematic survey of state aids. By the late 1980s the Commission was able to show that there was about €100 billion of state aid distributed yearly across the EU (a stable figure throughout the 1990s) (Allen, 1996, p. 180). Reviewing national practices allowed the Commission to enforce **regulations** in each member state and to require changes while it progressively implemented the ERDF.

The accession of Greece in 1981, and Spain and Portugal in 1986 further increased pressures on Italy and France (and also Greece, once it was a member), because these states had many regions that received support from the ERDF. With the accession of Spain and Portugal, these regions would face greater competition for EU funding: all of Greece; in Italy, the whole Mezzogiorno, Liguria, Tuscany, Umbria, Marche, parts of the north, the Apennines administered by Emilia Romagna, and the Adriatic lagoons; and in France, Languedoc-Roussillon, Corsica, Provence-Alpes-Côte d'Azur, Aquitaine, Midi-Pyrénées, Ardèche, and Drôme. In this situation, the Commission agreed to test new programs, called the Integrated Mediterranean Programs (IMPs). These programs were set for seven years with a budget of €6.6 billion for the period 1986–93. Their goals were to alleviate multiple market-related pressures on the regions of France, Greece, and Italy as they adapted to Spanish and Portuguese competition in agriculture, fisheries, and small and medium-sized businesses. There was also funding for training youth, women, and junior executives.

Under the IMPs, regional authorities submitted proposals through their respective member states to the Commission. These were assessed prior to being reviewed by a consultative committee made up of representatives of the then 12 member states of the EU, and included the Commission as chair. Notably, the Commission shared the burden of administrative efficiency and rapid implementation with the member states. It was granted large administrative powers to manage the program and to harness all local, regional, national, and EU forms of funding available. What was particularly innovative at the time was that (1) a uniform program was implemented across various locales, (2) the Commission engaged directly with local and regional authorities, and (3) it was able to work directly with a single committee of state representatives. Also (4), the Commission monitored and controlled the funding flows to regional and local authorities. In sum, the Commission took a stronger administrative leadership role. It is this new administrative leadership practice of the IMPs that led to the first partnership programs, which are called today multilevel governance and which form the core administrative system of regional policy (Commission of the European Communities, 1986). The assumption behind those policies was that local and regional authorities, as well as states, could learn from each other, that they could learn to work together better, and that they should implement systems of management that allow them to assess their success.

The successful experience with the IMPs and a positive review of the ERDF led the member states to agree that the Commission should take leadership toward organizing regional policy. Hence, the late 1980s marked a turning point: the Single European Act reasserted the importance of the "economic and social cohesion" of the EU, and the idea that regional policy should simply provide an annual reimbursement of existing member state projects was abandoned, given that this state-based system had clearly not worked in achieving balanced development across the EU member states.

The new and radical idea was that the EU needed a policy that would bring together regional authorities, member states, and the Commission to work in partnership on diverse regional strategies of development. The assumption was that broad, territorially grounded, multilevel partnerships would serve rich and poor regions equally well and would allow them to rally all the forces necessary for their development. In brief, the new goal was to organize regional development work, based on coordination and cooperation with member states and the Commission.

It was not until 1975 that EU member states genuinely started thinking about regional disparities and implementing a regional policy to address regional imbalances. Until 1988, the discussion focused on funding state-level development programs. Regional policy basically financed parts of state infrastructure programs, which were based on state-level priorities, which were not (or only modestly) influenced by local authorities or the Commission. Those policies were regional only in name; in practice, they were national-level structural development policies with a regional focus. Note that across other EU policies, such as agriculture (Chapter 11) or social policies (Chapter 10), the financing practices were similar. Thus, the EU institutions and policies at the time served primarily the member states' intergovernmental agendas. However, the IMPs introduced a new mode of administration in which member states shared decisions with, and delegated administrative powers to, the Commission. This enhanced the role of the Commission and local authorities; it was the first exception to strict state control (and hence to the principle of intergovernmentalism), while asserting the EU's economic legitimacy and mixed economic agenda.

### The Institutionalization of Cohesion Policy (1988–1993)

By 1988, all building blocks for the reform of regional policy were in place: regional policy formally became "cohesion policy." It was instituted by a regulation agreed upon by member states in the **Council** on June 24, 1988. The Commission restructured the structural funds (ERDF and ESF), reframing the funding amounts and periods to implement four general principles of administration (see Box 13.2), and five geographic priorities (called "objectives").

While some of the objectives focused on the poorest regions and were clearly linked to regional/territorial strategies, others covered the whole EU and focused on long-term and youth unemployment, and the transformation of rural areas. Importantly, though, most of the funding was placed in the objectives that related to the poorest regions: Objective 1, which focused on the development and structural adjustment of the regions whose

**Box 13.2**   The Commission's four general programming principles, 1988–1993

1. Funds are focused on the poorest people and regions (concentration).
2. Funding is organized in multiannual programs of activities that require sound public policy, analysis, planning, implementation, and evaluation (programming).
3. Member states, their regions and other local governments, and the Commission have to work together in the implementation of the policy (partnership).
4. European funds can come only in addition to state funding (additionality).

development was lagging behind, represented 64 per cent of the overall funding; the prime beneficiaries were Spain, Italy, Portugal, Greece, and Ireland. Selected regions in France, Germany, and the United Kingdom, in particular Northern Ireland, were also eligible. In all, about 87 million people or 25 per cent of the EU population lived in those regions. Objective 2 focused on regions seriously affected by industrial decline; it was designed to support job creation and help small and medium-sized businesses; the principal beneficiaries were the United Kingdom, Spain, France, and to a much smaller degree all other member states except Greece, Ireland, and Portugal. In all, about 57 million people lived in those regions. The other objectives, with a smaller share of the budget, focused on combating long-term unemployment, the occupational integration of young people, adjustment to agricultural reforms, and the development of rural areas.

Over the period 1988–93, the overall budget of the cohesion policy grew every year from €6.4 billion in 1989 to €20.5 billion in 1993; this represented an expansion from 16 per cent to 31 per cent of the total annual EU budget. The cohesion policy primarily targeted 39 regions of the 12 EU member states. Later evaluations of those policies show that the GDP per capita of those regions increased from 68.3 per cent to 74.5 per cent of the EU average, while EU funding helped create 600,000 jobs, with investments in 500,000 small and medium-sized businesses, and training or retraining of about one million individuals. Twenty-five per cent of the funding was focused on research and innovation and 30 per cent on combating climate change (European Commission, 2008a).

Clearly, this policy had to do with solidarity, the redistribution of wealth, and wealth creation. The fundamental policy assumption was that solidarity between rich and poor regions in the EU worked, diminishing economic imbalances and disparities while increasing regional involvement in policy-making processes, which also strengthened the role of the Commission. The Commission became the vector of development, and led all programs of cooperation—a clear erosion of states' intergovernmental agenda in favour of the Union. The primary breakthrough idea was the realization that there was a "geography of the EU" that was greater than the sum of all the member states, and that the EU regions made up a crucial part of this new geography. When the Commission started working on answering fundamental questions that arose from that realization, it was able to identify (1) which regions were most in need and (2) what their development issues were. In sum, there was a pan-European rediscovery of the regions of Europe; partners from inside and outside government, across local, regional, state, and EU levels started working together with a focus on regional issues.

### From 12 to 15: The Maastricht Treaty (1993–1999)

At Maastricht on February 7, 1992, the member states signed the **Treaty on European Union (TEU)**. The treaty came into force on November 1, 1993. It bolstered the cohesion policy in three ways. First, it created the Cohesion Fund, a new structural fund aimed at member states whose GNI per inhabitant was less than 90 per cent of the EU average. The Cohesion Fund was launched for a first generation of programs with a multiannual budget of €168 billion for the period 1994–99. Second, in response to growing demands from regional actors involved in EU policies, the **Maastricht Treaty** created a new institution called the Committee of the Regions to review and express opinions on all legislation that impacts local and regional authorities (about 75 per cent of all new legislation), to bridge EU-level decisions and citizens' concerns, and to give voice to local and regional issues in Brussels. Third, the Maastricht Treaty introduced the so-called subsidiarity principle. Defined in Article 5 TEU this principle specifies that the EU does not take action (except in the areas that fall within its exclusive competence), unless it is more effective than action taken at national, regional, or local level. Enshrined into the treaty, this principle compels governments across the EU to make policy closest to citizens.

On March 30, 1994, Austria, Finland, Sweden, and Norway, signed the **accession treaty**. All four countries held referendums; Norway's was not successful, with only 47.8 per cent of the votes in favour, and subsequently withdrew its candidacy. The economic impact of the three new members was limited, because they represented only about 6.3 per cent of the population of the EU15 and about 6.5 per cent of the EU GDP (in other words, they were a little richer than the EU average). However, they were very large countries with relatively small populations; indeed, they increased the land mass of the EU by about 35 per cent, nearly 900,000 square kilometres. Regional development issues in their very sparsely populated areas, particularly in the north (European Commission, 2008a), led to the amendment of regulations that defined a new funding objective favouring the regions with extremely low population density in Finland and Sweden and set a financial allocation for the three new member states. In other words, regional policies were modified yet again to accommodate concerns raised by EU enlargement, this time in favour of sparsely populated northern regions. This resulted in further side payments and an overall increase of the cohesion policy budget.

Later evaluations of the cohesion policy between 1994 and 1999 show that the GDP per capita of the main recipient states increased by anywhere from 1.3 per cent (Northern Ireland) to 4.7 per cent (Portugal), while the policy helped create 1,267,000 jobs, with investments in 800,000 small and medium-sized businesses, and the building of 4,104 kilometres of highways and 31,844 kilometres of roads (European Commission, 2008a).

## From 15 to 25: Making Enlargement a Success (2000–2006)

The end of the 1990s is particularly interesting because of the EU's eastern expansion, with 10 former members of the Eastern bloc working toward accession. This period marked a new turn in cohesion policy. The challenge of this new enlargement was to bring into the EU 20 per cent more population and 18 per cent more land mass, but only 5 per cent additional GDP: these countries were much poorer than the EU average. Also, they had a much lower proportion of actively employed population (56 per cent versus 64 per cent). In brief, with a GDP below 50 per cent of the EU average, these were the poorest countries of the EU, and this aggravated regional imbalances and raised a new challenge to the cohesion policy.

One of the core challenges was the transposition of the Cohesion Fund to those new countries; this impacted a large number of older EU member states, who as a result became net contributors to the EU annual budget for the first time. For this reason, the cohesion policy was once again thoroughly scrutinized, because it was clear that it would benefit new member states much more than older ones, whose regions would no longer be eligible. This result was not an unintended consequence of the accession policy, but a deliberate consequence of the goal of EU enlargement policy that was very clear from the beginning of the accession negotiations. Nevertheless, this situation constituted a test of solidarity that upset some governments (for instance the UK), but in the end it was successfully resolved with the decision to increase cohesion policy funding once again. Since the eastern enlargement, nearly 170 million EU citizens, one in three, live in the poorest regions—a tremendous challenge of solidarity and cohesion. Economic imbalances across the EU have never been greater. The per capita income in Central London, UK, is 290 per cent of the EU average, yet in northeastern Romania it is 23 per cent of the EU average.

To cope with this challenge, the cohesion policy budget for 2000–6 was increased to €213 billion (32 per cent of the EU budget), with €22 billion dedicated to the new member states. The six "concentration principles" for regional funding shifted back to three: Objective 1 still focused on regions whose development was lagging behind, Objective 2 supported regions faced with economic and social conversion, and Objective 3 focused on education, training, and employment. It is notable that the resulting program was as ambitious and as well funded as the post–World War II Marshall Plan—which demonstrates that the EU's commitment to the principle of a mixed economy was still going strong.

Over the period 2000–6, 0.4 per cent of the total EU GDP was invested in European regions, thanks to the cohesion policy. The policy targeted 271 regions in 25 EU member states. Later evaluations of those policies document that the GDP of recipient regions grew from 66 per cent of the EU average in 2000 to 71 per cent in 2006; the policy also contributed to the creation of 1,400,000 jobs in nearly one million businesses. In all, 230,000 small and medium-sized businesses received aid. Also, 20 million people were connected to main water systems, and 23 million were given access to wastewater treatment. The Cohesion Fund contributed to the construction of 1,200 kilometres of high-speed rails and funded 38,000 research and development projects (European Commission, 2008a).

The turn of the millennium marked, in a way, the end of an era and a new beginning for the EU's cohesion policy. By the end of 2006, the cohesion policy linked European actors from the public, private, and non-profit sectors in organized regional networks of policy-making that worked at both the local and regional levels while also integrating national and European priorities. The administration of the policies required more rigour and professionalism in the management of partnership and programming, and in particular the financial control of additionality. For this purpose, member states and regional authorities worked on "single programming documents." The networks of partnership were well understood as multi-partner, public-private, and non-profit-sector partnerships spanning various levels of government: they formed multilevel governance partnerships that designed and funded programs together, and in doing so defined the priorities of their locale and work, using pan-European management and evaluation standards.

## At 27 Members: The World's Largest Development Program (2007–2013)

In 2006, the **European Council** agreed to a seven-year budget, for the 2007–13 period, that contributed €347 billion (3.7 per cent of annual EU GDP) to cohesion policy, a clear increase to about 35 per cent of the annual EU budget. Eighty-six per cent of these funds were dedicated to "convergence" regions—these regions are where the poorest third of EU citizens live. The GDP per capita of those regions is lower than 75 per cent of the EU average. The three objectives for this funding period were defined as follows.

Objective 1 targeted 84 regions in 17 member states, a population of 170 million people. This included entire countries such as Bulgaria, the Czech Republic, Estonia, Greece, Cyprus, Latvia, Lithuania, Hungary, Malta, Poland, Portugal, Romania, Slovenia, and Slovakia. The total amount of funding available was €282.8 billion for the funding period. This objective focused on economic growth, targeting innovation, the knowledge-based economy, and adaptability to social change as vectors of success.

Objective 2 focused on 168 regions in 19 countries, or about 314 million Europeans. All the regions of a few countries were eligible (Bulgaria, Estonia, Latvia, Lithuania, Malta, Poland, Romania, and Slovenia), and a few specific regions in the wealthiest member states (France, Germany, Italy, Spain, and the United Kingdom) also had access to this objective. The goal was to enhance the attractiveness and competitiveness of those regions to business investors, in particular to promote the development of the infrastructure necessary to the information-communication society and the knowledge economy, and to increase job creation. Policies falling under this objective increased investment in human capital to foster innovation and entrepreneurship and also contributed funds to environmentally friendly ventures.

Objective 3 expanded on the idea of regional partnership networks by setting up the European Territorial Cooperation Policy, which encourages the formation of partnership networks across regions, across nations, and across borderlands. This new objective was concerned with 13 transborder areas or about 182 million Europeans. The funds were available only to regions within 150 kilometres of a border, whereas transnational cooperation and interregional cooperation included a vast grouping of regions across member states in the northern periphery, the Baltic Sea, the Northwest, the North Sea, the Alpine space, Central Europe, the Atlantic coast, the Southwest, the Mediterranean, Southeast

Europe, and included regions in the Caribbean, the Indian Ocean and the Atlantic Ocean. The goal of the European Territorial Cooperation objective was to strengthen cross-border cooperation at the local and regional levels, but also across pan-European networks of cooperation, to bring out exchanges of experiences leading to integration and regional development.

Interestingly, these three new objectives marked a priority shift. First, 86 per cent of all Objective 1 funds, or €282.4 billion, were earmarked for convergence regions (those whose GDP was less than 75 per cent of the EU average). Also, 25 per cent of all the funds were allocated to research and innovation and a further 30 per cent to climate change and environmental infrastructure—the highest funding level in the history of the cohesion policy for these policies, alongside job creation. As it was tying all three policy goals together, the Commission changed its cohesion policy strategy in a fundamental way. The new approach moved away from simply helping structurally backward regions, toward a policy of countering lagging development and promoting competitiveness and employment while leveraging both innovative and environmentally friendly policies for the purpose of job creation. This change in thinking is also visible in **Europe 2020**, the EU's 10-year growth strategy adopted in 2010, which states that the goal of the cohesion policy is "smart, sustainable and inclusive growth" (European Commission, 2010a).

In sum, the new structure of cohesion policy agreed upon in 2006 constituted a breakthrough that went beyond any previous cohesion policy reforms since the creation of the ERDF: while maintaining the fundamental principle of solidarity, it enshrined the ideas of smart, sustainable, and inclusive growth in the cohesion policy. But this was not all. Indeed, multilevel governance also faced reforms. Since 2007 the Commission has worked to persuade local authorities to develop integrated territorial approaches that link development policies into horizontal and vertical multilevel governance partnerships, with the goal of breaking through the traditional silos of policy coordination. The policy instruments take the forms of partnership investment and development contracts. These put the policy burden on local/regional-European networks. They are bottom-up networks that articulate local priorities within regional and national strategies as well as the Europe 2020 strategy. They require more policy capacity at the local level and in particular require better and clearer policy goals and measures, where every project, every contract is a self-generating data exercise as well. This approach forces much greater clarity on priorities up front and makes goals explicit.

## The Way Forward: Cohesion Policy in an EU of 28 Member States (2014–2020)

These new directions are confirmed in the cohesion policy program for the 2014–20 funding period. For this period, the cohesion policy budget amounts to €367 billion; if one includes leveraged member state contributions, it is expected to reach over €500 billion (European Commission, 2013b). The policy reasserts that goals need to be smart, inclusive, and sustainable, and they need to deliver growth and jobs in the EU's now 274 regions. As initiated in the previous agenda, the policy's centrepiece is its focus on enhanced local-regional partnership and governance methods that articulate both national and European goals. The policy now has 11 objectives, which fall into three broad categories, relating to innovation, **sustainability**, and social inclusion (see Table 13.1). The policy is designed to be data generating and result oriented, and it implements financial requirements. Also, it allocates nearly €100 billion toward specific growth sectors (innovation and research, digital agenda, support for small and medium-sized businesses, and the low-carbon economy). While the cohesion policy remains a redistributive policy, its character is no longer primarily defined

**Box 13.3**   Key elements of the cohesion policy, 2014–2020

1. Appropriate levels of investment (regions with GDP below 75 per cent of the EU average still receive most funds).
2. Targeted growth (€100 billion go to growth sectors and cities).
3. Accountability and results (local, regional, and national goals have to be clear and measurable—projects must be data generating).
4. Preconditions for funding (certain preconditions are mandatory, such as specific environmental laws).
5. Coordinated action (the "common strategic framework" provides the basis for funding coordination).
6. Simplification of procedures (less red tape and more measurable policy goals).
7. Expanded urban dimension (urban centres have earmarked funds).
8. Cross-border cooperation (cross-border projects enhanced).
9. Consistency and coherence (regional projects have to be coherent with national reform programs that are now part of the European Semester, see Chapter 7).
10. Financial instruments (target small and medium-sized businesses).

**Table 13.1**   Objectives of cohesion policy, 2014–2020

| Main focus | Innovation | Sustainability | Social inclusion |
|---|---|---|---|
| Objectives | 1. Strengthening research, technological development, and innovation | 5. Promoting climate change adaptation, risk prevention, and management | 8. Promoting sustainable and quality employment and supporting labour mobility |
| | 2. Enhancing access to, and use and quality of, information and communication technologies | 6. Preserving and protecting the environment and promoting resource efficiency | 9. Promoting social inclusion, combating poverty and any discrimination |
| | 3. Enhancing the competitiveness of small and medium-sized enterprises | 7. Promoting sustainable transport and improving network infrastructures | 10. Investing in education, training, and lifelong learning |
| | 4. Supporting the shift toward a low-carbon economy | | 11. Improving the efficiency of public administration |
| Funding | Investment from the ERDF supports all 11 objectives, but 1–4 are the main priorities. Main priorities for the ESF are Objectives 8–11, though the Fund also supports 1–4. The Cohesion Fund supports Objectives 4–7 and 11. | | |

by redistribution; rather, it has become a much more aggressive development policy that invests in European regions. The shift is both methodological (partnership/governance) and strategic (balancing smart, inclusive, and sustainable goals) (see Box 13.3).

## Debate: Does the Regional Policy Work?

Policies that redistribute funds between different regions are controversial by their very nature—not only in the EU but also at the state level (see Box 13.4 for a discussion of Canada). In the EU, regional policy has faced a barrage of questions and criticisms from various fronts, including academics and policymakers. These criticisms centre on the ongoing, and unresolved, issues regarding the policy's socio-economic impact and policy influence. There are two broad strands of criticisms: some suggest that the methods used feed into domestic, national policies and do not address local and regional issues

**Box 13.4**    Regional policy and multilevel governance in Canada

In Canada, regional policies exist as well but are understood from fundamentally different perspectives; they use a different vocabulary, and the ensuing debates are distinctively Canadian. Most importantly, the issue of redistributing resources between regions is framed almost exclusively in terms of federal-provincial intergovernmental relations. Canadian provinces have been fighting for greater power since World War II, and Quebec has advocated independence at times. Yet the federal government has maintained unity and inter-provincial equalization, which means that richer provinces pay for provincial programs in poorer provinces. Another aspect that makes regional policy in Canada distinctive is that relations between the provincial and federal governments are more competitive than collaborative. At the same time, a high degree of integration of the bureaucratic elite leads to active networking practices that counterbalance these competitive trends and allow for mechanisms of accommodation, or compromise, to be worked out. This results in partnerships (so-called collaborative **federalism**) that lead to economic development policies which link federal, provincial, and local governments.

A particularly important issue of multilevel governance in Canada is the role of municipalities. Historically, the relations of municipalities to provincial governments were unequal. Beginning in the first half of the twentieth century, and despite the 1849 Baldwin Act that gave municipal governments in Ontario important autonomy, provinces across Canada progressively restricted the autonomy of municipalities. The existence of municipalities was not (and still is not) guaranteed under the Canadian constitution, which left provincial governments free to create, modify, or destroy any and all units of local government. This statutory aspect of municipalities was important because it suggested that municipal governments were subordinate to provincial authorities. Today, federal-provincial-local political processes are made up of complex systems of relations; they have led to the understanding that municipalities—especially large cities—are not entirely subordinate. Political, cultural, demographic, and economic factors have encouraged the formation of entrepreneurial municipal coalitions, which benefit from the support of both provincial government largesse and local groups, allowing large municipalities to gain autonomy. For instance Toronto, the largest and richest city in the country, has its own City Act under Ontario law. Smaller municipalities, by contrast, are increasingly under provincial supervision.

effectively, while many others criticize them with regard to their expected economic and social impacts.

The debate about the success of EU regional policy first focused on the impact of the policy for the period 1989–99. Contributions to this debate generally suggest that the policy—in spite of the €247 billion spent between 1989 and 1999—had a number of serious flaws. Some studies suggest that the funds had limited impact (Garcia Mila & McGuire, 2001; De la Fuente & Vives, 1995; Rodríguez Pose & Fratesi, 2004). Others find an impact, but only with a delay (Beugelsdijk & Eijffinger, 2005; Ederveen, de Groot, & Nahuis, 2006). Also, they suggest that positive effects on the development of regions are due primarily to good regional governance and institution-building, rather than EU funding. Finally, there are studies that focus on inter-regional linkages and suggest that these are important and should be enhanced. Dall'erba & Le Gallo (2008), for instance, suggest that EU funds have limited impact on convergence because money targeted at peripheral regions does not spill over to neighbouring regions.

These studies posed a major challenge to the Commission's DG Regional Policy (DGRP). For a long time, the DG's answers were rather weak, but from about 2008–9, the DGRP took these criticisms seriously and addressed them with the development of two macroeconomic models (HERMIN and QUEST) to show that for the period 2000–6, the cumulative the impact of Objective 1 funds on regional GDP, employment, and capital stock was undeniable. The QUEST model shows clear GDP increases; HERMIN shows 819,000 jobs that result from the cohesion policy (European Commission, 2013a).

Also, the DGRP has started collecting and publishing numerical and qualitative indicators to measure the impact of the cohesion policy across the regions of the EU. All in all, it has been able to show that regional policy helps poorer regions to catch up—in particular, that regional policy accelerates growth—and that despite persistent unequal rates of development and growth, the entire EU is better off because of its cohesion policy. Its contributions include better transportation, more roads, railways, airports, and seaports, and also the development of sustainable connectivity policies. The DGRP also points to environmental projects—such as improvements in access to water and wastewater treatment for 20 million people, achieved at the end of 2006—as well as an increase in jobs that results not only from training, education, and research but also from investment in small and medium-sized businesses (European Commission, 2013a). What the DGRP has not been able to explain clearly, though, is why despite funding redistribution to the benefit of poorer regions and general regulatory integration, specific core regions of the EU seem to benefit much more from European integration than peripheral and generally poorer regions.

A number of insights result from these academic and policy debates. Most importantly, we observe that the Commission has increasingly pushed regions to manage policies of regional development across sophisticated partnership networks that are leading to improved local and regional governance. Such networks have to provide effective management systems for multi-year programs, broad stakeholder involvement, monitoring and evaluation, as well as effective implementation of EU legislation. The quality of partnerships turned out to be central to the most successful locally and regionally defined and nationally articulated projects. The mere availability of funding alone was insufficient to ensure the success of projects. Finally, evaluation should be an integral part of the oversight of regional policy, but is also a fundamental part of local, regional, and national partnerships.

The Territorial Agenda for the European Union (TAEU) 2020 is a response to some of those insights and a forward-looking answer to a number of issues identified in the debates about cohesion policy. TAEU 2020 emerged from the inter-institutional agreement between Parliament, Council, and Commission on budget discipline, which also led to a policy review on the four key challenges to the EU: globalization, demographic changes, climate change, and **energy security**. All four challenges are deemed to have impacts on the large regional disparities within the EU.

The answer to these challenges lies in the delivery of the smart, sustainable, and inclusive growth strategy of **Europe 2020**, which is explicitly applied to regional policy in the Commission's fifth report on economic, social, and territorial cohesion (European Commission, 2010b). This report underlines that the Europe 2020 strategy includes territorial cohesion. The strategy promotes competitiveness, convergence and innovation, infrastructure-building, and the strengthening of institutional capacity. Where partnerships are strategically planned, it focuses on quality of monitoring and evaluation of policy and seeks **spillover** across levels of government, because partnerships improve programs.

## Conclusion

The evidence presented in this chapter confirms that the EU's regional/cohesion policy has been driven by two of the three themes that organize this book: the EU is a mixed economic system, where solidarity and inclusiveness matter; and the legitimacy of the European project depends on its economic success. Today, legally enshrined principles of smart, sustainable, and inclusive growth are the foundation of regional policy. The policy started as an intergovernmental agreement between countries on compensation measures to alleviate the uneven spread of costs and benefits of economic integration. From 1975 to 2006, a principle of solidarity was developed, in the form of investments in infrastructures and human resources/job creation. Progressively driven by the Commission, a very effective partnership between local and regional authorities as well as member states was formed. Today, smart, sustainable, and inclusive growth principles drive partnership networks and organize growth bottom-up in architectures of public, private, and non-profit authorities that include national and European priorities; these change the nature of regional/cohesion policy fundamentally because the top-down process that drove funding with the ERDF, the ESF, and Cohesion Fund is altered. Regional policy is bottom-up and puts the onus on local capacity and strategy—it promotes competition for EU resources while requiring a strengthening of institutional capacity locally, including strategic planning, quality of monitoring, and evaluation. It is too early to know whether this strategy will improve EU regional policy.

## References and Further Reading

Allen, D. 1996. "Competition policy: Policing the single market." In *Policy-Making in the European Union*, edited by H. Wallace and W. Wallace, 157–83. Oxford: Oxford University Press.

Bachtler, J., and R. Michie. 1995. "A new era in EU regional policy evaluation? The appraisal of the structural funds." *Regional Studies* 29 (8): 745–51. https://doi.org/10.1080/00343409512331349353.

Bachtler, J., and C. Mendez. 2016. *EU cohesion policy and European integration: The dynamics of EU budget and regional policy reform.* Farnham, UK: Ashgate.

Bachtler, J., and I. Turok, eds. 2013. *The coherence of EU regional policy: Contrasting perspectives on the structural funds.* Philadelphia: J Kingsley Publishers.

Beugelsdijk, M., and S.C.W. Eijffinger. 2005. "The effectiveness of structural policy in the European Union: An empirical analysis for the EU 15 in 1995–2001." *Journal of Common Market Studies* 43 (1): 37–51. https://doi.org/10.1111/j.0021-9886.2005.00545.x.

Commission of the European Communities. 1986. *The integrated Mediterranean programmes.* European File 1/86. Brussels: Directorate for Information, Communication and Culture. http://aei.pitt.edu/14712/1/EUR-FILE-1-86.pdf.

Dall'erba, S., and J. Le Gallo. 2008. "Regional convergence and the impact of European structural funds over 1989–1999: A spatial econometric analysis." *Regional Science* 87 (2): 219–44. https://doi.org/10.1111/j.1435-5957.2008.00184.x.

De la Fuente, A., and X. Vives. 1995. "Infrastructure and education as instruments of regional policy: Evidence from Spain." *Economic Policy* 80: 13–51.

Commission of the European Communities. 1993. *Community structural funds 1994–1999: Revised regulations and comments.* Luxembourg: Office for Official Publications of the European Communities.

European Commission. 2008a. "EU cohesion policy 1988–2008: Investing in Europe's future." *Panorama Quarterly* 26. http://ec.europa.eu/regional_policy/sources/docgener/panorama/pdf/mag26/mag26_en.pdf.

European Commission. 2008b. "Regional policy and enlargement: Moving up a gear through pre-accession funding." *Panorama Quarterly* 27. http://ec.europa. eu/regional_policy/archive/information/panorama/index_en.cfm.

European Commission. 2010a. *Europe 2020: A strategy for smart, sustainable and inclusive growth.* Communication from the Commission, COM (2010) 2020 final. http:// eur-lex.europa.eu/legal-content/en/ALL/?uri=CELEX%3A52010DC2020.

European Commission. 2010b. *Investing in Europe's future: Fifth report on economic, social and territorial cohesion.* Report from the Commission. Luxembourg: Office for Official Publications of the European Communities. http:// ec.europa.eu/regional_policy/sources/docoffic/official/reports/cohesion5/ pdf/5cr_part1_en.pdf..

European Commission. 2013a. "Bringing communities together." *Panorama Quarterly* 45. http://ec.europa.eu/regional_policy/archive/information/panorama/index_en.cfm.

European Commission. 2013b. "Cohesion policy 2014–2020: Momentum builds." *Panorama Quarterly* 48. http://ec.europa.eu/regional_policy/archive/ information/panorama/index_en.cfm.

European Parliament. 1991. "Competition policy and the regions." Strasbourg: European Parliament, Directorate General for Research, Research and Documentation Papers.

Ederveen, S., H. de Groot, and R. Nahuis. 2006. "Fertile soil for structural funds? A panel data analysis of the conditional effectiveness of European cohesion policy." *Kyklos* 59 (1): 17–42. https://doi.org/10.1111/j.1467-6435.2006.00318.x.

Garcia Mila, T., and T. McGuire. 2001. "Do interregional transfers improve the economic performance of poor regions? The case of Spain." *Journal of Common Market Studies* 8 (3): 281–96.

Jeffery, C. 1997. *The regional dimension of the European Union: Toward a third level in Europe.* London: Frank Cass.

McCann, P. 2015. *The regional and urban policy of the European Union: Cohesion, result-orientation and smart specialization.* Cheltenham, UK: Edward Elgar Publishing. https://doi.org/10.4337/9781783479511.

Rodríguez Pose, A., and U. Fratesi. 2004. "Between development and social policies: Impact of structural funds in objective one regions." *Regional Studies* 38 (1): 97–113. https://doi.org/10.1080/0034340031000163226.

Wallace, H., M.A. Pollack, and A.R. Young. 2015. *Policy making in the European Union.* Oxford: Oxford University Press.

## Review Questions

1.  What is the European Regional Development Fund?
2.  What is the European Cohesion Fund?
3.  What country or countries triggered the need for the ERDF and then the Cohesion Fund?
4.  What is multilevel governance in regional policy?
5.  Is regional policy intergovernmental? Why?
6.  Do you think the smart, sustainable, and inclusive growth agenda has relevance for solidarity?

## Exercises

1. How has each of the following set of actors driven regional policy in the EU: member states, regional governments, and the EU institutions? What do the motivations of each set of actors tell us about multilevel governance in the EU?

2. Peruse the European Commission's website on regional policy. Examine the funding levels between countries and over time. Which member states are currently the main beneficiaries of regional policy funds? What variations have occurred over time?

# 14

# European External Trade Policy

VALERIE J. D'ERMAN

## Reader's Guide

This chapter discusses how the European Union (EU) handles trade with non-EU countries. The **Single Market** not only changed how EU members trade with each other, it also affected how the EU engages in trade with countries outside the EU (so-called third countries). The chapter outlines how EU policy competence began in this area and how it has evolved over the years in response to both internal and international developments. Ongoing issues in the area of EU trade revolve around the respective roles and responsibilities of each EU institution, the ongoing pursuit of free-trade agreements with non-EU countries, and the EU's role within the **World Trade Organization (WTO)**.

## Introduction

Trade policy in the European Union (EU) is an area in which the **supranational** level, rather than the national level of individual member states, has authority over policy-making. This chapter outlines the history of how authority in this policy area came to be at the EU level of decision-making. The members of the EU share a Single Market and a single trade policy; this means that when the EU begins trade negotiations with a non-EU country, the **European Commission** acts as the sole negotiator for the entire EU. The authority of the Commission in external trade negotiations raises questions of competencies and representativeness for any student of **European integration**. How did trade policy become delegated to the EU? What role do member states have in discussions and negotiations with external trading partners? How is conflict resolved between the national and supranational levels in debates over trade policy? Are there any parallels between the EU process of trade policy-making and the process of trade policy-making in other large, decentralized countries? This chapter attends to these questions, and discusses the institutional dynamics between EU institutions, member states, and interest groups.

This chapter also examines how EU trade policy affects—and is affected by—international developments. External events, such as the growth of other large markets in Asia, have also influenced the EU's approach to trade policy. The EU is the world's largest trading bloc, accounting for approximately 15 per cent of global trade (Eurostat, 2017). This gives the EU a significant amount of leverage when it participates as a single actor in international trade forums, such as the WTO, where the EU participates with a single voice representing all 28 EU member states. This chapter discusses how the EU has at times used the WTO to further its own international trade agenda, particularly in the areas of investment and **public procurement**. The chapter concludes with a brief discussion of the EU's emphasis on comprehensive free-trade agreements (FTAs) with other countries, including the **Comprehensive Economic and Trade Agreement (CETA)** with Canada and the **Transatlantic Trade and Investment Partnership (TTIP)** with the United States.

## The Evolution of EU Trade Policy

Trade policy refers to how the EU manages trade and investment relations with non-EU countries. It is the exclusive power of the EU, as set out in Article 207 of the **Treaty on the Functioning of the European Union (TFEU)**. "Exclusive power" means that individual member states are not able to independently legislate on trade matters and are not able to conduct individual international trade agreements. The exclusive power of the EU in trade was not conferred all at once, but rather evolved slowly in concert with the EU Single Market and other areas of EU competency, in response to political dynamics from domestic actors, policymakers, and international market forces. The precise boundaries of the EU's exclusive power remain contested. This section of the chapter (1) gives an overview of the history of integration in trade policy, (2) provides a description of the current steps of international treaty-making, and (3) discusses the EU's role in world trade in responding to international pressures.

### EC Common Commercial Policy

Trade as a community policy is emblematic of European integration arising out of the ashes of World War II. The central idea of interdependence among European countries was to make war unthinkable through member states agreeing to share **sovereignty** (Theme 1 of this book). The first steps in integration occurred in coal and steel production and atomic energy. As the integration of defence policy proved too contentious a policy area in early EU history (see Chapter 2), trade instead became a logical step in the process of making war materially unthinkable through economic interdependence.

Trade policy first began with the **Common Commercial Policy (CCP)** in Article 113 of the Treaty Establishing the European Community (TEEC), concluded in Rome in 1957. The newly created **European Economic Community (EEC)** developed a **customs union** among the six original members, for the purpose of removing **tariffs** on goods between EEC members with the stated intention of eventually establishing the full, free movement of goods, persons, capital, and services. The integration of the EEC into a customs union required that the members set common tariffs on goods arriving from non-EEC countries and to develop a community trade policy. This was for the simple reason that maintaining the integrity of the customs union, which required that member states greatly reduce internal barriers to trade through treating internal goods and services as *community* goods and services, needed a common policy for dealing with imports and exports with non-EEC members. During the time period surrounding the **Treaty of Rome**, commercial policy mostly attended to production and trade in industrial products (such as raw materials or manufacturing materials), with the Common External Tariff (CET). As the customs union extended to different areas (such as manufactured products and other types of goods), so did the CCP, in order to match the internal process of liberalization with common external action (EUR-Lex, 2000).

Before 1970, EEC members coordinated their activities with non-EEC members individually according to CET rules. An important exception to this took place with the EEC's participation as a single actor in the Kennedy Round of the General Agreement on Tariffs and Trade (GATT). The precursor to the WTO, the GATT provided a major international stage upon which the EEC began to interact in trade negotiations as a single bloc. As of January 1970, individual EEC members no longer coordinated their own activities; instead, decision-making within the **Council** concerning the CCP was made through **qualified majority voting (QMV)**. The **Court of Justice of the European Union (CJEU)**, then still called European Court of Justice (ECJ) (see Chapter 4), extended the scope of Article 113 in 1978 by stating that the article as written should not be interpreted as an exhaustive list, and that the CCP should be extended to areas beyond traditional trade. In doing this, the CJEU gave room to interpret community trade policy more liberally and to react more fluidly to changing trade situations, rather than having each new trade item become an issue of competence between the EU and member states (EUR-Lex, 2000).

During the early years of the EEC, the CCP made little distinction between trade with developed and developing countries in terms of the rules concerning general trade policy, but it did give special considerations to the former colonies, territories, and countries associated with EEC members. The period of decolonization during the 1960s brought about by political developments in Africa and elsewhere, combined with the first **enlargement** of the EEC in 1973 to include Denmark, Ireland, and the United Kingdom, greatly increased the number of countries receiving special considerations. Over time, both the enlargement of European integration and the increase of trading relationships around the world has shifted the relationships with trade partners around the world.

Aside from the CET and the preferential trading arrangements extended to certain developing countries, additional limitations to the EEC's ability to further a common trade policy were the rise of new economic protectionism in the 1970s and the slow pace of European integration. Economic stagnation and inflation during the 1970s prompted the EEC to introduce common policies such as **anti-dumping**, a tariff imposed on foreign imports priced below fair market value; and safeguard provisions, which allowed EEC members to temporarily restrict imports of a product in order to protect a specific domestic industry. What is more, European integration proceeded only slowly in the 1970s. Despite the EEC's original intent to complete the free movement of goods, services, labour, and capital in 12 years—which would have been 1969, dating from the signing of the Treaty of Rome (EEC Treaty)—the 1980s arrived without a complete single European market, and with many remaining barriers to both internal and external trade.

### Trade Policy and the Single Market

The completion of the Single Market through the Single European Act and the **Maastricht Treaty** made for important new institutional developments in EU trade policies. These were visible in voting procedures, the role of the EP, and the role of the Commission. First, a central change to the EU's external trade policy in the run-up to the completion of the Single Market was the shift in voting method within the **Council of the EU** from mostly unanimous voting (which effectively gave each member a veto) to mostly qualified majority voting. Some parts of the CCP—such as the area of services—remained under unanimous voting, but these, too, were gradually subject to QMV. Second, the Council and the Commission were now required to exchange information and consult with the EP at several stages throughout the decision-making process in trade agreements. In some instances of EU trade decisions, the EP was now also able to give (or withhold) "assent" by a simple majority. Third, the role of the Commission in EU trade policy was strengthened. A single EU market needed a single representative for the rest of the world, in particular with regard to international trade dynamics. Accordingly, the EU's member states began negotiating as one through the European Commission whenever the EU engaged in external trade affairs. Motivation for these changes came in part from the need to create a cohesive Single Market, and in part from a gradual shift of preferences from some member states and European businesses toward export-oriented interests (Young & Peterson, 2013). This was most visible when the legal personality of the European Communities (**Pillar** I under the 1993 Maastricht Treaty) gained membership in the WTO as a single actor (Meunier & Nicolaïdis, 1999).

Internally, the Single Market created more trade within the EU without any significant evidence of "trade diversion," that is to say, negative impacts on trade with non-EU countries. Externally, the EU Single Market contributed to momentum among developed nations to attend to deeper international trade liberalization. The GATT had made a great deal of progress since its establishment in 1947 toward reducing tariffs and other barriers to trade. As international trade moved beyond goods alone and began to include the exchange of services, ideas, and other non-tangible goods, and as other barriers to trade (such as environmental or health safeguards) began to take more prominence, the GATT became reinstitutionalized as the WTO in 1995. The timing of the EU Single Market, as finalized in the signing of the 1992 **Treaty on European Union (TEU)** at Maastricht, was a significant development for international trade at large. First, the Single Market created a powerful example of how trade in tangible and non-tangible goods could be liberalized according to the rule of law. Second, the Single Market created a very strong preferential trade agreement among EU members during a time of rising competition from Asian markets. These factors helped pressure other large, non-EU markets to consider deeper trade liberalization worldwide (Young & Peterson, 2013).

## The Lisbon Treaty and Europe 2020

The **Lisbon Treaty**, as noted in Chapter 4, made some sizeable changes in amending the TEU and the TEC, which is now the Treaty on the Functioning of the European Union (TFEU). Relevant to international trade, the consolidation of the prior three-pillar system into the single legal personality of the European Union meant that the EU as a whole gained membership in the WTO right after the Treaty of Lisbon was brought into force in 2009 (see Box 14.1).

The Lisbon Treaty introduced three main changes for EU trade policy: increased powers for the EU in negotiating international trade agreements, greater powers for the EP in trade policy, and QMV for almost all trade issues. First, the Lisbon Treaty created a solid legal basis for the EU as a whole

**Box 14.1**    Timeline of significant events in EU trade policy

- 1958* Treaty of Rome
  - Common Commercial Policy (CCP), Article 113, establishing trade as a supranational competency; Common External Tariff (CET)
  - EC becomes a single member of GATT, the precursor to the WTO.
- 1970 Council switched to joint decision-making for CCP through qualified majority voting.
- 1978 European Court of Justice (now the CJEU) ruling that Article 113 was not an exhaustive list, and thus that the CCP could be extended beyond areas of traditional trade.
- 1987* Single European Act (establishing completion of Single Market by 1992).
- 1993* Treaty on European Union (Maastricht).
  - Completion of EU Single Market for goods, services, people, and capital creates need for more elaborate CET to include services.
- 1995 EC becomes a member of WTO (World Trade Organization).
- 2009* Lisbon Treaty allows EU to adopt autonomous acts on trade.
  - EU becomes WTO member as a single legal personality.
  - Official launch of Comprehensive Economic and Trade Agreement (CETA) negotiations between Canada and the EU.
- 2013 Launching of negotiations between the EU and the US under TTIP (Transatlantic Trade and Investment Partnership).
- 2014 Conclusion of CETA negotiations.
- 2016 Signing of CETA.

*Date refers to the year in which the agreement came into force.*

to adopt autonomous acts on trade. "Autonomous" in this sense meant that the EU was able to negotiate and implement trade agreements on behalf of the entire union (at the time 27, now 28, member states). As well, the single legal personality of the EU now meant that the EU held trade authority for all areas of trade covered by the commercial aspects of the Single Market. This now included trade in services, **intellectual property**, and **foreign direct investment (FDI)**. In some cases, trade in protected services—such as cultural, audiovisual, educational, and social services—were also included under EU trade autonomy, although with the potential to be negotiated under different internal voting rules in the Council.

Second, the increased powers of the **European Parliament** under the Treaty of Lisbon meant that the EP became a full co-legislator with the Council on trade matters, using the new **ordinary legislative procedure (OLP)** (see Chapter 3). The EP is thus able to give all international trade activities a high degree of parliamentary scrutiny, as the Commission must transmit all documents and report regularly to the EP during trade negotiations. Once negotiations have concluded, all trade agreements have to be approved and ratified by the EP. As part of its budgetary powers, the EP also has a say on EU spending on trade policy (see Box 14.2).

Third, with the Lisbon Treaty, the Council now used qualified majority voting under the OLP. The relevance to EU trade policy is that almost all aspects of trade policy that fall under the exclusive competence of the EU are now decided upon by a qualified majority. However, in some particular areas of trade, unanimous voting is still required. Trade in areas that affect culturally sensitive goods or services, such as audiovisual services linked to the cultural and linguistic properties of different regions of the EU, must be subject to unanimous voting. This requirement is similar to laws in existence in Canada that concern Canadian content in national audiovisual broadcasting services, which exist in part to protect Canadian heritage and language. Furthermore, any trade in politically sensitive areas relating to social, educational, or health services might require unanimous voting, in order to prevent impeding the ability of national organizations to deliver these services (European Commission, 2009).

The **Europe 2020** strategy was introduced in 2010 by the Commission as a 10-year strategy geared toward advancing the economy of the EU with

**Box 14.2**  What does the EU spend on trade?

The budget title "Trade" in the EU budget included payments of €105,566 million in 2016, the great majority of which—€90,410 million—was allocated to administration (staff, buildings, communication technology, etc.). Only €15,150 million was allocated to trade policy, *inter alia* for legal advice, dispute settlement costs, conferences and training measures, communication policies, as well as support for trade policies of developing countries.

Source: Adopted budget for 2016, *Official Journal of the European Union*, L 48, February 24, 2016, 1285–94

"**smart, sustainable and inclusive growth**." While the targets and initiatives of Europe 2020 are not focused on trade policy specifically, the broad goal of economic legitimacy directly relates to some key areas of trade policy. In particular, the **Directorate-General (DG)** for Trade of the European Commission identified that open trade would benefit EU growth by boosting foreign demand for goods and services, giving EU consumers access to a wider variety of goods at lower prices and allowing EU companies to use FDI to increase their competitiveness internationally and to create more jobs both at home and abroad. The DG for Trade also identified that reaping the potential benefits of open international trade required a "spirit of reciprocity" and adherence to international rules (EUR-Lex, 2011). Since the launch of the WTO's Doha Round in 2001, the EU has been a central actor pushing for fair trading practices in many areas, most visibly the liberalization of public procurement and fair access to raw materials. In this regard, the EU's experience in designing, implementing, and constantly amending its own Single Market of 28 member states has given it strong international credibility for playing a dominant role in the formation of international trade rules.

### From Negotiation to Ratification

The process of achieving a trade agreement between the EU and a non-EU country first begins with the decision of whether to even consider a preferential agreement with the party in question. The Commission is in regular contact with the Council of the EU and the European Parliament about trade policy. Before any negotiations with a third country can begin, the Commission first holds a public consultation on the topic and conducts an assessment on the impact of any such deal on the EU and on the other country. At the same time, the Commission undertakes a "scoping" exercise on the country: it begins an informal dialogue with the country in question to ascertain what the range of issues in a trade agreement might look like and whether those issues are compatible with the EU's trade policy. Should both the public consultation and the scoping exercise prove fruitful, the Commission then requests formal authorization from the Council to begin negotiations within the guidelines of specific negotiating **directives**, which set out the objectives of a potential agreement. The Council then has the authority to discuss the negotiating directives and to suggest changes. Once the Council has approved and adopted the negotiating directives, the Commission is then able to proceed with negotiations (European Commission, 2013).

The process of negotiations depends to some extent on the depth of the deal proposed and the country the EU is negotiating with. These factors affect the size of the EU team involved in the dialogue, the length of the process, and the overarching objectives through the negotiations. The over-arching objectives of negotiations are broad in scope and also vary according to the agreement being proposed: free-trade agreements with developed countries are driven by economic gains, while agreements with less-developed countries aim primarily at supporting development (European Commission, 2013). The so-called second-generation agreements—agreements in which areas of trade go beyond basic reductions of tariffs and duties to include services and investment, and to provide for environmental safeguards and labour laws—are likely to necessitate more rounds of negotiation.

Once all topics (usually referred to as "chapters") under negotiations are "closed," meaning negotiations have successfully concluded, and the Council has been informed, finalized texts of the entire negotiating process are sent to the European Parliament and to each of the member states. At this stage, the texts undergo a "legal scrubbing"—which can take up to a year—a process where lawyers check for accuracy and consistency, but do not introduce any new substantive issues. The EU trade commissioner and the equivalent representative of the other party will then initial the "scrubbed" text; at this point, no new substantive issues can be introduced into the agreement, and the document can be made available to the public. The agreement is then translated into all official languages of the EU and of the other country (European Commission, 2013). The Council also legally screens the texts and holds internal debate on the final document before giving authorization for the agreement to be signed. The substance of the topics in the document may require the Council and the Parliament to pass additional legislative proposals, such as an area of an agreement that pertains to trade in services (European Commission, 2013).

Depending on the context of the trade texts, the agreement will either be approved as falling under the "exclusive competence" of the EU, or as a "mixed agreement" which partially falls into the shared competence of the member states. Articles 3 and 216 of the TFEU specify the external competencies of the EU and the areas in which the EU has the authority to conclude international agreements. Should the agreement meet the criteria of "exclusive competence," and after the Council gives final authorization, the agreement will be formally signed by the EU (usually by the European commissioner for trade) and by the other country. The agreement is then transmitted to the EP for consent, which must take place in a plenary session. However, if the agreement contains provisions that also fall under the responsibility of member states—an example here could be the provision of some liberalized trade of health care services—the agreement is "mixed" between the levels, and all EU member states will also need to sign and ratify the agreement before the EP can give formal consent (EUR-Lex, 2010).

After consent by all parties, the Council formally concludes the agreement by adopting the final decision. The decision is then published in the Official Journal of the EU, or EUR-Lex, becoming a legal act binding the EU. The agreement itself will come into force on a set date specified by both parties, or it will have a series of dates that different provisions of the agreement will adhere to accordingly; for example, some tariffs may be reduced gradually, or some areas of sectoral liberalization may occur in a specific order.

The case of CETA illustrates the difference between EU trade agreements that are the "exclusive" competence of the EU and those that are "mixed agreements" between the EU level and national levels. In the Commission's legal opinion, CETA's provisions fell into the legal category of EU-exclusive competence, and as such, ought to have required signing and ratification by the EP and EU trade ministers only. However, not all member states agreed with this assessment, and following the political climate of **Brexit**, the Commission decided to proceed with CETA as a mixed agreement, in order to appease a general political unease with Brussels at the time (European Commission, 2016b). This decision extended the process of approval and made it a more contentious process, as the new requirement of ratification by all national parliaments within the EU (as well as regional parliaments in some member states) opened up political space for local protest. This process was most visible in the Belgian region of Wallonia, which initially rejected CETA by the established signing deadline. Last-minute amendments to address protections for farmers and questions of foreign investors reversed the Wallonian rejection, and CETA was officially signed on October 30, 2016. This event provides an example of how political actors and societal interests can drive and shape the form of an EU trade agreement. At this stage, CETA is now "provisionally" in force, but still requires the full parliamentary ratification of the EP and all national and regional parliaments in Europe. The "mixed" competency of CETA demonstrates the political nuances of trade dynamics within the entire European Union.

## The EU and the World

While all EU member states have individual membership in the WTO, the EU itself also holds membership. As the EU is a Single Market, with a single tariff and an autonomous trade policy, the EU—through the European Commission—represents all EU member states at nearly all WTO meetings. This single representation is significant because the ability of the EU to have its own WTO membership, and speak with one voice, affords the EU greater leverage in WTO meetings and allows EU countries to further their shared interests. As the world's largest trading bloc, the EU as a whole is more competitive in international deliberations than the member states would be if they each participated independently (see Figure 14.1).

The EU has exercised its power in the WTO by pushing for stronger multilateral international trade rules. Its ability to do so comes from the size and strength of the EU market, as well as the precedent that the Single Market offers: in many areas of market integration, the EU provides a rare example of countries voluntarily opening up competition to each other, guided by rules and laws. One particular area of the EU's role in the WTO is in the WTO's "Agreement on Government Procurement." Procurement, which refers to public purchasing of goods and services, is a very large source of spending worldwide. The EU's own successes in liberalizing public procurement within its Single Market have had a significant influence on the design of the WTO procurement agreement. Many WTO efforts toward liberalizing procurement internationally have followed the EU's own directives on procurement in the areas of services and public works. The ability of the EU to influence the behaviour of the WTO suggests the strength of its global economic presence and its capacity as a trade entrepreneur (García, 2013).

The protracted period of the multilateral WTO Doha Round has resulted in many countries pursuing independent trade agreements,

**Figure 14.1** World trade in goods and services (2014; US $ billions)

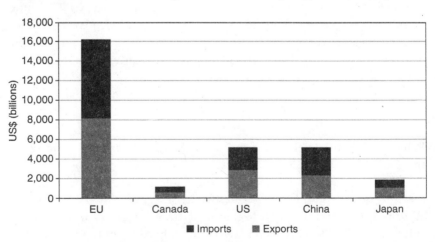

Source: European Commission (2014)

in order to create areas of "preferential" free trade between two or more countries. The EU has preferential-trade agreements or association agreements in place with numerous other countries around the world, including South Africa (2000), South Korea (2012), and Colombia (2012). CETA is the agreement in place between Canada and the EU that was adopted in October 2016. CETA negotiations began in 2007 and concluded in 2013, and the legal "scrubbing" (see above) of the final text took over a year after negotiations ended. CETA represents a notable achievement for both the EU and Canada, as it is the first major preferential-trade agreement that the EU has negotiated with a large, industrialized, developed country. As well, it also presents an example of a "second-generation" free-trade agreement. CETA's provisions extend well beyond the removal of tariffs to the liberalization of areas such as services, investment, procurement, and intellectual property (Young, 2016). For these reasons, the CETA negotiations were a very visible and political process in Canada. Some concerns raised during negotiations came from Canadian groups attached to the dairy industry, municipalities, and intellectual property proponents. However, the EU represents Canada's second-largest trading partner, and having access to the EU Single Market created powerful incentives for many Canadian businesses and consumers. Because of the inclusion of "second-generation" areas of trade, some of which directly affect local municipalities and businesses, Canadian provinces participated directly in CETA negotiations—a new precedent in Canada's international trade dynamics (see Box 14.3).

Similar to CETA, but much larger in scope, is the Transatlantic Trade and Investment Partnership (TTIP) between the EU and the United States. Whereas the CETA deliberations were not very newsworthy in EU member states during negotiations with Canada, TTIP has proven to be a much more political, controversial, and visible process. This salience is explained in part by economics—Canada is only the EU's 12th-largest trading partner, whereas the US is the EU's first trade partner for exports and second partner for imports, which greatly increases the risks and benefits of a potential agreement. Talks on TTIP began in 2013 but stalled after Donald Trump was elected US president; if and when TTIP negotiations conclude successfully, the EU and the US would represent the largest free-trade zone, comprising the two biggest markets, in the entire world. This would contribute to the EU's ability to influence world trade rules and to project its values globally (European Commission, 2016a).

Brexit, the United Kingdom's June 2016 referendum vote on leaving the EU, could potentially complicate the completion and implementation of the EU's various in-progress FTAs (see Chapter 7). Although (at the time

**Box 14.3**    Trade policy decision-making in Canada and the EU, compared

How do provincial-federal dynamics in Canada compare to the dynamics between member states and the Commission in the EU in the area of international trade? Generally speaking, there are a number of parallels between the two systems. Although the EU is not a federal state, it has many of the characteristics of a federal system. Its overlapping features makes comparisons with other federal states possible. Canada is a federal country that has a relatively large amount of decentralization. In both the EU and Canada, trade matters concerning customs, tariffs, and international agreements are the responsibility of the highest governmental level. Just as the EU Commission has the sole authority to initiate free-trade proceedings and conduct negotiations, the Canadian federal government in Ottawa holds this same power. For the EU, this is the Commission DG for Trade, and in Canada this is Global Affairs Canada. Furthermore, the president of the EU Commission makes the final decision on international trade agreements, as is the case in Canada where the prime minister has a similar power. However, given these similarities and despite the fact that Canada is a single country whereas the EU is a supranational polity of 28 member states, trade policy competences are actually significantly *more* centralized in the EU than in Canada. This is due to the level of integration of the EU's Single Market. There are fewer barriers to goods flowing freely between EU member states than there are between Canadian provinces and territories (see Chapter 7); as a result, the EU-level has more capability to negotiate trade deals as one cohesive Single Market. Trade policy is a prominent example of how the EU itself is much more than an international organization, even though it cannot meet the definition of a full federation (Theme 2 of this book).

In the EU context, individual member states have a role in trade policy through the Council of the EU. Although the Commission represents the EU during trade negotiations, the Council must first authorize the opening of negotiations and is later responsible for signing the agreement on behalf of the EU and adopting the final decision through which a trade agreement becomes law. In Canada, the Canadian Constitution limits the role of the provinces to merely an advisory one during international trade negotiations. However, recent trade agreements—such as CETA or the WTO Agreement on Government Procurement—have required provincial participation and consent, due to the nature of issues covered under "second-generation" treaties. Before opening CETA negotiations in 2009, the EU insisted that Canadian provinces be included in the negotiation process, in order to systematize a role for provinces that would both parallel internal EU trade dynamics and ostensibly reduce the possibility of last-minute regional protest (D'Erman, 2016). Involving provinces in this way has set a precedent that has made Canadian provinces more active members in international trade negotiations. It is unclear, however, to what extent this precedent may be repeated.

of writing) the process of Brexit has yet to be finalized, and what the UK's specific relationship to the EU might look like is unknown, both CETA and TTIP were negotiated with the fact of UK membership in the EU. Although Canada has done far more business with the UK than the rest of the EU in the past, part of the rationale for CETA was to create new market opportunities for Canadian businesses in parts of Europe where it lacks prior trading relationships. In this sense, Brexit should not affect the goal of CETA for either Canada or the EU. However, the CETA deal and the event of Brexit interact in two other notable arenas. First, the relationship between Canada and the EU under CETA might provide a possible template for UK–EU market relations in the future, depending on how Brexit unfolds. Second, the sentiments of Brexit might have echoes in other parts of the EU, as evidenced by the last-minute objections to CETA raised by the region of Wallonia in Belgium in October 2016. The "mixed-agreement" format of CETA (see above) makes CETA vulnerable to regional issues and societal interests with the trade agreement during the final national parliamentary ratification process.

## Debate: Issues with EU Trade Policies

While the EU Common Commercial Policy provides a strong and durable example of the achievements of European integration, there remain debates over the benefits and drawbacks of free trade (see Box 14.4), as well as about the specifics of EU trade policy. This section summarizes three specific issues. First, the exclusive competence of the EU institutions in managing trade for the entire bloc has on occasion chafed with national interests. Second, the position of the EU as the most powerful trading bloc in the world brings into question what *kind* of power the EU ought to be. Third, the actual substance of recent bilateral "second-generation" free-trade agreements has generated controversy in a number of EU members and EU interest groups.

**Box 14.4**   Benefits and costs of free trade: A critical viewpoint

Theoretically, free trade enriches all trading partners through the logic of comparative advantage. This means each country ought to specialize at producing/exporting what it is good at so that all trade partners will benefit from economic efficiency by trading their specialized goods with each other. However, the practical realities of mobile capital and unequal trading partners bolster the argument of national economic protectionism. Critiques of free trade highlight three important considerations. First, a rising GDP from free trade does not equal an increase in the material quality of life for all citizens or a reduction in income inequality. Second, the factors of production (capital and labour) are rarely mobile, making the theory of comparative advantage illusory. Third, the efficiency of free trade has negative consequences for the environment, social conditions, and **sustainability** of resources.

Inside the EU, the Single Market still contains barriers to completely free trade, particularly in the area of services. These barriers are the result of member states arguing for protectionism on the basis of cultural specificity, employment, and provision of social services. Critics of the EU's approach to trade liberalization—both internally in the Single Market and externally with other countries—argue that the EU's push for trade liberalization promotes economic efficiency and aggregate growth at the cost of local industry and natural resources.

These controversies have been most visible with some of the provisions (or lack of) in CETA and TTIP on **Investor State Dispute Settlement (ISDS)** mechanisms, intellectual property, and public procurement.

The common commercial policy, which governs EU trade policy, is the most prominent EU policy to have been under supranational competence from the very beginning of the EEC in the Treaty of Rome, yet this does not mean it is without debate (Meunier & Nicolaïdis, 2006). Meunier (2005) states that the EU external trade policy over time reflects a premium on efficiency in international bargaining over the impulse to protect national sovereignty. The strengthening of the European Parliament in the Lisbon Treaty has helped increase the legitimacy of the EU in many policy areas, including trade deals, but has not entirely removed tensions to do with delegation to supranational authority. One key example of this tension was the discussions over whether CETA should be ratified as falling under the EU's exclusive competence or as a mixed agreement. They revealed disagreements between the European

Commission and some key member states over the precise boundaries of the EU's exclusive competence. The CJEU clarified in May 2017 that all trade agreements, including ISDS provisions, must be ratified as mixed agreements. The debate over competency in many ways reflects ongoing debates about the legitimacy of European integration (Theme 3 of this book). EU trade policy provides a coherent response to the economic pressures of globalization, but—as the case of Wallonia during the signing of CETA illustrates—it faces criticisms of legitimacy and regional democratic input.

The size and strength of the EU market, combined with its role as the most powerful trading bloc in the world, gives the EU an enormous amount of leverage in shaping the multilateral rules of international trade. How the EU chooses to exercise that leverage, however, is not always clear or consistent (Meunier & Nicolaïdis, 2006). Different member state governments within the EU hold very different views on how to wield such power through trade; for example, whether the EU should concentrate on negotiating solely in its own market interest versus whether it should expend energy on shaping the entire multilateral framework. This dilemma is visible in the area of agriculture, an area of trade where the EU has been notoriously protectionist (see Chapter 12), despite its long-term commitment to using trade as a tool for economic development in less wealthy countries. This tension is also somewhat visible in the EU's surge in bilateral agreements with non-EU actors, despite the EU's advocacy of **multilateralism** as the primary recommended framework for international trade, although it could be argued that bilateral agreements serve as an indirect method of spreading multilateral norms.

Some of the newer areas of trade contained in both CETA and TTIP have proven to be very controversial for a variety of actors in European societies. ISDS mechanisms are temporary committees set up to help resolve disputes between foreign investors and states when there is a disagreement over investor rights. The draft CETA contained provisions for an ISDS system that followed precedents found in many other international agreements. However, once TTIP discussions began, many states and citizens in the EU objected strongly to the ISDS system proposed in both CETA and TTIP. The central concern has been that in neither agreement have national rights in environmental and labour regulations been given enough protections with regard to foreign investors. The resulting compromise in CETA has been to establish a permanent (rather than ad hoc) investment court with a tribunal to hear appeals. Intellectual property (IP) was a contentious issue during CETA negotiations primarily because of pharmaceuticals and copyright standards. The EU demanded extended patents on prescription drugs, to match what all other G8 countries (with the exception of Canada) provided for pharmaceutical research. Although this demand was met, it has triggered concerns in Canada that pharmaceutical costs will soar. The EU also demanded strict copyright provisions; these demands were softened as Canada passed the C-11 Copyright Modernization Act in early 2012. Public procurement—the purchasing of goods and services by public entities—was a long-standing issue with CETA and is likely to become one with TTIP. The EU demanded access to Canada's full procurement market, including provinces and municipalities. As procurement is often used as a tool to support local economies, there was widespread protest among Canadian municipalities. The result in CETA's final text was that Canada's municipal market would be open to EU bids, but with certain thresholds for spending in different sectors; conversely, Canadian bids have the same level of access to the EU procurement market as EU members have themselves, reinforcing the idea that internal EU market integration is matched by external actions. Whether the same level of procurement access will be included in TTIP remains to be seen.

## Conclusion

Trade policy in the EU is one of the longest-running policy areas for which the EEC, EC, and later EU have had **supranational** competence. Initially developed as a means to set common tariffs in accordance with the early customs union, it has since evolved into a near full delegation of authority to the EU institutions to set the terms of external trade with non-EU actors on behalf of the Single Market, and for the Commission to represent all 28 member states in international trade forums such as the WTO. Nevertheless, having supranational competence over trade policy has not prevented national interests from exercising their opposition on key issues, as the case of the signing and ratification of CETA demonstrates. In general, the pace of external EU actions on trade has matched the internal integration of the Single Market, with the result that a great deal of autonomy has been conferred on the supranational level—the strengthening of the EP is a qualification on this autonomy. Finally, the size of the Single Market and the actions of the EU internationally suggest that the EU has become a formidable trading power within the WTO and elsewhere, with the ability to create new norms and multilateral standards.

## References and Further Reading

D'Erman, V. 2016. "Comparative intergovernmental politics: CETA negotiations between Canada and the EU." *Politics and Governance* 4 (3): 90–9. https://doi.org/10.17645/pag.v4i3.565.

EUR-Lex. 2000. *Common commercial policy.* Summaries of EU legislation. http://eur-lex.europa.eu/legal-content/EN/TXT/?uri=LEGISSUM:a20000.

EUR-Lex. 2010. *International agreements and the EU's external competences.* Summaries of EU legislation. http://eur-lex.europa.eu/legal-content/EN/TXT/?uri=LEGISSUM:ai0034.

EUR-Lex. 2011. *Trade policy serving the Europe 2020 strategy.* Summaries of EU legislation. http://eur-lex.europa.eu/legal-content/EN/TXT/?uri=LEGISSUM:em0043.

European Commission (DG Development). 1995. *Trade relations between the European Union and the developing countries.* Luxembourg: Office for Official Publications of the European Communities.

European Commission (DG Trade). 2009. *Treaty of Lisbon enters into force—Implications for the EU's trade policy.* http://trade.ec.europa.eu/doclib/press/index.cfm?id=493.

European Commission (DG Trade). 2013. *Trade negotiations step by step.* http://trade.ec.europa.eu/doclib/docs/2012/june/tradoc_149616.pdf.

European Commission (DG Trade). 2014. *EU position in world trade.* http://ec.europa.eu/trade/policy/eu-position-in-world-trade/.

European Commission (DG Trade). 2016a. *About TTIP.* http://ec.europa.eu/trade/policy/in-focus/ttip/about-ttip/.

European Commission. 2016b. *European Commission proposes signature and conclusion of EU-Canada trade deal.* Press Release. http://europa.eu/rapid/press-release_IP-16-2371_en.htm.

Eurostat. 2017. *International trade in goods.* http://ec.europa.eu/eurostat/statistics-explained/index.php/International_trade_in_goods.

Fafard, P., and P. Leblond. 2013. "Closing the deal: What role for the provinces in the final stages of the CETA negotiations?" *International Journal* 68 (4): 553–59. https://doi.org/10.1177/0020702013509319.

García, M. 2013. "From idealism to realism? EU preferential trade agreement policy." *Journal of Contemporary European Research* 9 (4): 521–41.

Meunier, S. 2005. *Trading voices.* Princeton, NJ: Princeton University Press.

Meunier, S. 2007. "Managing globalisation: The EU in international trade negotiations." *Journal of Common Market Studies* 45 (4): 905–26. https://doi.org/10.1111/j.1468-5965.2007.00753.x.

Meunier, S., and K. Nicolaïdis. 1999. "Who speaks for Europe? The delegation of trade authority in the EU." *Journal of Common Market Studies* 37 (3): 477–501. https://doi.org/10.1111/1468-5965.00174.

Meunier, S., and K. Nicolaïdis. 2006. "The European Union as a conflicted trade power." *Journal of European Public Policy* 13 (6): 906–25. https://doi.org/10.1080/13501760600838623.

Smith, M. 2001. "The European Union's commercial policy: Between coherence and fragmentation." *Journal of European Public Policy* 8 (5): 787–802. https://doi.org/10.1080/13501760110083518.

Verdun, A. 2014. "Federalism in the EU and Canada." In *Understanding federalism and federation,* edited by A.G. Gagnon, S. Keil, and S. Mueller, 233–43. New York: Routledge.

Young, A.R. 2016. "Not your parents' trade politics: The Transatlantic Trade and Investment Partnership negotiations." *Review of International Political Economy* 23 (3): 345–78. https://doi.org/10.1080/09692290.2016.1150316.

Young, A.R., and J. Peterson. 2013. "'We care about you, but…': The politics of EU trade policy and development." *Cambridge Review of International Affairs* 26 (3): 497–518. https://doi.org/10.1080/09557571.2012.734782.

## Review Questions

1.  The Lisbon Treaty increased the authority of the European Parliament in shaping the trade policies of the EU. What is the value added of the new role of the EP?
2.  What role do international and non-EU actors have in shaping EU trade policy?
3.  Why does the EU have a single voice in the WTO?
4.  Why has CETA been difficult to approve?
5.  What are some of the areas in "second-generation" trade agreements?

## Exercises

1.  Collect information on CJEU opinions and rulings on the EU's ability to conclude free-trade agreements. What legal precedence is there for EU exclusive competence? What is the substance of the arguments against that competence, and when should trade agreements be approved as "mixed agreements"?
2.  CETA is the EU's first free-trade agreement with a wealthy, industrialized democracy. Undertake some research on other EU free-trade agreements already completed. What issues of negotiation are different with CETA?

# 15

# Enlargement

CHARLES C. PENTLAND

## Reader's Guide

Since its foundation, the European Union has grown from six to 28 members,
with more applicants at the door. Along the way, **enlargement** has evolved
from a series of distinct diplomatic episodes to a process integrated and consistent with EU institutions and governance. Often seen as a cumulative **foreign
policy** success reflecting the allure of the integration project, enlargement has
wrought change not only in applicants but also in the EU itself. Its future is
jeopardized by major EU crises, political instability both national and regional,
and rising concern that enlargement has been too much of a good thing.

## Introduction

States, like people, are attracted to successful groups and often seek to join
them. In turn, groups of states—global organizations such as the United
Nations (UN) or regional bodies such as the European Union (EU)—tend
to welcome others who share their goals and offer economic, geopolitical, and other assets. It is therefore not surprising that, from the 1960s on,
the early success and promise of the six-member **European Economic
Community (EEC)** (the forerunner of the EU) began to attract applicants from among its European neighbours. They were drawn to a project
of regional integration—neither a traditional international organization nor
a new federation—aiming to build a European zone of peace through an
innovative political-economic strategy (Themes 1 and 2 of this book).

Since 1961, when the United Kingdom first applied to join the EEC,
that organization and its successors have almost continuously—and often
simultaneously—been eyeing prospective applicants, negotiating with candidates for admission, and accommodating new members. Map 1.1 in this
book shows the EU's current member states as well as the states that are
currently recognized as candidates for membership. But while enlargement
is often cited as testimony to the magnetism of the European project, it has
rarely proceeded without controversy. A chronic concern has been whether
expansion will undermine the project's capacity to achieve its economic and
political aims at home and abroad. Mindful of that debate, among others, this

chapter describes the organization's growth from six to 28 members and the role of its main institutions in managing the enlargement process. It reviews discussions about the pros, cons, and consequences of expansion—past, present, and future.

## The First Three Enlargements

The enlargements of 1973, the 1980s, and 1995 expanded the **European integration** project from six to 15 members. Each was a discrete episode involving a distinctive cluster of applicants in unique historical circumstances. Each was viewed as a constructive interruption of the members' linear progress toward economic integration. Each aided the growth of common norms and practices to govern anticipated future enlargements (see Box 15.1).

### The United Kingdom, Ireland, and Denmark

In the 1960s, the opportunity to expand the six-member EEC arose from a historic change in British thinking about Europe. The United Kingdom had stepped away from the 1955–57 negotiations that produced the EEC, continuing to favour its ties with the Commonwealth, its "special relationship" with the US, and global trade liberalization. In 1960, it formed the **European Free Trade Association (EFTA)** with six other like-minded but smaller states as an alternative to the EEC. Within a year, however, the UK, along with two other EFTA members (Denmark and Norway) and the Republic of Ireland had begun negotiations for admission to the EEC.

Why this dramatic shift? First, contrary to British expectations, the EEC was surging ahead, propelled by rapid economic growth, while Britain's economy was languishing. Second, Britain's attempt to lure the EEC's members into a broader, EFTA-based free-trade system had failed. Its government thus concluded that the future lay with the markets of continental Europe, and that access and influence required joining the EEC as a full member. The Irish, two-thirds of whose trade was with the UK, decided to follow, as did the Danes and Norwegians.

The negotiations between the UK and the EEC largely determined the fate of the other three applicants. Talks soon became bogged down over sensitive issues such as agriculture, Commonwealth trade preferences, and the budget. Underlying these was a fundamental divide over the nature of the European project. The British and their companions were skeptical about grand schemes for an "ever-closer union" among Europeans, suspicious of a federalist agenda, regional protectionism, and potential rivalry with the US. Moreover, as a great power, the UK saw itself less as a supplicant than as an

**Box 15.1**    Enlargement: The basics

### Definition

For international organizations, the common-sense understanding of enlargement is the admission of one or more sovereign states as new members. Strictly speaking, the European Community was also enlarged in 1990 when German reunification embraced the territory and people of the former German Democratic Republic. Resolving a major **Cold War** issue, this was, however, an exceptional enlargement, different in purpose and process from those discussed in this chapter.

### Treaty Provisions: Rome and Lisbon

Article 237 of the Treaty Establishing the European Economic Community, the **Treaty of Rome** (1957), stated, "Any European state may apply to become a member of the Community." After obtaining the Commission's opinion, the Council had to decide unanimously if the application was to be accepted. The terms agreed upon in the negotiations and embodied in an **accession treaty** then had to be ratified by the applicant and all member states. These remained the core guidelines for the process up to and including the 1995 enlargement.

The experience of the eastern enlargement (1993–2007) influenced the revised provisions on enlargement incorporated in the Treaty of Lisbon (2009). Article 49 of the **Treaty on European Union (TEU)** states that any European state that "respects the values referred to in Article 2 and is committed to promoting them may apply to become a member of the Union." (Article 2 lists civic and moral values considered fundamental to the EU and "prevailing in the societies of all member states.") The accession process described in Article 49 resembles that in the Treaty of Rome, but adds the requirement of majority approval by the **European Parliament** and refers to "conditions of eligibility" determined by the **European Council**.

equal to the EEC, able to demand significant concessions at the bargaining table. Beneath the technical details of the negotiations lurked a growing French-British standoff, culminating in President de Gaulle's televised "veto" of the UK's application in January 1963.

In 1967 a second de Gaulle veto ended a brief revival of negotiations, but in 1970 new governments in both London and Paris generated a change of climate. French President Georges Pompidou signalled openness to UK membership and the Conservative government under Edward Heath responded. The other three applicants followed, and negotiations resumed. While the issues were familiar, circumstances had changed. The EEC was thriving: it initiated a **customs union** 18 months ahead of schedule, as well as free movement of labour and agreement on the **Common Agricultural Policy (CAP**; see Chapters 7 and 11). The UK economy, meanwhile, was stagnant, which weakened its bargaining position. Negotiations remained tough, but it was clear that Britain could no longer expect significant changes in EEC goals, policies, and institutions. Agreement was finally reached in 1972.

The four applicants signed accession agreements with the EEC, but only three were ratified: Britain's by Parliament, Denmark's and Ireland's by referendums and their national parliaments. In Norway's referendum, intense opposition from farmers and fishers defeated the agreement. On January 1, 1973, the EEC therefore admitted three new members. Five-year transition periods were set up for them to align themselves gradually with the tariff provisions of the customs union, the CAP, free movement of labour, and other EU policies, laws, and institutions.

Not only was the first enlargement prolonged and difficult, but its conclusion in 1973 proved less than final. The economic crisis of the 1970s stalled much of the EEC's agenda for Economic and Monetary Union, and Britain and Denmark witnessed growing skepticism about the European project. In 1974 Labour returned to power in the UK, promising a referendum on whether to stay in the EEC. With the government campaigning to stay, having won some minor concessions from Brussels, British voters agreed by a two-thirds majority to remain a member.

The United Kingdom, however, remained an "awkward partner" (George, 1994). After almost a decade of negotiations, it was granted a rebate on its contributions to the EU budget in 1984. Three decades later, in June 2016, a surge of **Euroskepticism**, especially in his own party, led Prime Minister David Cameron to put the choice of leaving or remaining in the EU to a referendum. A narrow and largely unexpected win by the "leave" side led the British government to begin formally negotiating its withdrawal from the EU (or **Brexit**).

## The Southern Enlargement

In the mid-1970s, three less-developed Southern European states applied to join what was by then called the European Community (EC). This second enlargement was, in many respects, different from the first, more akin to the eastern enlargement that would take place 20 years later. It saw the emergence of **conditionality** (the practice of tying membership to the fulfillment of explicit conditions) and the extended the use of transition periods, and it confirmed that in negotiations most of the concessions would be made by the candidates.

Greece had signed an association agreement with the EEC in 1961, which included trade concessions, development assistance, and the prospect of eventual membership. In 1967, however, the military seized power in Athens and the EC froze most components of its relations with Greece. Nevertheless, when the colonels' regime fell in 1974 and relations with Brussels resumed, Greece remained in a favourable position. It applied for membership in July 1975 and, despite the Commission's caution, negotiations began a year later. These were concluded in 1979, and Greece became the 10th member of the EC in 1981.

Negotiations with Portugal and Spain started later and took longer. Both countries had been under authoritarian rule since the 1930s, and had limited relations with the EC; both had recent trade agreements, and Portugal was a member of EFTA. They were less familiar than Greece with the EC and less prepared for complex negotiations with it. In both countries, the collapse of an authoritarian regime was followed by two years of political instability and uncertainty.

In Portugal, the crisis was resolved by elections in July 1976. The following March, the new democratic government in Lisbon filed its application for EC membership. Negotiations ran from October 1978 to June 1985. In Spain, a difficult political transition following the death of Generalissimo Franco ended with the election of a democratic government in June 1977. An application to the EC followed swiftly and, with a favourable opinion from the Commission, negotiations commenced in February 1979. Running almost parallel to those with Portugal, they resulted in a simultaneous accession on January 1, 1986.

All three southern candidates presented similar profiles. Economically, they were underdeveloped compared to most of the EC member states, with large agricultural sectors, outdated industries, and high unemployment. Politically, they were new and fragile democracies, with deep internal divisions and untested institutions. Strategically, the Mediterranean region seemed increasingly sensitive, given its proximity to the Middle East and North Africa. Common themes in all three negotiations reflected this, among them agriculture, textiles, labour migration, fisheries, and regional aid. While the interests of the three applicants were broadly similar, the nine EC members did not always agree on the issues.

In the end, the political and strategic arguments for enlargement prevailed over the economic reservations of some member states. Despite their concerns about agriculture, France and Italy welcomed the "rebalancing" of the EC through the admission of states sharing their Latin cultures. While sensitive to the increased financial burden, EC members welcomed democracy and stability on Europe's southern flank, along with a responsibility to legitimize and otherwise support political reform. All parties embraced the use of transition periods (five, seven, or 10 years) to ease their adjustment to the terms of accession. With membership at 12, however, some were already asking whether the EC would be "wider but weaker" (Wallace, 1976).

## The EFTA Enlargement

Within five years of the southern enlargement, new requests for EC membership arrived—from Turkey in 1987 and from Cyprus and Malta in 1990. These were temporarily shelved as the end of the Cold War brought a wave of new demands for admission. Initially, these came from four of the remaining members of the EFTA—Austria, Sweden, Finland, and Norway. The first three, geopolitically neutral but with close economic and cultural ties to the West, had remained outside the EC during the Cold War. They were now free to reinterpret their neutrality. Norway was a member of the North Atlantic Treaty Organization (NATO). All four governments wished to enhance their access to EC markets with a seat at the Brussels table, where decisions affecting them were being made.

These wealthy, stable democracies were, as potential net contributors to the EC's budget, a welcome change from some previous candidates. Denmark supported its three Nordic neighbours, while Germany backed Austria. Although the negotiations raised a few difficult issues, they were brief compared to their precursors. Reservations tended to be found more in the candidates than in the EC.

As in previous cases, the accession processes for the individual applicants were separate, although running roughly in parallel, similar in substance, and concluding (except for one) with admission on the same date. Austria applied first (in July 1989), followed by Sweden (July 1991), Finland (March 1992), and Norway (November 1992). All four negotiations concluded in the spring of 1994. Their relative brevity reflected the fact that many barriers had already been removed through existing economic agreements between EFTA members and the EC. All four candidates then sought ratification of their accession treaties by referendum. Three succeeded, while—in a repeat of 1972—the combination of fish, farming, and oil defeated the accession treaty in Norway. Austria, Finland, and Sweden joined what was by then the EU on January 1, 1995, bringing its total membership to 15.

## The EU Looks Eastward

The EU's biggest enlargement saw it admit eight countries in Central and Eastern Europe (CEE) plus Cyprus and Malta in 2004, and two more former Soviet-bloc countries in 2007, bringing its membership to 27 (see Box 15.2). Formally initiated by the Copenhagen summit of 1993, this process differed from its predecessors in at least three respects. The first was scale—there were 13 candidates. As 12 of them (all but Turkey) negotiated entry between 1996 and 2007, the prospect of so many states—mostly small and relatively poor—entering the EU escalated the "wider but weaker" debate.

Second, if the Union was indeed reaching the upper limits of membership, its institutions might become overburdened. Increased diversity, while otherwise admirable, could hinder effectiveness. Major institutional reforms to the ways in which decisions were made and budgets allocated would thus be needed if enlargement was to proceed, and succeed.

Third, this accession process went further than its predecessors in imposing on each candidate the full burden of adjustment. Each had to incorporate into its legislation the full *acquis communautaire* (see Box 15.3). Doing so required that it engage in negotiations covering 31 areas of policy ("chapters" in EU jargon). Given that most candidates perceived the EU as their only real option, Brussels held a strong hand.

The Copenhagen summit was a belated response to Europe's post–Cold War political realities. The CEE countries, newly free to chart their own course, were demanding access to Western institutions on a combination of moral and prudential grounds. The moral claim was that the West should

---

**Box 15.2**    Enlargement timeline

| | |
|---|---|
| 1958 | Founding members: Belgium, France, Italy, Luxembourg, the Netherlands, West Germany |
| 1973 | Denmark, Ireland, United Kingdom |
| 1981 | Greece |
| 1986 | Portugal, Spain |
| 1995 | Austria, Finland, Sweden |
| 2004 | Estonia, Latvia, Lithuania, Czech Republic, Hungary, Poland, Slovakia, Slovenia, Cyprus, Malta |
| 2007 | Bulgaria, Romania |
| 2013 | Croatia |

**Box 15.3**   Conditionality and enlargement

## Conditionality

This term refers to the obligation of applicant states to adopt the EU's legal, administrative, economic, and political standards, embodied in the *acquis communautaire* and summarized since 1993 in the **Copenhagen Criteria**. Conditionality was first applied by the EC in the 1970s during enlargement negotiations with Greece, Portugal, and Spain. In a more structured form, it became central to the negotiations for the 1993–2007 eastern enlargement. It is the governing principle of the preparatory partnerships—European Partnership Agreements (EPAs) and Associate Partnerships (APs)—and Stabilization and Association Agreements (SAAs).

## The Copenhagen Criteria

Emerging from the 1993 Copenhagen summit initiating the eastern enlargement, these criteria summarize the standards and expectations to be met by all applicants: first, stable institutions that guarantee democracy, the rule of law, human rights, and respect for minorities; second, a functioning market economy and the capacity to cope with competition and market forces in the EU; third, the will and ability to assume the aims and obligations of EU membership as represented by the *acquis communautaire*.

## The *acquis communautaire*

This term refers to EU treaties, legal principles, legislation, declarations and resolutions, case law, and international agreements, incorporated in over 100,000 pages of documents, which applicants must commit to adopting and applying. The *acquis* illustrates the essential asymmetry of accession negotiations, which require most reforms and adjustments to be made by the applicant, in exchange for modest concessions by the EU. Success in assimilating the *acquis* leads to the big prize—membership.

## Chapters

Chapters are categories of the *acquis*—30 to 35 in number—corresponding to the main policy areas of the EU. Chapters provide the framework for accession negotiations. Each is opened as the applicant's preparation meets the Commission's approval. Negotiations then proceed, often involving several chapters in parallel. When the Commission is satisfied that the applicant has met EU standards in that policy field, it recommends to the Council that the chapter be closed. Some chapters are settled quickly; others can take years and may even be "frozen" for political reasons. Accession cannot proceed until all are closed.

deliver on promises it had made to encourage those struggling against Soviet domination. The prudential argument was that an eastward extension of Western institutions would promote prosperity and security, the best guarantee against a reversion to anarchy or domination. Preoccupied with internal developments and unsure how to respond to these pressures, Brussels had initially offered trade agreements with no mention of eventual membership. By 1993, however, it recognized that it had to act more creatively.

At Copenhagen, the EU laid down six conditions that applicants would have to meet before being admitted. In time, these became condensed into three Copenhagen Criteria (see Box 15.3). Not officially part of this triad, but no less real, was a concern for the EU's capacity to absorb new members while maintaining the momentum of European integration. This condition, clearly beyond the control of the candidates, reflected some EU members' anxieties about the unprecedented scale of this enlargement.

From 1993 until late 1996, the EU received applications from 10 CEE states—the three Baltic states (Estonia, Latvia, and Lithuania), four Central European states (Poland, Hungary, the Czech Republic, and Slovakia), and three Balkan states (Slovenia, Romania, and Bulgaria). Combined with the applications received earlier from Turkey, Cyprus, and Malta, this promised a large and complex agenda. Such a throng of applicants would be difficult to manage unless the Copenhagen Criteria could be translated into specific, objective, and measurable indices of progress. Furthermore, the EU could no longer avoid the matter of reforming itself.

The issue of enlargement dominated EU decision-making in the late 1990s and early 2000s. Two major reforms aimed to adapt EU institutions to a larger number of member states: the Treaties of Amsterdam (signed in 1997) and Nice (signed in 2000). Various European Council summits adjusted the EU's enlargement strategy. In 1997, applicants were divided into two tiers of six states each according to their progress and prospects to date, with Turkey omitted for the moment. Two years later, at Helsinki, this two-tier strategy was replaced by a "regatta" in which applicants would cross the finish line individually or in clusters as they fulfilled the EU's criteria.

The EU also made peace with Turkey, whose outrage at having been set aside was creating problems in NATO and over Cyprus. It was formally accepted as a candidate, with an appropriate "to do" list, although no date was set for the opening of negotiations. From early 2000 on, the applicants made rapid, if uneven, progress in their 12 parallel accession talks. The EU was determined to bring the accession negotiations to a successful conclusion by the end of 2002 so that the new members could take part in the European Parliament elections of 2004. A final push led to agreement at a 2003 summit in Athens that 10 of the 12 would be admitted in May 2004. Bulgaria and Romania followed in 2007. As in previous enlargements, transition periods were negotiated, notably for phasing in CAP payments to the new members (10 years) and for restricting free movement of labour (maximum of seven years). Bulgaria and Romania were subject to post-admission monitoring by the Commission concerning issues of judicial reform, corruption, and organized crime, under the so-called Cooperation and Verification Mechanism.

## Managing Enlargement: From Improvisation to Governance

In the succession of enlargements described above, norms, institutions, and procedures developed as member states responded to demands for admission. By the late 1990s, enlargement had become institutionally embedded as a distinct field of EU policy.

In this field, the **intergovernmental** institutions—European Council, **Council of the EU**—provide a framework in which member states, as the ultimate arbiters of enlargement, exercise power and pursue their interests, but those institutions are also actors in their own right. The **supranational** institutions—Commission, European Parliament—exhibit a similar duality: each is a political arena in which national and EU-level forces are in play, but also an actor whose collective positions carry weight, based on technical and political legitimacy.

### Intergovernmental Institutions and Actors

The role of the European Council—the regular summits of the heads of state or government—in framing enlargement strategy, overseeing negotiations, and deciding on their outcomes, underlines the formally intergovernmental character of this policy area. In 1961, when Britain's application initiated the first enlargement, it was already accepted that, as Article 237 of the Treaty of Rome (EEC Treaty) indicated, the matter would be managed by the governments of the six original members and ultimately decided by **consensus**. Any doubts about this were removed by President de Gaulle's vetoes in 1963 and 1967. Although the other five governments opposed these unilateral actions, they accepted the premise that for enlargement to proceed, all members had to be on side.

The inauguration of the European Council as a regular EC practice coincided in the mid-1970s with the southern enlargement. These summit meetings oversaw negotiations and provided a venue for the occasional high-level decision, while the Council of Ministers (now Council of the EU) managed things between summits. In assessing and pronouncing on the state of negotiations at various stages, and in formally marking their conclusion, the European Council legitimized the process and the outcome.

The eastern enlargement showed the degree to which the summits had solidified their role in defining the strategy, managing the process, and endorsing its results. The Copenhagen summit of 1993 confirmed the decision of the then 12 member states to invite applications from the CEE countries, laid down the track along which the negotiations should proceed, and set out the standards all applicants would have to meet. Subsequent European Councils made important decisions, differentiating among **candidate states** with respect to commencing accession talks and assessing their progress. Another Copenhagen summit in 2002 formalized the conclusion that 10 of the 12 candidates had met the requirements of membership. The accession treaty, signed in Athens, required ratification by the candidates and all 15 members.

In between the meetings of the European Council, the member states manage the enlargement process at the ministerial level through the Council of the EU and at the "deputy" level though their ambassadors to the EU, who constitute the **Committee of Permanent Representatives (COREPER)**. Ministers or deputies meet to deliberate on reports or opinions from the Commission and to develop the EU's collective negotiating position.

The **Lisbon Treaty** created two versions of the Council in which enlargement issues may be discussed. The **General Affairs Council (GAC)** is chaired by the member state holding the Council's six-month rotating presidency. While broad issues related to enlargement can be discussed there, specific issues related to negotiations over the chapters tend to surface in the more focused configurations of the Council—agriculture ministers, for example. And while the presidency can help provide continuity, it is limited by the brevity of its term.

The Foreign Affairs Council consists of foreign ministers or their deputies and is chaired by the High Representative for Foreign Affairs and Security

Policy. This helps resolve an institutional problem peculiar to enlargement: unlike most other EU policy areas, enlargement is not managed at the national level by a dedicated governmental department. Instead, that task has usually been assumed by the foreign ministry, partly because of enlargement's proximity to foreign policy, partly because of its comprehensive content. Foreign ministers meeting as the Foreign Affairs Council with the High Representative—who is also a member of the Commission—thus provide continuity and intergovernmental oversight of accession negotiations. This matters because accession negotiations are essentially a set of continuing, parallel intergovernmental meetings involving each individual applicant, the Commission, and all the member states.

### Supranational Institutions and Actors

The Commission plays a vital part in enlargement, based on the provisions of the Rome and Lisbon Treaties and on its general power to propose policy. The Commission's findings from its extensive investigation of each applicant, embodied in a formal opinion presented to the Council, are critical in determining whether and when accession talks might begin. During negotiations, the Commission provides the Council with a continuous flow of information and evaluations. It issues annual reports on the progress of each candidate, including estimates of when some chapters should be opened for negotiations and others might be closed. In effect, the Commission keeps a scorecard for each candidate; its findings provide ammunition for the member states and incentives to the applicants. Its role is thus both technical and political.

The Commission's political influence becomes more apparent if we consider the broader context in which enlargements happen. In the late 1980s, even before the collapse of the Soviet system, the Commission began to extend economic and technical assistance to the CEE states, signing Trade and Cooperation Agreements (TCAs) with them and beginning a "political dialogue." In 1992, it began to upgrade the TCAs to Association Agreements (called Europe Agreements), creating a political momentum toward enlargement that hesitant member states found difficult to resist. The Commission's introduction of the Copenhagen Criteria in advance of the summit itself illustrated its capacity to frame the issues, set the agenda, and design the procedures for accession.

As accession unfolded, the Commission continued to exercise political influence, outlining changes the EU would have to undertake to prepare for enlargement. This was the Commission in its classic brokering role, linking the requisites of enlargement to politically sensitive EU reforms that needed doing for their own sake.

The Commission itself had to adapt to cope with the unprecedented scale of the eastern expansion. Faced with 13 applications, it could no longer rely on the traditional practice of providing data and assessments from the various **Directorates–General (DGs)** in a relatively uncoordinated way. To maintain its influence over enlargement policy, it would have to restructure to better manage the flow of information, oversee the process, and shape its own strategy. In 1999, it therefore created a new DG dedicated to enlargement and headed by a forceful commissioner prepared to comment on the prospects of the negotiations and the conduct of individual applicants.

After 2004, the number of parallel accession talks shrank from 12 to a more manageable four—the end games with Bulgaria and Romania and the early stages with Turkey and Croatia. The Commission nevertheless retained DG Enlargement, subsequently relabelled DG for Neighbourhood and Enlargement Negotiations (DG NEAR) and given responsibility for the European Neighbourhood Policy as well. It continues to provide frank annual assessments of candidates' progress. It also manages the budget allocated to the enlargement policy field (see Box 15.4).

The Treaty of Lisbon formalizes the powers gradually acquired by the European Parliament (EP) with respect to enlargement. The EP must be notified of each application, and the consent of an absolute majority of its members (MEPs) is required for final approval of the accession agreement, prior to its ratification by member states. In addition, the EP has played an active part in all phases of enlargement. Its resolutions can influence

**Box 15.4**   Budget allocation for enlargement policy

The total budget allocation to DG NEAR in the 2016 EU budget was €3,555 million, including costs of administration. Enlargement process and strategy received an allocation of €1,065 million almost half of this budget item was used to complete former pre-accession assistance to states that have since joined the EU, and the rest was used for support to current and potential candidate states. The largest item in the budget of DG NEAR was the European Neighbourhood Instrument, with a budget of €2,346 million, used to finance the **European Neighbourhood Policy**.

Source: Adopted budget for 2016, *Official Journal of the European Union*, L 48, February 24, 2016, 1387–1428

the selection of candidates and the timing, pace, and agenda of negotiations. Pronouncements by its party groups or individual MEPs shape the political climate in which individual applications, and enlargement in general, are debated. In the early 1990s, the EP was more generous with aid and keener to proceed with enlargement than were most member states. Between the Amsterdam and Helsinki summits, it persuaded the European Council to negotiate with all 12 applicants at once—not just the six most advanced—and to recognize Turkey as a candidate. After 2004, some MEPs called for a moratorium on further expansion, reflecting the "**enlargement fatigue**" emerging in European governments and public opinion.

## Debate: Assessing Enlargement

In retrospect, enlargement may appear to have been smooth and inevitable. As we have seen, however, each expansion raised disagreements among member states, reflecting differences in their domestic politics and their national economic and strategic interests. The same was true for the applicants. The debates that ensued were sometimes specific to one enlargement; more often they were variations on recurrent themes: would enlargement enhance prosperity, democracy, and security for current members, applicants, and wider Europe?

### The Past to 1995

Fundamental differences between the United Kingdom and de Gaulle's France blocked the first enlargement for a decade. De Gaulle dismissed the UK as "insular and maritime"; the UK was wary of the EEC as a project for French continental domination. Although shifts in the domestic conditions of each country calmed that debate, disputes arising from the UK accession continued past the 1975 referendum and up to the 1984 budget agreement—indeed debates over finances and **sovereignty** marked the 2016 Brexit campaign. But membership spurred economic transformation in all three new members and helped resolve Northern Ireland border issues between the Republic and the UK.

The southern enlargement saw French and Italian agricultural interests opposed to opening EC markets to imports from the three Mediterranean candidates, while Ireland and Italy feared the diversion of rural development aid. A shared concern for political and strategic stability helped reconcile these differences. Until the euro crisis, the economic benefits of this enlargement were clear and largely uncontested. Democracy was vibrant, and security on the EU's southern flank ensured, reinforced by Spain's accession to NATO.

The EFTA enlargement of 1995 was relatively smooth, although it sparked lively debates in Sweden and Norway. For Finland, EU membership was crucial in overcoming the loss of its once-lucrative ties to the Soviet economy and transforming it into a modern state. Austria, too, prospered, although in 2000 its inclusion of a far-right party in government produced a political crisis and a test for democratic values in the EU, which briefly imposed sanctions.

Up to this point it was tempting—indeed commonplace—to celebrate enlargement as a series of foreign-policy successes demonstrating and enhancing the attractiveness of the European project. The ensuing expansion cast doubt on that optimistic view.

### The "Big Bang" and After

The eastern enlargement raised concerns in France, which suspected that the CEE states would align economically with Germany and politically with Britain. The Germans argued for enlargement on moral and strategic grounds, while the British hoped that independent-minded new members freed from Moscow's control would help resist the federalist quest for an "ever-closer union" (see Box 15.5).

Three features of that dramatic expansion from 15 to 27 members make it difficult to assess. First, it involved an unprecedented number of new members. Second, it is too soon to evaluate the long-term economic and political effects of their accession. Third, it is sometimes hard to discern these effects amid the crises that have beset Europe since 2008: the euro, migration, Russia's challenge, and Brexit.

The decade since the "big bang" has, however, seen impressive economic growth in most new members, bettering that of the older ones (Vachudova, 2014, pp. 126–28). Eastward investment and westward labour migration have—not without controversy—transformed their economies. Democracy is robust in most new members, although questions of human rights, rule of law, and corruption persist in some, including Poland, Hungary, Romania, and Bulgaria. EU membership has given these issues prominence, generating pressures for change but also weakening Brussels' leverage. Ten of the 12 also joined NATO, adding an explicit security guarantee to that implicit in EU membership. But Russia's hostility to this dual eastward expansion has raised new tensions. Thus, while the net gains from enlargement are clear for prosperity, democracy, and security, new debates about all three have arisen in both the individual new member states and the EU as a whole.

**Box 15.5**    Explaining enlargement

1. *The EU's "vocation"*: Belief in the desirability of extending integration to other European states when circumstances permit; the normative vision of Europe "whole and free" can best be realized through the Brussels institutions. Critique: some EU members have been unprepared or reluctant when faced with opportunities for expansion.

2. *Soft-power attraction*: The image of European integration as positive and inevitable attracted many applicants, including the southern candidates (for democratic and economic reasons) in the late 1970s and, more recently, the CEE and Western Balkans. Undermined by current crises (**Euro Area**, migrants, Brexit, Russian challenge).

3. *Global change*: Gradual or sudden shifts in the international system can eliminate some options and create new opportunities. In the 1960s, global economic growth and trade liberalization pushed the first enlargement. Decolonization reduced the alternatives available to the United Kingdom and, later, Portugal and Spain. The fall of the Berlin Wall removed an obstacle to Eastern Europe's engagement with the EU. But the Brussels-centred, post–Cold War order is now challenged by Russia and growing Euroskepticism.

4. *External demand*: National interests drive European states to apply for membership. Broad strategic and economic calculations—the UK's historic shift in 1961, the southern three's quest for democracy and development, and the CEECs' escape from Russia's sphere—reflect pressures from domestic interests. A liberal-institutional account, portraying a demand-driven process to which the EU reacts.

5. *EU member states' national interests*: Can work for or against enlargement in general, and the admission of specific candidates. Examples: early French opposition to UK accession; member states' concern for security and democracy on their southern flank (Greece, Spain); German and UK support for CEE in the 1990s; Greek opposition to Turkey. Essentially a "realist" interpretation centred on calculations of power and relative advantage, as well as prospects of economic gains from expanded trade.

## Turkey

In 1963, Turkey signed an association agreement with the EEC. Its 1987 membership application was relegated to the bottom of the list as three EFTA states and then 12 others joined over the next 20 years. Finally, in 2005, negotiations began. They proceeded fitfully, hampered by disputes over the divided island of Cyprus and opposition from some EU states. Talks stalled in 2010 amid growing frustration and opposition in Turkey, reopening in late 2013. That almost 30 years have passed since Turkey's initial application highlights the difficulty of this relationship.

Turkey's history, location, population, modernizing economy, military strength, and NATO membership make it a weighty candidate. But EU governments worry about its record of military coups, authoritarian rule, civil-rights abuses, and harsh treatment of its Kurdish minority. Barely concealed anxiety that Sunni Muslim Turkey would eventually become the largest EU member by population reinforces Europe's recent "enlargement fatigue."

Cyprus remains a critical issue. In 1974, responding to an attempted coup by Greek officers, Turkey invaded and occupied the north of the island. It created the Turkish Republic of Northern Cyprus, a state which, to this day, only Ankara recognizes. Turkey refuses to recognize the Greek-Cypriot-led government in Nicosia as the legitimate government of all Cyprus. Notwithstanding this ongoing conflict, Cyprus joined the EU in 2004. It now wields a veto over Turkish membership.

War in Syria, and the flow of refugees via Turkey to Europe, have intensified the debate over Ankara's EU future. An agreement in March 2016 recognized a shared interest in managing the crisis (and earned Turkey some concessions on membership) but is legally flawed and fragile.

### The Western Balkans

The EU has assumed the leading role in the postwar reconstruction of the Balkans. Slovenia joined in 2004. Croatia opened accession negotiations in the fall of 2005 and became the EU's 28th member in 2013. At the 2003 Thessaloniki summit, the states of the Western Balkans were granted a "European perspective": they would be invited to apply when their economies, laws, and political practices approached EU standards. The remaining six are less advanced than Slovenia and Croatia; in addition to needing fundamental political, legal, and economic reforms, several have outstanding issues relating to borders, war criminals, international recognition (Kosovo), or a recognized name (Macedonia). For each, a Stabilization and Association Agreement (SAA)—the framework for working toward formal recognition of candidacy, application for membership, and eventual negotiations—is now in force (see Table 15.1). Two have begun negotiations—Montenegro (2012) and Serbia (2015)—while Bosnia-Herzegovina and Kosovo trail the pack, not yet recognized as candidates. The prize for all Europe is the pacification and development of a notoriously troubled region.

**Table 15.1** Progress chart: Current applicants (to April 2017)

| Stages of Accession | SAA and/or other preparatory agreements | Visa liberalization | Application | Candidate status granted | Negotiations opened (or preliminary dialogue) | Chapters opened | Chapters closed (provisional) |
|---|---|---|---|---|---|---|---|
| Turkey | Association Agreement 1963; Customs Union 1995; AP 2001, 2008 | Dialogue 2013– | 1987 | 1999 | 2005 | 15/35 | 1 |
| Montenegro | EPA 2007; SAA signed 2007; in force 2010 | 2009 | 2008 | 2010 | 2012 | 19/33 | 1 |
| Serbia | EPA 2008; SAA signed 2008; in force 2013 | 2009 | 2009 | 2012 | 2014 | 7/35 | 2 |
| Macedonia (FYROM) | EPA 2006; AP 2008; SAA signed 2001; in force 2004 | 2009 | 2004 | 2005 | High-Level Accession Dialogue 2012– | | |
| Albania | EPA 2004; SAA signed 2006; in force 2009 | 2010 | 2009 | 2014 (Commission Recommendation 2012) | High-Level Dialogue 2013– | | |
| Bosnia–Herzegovina | EPA 2008; SAA signed 2008; in force 2015 | 2010 | 2016 | potential candidate: "meaningful progress needed" | High-Level Dialogue 2012– | | |
| Kosovo* *Independence not recognized by five EU states | SAA signed 2015 | Dialogue and Roadmap 2012– | | potential candidate, pending progress in reforms | Kosovo-Serbia High-Level Dialogue 2012– | | |

AP: Association Partnership; EPA: European Partnership Agreement; SAA: Stabilization and Association Agreement

**Box 15.6**    Enlargements compared: Europe and Canada

*Confederation*: Canada emerged in 1867 from negotiations among Britain's eastern North American colonies. Ontario and Quebec were the West Germany and France of this integration project, while New Brunswick, Nova Scotia, and (after 1873) Prince Edward Island resembled Benelux, a customs union of three small European states that helped to found the EEC. Both projects had external support (Britain for Canada, US for the EEC) and perceived external threats (US to Canada, Soviet Union to Europe).

*The accession of Manitoba* in 1870 was driven by a combination of eastern Canadian interests and the demands of settlers in the Red River region. That of *British Columbia* (BC) in 1871 reflected similar economic and political developments and a shared concern to prevent northward incursions by an expansionist US. There are some parallels with the EU's post–Cold War enlargement, although that took place when the potential regional rival, Russia, was relatively weak and represented no apparent threat.

*The disposition of the Northwest Territory* (south of the 60th parallel) was settled by the creation of Saskatchewan and Alberta in 1905, filling the gap between Manitoba and BC. These two new provinces emerged from eastern Canadian economic interests, concern about American pressures, and new facts on the ground created by immigration. This decisive act of territorial expansion by ambitious (but insecure) Canada, can be contrasted with European enlargements sometimes lacking broad support among member states.

*Newfoundland joined Canada* in 1949 after a hard-fought referendum, illustrating that, when they are part of an accession process, referendums introduce the uncertainties of direct democracy. Recall the two Norwegian defeats (1972, 1994) of accession agreements, but also the substantial victories in Denmark (1972) and in the UK's 1975 vote to stay in the EC. Brexit reminds us that referendums, like the two held in Quebec (1980 and 1995), may also be about secession.

*Yukon* became a territory in 1898. The Arctic territory of *Nunavut* was carved out of the Northwest Territories in 1999. These were not enlargements, but political-administrative rearrangements.

## Conclusion

The progressive addition of new member states or subunits is, in principle, a sign of a polity's success (see Box 15.6 for a comparison with Canada). However, since 2004 much of the energy that marked the EU's post–Cold War expansion has dissipated. The wider EU has become, if not weaker, certainly more cumbersome in its decisions and actions. Its impressive economic and geopolitical presence is often countered by the quarrelsome diversity of its broadened membership. Moreover, enlargement fatigue now displays two distinct components: the "morning after" regrets expressed since 2004 by some members, and deepening frustration with conditions in the Western Balkans.

Broader European developments also pose questions about the future of EU enlargement. First, Europe's underperforming economy, the troubles of the Euro Area, its response to mass migration from the south, and the likelihood of Britain's departure, have weakened the **soft-power** attraction of the European project. The Brussels narrative—that integration is both progressive and inevitable—is further challenged by the rise of populist anti-EU parties in many member states. The less attractive the EU appears, the less it can demand of prospective applicants, some of whom may be tempted by other options.

Second, Russia's actions since the autumn of 2013 have revealed flaws in the liberal assumptions underpinning the eastward expansion of Western-based institutions such as the EU. What seems a benign "win-win" situation when viewed from Brussels resembles a zero-sum game of *realpolitik* when viewed from Moscow. The comfortable belief that enlargement has been a triumph of EU external policy is challenged by Russia's responses in Ukraine and the Balkans, the mixed aftermath of the 2004–7 enlargement, and second thoughts throughout the EU about the wisdom of continuing expansion.

## References and Further Reading

Asmus, R. 2008. "Europe's eastern promise: Rethinking NATO and EU enlargement." *Foreign Affairs* 87 (1): 95–106.
Baun, M.J. 2000. *A wider Europe: The process and politics of European Union enlargement.* Lanham, MD: Rowman and Littlefield.
Epstein, R., and W. Jacoby. 2014. "Eastern enlargement ten years on: Transcending the East-West divide?" *Journal of Common Market Studies* 52 (1): 1–16. https://doi.org/10.1111/jcms.12089.
Fouéré, E. 2014. The EU's enlargement agenda – Credibility at stake? *CEPS policy brief no. 324, 31 October 2014.* Brussels: Centre for European Policy Studies.

Friis, L., and A. Jarosz-Friis. 2002. *Countdown to Copenhagen: Big bang or fizzle in the EU's enlargement process?* Copenhagen: Danish Institute of International Affairs.

George, S. 1994. *An awkward partner: Britain in the European community.* Oxford: Oxford University Press.

Grabbe, H. 2014. "Six lessons of enlargement ten years on: The EU's transformative power in retrospect and prospect." *Journal of Common Market Studies* 52 (S1): 40–56. https://doi.org/10.1111/jcms.12174.

Granell, F. 1995. "The European Union's enlargement negotiations with Austria, Finland, Norway and Sweden." *Journal of Common Market Studies* 33 (1): 117–41. https://doi.org/10.1111/j.1468-5965.1995.tb00520.x.

Kelemen, R.D., A. Menon, and J. Slapin. 2014. "Wider and deeper? Enlargement and integration in the European Union." *Journal of European Public Policy* 21 (5): 647–63. https://doi.org/10.1080/13501763.2014.897745.

Kitzinger, U. 1973. *Diplomacy and persuasion: How Britain joined the Common Market.* London: Thames and Hudson.

Mayhew, A. 1998. *Recreating Europe: The European Union's policy towards Central and Eastern Europe.* Cambridge: Cambridge University Press.

Miles, L., and J. Redmond. 1996. "Enlarging the European Union: The erosion of federalism?" *Cooperation and Conflict* 31 (3): 285–309. https://doi.org/10.1177/0010836796031003002.

Mungiu-Pippidi, A. 2014. "The transformative power of Europe revisited." *Journal of Democracy* 25 (1): 20–32. https://doi.org/10.1353/jod.2014.0003.

O'Brennan, J. 2006. *The Eastern enlargement of the European Union.* London: Routledge.

Prifti, E. 2013. *The European future of the Western Balkans.* Paris: EU Institute for Security Studies.

Tsoukalis, L. 1981. *The EC and its Mediterranean enlargement.* London: Allen and Unwin.

Vachudova, M.A. 2014. "EU leverage and national interests in the Balkans: The puzzles of enlargement ten years on." *Journal of Common Market Studies* 52 (1): 122–38. https://doi.org/10.1111/jcms.12081.

Verdun, A., and O. Croci. 2005. *The European Union in the wake of Eastern enlargement: Institutional and policy-making challenges.* Manchester: Manchester University Press.

Wallace, W. 1976. "Wider but weaker: The continued enlargement of the European community." *World Today* 32 (3): 104–11.

Zielonka, J. 2015. *Europe unbound: Enlarging and reshaping the boundaries of the European Union.* London: Routledge.

## Review Questions

1. What trends and events in international political and economic relations influenced each round of enlargement and helped to shape its outcome?

2. Analyze the main ideas and national interests motivating the applicants and the member states in any of the rounds of enlargement discussed in this chapter.

3. What roles are typically played in the enlargement process by each of the EU institutions identified in this chapter? How have those roles evolved, and on what legal powers and political resources are they based?

4.   To assess the effects of enlargement on applicant states, established members, or on the European project in general, what kind of evidence would you look for?

## Exercises

1.   Access the **European Commission**'s Neighbourhood Policy and Enlargement website. Compare the status of current candidate countries. What progress has each candidate made toward accession, and at what speed? What are the most important obstacles to accession that remain in each case? Based on this, where is the EU most likely to enlarge to next?

2.   Consider the role of "conditionality" in applying the EU's enlargement criteria. Do some research on the theoretical debates surrounding the EU's power as leverage on the European continent. What do these debates tell us about the EU as a source of economic, political, and normative power?

# 16
# European Neighbourhood Policy

GABRIELA CHIRA AND ASSEM DANDASHLY

## Reader's Guide

In the wake of its expansion to the east and south in 2004, the European Union (EU) has faced complex external challenges, acquiring frontiers with countries that are less developed economically, often do not have consolidated democratic systems, and might pose security concerns. The EU has attempted to address these challenges through a policy of association, called the **European Neighbourhood Policy (ENP)**. The ENP provides assistance to neighbouring states and seeks to export EU values, but does not promise eventual EU membership. The EU vision is that of a ring of neighbouring countries that strengthen their relations with the EU, sharing everything but the institutions. This chapter discusses the origins, areas of focus, and instruments of the ENP.

## Introduction

The European Neighbourhood Policy (ENP) is an external relations instrument of the European Union (EU) that was launched in 2003 and began to take shape in the years following the 2004 EU enlargement. The ENP is based on fundamental EU principles: a commitment to democracy, the rule of law, and respect for human rights. In addition to sharing elements with EU trade and development policy, it adopts major elements of the policy framework developed for EU enlargement. The main goal of the ENP is to strengthen the EU's relation with its eastern and southern neighbours at both bilateral and multilateral levels. The policy follows in the footsteps of enlargement in that the EU aims to influence political and economic changes in the targeted countries and seeks to help them to become more integrated into the EU system. However, in contrast to enlargement, the ENP does not promise future EU membership.

With the so-called big bang enlargement of 2004, the EU acquired borders with Ukraine, Moldova, Belarus, and Russia, in addition to getting closer to Middle Eastern and North African (MENA) countries through the accession of Cyprus and Malta. In the wake of those expansions, the EU has sought to avoid the emergence of new dividing lines between itself and its new neighbours. The ENP is the EU's answer to this challenge. Its ambition is regional and geopolitical. The EU aims at being surrounded by stable and well-governed states, which help the EU secure its borders from irregular migration and terrorism and allow productive economic exchange, but are not seen as future EU member states. The ENP includes 16 countries:

- In the south: Algeria, Egypt, Israel, Jordan, Lebanon, Libya, Morocco, the Palestinian Authority, Syria, and Tunisia.
- In the east: Armenia, Azerbaijan, Belarus, Georgia, Moldova, and Ukraine.
- Russia has not participated in the ENP; it enjoys a special status through the EU–Russia Common Spaces that is governed by a "strategic partnership" (see Chapter 18).

Through the ENP, the EU puts in place specific policy measures (so-called Action Plans) applied to each participant country. The main challenge of the ENP, from the outset, has been to deal with very heterogeneous countries, including some in which revolutions and wars have been raging. With the Arab uprising that started in Tunisia in December 2010 and spread to the rest of the MENA, the pressure on the EU has increased in terms of security, the **refugee crisis** (as a result of the Syrian civil war), and illegal migration.

This chapter asks three main questions: What are the origins of the ENP, and how has it developed? What instruments has the EU used? What are the main areas of focus? In the following sections, the chapter answers each of these questions.

## The Origins of the ENP

Relations between the EU and its neighbours have developed significantly over the past two decades. Following the dissolution of the Union of Soviet Socialist Republics (USSR) in 1991 and the war in Yugoslavia in the mid-1990s, the EU could not turn its back on Central and Eastern Europe (see also Chapter 15). There were important political, economic, and social issues at stake with the collapse of communism across the region. The EU had to work on the geopolitical stabilization and economic revitalization of the European borderlands to curb nationalist conflict and counteract irregular migration. The EU's vision has been that of creating democratic countries with somewhat similar human rights and democratic values, and functioning market economies that can be closely aligned with the EU's political and economic system without their becoming full EU members. In its own way, the ENP hence forms part of a strategy to consolidate geopolitical stability (Theme 1 of this book) and to reduce the chance of war in the area. The effective resolution of security threats emerging from the neighbourhood is also important for the EU's legitimation in the eyes of its population (Theme 3 of this book).

The ENP supports institutional development and capacity-building in these countries and provides financial support. Central to this assistance is the fulfillment of democratic and human rights standards; in this respect, the ENP builds on the approach developed when EU enlargement to Eastern Europe was first discussed. Already in January 1989, the **European Parliament (EP)** demanded that reference be made to human rights protection as part of the Trade and Cooperation Agreements (TCAs) that the EU was starting to negotiate with the Central and Eastern European countries (CEECs). Following the demise of the USSR, the **European Commission** demanded that new types of economic agreements be subject to political conditions, including institutions guaranteeing democracy, the rule of law, human rights and democratic freedoms, as well as the protection of minorities. These principles were further confirmed in the **Copenhagen Criteria**, drafted in 1993, which define the formal conditions of accession to the EU (see Chapter 15).

In the 1990s, the EU's focus was not directed toward eastern neighbours only; the EU also wanted to strengthen its relations with its southern neighbours and move beyond the old bilateral commercial agreements that went back to the 1960s and 1970s (see Table 16.1). For this purpose, the Global Mediterranean Policy (GMP), first formulated in 1972, was replaced by the Renewed Mediterranean Policy (RMP) in 1992. The main focus of the new framework was to prioritize economic and structural reforms, development, regional cooperation, and environmental policies. With the launch of the Euro-Mediterranean Partnership, established in Barcelona (Spain) in November 1995 under the Spanish Council presidency, relations with the

**Table 16.1** EU-MENA relations

| 1957–1971 | 1972–1991 | 1992–1995 | 1995–2003 | 2003–present |
|---|---|---|---|---|
| Mediterranean Policy | Global Mediterranean Policy | Renewed Mediterranean Policy (RMP) | The Euro-Mediterranean Partnership (EMP) or Barcelona Process | The new European Neighbourhood Policy |
| Post-Colonialism | Cooperation | Co-Development | Partnership "Rings of solidarity" | Neighbourhood "Rings of friends" |

Source: Adapted from Amoroso (2006)

MENA countries took on a new trajectory and became more comprehensive. The Barcelona meeting focused on three main areas: (1) political and security partnership, (2) economic and financial partnership, and (3) partnership in social, cultural, and human affairs.

With the completion of the accession negotiations with the CEECs, discussions regarding the impact of enlargement on neighbouring states that remained outside the EU became more intensive. The Commission pushed for serious steps to be taken; these took the form of a Communication on "Wider Europe" in March 2003 (European Commission, 2003), followed by a more developed Strategy Paper on the European Neighbourhood Policy, published in May 2004 (European Commission, 2004). The "Wider Europe" Communication stated that the EU and its new neighbours had an "equal stake in furthering efforts to promote transnational flows of trade and investment as well as even more important shared interests in working together to tackle transboundary threats—from terrorism to air-born pollution" (European Commission, 2003, p. 3). In Thessaloniki, Greece, in June 2003, the EU heads of state or government endorsed the initiative with a view to developing these new policies, enabling the furthest possible form of association short of membership. With the 2004 Strategy Paper, actions were defined according to each partner, and some concrete instruments were brought into effect (including the TACIS and MEDA programs, which have since been absorbed into the ENP).

### The Development of ENP since 2004

Meeting in Copenhagen in December 2002, the **European Council** decided that the Union should enhance relations with its neighbours. The wish of the European Commission was that the EU's external border should not become a "new dividing line" (European Commission, 2004, p. 3); rather, the EU aspired to become a player working together with those states who share a land or sea border with the EU, to increase their prosperity and stability. The EU intended to reach out to its neighbours in order to help them attain the same standard of living and level of stability and security. It intended to do so by building a "ring of friends," as Commission President Prodi put it at the time (Prodi, 2002b). With the difficulties facing ENP, this became more of an attempt to manage a neighbouring "ring of fire." Indeed, when one looks at the countries under the purview of this policy, the geography (Map 1.1), as well as the situation in which each country finds itself from a political and ethnic point of view, it is clear that the ENP has been faced with many challenges.

The objective of forging closer relations with the EU's neighbours called first for a strengthening of relations with Russia, as well as for enhanced relations with Ukraine, Moldova, Belarus, and the Southern Mediterranean. However, Russia declined to be incorporated into the ENP and opted for developing bilateral cooperation with the Union on an allegedly more "equal" basis (see also Chapter 18). In June 2004, after the "Rose Revolution" in Georgia, the ENP was further extended to the South Caucasus republics of Armenia, Azerbaijan, and Georgia. States that are formal candidates for EU membership are not part of the ENP.

The extreme variety of the countries involved in the ENP made it challenging to develop a coherent policy. There was a need to adapt the cooperation mechanisms to the particularities of each country. The mechanism of **conditionality**—first developed in the context of enlargement—was used as the main tool to get the ENP countries to comply with EU rules. The EU's main condition for cooperation was the partner countries' willingness to carry out reforms, to improve their standards of democracy and human rights, to increase their access to the Union's **Single Market**, to improve the environment, as well as to step up their cooperation with the EU on issues such as energy, transport, and migration. In exchange, the EU offered assistance, technical help, and political support. The EU was designed to adapt to the specific situation of each country, but many of the partner countries would have desired even more flexibility.

Of the 16 ENP countries, 12 are currently participating fully as partners in the ENP, having concluded a bilateral agreement (called "Action Plan" or "Association Agenda") with the EU. No agreements have been concluded with Belarus, Algeria, Libya, or Syria. While the ENP proposes the same policy instruments to the southern and eastern partners, it is important to distinguish between the two groups of countries, with each group having had specific EU member states advocating on their behalf inside the EU. The southern partners found a loyal ally in France, whereas the eastern partners were strongly supported by the Nordic states. Within the ENP, a differentiation emerged between the two groups because each bloc lobbied for its protégés' interests, leading the ENP toward further disparity.

The **Lisbon Treaty**, which came into force in 2009, for the first time introduced an article in EU **primary law** which explicitly stated that "the Union shall develop a special relationship with neighbouring countries … founded on the values of the Union" (Article 8 TEU). The creation of the High Representative and vice-president of the Commission (HR/VP) and the **European External Action Service (EEAS)** changed little in the design and implementation of the ENP, which still had its own budget line and dedicated commissioner, albeit under the potential "supervision" of the HR/VP.

After 2010, external circumstances significantly changed the context in which the ENP was implemented. In the southern neighbourhood, the main change was the so-called Arab Spring, beginning in early 2011, which led to the toppling of a number of regimes in the MENA. The Arab Spring triggered a first rethinking of the ENP, encapsulated in a Joint Communication by the Commission and the EEAS released in May 2011. It proposed both a more differentiated approach to the neighbours, based on the principle of "more for more" conditionality, and a better tailored policy. In the eastern neighbourhood, the main change was an increased assertiveness of Russia, which in 2013 began to put pressure on the Eastern European neighbours to join the new Russian-dominated Eurasian Economic Union, rather than signing the association agreements proposed by the EU. The situation escalated in late 2013 when the standoff led to pro-EU demonstrations and civil unrest in Ukraine (referred to initially as #EuroMaidan on Twitter), which culminated in the ouster of the country's Russia-friendly president, the annexation of Crimea by Russia, and a violent conflict in the eastern part of Ukraine between government forces and separatist groups. The following two subsections of this chapter elaborate further on each of the two "groups" of neighbours (eastern and southern) in the ENP.

### The Eastern Partnership (EaP)

The idea of an Eastern Partnership (EaP), bringing together all EU countries and all the eastern neighbours in the ENP, was first proposed by Sweden and Poland in 2008 and formally launched in Prague (Czech Republic) in May 2009. It addresses the six Eastern European partners: Armenia, Azerbaijan, Belarus, Georgia, Moldova, and Ukraine. The EaP relies on the ENP in terms of resources, but creates distinct institutions within the ENP framework (Gaub & Popescu, 2015, p. 9) and, most importantly, new association agreements. These include Deep and Comprehensive Free Trade Area Agreements (DCFTAs, for those willing and ready to take on the far-reaching commitments); comprehensive programs funded by the EU to improve partners' administrative capacity; as well as "mobility and security pacts," allowing for easier travel to the EU while at the same time stepping up efforts to combat corruption, organized crime, and illegal migration. These pacts also cover the upgrading of asylum systems to EU standards and the establishment of integrated border-management structures. The long-term goal is full visa liberalization, provided that conditions for well-managed and secure mobility are in place. Other aspects of the agreements include labour mobility (with the aim of further opening the EU labour market); enhanced **energy security** (support for investment in infrastructure, better regulation, energy efficiency, and early warning systems to prevent disruption of supply); as well as "multilateral policy platforms" for dialogue on democracy, good governance, and stability. In addition, the EaP foresees more cooperation on specific issues within the EU's **Common Foreign and Security Policy (CFSP)** and **Common Security and Defence Policy** (**CSDP**; see Chapter 9), including the participation of partner countries in EU missions and the coordination of diplomatic activities. The EaP maintains the core principle of the ENP. How far the EU advances in relations with each country depends on the progress made by that country in its reform and modernization efforts.

### The Mediterranean Initiative

On his election to the French presidency in May 2007, Nicolas Sarkozy launched the idea of a Mediterranean Union, encompassing all the littoral states in a single political community. The idea was later refined and translated shortly afterward into what would become the Union for the Mediterranean (UfM) in July 2008, a bi-regional international organization encompassing 43 member countries. The UfM is institutionally separate from the EU but includes all EU member states and the European Commission as members (see Box 16.1); it is based in Barcelona and endowed

**Box 16.1** Members of the Union for the Mediterranean

- European Union:
  - The 28 EU member states
  - The European Commission

- Mediterranean Partner countries:
  - 15 member states: Albania, Algeria, Bosnia and Herzegovina, Egypt, Israel, Jordan, Lebanon, Mauritania, Monaco, Montenegro, Morocco, Palestinian Authority, Syria (self-suspended on June 22, 2011), Tunisia, and Turkey
  - Libya as an observer state
  - The League of Arab States involved in all meetings and preparatory meetings

with its own staff and resources to carry out specific projects in various domains. The main objectives of the UfM are to enhance multilateral relations, increase co-ownership of the process, and launch concrete projects visible to the citizens.

The UfM focuses on the four priority areas that build on those defined in the Euro-Mediterranean Partnership: politics and security; economics and trade; socio-cultural affairs; and justice and interior affairs. In addition to these four areas of cooperation, the UfM's Marseilles Summit in 2008 identified six specific projects: depollution of the Mediterranean; maritime and land highways; civil protection; alternative energies; higher education and research; and the Mediterranean business development initiative. Despite the political capital invested, the UfM has thus far produced very limited results. The complex institutional arrangement has created more obstacles, rather than easing political cooperation. Furthermore, the prioritization of economic cooperation pushed political values to the back seat. In addition, the complicated MENA regional conflicts, especially the Arab-Israeli conflict, did not make it easy for UfM to succeed in the area of political cooperation.

### Main ENP Tools: Conditionality Based on Shared Values?

Although the EU presents the ENP as a "jointly owned initiative" of the Union and the partner countries, and its implementation requires action by both parties, the ENP has been criticized as being unilaterally oriented toward the ambitions of the EU. The ENP is explicitly based on the EU's values, as defined in Articles 2 and 3 of the **Treaty on European Union (TEU)**: "The Union is founded on the values of respect for human dignity, liberty, democracy, equality, the rule of law and respect for human rights. These values are common to the Member States.... In its relations with the wider world, [the Union] aims at upholding and promoting these values."

As the European Commission pointed out in its 2004 Strategy Paper on the ENP, "The Union's neighbours have pledged adherence to fundamental human rights and freedoms, through their adherence to a number of multilateral treaties as well as through their bilateral agreements with the EU." These mutual commitments form the basis for the dual role of democracy and human rights in the ENP: first, as a precondition for participation in ENP, and second, as an objective of ENP actions (European Commission, 2004).

First, the Strategy Paper stated explicitly that the "level of ambition of the EU's relationships with its neighbours will take into account the extent to which [the EU's] values are effectively shared." It also outlined a clear political conditionality for the participation of those neighbouring countries in the ENP that are not yet considered ready. For instance, with regard to countries of the Southern Caucasus, the Commission proposed that the "EU should consider the possibility of developing Action Plans ... in the future on the basis of their individual merits with respect to the strengthening of democracy, the rule of law and respect for human rights." With regard to Belarus, it promised to "reinforce its lasting commitments to supporting democratic development" and stated that "when fundamental political and economic reforms take place, it will be possible for Belarus to make full use of the ENP" (European Commission, 2004).

Second, the Strategy Paper outlined a number of priorities for the individual ENP Action Plans, which were designed to strengthen commitment to EU values. These included "strengthening democracy and the rule of law, the reform of the judiciary and the fight against corruption and organised crime; respect of human rights and fundamental freedoms, including freedom of media and expression, rights of minorities and children, gender equality, trade union rights and other core labour standards, and fight against the practice of torture and prevention of ill-treatment; support for the development of civil society; and co-operation with the International Criminal Court" (European Commission, 2004, p. 13).

In addition to the emphasis on EU values, security concerns have also played a major role in the ENP. Various terrorist attacks in Europe have motivated more cooperation in the political and security arena in addition to the fields of democracy promotion, economy, and trade. In the EU's analysis, economic, political, and social failures of local regimes have contributed to the increase in terrorist behaviours and attacks all over the globe (Youngs, 2006). With the launch of the European Security Strategy (ESS) in 2003, the EU has emphasized that the ambition to share borders with stable and well-governed states to the east and south of the EU is also a matter of security (Council of the European Union, 2003).

With the European Union Global Strategy (EUGS), the EU aims to follow a more pragmatic approach. It aims to build on areas discussed in previous agreements and to support cooperation on issues such as security, socioeconomic problems, infrastructure, and disaster management. By solving those conflicts (mainly in the southern neighbouring countries) and promoting development and human rights, the EU aims to contribute to solutions for the root problems of terrorism, demographic challenges, illegal migration, as well as energy and climate change (European Union, 2016, p. 34). There is less focus on democracy in the EUGS, which the EU plans to promote where the situation is more favourable (Georgia and Tunisia). One of the main aspects highlighted in the EUGS is the clear differentiation among ENP countries; the EU expresses a willingness to be more involved in areas of common concerns with countries that show more openness to cooperation.

## Types of Agreements and Associations

How does the ENP work in practice? Partner countries agree with the EU on an ENP Action Plan or an Association Agenda, declaring their commitment to democracy, human rights, rule of law, good governance, market economy principles, and sustainable development. While following a similar template and drawing on the same toolkit (see Box 16.2), each individual agreement is different and reflects, on most key policy dimensions—democratization, trade, visas, energy links, and security—the specific realities in each of the eastern and southern neighbours and their willingness to engage more closely with the EU.

The ENP Action Plans (called Association Agendas for the EaP countries) set out the partner country's agenda for political and economic reforms, with short- and medium-term priorities of three to five years, reflecting the country's needs and capacities, as well as its interests and those of the EU. The Action Plans build on existing legal agreements with the EU: Partnership and Cooperation Agreements (PCAs) or Association Agreements (AAs). Implementation is monitored through committees set up by these agreements. Once a year, the EEAS and the European Commission publish ENP progress reports, assessing the progress made toward the objectives of the Action Plans and the Association Agendas.

Following the 2010–11 review of the ENP, the EU introduced the "more-for-more principle." It states that the EU will develop stronger partnerships and offer greater incentives to countries that make more progress toward democratic reform—free and fair elections, freedom of expression, freedom of assembly and freedom of association, judicial independence, a continued fight against corruption, and democratic control over the armed forces. Partners decidedly embarking on political reforms should be offered—in addition to the incentives available to other partners—the "3Ms": money, markets, and mobility:

- Money: A greater share of EU financial support
- Market: Economic integration and development through Deep and Comprehensive Free Trade Area Agreements (DCFTAs)
- Mobility: Mobility partnerships and visa facilitation

In this context, the Commission has decided recently to set up specific programs for both the eastern (EAPIC) and southern (SPRING) neighbours that will allocate extra financial support only to those neighbours taking clear and concrete steps toward political reforms. In addition, a new Civil Society Facility was created in September 2011 to strengthen the

**Box 16.2**   ENP Action Plans and financial instruments

- Action Plans
  - Main instrument of the ENP; backed by financial and technical assistance
  - List of different priorities for engagement and reforms the partner country should undertake
  - Developed for each individual partner country, defined by common consent, thus varying from country to country
  - Cover periods of three to five years
  - Focused on several priorities:
    - Commitment to shared values
    - More effective political dialogue
    - Economic and social development policy (legislative and regulatory approximation to the Internal Market)
    - Trade and Internal Market (approximation to the Internal Market, regulatory convergence, market opening)
    - **Justice and Home Affairs** (border management)
    - Connecting the neighbourhood (safety and security of energy supply, transport links and the environment, information and communications technology, research and innovation)
    - People-to-people, programs, and agencies
  - EU offers expert advice, financial assistance programs, and monitoring and evaluations on progress achieved

- Main Financing Instruments
  - European Neighbourhood Instrument (ENI), introduced in 2014, replacing the European Neighbourhood and Partnership Instrument (ENPI)
  - Facility for Euro-Mediterranean Investment and Partnership (FEMIP)
  - Neighbourhood Investment Facility

- Main Technical Assistance Instruments
  - Technical Assistance & Information Exchange (TAIEX)
  - Twinning Mechanism
  - Competitive and Innovation Program (CIP)
  - 7th Research Framework Program (FP7)

**Box 16.3**    Budget for the ENP

The EU's budget for 2016 allocated €3,565 million to the Commission's DG NEAR, which manages the ENP. This includes administrative expenses. The European Neighbourhood Instrument (ENI) was the DG's largest spending item, with a total budget allocation of €2,346 million (1.6 per cent of the total EU budget). Of this money, €930 million was spent for support to Mediterranean countries (mainly for projects related to human rights, poverty reduction, and conflict settlement), €214 million for support to Eastern Partnership countries, and €135 million for projects on cross-border cooperation. A large chunk of the budget (€950 million) was allocated for the completion of ongoing ENP actions that were begun prior to 2014.

Source: Adopted budget for 2016, *Official Journal of the European Union*, L 48, February 24, 2016, 1387–1428

capacity of civil society to promote and monitor reforms and to increase public accountability.

The outcome of the ambitious "3Ms" remains debatable: While the 2014–20 **Multiannual Financial Framework (MFF)** allocates €15.4 billion to the European Neighbourhood Instrument (ENI), the main funding vehicle of the ENP, the ENI constitutes only a relatively small share of the overall EU budget (see Box 16.3). This financial allocation may prove insufficient to compensate the massive injection of resources invested by other regional players (Russia, the Gulf monarchies, Iran, etc.). In addition, a certain competition over resources has emerged between the EU's eastern and southern partners and their respective mentors inside the Union.

Questions can also be raised about the other two elements of the "3Ms." With respect to markets, the opening of the EU to goods from neighbouring countries (especially from the south) has become politically more contentious in light of the economic crisis. Regarding mobility, growing fears of irregular migration in light of the refugee crisis and various terrorist attacks have made the EU's pledge of visa facilitation ever more complex to deliver on. In addition, the crisis in and over Ukraine has laid bare the fact that the predominantly technocratic approach represented by the DCFTAs could no longer compensate for the lack of a solid foreign and security policy framework in which the ENP is embedded (see also Chapter 18). Furthermore, the original uniformity of the ENP policy does not allow for differences to be

implemented in the eastern and southern neighbourhoods of the EU. Originally policies developed for the East have been imposed upon southern neighbours, though those neighbours have learned how to use migration policies as
bargaining chips to get the partnership to work in their favour.

### The ENP as an External Governance Approach

Through enlargement and through the ENP, the EU exports rules and institutional models, and it thus exercises what can be described as "external
governance" over its partners. Schimmelfennig and Sedelmeier (2004) argue
that the EU adopts an external incentive model when dealing with other
countries. The targeted state receives rewards for adopting EU rules and ful-
filling their commitments to the EU. In the case of enlargement policy, the
ultimate reward is EU membership. Targeted countries that have a membership perspective usually comply with the EU rules, as the reward is significant (see Chapter 15). By contrast, under the ENP, membership is not among
the incentives the EU has to offer. Rather, the EU offers other rewards, such
as (relatively limited) access to the Single Market, financial support, and trade
liberalization. These rewards are not as attractive as the membership incentive. This creates a very asymmetric structure in which the EU has the upper
hand and seems to gain more benefits from the ENP than many neighbouring countries do (see Box 16.4).

The external governance framework thus helps to decode mechanisms,
institutional models, and conditions of effectiveness of the ENP. It assesses
the transfer and extension of the EU's internal rules and policies short of
formal membership. Thus, this approach is fitting to a situation in which
the EU seeks to transfer some of its internal rules, while EU membership is
ruled out. The external governance framework also allows for an analysis of
the considerable variation and lack of uniformity of this transfer of rules and
institutional frameworks across countries, regions, and policy fields (Lavenex
& Schimmelfennig, 2009). It also makes it possible to place the ENP in a
broader discussion of EU external relations, which include not only enlargement and policies toward the EU's neighbourhood but also external trade
policies (see Chapter 14), the Common Foreign and Security Policy (see
Chapter 9), and the external dimensions of EU Justice and Home Affairs
policies (see Chapter 8).

## Debate: How Successful Has the ENP Been?

How should we assess the success of the ENP since its inception in the mid-
2000s? In spite of the asymmetry of the policy, some of the new neighbours

**Box 16.4**    Relations with one's closest neighbours in the EU and in Canada

The challenges that the EU and Canada face in governing relationships with their neighbours are extremely different. First, Canada shares its borders with only one direct neighbour, the United States (US), while the EU has land or sea borders with the 16 ENP states, Russia, the EU **candidate states** in the Balkans, and Turkey. Second, Canada's sole neighbour is a country with a highly developed economy and stable democratic institutions that does not pose any security challenges for Canada, while many of the EU's neighbours have deficiencies in all these respects. These different realities on the ground explain why the ENP includes elements of development policy and a focus on value transfer, which one does not find, of course, in Canada's relations with the US.

Nevertheless, the need to foster close cooperation with one's neighbours can be illustrated in both cases. The EU has to stabilize relations with a geographically very large neighbourhood that recently has been very unstable from both an economic and political point of view (a situation that might become even more challenging in the future with the rise of Russia as a major geopolitical player), whereas Canada has a long-standing security partnership with an economic partner that has a much bigger economy, the US. With the election of Donald Trump as US president, and his "America first" agenda, Canadian **foreign policy** toward the US has become much more politically sensitive than in the past decades. Given the importance of trade with the US, it is noteworthy that Prime Minister Justin Trudeau worked very hard to establish a positive working relationship with the US administration (even replacing his foreign minister with a politician seen as more in tune with the US), in spite of clear ideological disagreements.

Another interesting angle of comparison between the ENP and Canada could address the idea of the transfer of values in international development policy, and the use of conditionality in Canada's external relations. Canada's international development policy, conducted until 2013 by the Canadian International Development Agency (CIDA) and now part of the mandate of Global Affairs Canada, aims to support sustainable development in developing countries in order to reduce poverty and to contribute to a more secure, equitable, and prosperous world. Like the ENP, this policy is guided by normative ambitions, including the protection of basic human needs, the full participation of women, infrastructure for the poor, human rights/democratic development/governance, private-sector development, and the protection of the environment.

of the enlarged EU have clearly been attracted by the idea of economically cooperating with the EU and having access to its market. At the same time, countries like Ukraine and Moldova, which aimed for more, hoping that faithfully applying EU's conditionality might open up the door to membership, have seen their hopes shattered (Verdun & Chira, 2008). The EU has not been willing to renegotiate the terms of what the ENP offers: close cooperation with the EU ("all but institutions"), but no EU accession.

The results of the ENP have been relatively positive in the domain of trade. If we look to the east, trade patterns with the EU have been encouraging. For example, between 2004 and 2014, Azerbaijan's exports (mainly oil) to the EU increased by 918 per cent. By comparison, Azerbaijan's exports to Russia increased by only 362 per cent in the same period. Moldova's exports to the EU more than doubled between 2004 and 2014, while the country's exports to Russia declined by 15 per cent (Gaub & Popescu, 2015, p. 50).

Trade is also an area where improvements are substantial in the relation between EU and its southern neighbours. The EU is the main trading partner of the MENA countries; it absorbs 60–75 per cent of their exports. Almost all of the states in the region have doubled, and sometimes tripled, the volume of their trade with the EU over the last two decades. In general, all states have evolved in a positive direction in this regard, with the exception of Syria, which has been subject to economic sanctions due to the ongoing civil war. Even when focusing only on European imports, the picture is positive; this is particularly the case with oil-exporting countries such as Algeria and Libya, but non-oil states fare well too. For example, exports from non-oil North African countries (Morocco and Tunisia), as well as from Israel, have been high.

At the same time, the partnership with the EU has been undermined by the security worries (such as terrorism) and increasingly pressing migration concerns as a result of the Arab uprisings. The perceived security threat is due to both external threats—such as the conflict between Ukraine and Russia—and the internal political instability in the neighbourhood countries: their problems with terrorism, crime, religious extremism, political oppression, violations of human and civil rights, corruption, and the like. In addition, there are problems of migratory pressure arising from these countries' poor economic performance. Especially the terrorist attacks in the past two decades have contributed to the feeling among EU policymakers that more cooperation is needed in the political/security arena and not only in the field of economics and trade.

These examples indicate that, when examining the ENP Action Plans, it is important to assess the impact of the conflicts affecting the region with regard to the economic and financial dimensions. In the last two decades, many countries in the region were affected by war, terrorism, and civil conflict. There were direct impacts, such as human casualties and infrastructural damage, as well as indirect impacts, such as forced migration, reduction in investment flows and loss of economic opportunities, fragile economic growth, and diversion of resources away from sectors such as education or infrastructure development.

Moreover, non-violent political conflict, at the national or international level, has also impacted the region both directly and indirectly. Examples include states of emergency with detrimental economic and social consequences (e.g., in Egypt from 1981 to 2012, in Syria from 1963 to 2011, and in Algeria from 1992 to 2011) as well as the imposition of sanctions or the closing of borders as a result of conflict. These conflicts have had a cost and have affected not only the country directly involved but also neighbouring countries. Israel and Algeria, for instance, are barely integrated into the regional economic structure surrounding them; conflicts in both states therefore generate mostly direct costs for their national economies as well as indirect costs in terms of lost opportunities for either country to engage with trade partners.

In short, almost all ENP countries had to meet the EU's targets in various highly conflictual political contexts, which led to the diversion of resources, destruction of capital, and a realignment of political priorities (Gaub & Popescu, 2015). There can be no doubt that all states would have developed further without the continuous cycle of violence. Ending internal and external conflict will therefore be a critical prerequisite to unlocking the potential that exists in the region. This places the EU in a serious dilemma: It cannot offer further enlargements and it has to accept the closeness of unsecure, unprosperous territories in its vicinity. This constellation forces the EU to decide what to prioritize: security, which it needs, or democracy, which it would like to promote globally, but which might have negative side effects on security. Given what is happening in the MENA at the moment, security seems to have emerged as the EU's priority.

## Conclusion

The ENP may not provide a comprehensive answer to the EU's goals and worries regarding its neighbours' prosperity, stability, and security, as well as the impact of current developments in its neighbourhood countries on EU affairs. The ENP has also not offered a security blanket for peace and stability even if it was intended that way (Theme 1). Furthermore, there are ongoing concerns about keeping eastern "apples" and southern "pears" in the same basket. In terms of effectiveness, there are large disparities between countries and groups of partner countries. These disparities create tensions over policy priorities and financial allocations. It is therefore virtually impossible to assess how "successful" and "effective" the ENP has been in advancing the declared EU objectives. What is certain, however, is that the ENP has constructively supported pre-existing reform processes in some participating countries.

While cooperation in the areas of economics and trade as well as security has been advanced, the same is not true of the area of democracy promotion, human rights, and civil liberties. The EU has shied away from seriously pushing for democratization, due to the ongoing fear of terrorism and security threats and recently the chaos unleashed in some countries on its southern borders in the wake of the Arab Spring. This fear has pushed the EU to apply a very soft approach instead of strict negative conditionality. As security is currently the main concern for the EU, it continues to avoid imposing sanctions on ENP countries with problematic democratic and human-rights situations. Instead it focuses more on the **soft-power** approach and on socialization. For most parties involved (both the EU and ENP countries), the current cooperation is a win win situation. ENP countries gain economic and institutional benefits, while the EU maintains secure borders and guarantees the cooperation of the neighbouring countries on immigration, organized crime, and border-control issues.

The ENP remains a policy in the making, but with potential for development. The ENP was not conceived as, nor is it, a launch pad for greater expansion of the EU. This explains why the EU could not use the ENP to exercise strong conditionality for democracy, human rights, and the rule of law, as it did during the eastern enlargement in the 1990s and early 2000s. The ENP is also not formally a part of the EU's Common Foreign and Security Policy, where the focus is less on values and more on pragmatism. Instead, it encompasses elements of both. Given the various challenges in its neighbourhood, as outlined in this chapter, it is clear that the ENP needs to become less compartmentalized, more comprehensive, and, above all, more consistent. The EU has acknowledged this need for more consistency in its 2016 Global Strategy, which states that the security of the EU "at home entails a parallel interest in peace in our neighbouring and surrounding regions" (European Union, 2016). This implies an increased interest in dealing with problems at their source, by preventing conflicts, promoting human security, and addressing the root causes of instability in the MENA and the eastern neighbours.

## References and Further Reading

Amoroso, B. 2006. *European construction and the Mediterranean region: Neighbourhood policy or common project?* Research report/Federico Caffè Centre, No. 1. Roskilde, Denmark: Roskilde University.

Bouris, D., and T. Schumacher, eds. 2017. *The revised European Neighbourhood Policy: Continuity and change in EU foreign policy*. Basingstoke, UK: Palgrave Macmillan. https://doi.org/10.1057/978-1-137-47182-6.

Börzel, T., A. Dandashly, and T. Risse. 2015. "Responses to the 'Arabellions': The EU in comparative perspective—Introduction." *Journal of European Integration* 37 (1): 1–17. https://doi.org/10.1080/07036337.2014.975986.

Council of the European Union. 2003, December 12. *A secure Europe in a better world: European Security Strategy*. Brussels: European Council. http://www.envirosecurity.org/ges/ESS12Dec2003.pdf.

Cremona, M. 2008. "The European Neighbourhood Policy: More than a partnership?" In *Developments in EU external relations law*, edited by M. Cremona. New York: Oxford University Press. https://doi.org/10.1093/acprof:oso/9780199552894.003.0007.

Del Sarto, R.A., and T. Schumacher. 2005. "From EMP to ENP: What's at stake with the European Neighbourhood Policy towards the southern Mediterranean?" *European Foreign Affairs Review* 10: 17–38.

Delcour, L., and E. Tulmets, eds. 2008. *Pioneer Europe? Testing EU foreign policy in the neighbourhood*. Baden-Baden, Germany: Nomos. https://doi.org/10.5771/9783845212272.

European Commission. 2003, March 11. *Wider Europe – Neighbourhood: A new framework for relations with our Eastern and Southern neighbours*. Communication from the Commission to the Council and the European Parliament, COM(2003) 104 final. Brussels: Commission of the European Communities. http://eeas.europa.eu/archives/docs/enp/pdf/pdf/com03_104_en.pdf.

European Commission. 2004, May 12. *European Neighbourhood Policy: Strategy paper*. Communication from the Commission, COM(2004) 373 final. Brussels: Commission of the European Communities. http://eur-lex.europa.eu/legal-content/EN/TXT/PDF/?uri=CELEX:52004DC0373&from=EN.

European Union. 2016. Shared vision, common action: A stronger Europe. A global strategy for the European Union's Foreign and Security Policy. http://eeas.europa.eu/archives/docs/top_stories/pdf/eugs_review_web.pdf.

Freyburg, T., S. Lavenex, F. Schimmelfennig, T. Skripka, and A. Wetzel. 2009. "EU promotion of democratic governance in the neighbourhood." *Journal of European Public Policy* 16 (6): 916–34. https://doi.org/10.1080/13501760903088405.

Gaub, F., and N. Popescu. 2015. *The EU neighbours 1995–2015: Shades of gray*. Chaillot papers. Paris: EU Institute for Security Studies.

Kelley, J. 2006. "New wine in old wineskins: Promoting political reforms through the new European Neighbourhood Policy." *Journal of Common Market Studies* 44 (1): 29–55. https://doi.org/10.1111/j.1468-5965.2006.00613.x.

Kochenov, D. 2008. "The ENP conditionality: Pre-accession mistakes repeated." In *Pioneer Europe? Testing EU foreign policy in the neighbourhood*, edited by L. Delcour and E. Tulmets, 103–20. Baden-Baden, Germany: Nomos. https://doi.org/10.5771/9783845212272-103.

Lavenex, S. 2008. "A governance perspective on the European Neighbourhood Policy: Integration beyond conditionality?" *Journal of European Public Policy* 15 (6): 938–55. https://doi.org/10.1080/13501760802196879.

Lavenex, S., and F. Schimmelfennig. 2009. "EU rules beyond EU borders: Theorising external governance in European politics." *Journal of European Public Policy* 16 (6): 791–812. https://doi.org/10.1080/13501760903087696.

Noutcheva, G. 2015. "Institutional governance of European Neighbourhood Policy in the wake of the Arab Spring." *Journal of European Integration* 37(1): 19–36.

Prodi, R. (2002a). "L'Europe et la Méditerranée: Venons-en aux faits." Address at Université Catholique de Louvain-la-Neuve. Louvain-la-Neuve, November 26. IP/02/589.

Prodi, R. (2002b). "A wider Europe—A proximity policy as the key to stability." Address at the Sixth ECSA-World Conference, "Peace, Security and Stability International Dialogue and the Role of the EU," Brussels, December 5–6. IP/02/619.

Schimmelfennig, F., and U. Sedelmeier. 2004. "Governance by conditionality: EU rule transfer to the candidate countries of Central and Eastern Europe." *Journal of European Public Policy* 11 (4): 661–79.

Sedelmeier, U. 2007. "The European Neighbourhood Policy: A comment on theory and policy." In *Governing Europe's Neighbourhood: Partners or periphery?* edited by K. Weber, M.E. Smith, and M. Baun, 195–208. Manchester: Manchester University Press.

Smith, K.E. 2005. "The outsiders: The European neighbourhood policy." *International Affairs* 81 (4): 757–73. https://doi.org/10.1111/j.1468-2346.2005.00483.x.

Verdun, A., and G.E. Chira. 2008. "From neighbourhood to membership: Moldova's persuasion strategy towards the EU." *Journal of Southeast European and Black Sea Studies* 8 (4): 431–44. https://doi.org/10.1080/14683850802556418.

Whitman, R.G., and S. Wolff. 2012. *The European Neighbourhood Policy in perspective: Context, implementation, and impact.* Basingstoke, UK: Palgrave Macmillan.

Youngs, R. 2006. *Europe and the Middle East: In the shadow of September 11.* Boulder, CO: Lynne Rienner.

## Review Questions

1. Why does the EU have an interest in forging close relations with states in its neighbourhood, even when it does not want to offer these states EU membership?

2. How does the EU's conditionality exercised under the ENP differ from conditionality under enlargement policy? What impact does this difference have on the likelihood of encouraging reform in the targeted states?

3. What are the advantages and disadvantages of governing the relationships with the 16 ENP countries based on the ENP's unitary framework?

4. While the commitment to values like democracy and the rule of law is very prominent in the EU's programmatic documents on the ENP, these values have in practice often been subordinated to security concerns. Why did this happen?

## Exercises

1.  Peruse the European Commission's ENP and Enlargement website. Select a country covered under the Eastern Partnership (EaP) and a country covered under the Mediterranean Initiative (UfM). Compare the Action Plan and Association Plan for the two countries. What issues are prominent in both countries? What issues are country specific?

2.  Partner with another student to debate the success of the ENP. Should conditionality always be linked to eventual membership? Should the EU concentrate its efforts on economic partnership only, or is it obliged to stipulate criteria for "good governance" in the non-EU region?

# PART III

# Challenges

## Introduction to Part III

IT IS SOMETIMES SAID THAT THE EUROPEAN UNION (EU) is perpetually in crisis. Throughout its existence, the EU has been confronted with internal and external challenges that seemed to put its future into doubt. In the 1950s, the failure of the **European Defence Community (EDC)** was an early setback. In the 1960s, the integration process appeared stalled after the French government decided to adopt its "policy of the empty chair," refusing to take a seat in the **Council** meetings. During the 1970s and 1980s, there was talk of "eurosclerosis"—a stalemate in **European integration**—because EU decision-making was painfully slow. When *The Economist*, an influential British weekly, ran a report in 1982 on the 25th anniversary of the **European Economic Community (EEC)**, as the EU was then called, its editors decided to put a tombstone on the cover.

And yet, time and again, the EU has been able to recover from such crises. This history serves as a warning to over-eager commentators today who see the EU's current crises as a harbinger of its upcoming demise. At the same time, the severity of the crises that have faced the EU in the past few years—such as **Brexit**, the financial crisis of the **Euro Area**, or the **refugee crisis**—should not be underestimated. These crises are fast moving, and new developments will surely have occurred between the time of writing (spring 2017) and the time this book is read or used in university courses. Especially in their combination, these crises have raised concerns about the capacity of the EU to cope successfully with internal and external challenges. Together, they have thus contributed to debates about the EU's legitimacy (Theme 3

337

of this book). All of them point to core EU policies, such as the **Single Market**, **Economic and Monetary Union (EMU)**, and the **Area of Freedom, Security and Justice (AFSJ)**. Hence, when conceptualizing this textbook, we decided to discuss these crises at the first introduction of the policies in question (see, for instance, Chapters 7 and 8).

In addition to short- and medium-term crises, the EU faces a number of longer-term challenges that have affected European integration more or less continuously since its inception. This third section of the textbook deals with two of the most important challenges of this nature: first, the democratization of EU decision-making, and second, the EU's attempt to carve out its role as a global power. While perhaps less pressing in the short term than events like Brexit and the refugee crisis, these challenges point to steps in the political development of the EU that will determine the longer-term fate of the European integration project. If the EU were able to address both challenges successfully, it would firm up its legitimacy and would become less susceptible to short-term crises emerging from internal political processes or external developments. Yet as we show in the following two chapters, the EU faces serious dilemmas in both domains, which make easy and quick solutions unlikely.

# 17

# Democracy in the European Union

ACHIM HURRELMANN

## Reader's Guide

The alleged **democratic deficit** of the EU is a prominent theme of Euro-skeptic political arguments. In light of the recent popularity of these arguments, this chapter examines the EU's democratic processes and the way citizens make use of them in practice. In a first step, it takes stock of the existing mechanisms for citizen participation: the **European Parliament**, elections and referendums at the national level, and procedures for civil society involvement. In a second step, the chapter returns to the normative question of whether there is a democratic deficit in the EU. It reviews some of the most important arguments in this debate and examines proposals for making the EU more democratic.

## Introduction

When the predecessor institutions of today's European Union (EU)—the **European Coal and Steel Community (ECSC)**, the **European Economic Community (EEC)**, and the **European Atomic Energy Community (Euratom)**—were created in the 1950s, their powers did not extend beyond the regulation of limited and relatively technical aspects of economic life. As these institutions were more bureaucratic than political in nature, concerns about their democratic quality were not considered particularly pressing. In the following decades, more and more legislative powers were transferred to the European level and **European integration** began to affect an increasing number of policy fields. Although there was never a significant "democracy movement" in the citizenry, the architects of European integration concluded that a democratization of EU institutions was unavoidable if political support for the integration project was to be safeguarded (Rittberger, 2005). This perception led to successive rounds of reforms aimed at improving the democratic quality of EU decision-making.

As a result of these reforms, the EU now possesses more mechanisms for democratic input than any other regional or global institution. Many of these mechanisms have obvious similarities to the institutions of state-based democracy, but as we shall see in this chapter, the way in which they operate—and in which politicians, parties, and citizens make use of them—reflects the peculiar non-state character of the EU (Theme 2 of this book). This peculiarity of democratic institutions and practices in the EU has given rise to debates about whether the EU is sufficiently democratic. As public controversies about European integration have become more intense (Theme 3 of this book), democracy has emerged as one of the main issues of contention. While some observers praise the EU's democratic achievements, others portray EU governance as lacking meaningful mechanisms of participation and accountability.

This debate is of more than just academic significance. For the growing Euroskeptic movement, the EU's alleged democratic deficit has become an important rallying cry. In the **Brexit** campaign of 2016, depictions of the EU as an undemocratic "superstate" that takes away power from the member states' democracy were a prominent theme. The referendum result in favour of Brexit—the withdrawal of the United Kingdom from the EU—suggests that such arguments strike a chord with many voters (see also Chapter 7). As will be discussed below, referendums in other member states have also repeatedly resulted in majorities against deeper European integration. These referendum results indicate that the democratization of the EU has not alleviated many citizens' concerns about a loss of democratic quality due to European integration.

In light of these concerns, this chapter approaches the question of democracy in the EU from two angles. The first part of the chapter looks at the existing mechanisms for democratic input in EU politics—such as elections at the European and national levels, referendums on EU issues, and other opportunities for citizen participation. It also discusses how Europeans have made use of these opportunities in practice. The second part then turns to normative debates about the EU's democratic quality. It reviews competing positions on whether there is a democratic deficit in EU politics and introduces proposals for making the EU more democratic.

## Democratic Life in the EU

Democracy means "government by the people." In the context of modern, large-scale polities where day-to-day decisions cannot be taken by the citizens directly, it consists of institutionalized procedures that enable citizen participation in selecting political leaders, making substantive policy decisions, and holding politicians to account for their performance in office. Democratic states usually possess a considerable range of such procedures. In Canada, for instance, citizens can vote in elections at the municipal, provincial, and federal level. In addition, they can also seek to influence politicians between elections, for instance by forming associations or interest groups that lobby for specific policies. The citizens of EU member states have similar options, but for them, the EU constitutes an additional political level at which participation might be warranted.

What options do citizens have to influence politics at this level? This section discusses three channels of democratic input in the EU: (1) elections to the European Parliament (EP); (2) national elections and referendums that shape a member state's position in EU decision-making; and (3) formalized procedures for civil society input between elections. We discuss each of these channels in turn and then examine how citizens make use of them in practice.

### European Parliament

The EP is a **supranational** legislature composed of 751 members from all 28 member states. Since 1979, its members have been directly elected every five years. EP elections take place at the same time in all member states, usually over a period of four days. Details of the election differ from one member state to the next. Electoral rules vary somewhat, though all member states now use proportional representation systems. Different parties appear on the ballot in each state—usually the same ones that also dominate national politics—but most of them are associated with a European political party that brings together ideologically like-minded national parties. The party groups currently represented in the EP are discussed in Chapter 3. While most EP groups—including the two largest ones, European People's Party (EPP) and Socialists and Democrats (S&D)—are firmly in favour of European integration, it is noteworthy that the EP includes two radically Euroskeptic groups, which argue that the EU—at least in its current form—should be abolished.

EP elections are significant in EU politics for two main reasons. First, they influence the nomination of the President of the **European Commission**. Article 17(7) TEU, requires that the **European Council** "take into account" the EP elections when deciding on its nominee. Referring to this article, most European political parties in the run-up to the 2014 EP election nominated their respective *Spitzenkandidaten* (lead candidates) for the office of Commission president and insisted that the candidate of the largest party be nominated for the office. After the election, the European Council accepted this demand when it appointed Jean-Claude Juncker, the candidate of the EPP, to lead the Commission. It is unclear whether this process established a precedent that will be respected in future EP elections. Yet even if this practice were to continue, it is important to note that the EU—unlike Canada and most of its own member states—is not a parliamentary system in which the executive (the Commission) is responsible to the legislature (see Box 17.1). Once the Commission has taken office, its political survival is not dependent on continuous EP support.

**Box 17.1**    Parliamentarianism in Canada, the United States, and the EU

Parliaments play different roles in relation to the executive, depending on whether they operate in a parliamentary or in a presidential system. In parliamentary systems, such as Canada, citizens elect the (lower house of) parliament (House of Commons), which in turn elects the head of the executive (prime minister). Thus, the head of the executive is dependent for his or her political survival on parliamentary support. The parliament may vote him or her out of office with a simple majority. If this happens, the government falls.

By contrast, in presidential systems, such as the United States, both the parliament (Congress) and the head of the executive (president) are elected by the citizens, in separate elections. Here the parliament is restricted in its activities to legislative functions. It cannot bring down the head of the executive. The only exception is a process of impeachment, a special procedure reserved for crimes committed in office that requires more parliamentary support than a simple majority.

The EU displays elements of both systems. As in a parliamentary system, the head of the EU's main executive actor—the Commission president—is not directly elected. Rather, Article 17 TEU, establishes an explicit link between EP elections and the Commission presidency. However, while the EP must give its consent to the Commission president (as an individual) and to the College of Commissioners (as a group), it may not nominate the president or the individual commissioners. (The Commission president is nominated by the European Council and the individual commissioners by the member states.)

Once the Commission has taken office, it does not require continuous backing by an EP majority. Therefore, the Commission—which tends to be politically heterogeneous, as its members come from a range of different parties—does not need to cater its policies to a specific parliamentary majority. Rather, it can seek to find majorities for its legislative proposals on a case-by-case basis. The EP can bring down the Commission only through a motion of censure, a procedure reserved for cases of gross misconduct that requires a majority of two-thirds of the votes cast (Article 234 TFEU). Overall, the EP thus operates more like a parliament in a presidential system.

The second reason for the significance of EP elections lies in the legislative powers of the EP. While the EP originally had only a consultative role in EU legislation, the EU's **ordinary legislative procedure** (OLP; Article 294 TFEU) that became the norm with the **Lisbon Treaty** requires that legislative acts be approved by both the EP and the **Council**. The EP also possesses co-decision powers over the EU budget (see Box 17.2). In EP committees and in the plenary, legislative proposals are carefully scrutinized and may be substantially amended or even blocked. EP party groups have emerged as powerful and remarkably cohesive legislative actors. There are only two remaining aspects in which the EP's legislative powers fall short of those of typical parliaments at the state level. First, the EP cannot formally initiate EU legislation. This role is left to the European Commission. Second, in a small number of policy fields, the Council remains the main decision-maker. These fields include areas that are considered particularly sensitive to member state **sovereignty**, for instance, tax harmonization or police cooperation. In these areas, the ordinary legislative procedure is not applied. However, over the past decades the number of such exceptions has been continuously reduced.

Given how much the influence of the EP on EU decision-making has increased in recent years, the main limitations of EP elections, as a mechanism of democratic control over EU politics, no longer lie in insufficient parliamentary powers. Rather, they stem from the way in which EP elections have been treated by political parties and voters. EP elections have traditionally been characterized as **second-order national elections**

**Box 17.2**   The EP and the EU budget

The EU's annual budgetary process is laid out in Article 314 TFEU. While defined as a special legislative procedure, this provision gives the EP full co-decision over the EU budget, most notably the power to amend the Commission's draft and to reject the budget if no satisfactory compromise with the Council can be found. The EP also has to give its consent to the **Multiannual Financial Framework (MFF)**, the EU's seven-year budget plan that sets the parameters for each year's budget. However, it cannot amend the MFF (Article 312 TFEU). The budgetary powers of the EP are also restricted by the fact that the EU has no taxation powers—its budget is financed largely by member state contributions—and is explicitly prohibited from running a budget deficit (Article 310 TFEU).

(Reif & Schmitt, 1980), which are dominated by considerations of domestic politics and elicit little voter interest (see Box 17.3). This attitude toward EP elections derives from the fact that most voters still consider the member states as the primary political arena. The second-order character of EP elections weakens the representative connection between Members of the European Parliament (MEPs) and their voters, as MEPs tend to win or lose their seats not because of their position on important EU-level controversies, but because of domestic factors such as the current popularity or unpopularity of the national government. Hence, EP elections do not provide MEPs with a strong mandate to use the EP's powers in any particular way. Recent innovations such as the *Spitzenkandidaten* system, along with proposed reforms that would make the European political parties more prominent on the ballot, are intended to strengthen the "European" element in EP elections. The aim of these innovations is to make the EP elections stand on their own, so that voters no longer treat them as secondary. This process will take time.

### National Democratic Processes

The second channel of democratic input in the EU relies on democratic processes at the member state level; these include not only national elections

**Box 17.3**    Why have EP elections been described as second-order national elections?

1.  Dominance of national politics: EP election campaigns are not really about the EU, but focus on issues relevant to the national political arena, where "first-order elections" are held.
2.  Lack of voter engagement: From the voters' perspective, there is little at stake in EP elections. Voters have few incentives to become informed, and voter turnout is low.
3.  Protest votes: Since EP elections are seen as unimportant, voters often use them as a way to cast a protest vote (for instance, by voting for new or extreme parties), thereby giving a signal to national governments.
4.  Significance of national electoral cycles: EP elections are accorded the greatest significance by politicians and voters if they take place shortly before a national election and can hence be seen as a "bellwether" for the national election result.

but also referendums on EU affairs that have recently generated much attention. Let us examine both in turn.

*National elections* are relevant in the EU context because they may bring to power a government that promises to take a particular position on EU affairs, especially through its participation in the EU's **intergovernmental** institutions (Council and European Council). While the life and death of national governments in EU member states was traditionally only tangentially affected by EU politics, as EU-level issues played a subordinate role in national election campaigns, this pattern has slowly begun to change in recent years. Particularly in the context of the **Euro Area financial crisis**, incumbent national governments have sometimes become targets of electoral punishment for their EU-level policy choices. It is important to note, however, that the EU's decision-making system greatly limits the ability of any one national government to bring about change in EU policies, especially if **qualified majority voting (QMV)** rules are applied. As a result, changes in national governments matter for EU policy-making only to a limited extent.

National elections also influence the composition of national parliaments, which are tasked with holding their governments to account for their behaviour at the EU level. National parliaments are often seen as "losers" of European integration, as some of their legislative powers have been shifted to the EU. In response, they have sought to play a more active role in legislative processes at the supranational level. All national parliaments in the EU have established European Affairs Committees (EACs) that monitor EU legislative activities with respect to potential implications for domestic policies. In advance of key decisions in the Council or European Council, EACs consult with government ministers. In some member states, they can issue binding mandates for the government's voting behaviour. Ultimately, if such mandates are not respected, parliaments may withdraw their support from the government. Nevertheless, governments usually retain a large room for manoeuvring in the EU's intergovernmental procedures. One reason is that national parliaments are often unable to keep track of the EU's complicated policy processes. A second reason is that even in parliaments that have adequate information, parliamentary majorities may hesitate to tie their own government to overly restrictive mandates, which could limit the government's negotiating flexibility.

In light of these limitations of parliamentary control over national governments, an additional procedure was introduced with the Lisbon Treaty in 2009: an "early warning mechanism" that allows coalitions of national parliaments to level a direct protest against legislative initiatives at the EU level (see Box 17.4). This procedure requires the cooperation of various national

**Box 17.4**    The "early warning mechanism"

Protocols No. 1 and No. 2 to the TFEU allow national parliaments to protest directly against legislative initiatives proposed by an EU institution (usually the Commission). Such protests must be grounded in the principle of subsidiarity, which states that the EU should legislate only on issues that cannot be addressed at a lower political level. According to the early warning procedure, the national parliaments of all member states have eight weeks to review each proposal for EU legislation. If one-third of them raise objections, the proposal must be reviewed ("yellow card"). If a majority of national parliaments protest, the proposal can immediately be voted down, either by the Council or by the EP ("orange card"). However, the mechanism does not compel the EU's legislative institutions to drop the proposal in question.

parliaments, which in practice can be difficult to bring about within the required time frame.

While national elections are at best an indirect mechanism for democratic control over EU decision-making, *national referendums* are a device to give citizens a direct voice on EU-related issues. Such referendums have been held in 20 of the 28 member states (see Table 17.1). While they are sometimes influenced by the popularity of national governments, they usually involve spirited—though not always well-informed—debates about fundamental questions of European integration. They can thus be interpreted as important statements about the EU's legitimacy.

In the last two decades, national referendums have repeatedly resulted in national citizens' rejection of European integration. In some cases (such as the Danish referendum on the **Maastricht Treaty** and the Irish referendums on the Nice and Lisbon Treaties), the member state in question ended up holding a second vote on a slightly revised proposal, containing certain clarifications or **opt-outs**. In other cases, the rejection was more consequential. The negative vote on the proposed EU Constitution (formally the Treaty Establishing a Constitution for Europe) in France and the Netherlands in 2005 put an end to the EU's constitutional project. Similarly, the Brexit referendum of 2016 is on course to result in the first-ever case of a member state leaving the EU. These cases illustrate that EU-related referendums provide a highly consequential opportunity for national electorates to leave their imprint on EU politics—an opportunity that has repeatedly been seized by Euroskeptic mobilization. When assessing the value of referendums as a democratic

**Table 17.1** EU-related referendums in the member states (rejections highlighted)

| Member state | Year | Subject | Yes vote | Turnout |
|---|---|---|---|---|
| Austria | 1994 | Accession to the EU | 67% | 82% |
| Croatia | 2012 | Accession to the EU | 66% | 44% |
| Czech Republic | 2003 | Accession to the EU | 77% | 55% |
| Denmark | 1972 | Accession to the European Communities | 63% | 90% |
| | 1986 | Single European Act | 56% | 75% |
| | 1992 | Maastricht Treaty | 49% | 83% |
| | 1993 | Maastricht Treaty, Edinburgh agreement | 57% | 87% |
| | 1998 | Treaty of Amsterdam | 55% | 76% |
| | 2000 | **Economic and Monetary Union** | 47% | 88% |
| Estonia | 2003 | Accession to the EU | 67% | 64% |
| Finland | 1994 | Accession to the EU | 57% | 74% |
| France | 1972 | Accession of Denmark, Ireland, and the UK to the European Communities | 68% | 60% |
| | 1992 | Maastricht Treaty | 51% | 70% |
| | 2005 | Constitutional Treaty | 45% | 69% |
| Hungary | 2003 | Accession to the EU | 84% | 46% |
| Ireland | 1972 | Accession to the European Communities | 83% | 71% |
| | 1987 | Single European Act | 70% | 44% |
| | 1992 | Maastricht Treaty | 69% | 57% |
| | 1998 | Amsterdam Treaty | 62% | 56% |
| | 2001 | Nice Treaty | 46% | 35% |
| | 2002 | Nice Treaty | 63% | 50% |
| | 2008 | Lisbon Treaty | 45% | 53% |
| | 2009 | Lisbon Treaty | 67% | 58% |
| | 2012 | European Fiscal Compact | 60% | 51% |
| Latvia | 2003 | Accession to the EU | 67% | 73% |
| Lithuania | 2003 | Accession to the EU | 91% | 63% |
| Luxembourg | 2005 | Constitutional Treaty | 57% | 88% |
| Malta | 2003 | Accession to the EU | 54% | 91% |
| Netherlands | 2005 | Constitutional Treaty | 39% | 63% |
| | 2016 | Association Agreement with Ukraine | 38% | 32% |

*(continued)*

**Table 17.1**    (Continued)

| Member state | Year | Subject | Yes vote | Turnout |
|---|---|---|---|---|
| Poland | 2003 | Accession to the EU | 77% | 59% |
| Sweden | 1994 | Accession to the EU | 53% | 83% |
|  | 2003 | Economic and Monetary Union | 42% | 83% |
| Slovenia | 2003 | Accession to the EU | 90% | 60% |
| Slovakia | 2003 | Accession to the EU | 92% | 52% |
| Spain | 2005 | Constitutional Treaty | 77% | 42% |
| UK | 1975 | Continued membership in European Communities | 67% | 64% |
|  | 2016 | Continued membership in the EU | 48% | 72% |

device, however, it is important to keep in mind that the range of issues on which referendums are held is limited. Usually they are called in individual states to decide on questions of a constitutional nature, such as membership, treaty amendments, or euro adoption. Referendums have never taken place simultaneously in all member states. They are not available as an avenue of democratic participation on day-to-day EU policy-making.

### Procedures for Civil Society Participation

In addition to calling on the whole population to vote in regular elections (and occasionally in referendums), democratic political systems have established procedures that are designed to allow groups of citizens to voice—and infuse into the decision-making process—their opinions about political issues about which they care particularly strongly. Such procedures for direct, policy-specific input from civil society supplement, but cannot replace, the electoral mechanism.

In the EU, procedures of this kind are widely used. Consultation mechanisms by the European Commission have the longest tradition. They aim primarily at *interest associations* active at the EU level. Such associations include business organizations (e.g., Business Europe), trade unions (e.g., the European Trade Union Confederation), or civil society groups (e.g., the European Anti-Poverty Network). In addition to groups with a formal EU-level organization, individual corporations, national interest groups, regions of the member states, international organizations, think tanks, as well as private law firms and consultants are also active in lobbying EU institutions. The Commission follows a long-standing policy of systematically incorporating them in the policy-making process by asking them to provide information, as well as by inviting them to serve on advisory committees. From the Commission's perspective, their inclusion not only improves the substantive quality of its legislative proposals but also opens up an avenue for civil society participation. To level the playing field for competition between various interests (e.g., business and consumers), the Commission provides some financial assistance to less well-organized groups to assist them in setting up structures at the EU level. In recent years, the Commission has enacted a number of reforms that seek to improve the transparency of its consultation procedures, among them a Transparency Register that lists organizations active in Brussels (see Box 17.5).

In addition to the incorporation of interest associations into the policy-making process, the EU also possesses a number of mechanisms that allow for the participation of *individual, non-organized citizens*. One such mechanism is the Commission's online consultations on legislative initiatives (https://ec.europa.eu/info/law/contribute-law-making_en), which invite submissions by both individuals and organizations. Another is the European Citizens' Initiative (ECI, http://ec.europa.eu/citizens-initiative/public/welcome). This procedure, introduced with the Lisbon Treaty (Article 11 TEU), allows one million EU citizens, by signing a petition, to invite—but not to compel—the Commission to make a specific legislative proposal. The procedural requirements for ECIs are demanding, and only a small number have been successful in collecting the required number of signatures.

Procedures for the direct participation of associations and individuals in the EU are unquestionably diverse and innovative, yet they face limitations when it comes to securing an unbiased connection between the preferences of citizens and the outcome of EU decision-making. Well-organized interest groups, including professional lobbyists—especially those from Northern and

**Box 17.5**   The Transparency Register

The Transparency Register lists more than 10,000 organizations (as of December 2016) that interact with EU institutions to conduct lobbying and policy advice activities (http://ec.europa.eu/transparency register/public/homePage.do). Registration is voluntary; organizations that register must sign up to a "code of conduct" that bars unethical lobbying practices. In return, the organizations listed in the database receive invitations to all consultations that the Commission initiates within their fields of interest.

Western Europe—dominate the process. The positions voiced by them do not reflect the breadth of preferences that exist in society. What is more, EU institutions are selective in incorporating civil society proposals into legislative documents. Thus, mechanisms of civil society participation are primarily an agenda-setting device; they do not ensure democratic accountability.

### EU Democracy and the Citizens

Our overview of mechanisms for democratic input in EU decision-making confirms that over the past decades, the EU has taken important steps toward democratization. We have also seen, however, that each of the mechanisms has specific limitations when it comes to securing effective citizen participation in selecting political leaders, making substantive policy decisions, and holding leaders to account.

Some of these limitations are due to the institutional setup of the EU. It is important to understand that the EU is not a *majoritarian democracy* (like Canada or other Westminster systems), in which a parliamentary majority faces few obstacles in shaping policies to its liking. Rather, the EU is a *consensus democracy*, with extensive checks and balances designed to protect minorities (Lijphart, 1999). This system was adopted because the EU's population is much less homogeneous than that of most nation-states; most importantly, the member states vigorously seek to protect their interests and identities in EU decision-making. As a result, EU decision-making proceeds through protracted negotiations, involving the member states (inside and outside of the Council), the European Parliament, and the Commission. For democratic participation, this system implies that none of three democratic mechanisms distinguished above is able to shape EU decision-making in a direct and unmediated way. All of them feed democratic input into the EU's consensus democracy, but the final version of most EU policy documents is ultimately hammered out in negotiations behind closed doors, such as **trilogues** and meetings of conciliation committees under the ordinary legislative procedure (see Chapters 3 and 5 for more details). Perhaps unavoidably, this process of building inter-institutional compromise remains non-transparent and inaccessible to outside influence.

In addition to these institutional factors, the limitations of the EU's democratic mechanisms also derive from the specific ways in which citizens, political parties, and interest groups participate in EU-level politics. These participation patterns are shaped by the non-state character of the EU. Until little more than two decades ago, most observers argued that EU-level politics elicited a vague form of generalized support, but very little detailed interest among the population. This constellation was described as a **permissive consensus** (Lindberg & Scheingold, 1970). In this model, the European population supports the broad goals of the European integration project but cares little about the details, thus leaving political elites far-reaching discretion over EU policy choices. Since the early 1990s, the EU has become more explicitly politicized—that is, salient and controversial—in the population. This **politicization** has coincided with the rise of **Euroskepticism** as a political force (Box 17.6). Some say that the permissive consensus has been replaced by a "constraining dissensus" (Hooghe & Marks, 2009), that is, societal controversies about European integration have become so heated that political leaders no longer dare to push the integration project forward. At the same time, the politicization of EU governance has clearly been much more pronounced in political parties, interest groups, and the media than it has been among regular citizens without a professional interest in politics. With the partial exception of EU-related referendums, there are few instances of EU issues capturing the imagination of a sizeable proportion of the people. Most citizens are well aware of the political importance of the EU, but many feel that they do not fully understand its peculiar, non-state political system and policy processes. These knowledge deficits deter a significant portion of citizens from participating more actively in EU democracy.

## Debate: Is There a "Democratic Deficit" in EU Politics?

While the characteristics of democratic life in the EU have been analyzed fairly comprehensively, there is no consensus in EU studies on how they

**Box 17.6**   Euroskepticism

The term "Euroskepticism" is used to describe parties, social movements, and political attitudes that explicitly oppose European integration, either in principle ("hard Euroskepticism") or in its current form ("soft Euroskepticism"). Euroskeptic positions can be found on both the left and the right of the political spectrum. They are usually grounded in the perception that European integration has undermined national sovereignty and identity, democracy, and/or established systems of social protection. Ironically, the EU's own democratic mechanisms—including EP elections and EU-related referendums—have provided some of the clearest examples of the Euroskeptics' political influence.

should be interpreted from a normative vantage point. The question here is whether the limitations of the EU's democratic mechanisms seriously undermine the quality of EU decision-making. When answering this question, we should keep in mind that even consolidated democracies at the state level—such as Canada, the US, or the EU's own member states—can be criticized for certain democratic imperfections. Citizens do not all participate in politics, some interest groups have privileged access to power, and various decision-makers are not directly accountable to the voters. Is the situation in the EU significantly worse?

One of the most prominent authors who has answered this question with a resounding "no"—and hence argues against the democratic deficit thesis—is Andrew Moravcsik (2002). He advances three main arguments. First, he claims that there is less of a need for democratic control in the EU than in typical Western states, given that the EU's legislative and executive powers are more constrained, its budget and bureaucracy are smaller, and its decision-making processes include more extensive checks and balances. Second, he points out that EU decision-makers are not unaccountable, especially due to the existence of EP and national elections that serve as mechanisms of democratic control. Third, he argues that the main reason why citizens are not more involved in the EU is not a deficiency of the EU's democratic institutions, but rather derives from the fact that the EU's main powers—trade liberalization, technical regulation, agricultural policy, and so on—generate little interest among the population. By contrast, most of the issues that citizens typically care more about, such as social policy, law and order, or taxes, are dealt with primarily at the member state level. Unless the EU gains powers in such areas, Moravcsik argues, it is unrealistic to expect more participation from the citizens.

Most scholars are less optimistic about the state of democracy in the EU than Moravcsik. Two authors who have explicitly contradicted his claims are Andreas Føllesdal and Simon Hix (2006). They argue that the most important democratic deficiency of the EU is the *lack of meaningful political competition* about EU personnel and policy choices. As we have seen, EP elections do not generate a mandate for politicians at the EU level to pursue specific policies. In spite of the new *Spitzenkandidaten* process, they also do not serve as a forum in which rival European elites—a European government and a European opposition—would battle for leadership positions. The most relevant decisions about EU policy and personnel are, therefore, not made electorally. In addition, a second dimension of the democratic deficit exists at the national level. As member states lose more and more powers to the EU, *national democratic processes are hollowed out*. The limited powers that national parliaments have acquired in EU decision-making do not fully compensate for this loss. The resulting system of decision-making at the EU level can thus be described as "policy without politics" (important decisions are made without adequate democratic debate), while national decision-making increasingly turns into "politics without policy" (intensive debates are conducted, but crucial decisions are taken elsewhere) (Schmidt, 2006).

This more pessimistic view of the state of democracy in the EU raises the question of what (if anything) can be done to make the EU more democratic. Three types of answers have been given to this question in the EU studies literature:

1. The first answer claims that is it impossible, at present, to democratize the EU further, as the European population is just not ready for more EU-level democracy. The main reason is that Europe lacks a cohesive demos, that is, a community of citizens who identify strongly with the EU, and all other Europeans, and who are willing to make personal concessions for the EU's greater good. Authors arguing for this *no-demos-thesis* point out that the identification of citizens with the EU is substantially weaker than their attachment to their individual nation-states (see Figure 17.1). This weakness of a European demos, in their view, is the main reason why democratic processes at the EU level remain impoverished. Citizens who do not feel attached to the EU are not motivated to participate in meaningful ways in EU decision-making. Furthermore, they will be unwilling to contribute resources for the benefit of other Europeans and would not accept majority decisions in which they are overruled by the nationals of other member states (Greven, 2000). According to the no-demos theorists, there is little that can be done about this conundrum. Since collective identities change only in the long run, there are no short- or medium-term solutions to the EU's democratic deficit.

2. The second answer takes a more optimistic view; it argues that targeted institutional changes at the EU level can *encourage greater citizen participation* in EU politics. Before the failure of the EU Constitution in 2005, advocates of this position placed great hopes in the constitutional project, which they expected would trigger more intensive debates about European politics, inspire enthusiasm for Europe, and ultimately lead to the formation of a European political community (Habermas, 2001). The failure of the Constitutional Treaty has greatly reduced the appetite of politicians and academics for large-scale treaty reform. However, some commentators—most prominently Simon Hix (2008)—claim that greater citizen involvement in EU politics can be triggered even without changing the treaties. One way of achieving this

**Figure 17.1** European and national identities in EU member states (2016)

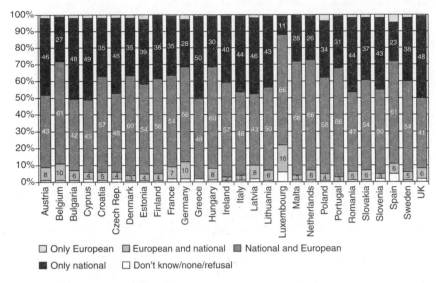

Question: "Do you see yourself as…?"

Source: *Eurobarometer 86*

is the above-mentioned *Spitzenkandidaten* process in EP elections, of which Hix was an early proponent. Further modifications of the current system that he suggests include rewarding the largest EP party group with a disproportionate number of committee chairs, and putting all legislative proposals to a formal vote in the Council. Hix's hope is that such changes, which would infuse more majoritarianism into the EU's consensus-based system, would encourage more visible competition between different political agendas. Such competition, in turn, would make it easier for the citizens to understand what is at stake in EU decisions, would encourage more active participation, and would ultimately lead to a stronger European identity.

3.  The third answer seeks to define an intermediate position between the first two views. It rejects as unrealistic (and potentially dangerous) the hope that institutional changes can fundamentally change patterns of political engagement and collective identity, but also opposes the fatalistic pessimism of the "no-demos" theorists who consider EU democracy impossible in the absence of such changes. Rather, it proposes to conceptualize the EU as a **demoi-cracy** (*demoi* being the Greek plural of *demos*), that is, as a political system composed of multiple political communities at different political levels (Nicolaïdis, 2013). In such a system,

people participate democratically in multiple roles: as citizens of the EU (Europeans), as nationals of their member states (statespeoples), and as members of functional communities (farmers, business owners, university students, etc.). As the interests of the various political communities must be respected, such a system is necessarily consensus oriented. The EU's democratic system reflects this diversity by setting up multiple, interdependent channels of democratic input. However, according to the demoi-cracy theorists, the interplay of these channels can be made more effective and transparent. Some authors suggest a more extensive use of member state opt-outs from EU legislation. Others propose the creation of horizontal channels of influence through which citizens from various member states can influence each other's decision-making in areas of mutual interdependence. This idea could mean, for instance, that Greek citizens would be given a say in German politics, and vice versa, since both countries clearly influence each other in decision-making on issues such as the **Euro Area** and the **refugee crisis**. Hence, a fully developed demoi-cratic system for the EU would look very different in institutional terms from a conventional state-based democracy. As most demoi-cracy theorists admit, navigating it might be a considerable challenge for citizens accustomed to state-based systems. In other words, the task is not only to build demoi-cratic institutions, but also to foster demoi-crats who can use these institutions in an informed and effective way.

The positions summarized above cannot easily be proven right or wrong. They are rooted in different normative conceptions of democracy—for instance, different degrees of emphasis put on negative liberty (individual freedom and restraint on power holders) as opposed to positive liberty (participation in collective self-government). They also reflect different assumptions about the malleability of the citizens' participation patterns and collective identities. Thus, there is not one correct answer to the question of whether a democratic deficit exists in the EU, or whether it is merely the invention of overly demanding theorists. Similarly, none of the democratization proposals is objectively superior to another.

## Conclusion

As this chapter has shown, the EU has developed a large array of procedures that allow EU citizens to contribute to its decision-making processes. These developments have addressed some of the concerns of those who argue that the EU suffers from a democratic deficit. However, the specific character of the EU as a polity—the non-state character of its institutions as well as the heterogeneity of its society—implies that the EU's democratic institutions and practices look different than those in most member states. When it comes to realizing the participation of citizens in selecting the EU's political leaders, making substantive decisions on EU policy, and holding EU politicians to account, limitations undeniably remain. While some authors argue that the overall democratic quality of the EU is nevertheless satisfactory, these limitations will likely continue to fuel political criticism of the EU and scholarly debates about its "democratic deficit." This political and scholarly contention should not necessarily be seen as a bad thing, since such debates are themselves an important driving force for democratization. With regard to its democratic quality, the EU has come a long way, but there is surely room for further improvement.

## References and Further Reading

Farrell, D.M., and R. Scully. 2007. *Representing Europe's citizens? Electoral institutions and the failure of parliamentary representation.* Oxford: Oxford University Press. https://doi.org/10.1093/acprof:oso/9780199285020.001.0001.

Føllesdal, A., and S. Hix. 2006. "Why there is a democratic deficit in the EU: A response to Majone and Moravcsik." *Journal of Common Market Studies* 44 (3): 533–62. https://doi.org/10.1111/j.1468-5965.2006.00650.x.

Franklin, M., and S. Hobolt. 2015. "European elections and the European voter." In *European Union: Power and policy-making,* 4th ed., edited by J. Richardson and S. Mazey, 399–418. London: Routledge.

Greenwood, J. 2011. *Interest representation in the European Union.* 3rd ed. Basingstoke, UK: Palgrave Macmillan.

Greven, M.T. 2000. "Can the European Union finally become a democracy?" In *Democracy beyond the state: The European dilemma and the emerging global order,* edited by M.T. Greven and L.W. Pauly, 35–61. Toronto: University of Toronto Press.

Habermas, J. 2001. "Why Europe needs a constitution." *New Left Review* 42 (11): 5–26.

Habermas, J. 2017. "Citizen and state equality in a supranational political community: Degressive proportionality and the *pouvoir constituant mixte.*" *Journal of Common Market Studies* 55 (2): 171–82. https://doi.org/10.1111/jcms.12517.

Hix, S. 2008. *What's wrong with the European Union and how to fix it.* Cambridge: Polity Press.

Hix, S., and B. Høyland. 2013. "Empowerment of the European Parliament." *Annual Review of Political Science* 16 (1): 171–89. https://doi.org/10.1146/annurev-polisci-032311-110735.

Hobolt, S.B. 2009. *Europe in question: Referendums on European integration.* Oxford: Oxford University Press. https://doi.org/10.1093/acprof:oso/9780199549948.001.0001.

Hooghe, L., and G. Marks. 2009. "A postfunctionalist theory of European integration: From permissive consensus to constraining dissensus." *British Journal of Political Science* 39 (1): 1–23. https://doi.org/10.1017/S0007123408000409.

Hurrelmann, A. 2007. "European democracy, the 'permissive consensus' and the collapse of the EU Constitution." *European Law Journal* 13 (3): 343–59. https://doi.org/10.1111/j.1468-0386.2007.00369.x.

Hurrelmann, A. 2014. "Democracy beyond the state: Some insights from the European Union." *Political Science Quarterly* 129 (1): 87–105. https://doi.org/10.1002/polq.12143.

Hurrelmann, A., A. Gora, and A. Wagner. 2015. "The politicization of European integration: More than an elite affair." *Political Studies* 63 (1): 43–59. https://doi.org/10.1111/1467-9248.12090.

Kohler-Koch, B., and C. Quittkat. 2013. *De-mystification of participatory democracy: EU governance and civil society*. Oxford: Oxford University Press. https://doi.org/10.1093/acprof:oso/9780199674596.001.0001.

Lijphart, A. 1999. *Patterns of democracy: Government forms and performance in thirty-six countries*. New Haven, CT: Yale University Press.

Lindberg, L., and S. Scheingold. 1970. *Europe's would-be polity: Patterns of change in the European community*. Englewood Cliffs, NJ: Prentice-Hall.

Moravcsik, A. 2002. "In defence of the 'democratic deficit': Reassessing legitimacy in the European Union." *Journal of Common Market Studies* 40 (4): 603–24. https://doi.org/10.1111/1468-5965.00390.

Nicolaïdis, K. 2013. "European demoicracy and its crises." *Journal of Common Market Studies* 51 (2): 351–69. https://doi.org/10.1111/jcms.12006.

Reif, K., and H. Schmitt. 1980. "Nine second-order national elections: A systematic framework for the analysis of European election results." *European Journal of Political Research* 8 (1): 3–44. https://doi.org/10.1111/j.1475-6765.1980.tb00737.x.

Rittberger, B. 2005. *Building Europe's Parliament: Democratic representation beyond the nation state*. Oxford: Oxford University Press. https://doi.org/10.1093/019927 3421.001.0001.

Schmidt, V. 2006. *Democracy in Europe: The EU and national polities*. Oxford: Oxford University Press. https://doi.org/10.1093/acprof:oso/9780199266975.001.0001.

Usherwood, S., and N. Startin. 2013. "Euroscepticism as a persistent phenomenon." *Journal of Common Market Studies* 51 (1): 1–16. https://doi.org/10.1111/j.1468-5965.2012.02297.x.

Winzen, T. 2012. "National parliamentary control of European Union affairs: A cross-national and longitudinal comparison." *West European Politics* 35 (3): 657–72. https://doi.org/10.1080/01402382.2012.665745.

## Review Questions

1.  What are the three channels of democratic input distinguished in this chapter? How does democratic participation occur in each of these channels? What are their limitations when it comes to ensuring the effective participation of citizens in selecting political leaders, making substantive policy decisions, and holding leaders to account?

2.  Why does the chapter argue that the limitations of the EU's democratic mechanisms are due to not only institutional factors but also participation practices

by political parties, interest groups, and citizens? Provide illustrations from the material discussed in this chapter.

3. What arguments can be used to dispute the claim that the EU suffers from a "democratic deficit"? How convincing do you find these arguments? Which counter-arguments can be used to criticize this position?

4. The chapter discusses three perspectives on the potential for further democratization in the EU and the strategies which could be used to achieve it. Summarize the main arguments of each perspective. Which one do you find the most convincing?

## Exercises

1. Collect information on the most recent EP election, examining factors such as voter turnout, and results in various member states, as well as election campaign activities at both the European and member state level. Does this research provide any evidence that EP elections are losing their "second order" characteristics?

2. Explore the Transparency Register. What types of organizations are listed? What information is provided about them? Which aspects of the organizations' lobbying activities are not disclosed? How would you assess the democratic value of the Register?

# 18

# Geopolitics of the European Union

JOAN DEBARDELEBEN

## Reader's Guide

This chapter elucidates how the changing nature of the EU's global and regional environment poses new challenges for the Union and affects its responses to **foreign policy** issues. The author identifies resources that the EU has to exert international influence and considers obstacles that limit the EU's ability to exercise geopolitical power. Specific issues are examined, including frozen conflicts in the post-Soviet countries, challenges emanating from the Middle East, and the growing influence of emerging powers. The chapter provides background on the rise in tensions between the EU and Russia following eruption of the Ukraine crisis in 2014 and examines debates over the way forward.

## Introduction

This chapter explores the nature of the global influence of the European Union (EU) and the manner in which the EU has responded to challenges in its geopolitical environment. **Geopolitics** refers to the exercise of power within a particular spatial or geographic context. The EU's regional and global environment is one of flux and change; at the same time, the EU's progressive **enlargement** has brought new countries into the Union, and with them, new perspectives and priorities about foreign policy. Only slowly and unsurely has the EU come to see itself as an actor potentially capable of exercising geopolitical power.

Three factors are of key importance in understanding the geopolitical forces that have shaped the EU's understanding of itself as a regional and global force. The first involves changing circumstances in Europe itself. As discussed in Chapter 1, **European integration** was initiated as an effort to create a viable and stable system based on economic interdependence, to assure the maintenance of peace in Europe (Theme 1 of this book). With the collapse of the Soviet Union in 1991, however, the geopolitical context changed radically. The bipolar structure termed the **Cold War**, which was characterized by rivalry between the Union of Soviet Socialist Republics (USSR) and the West, came to an end. The Soviet collapse resulted in the emergence of a large number of newly independent countries, including the Russian Federation, which had to find their place in the international sphere. Relations between the EU and these new countries have presented both opportunities and challenges. The second set of factors has to do with the altered structure of the larger global geopolitical environment in the last two decades. Countries such as China, India, and Brazil are taking on increased importance, challenging the previous structures of international relations. With Russia and South Africa, these are referred to as the **BRICS** countries. A third factor is continuing instability in the Middle East, which involves not only the ongoing tensions between Israel and its Arab neighbours but also the impacts of the so-called Arab Spring, anti-government uprisings beginning in 2011 that spread across a range of Middle Eastern countries. Other developments, such as climate change, disputes over the Arctic, and worries about **energy security** have also affected Europe's geopolitical position.

In areas clearly within the jurisdiction of EU institutions or where EU member states have been able to agree on priority objectives, such as trade, non-proliferation of nuclear weapons, humanitarian assistance, and climate change policy, the EU has achieved the status of a global power. By contrast, in terms of a range of other concerns, particularly relating to security issues, the EU's global, and even regional, influence has been more limited. Because many foreign policy functions are retained by the member states, the EU often lacks the capability and instruments to react effectively to geopolitical challenges or to accept the geopolitical power that it potentially commands. This reality sometimes contributes to unpredictable outcomes, such as the Ukraine crisis that erupted in 2014, difficulties in handling a huge influx of Syrian refugees, and the rising threat of terrorism in Europe.

## The EU: An "Accidental" Geopolitical Actor?

The EU operates in a geopolitical environment, but the EU itself is not a traditional geopolitical actor. This disjunction can lead the EU to overlook the geopolitical implications of its actions or to underestimate geopolitical challenges at an early stage. We coin the phrase "accidental geopolitical actor" to describe the EU because, to a large extent, the Union has defined itself in terms of a set of normative objectives rather than as an international actor promoting its own political interests. The EU's normative objectives derive from its basic value commitments, for example promoting democracy, **multilateralism**, and good governance. However, over time, the EU has been pressed, without having any clear strategy, to consider the geopolitical implications of its policy choices, due to the expanded range of its activities, its greater geographical span, the unexpected impacts of its economic influence, and the interconnectedness of social, economic, and political processes in the region and across the globe. This is most visibly evident in the events that unfolded as a result of the EU's relations with Ukraine, discussed later in the chapter.

Unlike nation-states that formulate foreign policy goals reflecting their own understandings of national interest and capabilities, EU decisions also represent a compromise between various member state positions. On the other hand, compared to most international organizations, the EU has a broader mandate as well a stronger capacity to make decisions binding on its members in particular policy arenas (Theme 2 of this book). EU documents provide guidance in understanding how the EU's geopolitical position is understood in Brussels. However, to provide a clear picture, these EU documents need to be placed alongside similar policy documents of key member states such as France, Germany, the United Kingdom (until **Brexit**), Poland, and Spain. These national conceptions can differ significantly from one another on key issues such as relations with Russia, responses to immigration flows resulting from the Syrian civil war, and reactions to US actions (e.g., the American intervention in Iraq in 2003). In general, individual member states quite readily acknowledge geopolitical (national) interests. One exception is Germany, which has been a reluctant geopolitical actor, similar to the EU itself. German elites are unsure about how assertively their country can wield its power without evoking distrust and suspicion among other countries. Given that Germany has often filled a leadership vacuum in recent years in addressing a range of European problems, this reluctance has reinforced the EU's difficulties in acknowledging its own geopolitical role.

In June 2016 the EU adopted a document outlining its global strategy, called *Shared Vision, Common Action: A Stronger Europe* (European Union, 2016). This document identifies key EU priorities and suggests a general approach termed "principled pragmatism." This involves a reassertion of the EU's basic value commitments to democracy, human rights, global governance, and the rule of law, while also prioritizing the EU's domestic and international security, assuring the resilience and strength of neighbouring countries, addressing challenges of conflict management in unstable regions, and supporting regional cooperation mechanisms in particular parts of the world. Just like its predecessor, the 2003 Security Strategy (European Union, 2003), the 2016 document reveals that EU leaders, including national heads of states, recognize important geopolitical realities that are present in the EU's environment and acknowledge that they warrant attention and a response.

The tools that the EU commands to influence its external environment are more limited than those that a country of similar size and economic importance would be expected to have. For example, the EU lacks a credible military capacity, and most member states rely heavily on the North Atlantic Treaty Organization (NATO) as their security guarantor. The 2016 EU strategy document suggests that the EU's military capability should be reinforced, but there are likely to be both budgetary and political obstacles to realizing this objective. As early as 1993, Christopher Hill, in an influential article, identified the "capability-expectations gap," referring to the distance between the EU's aspirations and the tools it has to realize these goals. This disparity continues to plague EU efforts to realize its objectives.

Nonetheless, the EU still has significant sources of power, primarily of two types, normative power and economic might. The political scientist Joseph Nye (2004) developed the concept of **soft power** to depict the manner in which non-material resources can be deployed to effectively establish international influence. Among the EU's most important soft-power tools is normative power, a notion explored by Ian Manners in a seminal article in 2002. Normative power refers to the "ability to shape conceptions of 'normal'" (Manners, 2002, p. 240), that is, to influence ideas and opinions about appropriate norms and values governing decisions and actions. Manners argued that the EU is often able to achieve its objectives by using the "soft" powers of persuasion, example, and socialization, convincing leaders and publics in other countries that the European model is desirable, both due to the intrinsic values it represents as well to the security and prosperity that it has brought for its citizens. The values that underlie the European model in exercising normative power are concepts such as democratic governance, the rule of law and universal human rights, as well as the proclaimed superiority of a liberal competitive market economic system to promote prosperity and human welfare. These, of course, are the very values that form the legitimizing basis of the EU itself, and they have indeed gained wide adherence, ascribed to, at least rhetorically, by leaders worldwide, even when they are not honoured in practice. More recently, values like sustainable development and limiting climate change have been taken on board by the EU. The use of normative power as a resource to influence other countries, however, has some pitfalls, in that it easily opens the door to charges of hypocrisy if those values are not realized at home. It can also engender resistance, as, for example, some countries in the EU's eastern neighbourhood resent the EU's efforts to export its values.

The EU's normative power is augmented by its economic force. With a gross domestic product (GDP) of $18.51 trillion and a population of 510.1 million at the start of 2016, according to Eurostat, the European

Union represents one of the largest potential markets in the world as well as a source of **foreign direct investment (FDI)** for partner countries. While the average level of GDP per capita for the EU overall is well below that of Canada and the United States (US), it exceeds that of other potentially influential countries in the region, such as Russia and Turkey. Furthermore, the more affluent countries of the EU stand at the top of the World Development Index. Countries of the former Soviet bloc that have joined the EU have experienced a much clearer upward economic trajectory compared to those that have remained outside. This combination of factors has accorded the EU credibility and attractiveness as an economic model, forming part of its soft-power resources and giving the EU the capacity to generate support for free-trade agreements and other forms of partnership that other countries believe will be beneficial in economic terms.

The EU's soft-power tools, namely reliance on its "power of attractiveness," are generally effective only if viewed in the medium-to-long term, since the underlying socialization effects and benefits of association with the EU do not take place immediately. Furthermore, the economic problems that the EU and the **Euro Area** have experienced since 2008, along with generally low rates of economic growth and high unemployment rates in some EU member countries, have also, to a degree, begun to undermine the credibility of the EU economic model. Despite these issues, EU spokespersons sometimes overlook the fact that soft-power resources and associated economic strength, while compelling resources of geopolitical influence, can also be perceived as threatening to other countries, a theme we will return to later in this chapter.

An important element of the EU's geopolitical reality is the relationship of Europe to the United States (US), and, by extension, to Canada. A key vehicle for securing this transatlantic connection has been the North Atlantic Treaty Organization (NATO). With the 1991 collapse of the USSR—the adversary that triggered NATO's original formation after World War II—NATO has had to find a new mandate. It now includes **crisis management** and disaster relief activities in conflict zones, as well as combating terrorism. NATO has helped maintain the US security commitment to Europe through Article 5 of the NATO treaty, which provides that for collective defence, "armed attack against one or more of them in Europe or North America shall be considered an attack against them all." The bulk of NATO forces and expenditures have come from the US, whose contributions are considerably higher as a percentage of GDP and on a per capita basis than for any of the EU countries. The admission of 10 post-communist countries to NATO—the Czech Republic, Hungary, and Poland in 1999; and Bulgaria, Estonia, Latvia, Lithuania, Romania, Slovakia, and Slovenia in 2004—while ostensibly unrelated to any definable Russian threat to them, was viewed by Moscow as a hostile action that violated an unwritten agreement at the end of the Cold War. While the EU itself did not play any explicit role in NATO's decision to enlarge, the vast majority of EU member states are NATO members and the processes of EU and NATO enlargement generally went hand in hand in Central and Eastern Europe, reinforcing Russian perceptions of a concerted intrusion into its own sphere of influence. Russian leaders have also complained loudly and consistently about the emergence of a unipolar geopolitical structure, where the US, with European acquiescence, has regularly circumvented approval by international institutions to pursue its own geopolitical objectives.

While the US has been the most important ally of the EU, areas of tension also exist, including differences over climate change policy, various trade disagreements, and the tendency of the US to take unilateral action outside the framework of international organizations. Controversial and unpredictable positions taken by US President Donald Trump on a variety of international issues have the potential to increase such areas of disagreement but also might reinforce solidarity between EU member states, if US positions question the legitimacy of the EU.

## Regional Geopolitical Challenges: The Larger European Context

Until the collapse of the Soviet Union in 1991, the postwar geopolitical environment in which European integration was unfolding was marked by the division of Europe into two clearly defined blocs that stood in a competitive relationship to one another and which formed the basis of the Cold War. Nonetheless, despite the arms race and the Cold War context, the situation took on a certain stability and predictability that allowed the European integration project to progress within relatively clearly defined geographic boundaries. The fall of the Berlin Wall in 1989 and the subsequent reunification of divided Germany, followed by the collapse of the USSR in 1991, represented a major earthquake in the geopolitics of Europe, unsettling the terms of the postwar settlement and introducing the possibility of instability and uncertainty to the continent. The fact that this transition occurred in a largely peaceful manner astounded many observers, with the main areas of violent conflict in the former Yugoslavia (the West Balkans), where interethnic wars broke out in the 1990s. Those conflicts served as a wake-up call to Europe, as the EU was not able to develop an effective and unified strategy for responding to that challenge. Subsequently the EU, in conjunction with the US, put in place a number of measures to support political reform and ethnic accommodation in the West Balkans.

From the 1990s and into the 2000s, the EU's policy in relation to Eastern Europe was largely premised on an enlargement logic (see Chapter 15), culminating in the addition of 10 new members in 2004, two in 2007, and one in 2013. In relation to the West Balkans as well, the EU offered a clear membership perspective as an incentive for the countries of the region to adopt appropriate reform strategies. Croatia was in fact admitted to the EU in 2013, with other countries either receiving candidate status (Albania, Macedonia, Montenegro, and Serbia) or aspiring to it (Bosnia-Herzegovina).

However, in other regards, using enlargement as a foreign policy tool has brought with it geopolitical implications that were not adequately foreseen. One of these is what Tom Casier (2008) has called the enlargement paradox: namely, as more countries join the EU, it becomes more costly for others to remain outside. This is because the benefits of being in such a strong free-trade and customs zone are largely restricted to members. Thus, through enlargement, the EU has indirectly affected the economic and geopolitical calculations of its new eastern neighbours, strengthening the desire for membership in countries such as Moldova and Ukraine. The EU's response, in the EU's **European Neighbourhood Policy (ENP),** has been to encourage neighbours to adopt EU regulatory standards and to seek greater integration to achieve trade access, even though the EU has not been prepared to offer the carrot of eventual membership (see Chapter 16).

These policies, intended to create a stable and secure environment for democratic and market development, also failed to address the three "frozen conflicts" that had developed in the post-Soviet space. The term "frozen conflicts" refers to international disputes that have proven intractable to resolution; while the regions may appear relatively calm for some period of time, they are capable of erupting into violent conflict in response to only minimal provocation. Each of the three frozen conflicts in Europe involves countries that emerged as newly independent states following the Soviet collapse. First is the contested region of Nagorno-Karabakh, located geographically within Azerbaijan, but claimed by Armenia due to the strong Armenian population base and for historical reasons. Second are two secessionist regions, South Ossetia and Abkhazia, located in Georgia. The third case is Transnistria, a region with a Russian majority population located in the eastern part of Moldova. The EU has, for a variety of reasons, proven largely unable to contribute to sustainable solutions to these problems. A strong EU role could risk mobilizing a Russian objection, because Russia perceives clear interests in the region, or in alienating one or another of the parties to the conflicts. Because the EU is a relatively risk-averse actor, these considerations may underlie its reticence in addressing these conflicts. In some cases, however, the EU has taken action. In 2008, when Russia intervened to support secessionist forces in Georgia, Nicolas Sarkozy, the French president, stepped forward to mediate the conflict (France held the rotating presidency of the **European Council** at that time); following that, the EU sent observers to monitor the situation. Since 2005, through the EU Border Assistance Mission to Moldova and Ukraine (EUBAM), the EU has been engaged in monitoring the Transnistrian conflict and facilitating confidence-building measures. Despite these efforts, all three conflicts remain frozen, with the potential for new outbreaks of violence at any time.

An even greater problem, however, arose in Ukraine in 2014. The crisis emerged when Russia annexed Crimea, previously part of Ukraine. The concrete trigger was, in fact, related to the EU's Eastern policy. In late 2013, under heavy Russian pressure, the president of Ukraine (Viktor Yanukovych) suddenly shifted Ukraine's trajectory when he unexpectedly stepped back from signing a long-planned Association Agreement (AA) and free-trade agreement with the EU. The surprisingly strong attractive power of the EU in Ukraine was then graphically demonstrated in the weeks that followed when hundreds of thousands of Ukrainians took to the streets of Kiev, at the so-called Euromaidan, to protest their government's reversal. EU officials were themselves surprised by the power that their model and the offer of association with the EU had commanded among a substantial element of the Ukrainian public. The demonstrations triggered a political crisis in Ukraine in which Yanukovych was ultimately toppled, to be replaced by a pro-Western interim government. The Russian political leadership reacted strongly, intervening in support of Crimea's secession from Ukraine and its annexation to Russia. But the conflict did not stop there; civil war broke out in eastern Ukraine, as rebels in Ukrainian regions with a large Russian-speaking population (Luhansk and Donetsk) condemned the new Kiev government and demanded regional autonomy, while receiving material backing from Russia. This situation led to a spiral of Western sanctions against Russia and Russian counter-sanctions against the West. In the final section of this chapter, we return to the implications of this conflict for EU–Russian relations.

What these cases illustrate is the mixed capacity of the EU to act as an effective regional actor in Europe. While enlargement was a highly successful strategy with some countries, the EU has shown a limited capacity to respond effectively to challenges in other parts of the post-Soviet space. With the Ukraine crisis, the EU was forced to deal with the consequences of its unexpected geopolitical power.

## Global Geopolitical Challenges: The EU's Geopolitical Role outside of Europe

At the same time that the broader European geopolitical environment has undergone radical change, the balance of power on the global scale has also seen significant alteration. The increasing economic and political importance of countries such as China, India, Brazil, and South Africa has led the EU to focus on intensified relations with them. One of the tools that the EU has developed is the notion of strategic partnership. But much of the EU's attention has also been devoted to particular world regions— such as the Middle East—and pressing global problems such as terrorism.

### The EU's Strategic Partnerships

While there are no clear criteria defined to determine which countries should be designated as strategic partners, clearly these are countries that are considered to be of long-term importance to the EU's objectives. Of the 10 strategic partnerships that the EU has designated, several are with countries that share a common values agenda, such as the US, Canada, Japan, and South Korea, but five major newly emerging countries referred to as the BRICS (Brazil, Russia, India, China, and South Africa) are all also included. (The 10th strategic partnership is with Mexico.) The strategic partners of the EU are all members of the G20, a group created in 2009 to bring together the world's strongest economies. No doubt an important motivation for identifying strategic partnerships has to do with reinforcing the EU's global economic position, as four of the five BRICS are among the EU's 10 largest trading partners (see Table 18.1).

Whether there are geopolitical motivations as well as economic ones for the EU's selection of strategic partners is hard to say. With the exception of Russia, none of the other strategic partners are in the immediate geographic neighbourhood of the EU. At the same time, other bases for the partnerships may be to mobilize increased support for key EU values such as multilateralism, and to gain cooperation in addressing global or regional issues such as climate change or regional conflicts. In short, the EU seeks to extend its trade and investment capacity, as well as elements of its foreign policy agenda, through such agreements. An important concern would be to maintain the EU's economic leadership role, as this is an important element of political influence. Box 18.1 takes a closer look at the strategic partnership with Canada.

The partnership with China has taken on particular importance due to the fact that China is the EU's second-largest trading partner, after the US;

**Table 18.1**    EU top trading partners, as % of merchandise extra-EU trade

|  | 2006 | 2011 | 2015 |
|---|---|---|---|
| US | 17.7 | 13.8 | 17.6 |
| China | 10.3 | 13.3 | 14.8 |
| Switzerland | 6.3 | 6.6 | 7.2 |
| Russia | 8.5 | 9.5 | 6.0 |
| Turkey | 3.7 | 3.7 | 4.0 |
| Norway | 4.7 | 4.4 | 3.5 |
| Japan | 4.9 | 3.6 | 3.3 |
| South Korea | 2.5 | 2.1 | 2.6 |
| India | 1.9 | 2.4 | 2.2 |
| Brazil | 1.8 | 2.3 | 1.9 |
| Canada | 1.8 | 1.6 | 1.8 |
| Saudi Arabia | 1.6 | 1.7 | 1.8 |

Source: European Commission, Directorate-General for Trade: http://trade.ec.europa.eu/doclib/
docs/2006/september/tradoc_122529.pdf;
http://trade.ec.europa.eu/doclib/docs/2006/september/tradoc_122530.pdf

**Box 18.1**    Canada's transatlantic connections

Canada is closely tied to the US, by trade, geography, and history.
While 75 per cent of Canada's exports went to the US in 2015, only
7.5 per cent went to the EU; for imports, the figures were 66.3 per
cent and 9.7 per cent. Canada's membership in the North Atlantic
Treaty Organization (NATO) provides a critical link to both the US
and Europe in the security sphere, but Canada's role there is often
overshadowed by the greater international political weight of the US.
Therefore, Canada's direct bilateral ties to the EU are an important
vehicle in Canadian efforts to diversify its trade and international pro-
file beyond is relationship with the US.

To reduce Canadian dependence on the US economy and to
expand Canada's links with Europe, a **Comprehensive Economic
and Trade Agreement (CETA)** was negotiated over several years
and signed in 2014 (see Chapter 14). Alongside CETA, the EU and
Canada also negotiated a Strategic Partnership Agreement (SPA),
which reaffirms a broad range of shared commitments, including in
the areas of political values, sustainable development, anti-terrorism,

non-proliferation of weapons of mass destruction, and the important role of effective multilateralism. Already Canada has supported several EU activities, including EU missions in Afghanistan, the Palestinian Territories, Kosovo, and Ukraine, as well as providing financial support to the EU's training mission in Mali.

As noted in this chapter, the EU's 10 strategic partnerships are viewed as important instruments for the EU in terms of achieving its foreign policy objectives. But among those partnerships, EU officials frequently emphasize the important place of Canada in this group. In a visit to Canada in 2016, the EU's High Representative for foreign and security policy stated, "We really see Canada as a key partner in multilateralism, in conflict management and conflict prevention, for stabilizing the different crises we have around us," referring to Canada as a "like-minded partner" (Delegation of the European Union to Canada, 2016). In particular, Canada has traditionally shared the EU's strong commitment to multilateralism, which involves support for international law, a rule-based international order, and strong international institutions, most importantly the United Nations. While many observers felt that Canadian support for these principles waned during Stephen Harper's terms as prime minister in favour of a policy prioritizing Canadian economic interests, support for multilateralism has been reaffirmed under the Trudeau government elected in the fall of 2015. Former foreign minister Stéphane Dion dubbed the approach one of "responsible conviction," contrasted with the "disengagement" of the Harper period, and, along with other government spokespersons, he has emphasized that Canada "is back" in world affairs. One could expect that this trajectory would provide reinforced opportunities for EU-Canada coordination in addressing global problems.

imports from China significantly exceed exports, leaving the EU with a significant negative trade balance with China. Efforts to negotiate a Partnership and Cooperation Agreement, launched in 2007, as well as an EU-China Investment Agreement, launched in 2013, have so far been unsuccessful. The EU has significant concerns regarding China's alleged "dumping" of products at prices below their value on the export market, and so far the EU has not granted China "market economy status," thus disadvantaging some Chinese imports. The EU also remains concerned about human rights violations in China, exemplifying the EU's difficulties in balancing economic and normative concerns in its foreign policy relations with emerging powers.

## The Middle East and the Arab Spring

The geographic proximity of the Middle East to Europe lends special importance to issues in this region. Instability in this region can have dramatic consequences for Europe. Moreover, several European countries have particular historical ties to countries in the Middle East. In 1995, well before the European Neighbourhood Policy was set out, the so-called Barcelona Process formed the basis for a Euro-Mediterranean Partnership with 12 countries from the region and involved attention to issues of economic and social development, cultural ties, and political stability and security. In 2008, the process was relaunched as the Union for the Mediterranean (see Chapter 16). The policy framework is complex, with varying membership of countries in different EU policy initiatives relevant to the region. Critics of the policy argue that the EU has prioritized stability and European economic interests over the proclaimed goals of democratic and market reform in the countries involved. Nonetheless, when the Arab Spring erupted in December 2010, the EU welcomed the civil society activism and the democratic impulse that underlay it. The main thrust of the EU response was to provide assistance to support the economic development of the countries involved and to begin negotiations on free-trade agreements with selected partner countries.

The civil war in Syria and the associated influx of hundreds of thousands of asylum seekers into the EU took over first place as the primary geopolitical concern of the EU in 2015. The particular challenge here is that the refugee flood falls outside the authority of any political jurisdiction. The crisis demonstrates graphically how political unrest in adjacent regions can dramatically affect the political and social situation inside the EU itself. Disagreements over an appropriate response have raged both within particular member states and EU institutions. Debate has centred on the relative weight of the EU's humanitarian obligations to asylum seekers and international commitments under the Geneva United Nations Convention relating to the Status of Refugees, on the one hand, and concerns about the EU's or national absorptive capacities and associated political risks, on the other. On another level, the issue crystallized the differing positions of the member states as to whether the EU could, or should, impose obligations on its member states to share the burden of accepting refugees. An agreement reached with Turkey in early 2016 regarding the return to Turkey of irregular migrants arriving in Greece in exchange for various concessions from the EU has come under threat as tensions have risen over Turkey's a drift toward authoritarianism under President Recep Tayyip Erdoğan. This issue again highlights the difficulties the EU faces in balancing its normative concerns (related to democratic governance in Turkey as well as Convention commitments to refugees) with its geopolitical interests (bringing massive refugee flows to Europe under control).

In terms of the Arab-Israeli conflict, another dimension of the Middle Eastern geopolitical environment, the EU has recognized its resolution as a key foreign policy priority. The EU has supported a two-state solution (i.e., security for the State of Israel alongside a viable Palestinian state), but it has not been effective in helping to realize this objective. In 2002, the EU became a member of the so-called Quartet (along with the United Nations, the US, and Russia), an entity involved in seeking a solution to the conflict. While the EU has played a role in crisis management and mediation in several instances, it has been hampered in its effectiveness by differing EU member state positions; in fact, European actors have taken a secondary role to the US in the peace process.

A notable success in EU foreign policy has involved efforts to prevent Iran from developing a nuclear weapons capacity. Non-proliferation of weapons of mass destruction has been a key policy goal of the EU, and one on which all member states remain highly united. It may be for this reason that EU efforts, since 2003, to mobilize the diplomatic resources of the EU, in conjunction with key EU member states (France, Germany, and the United Kingdom), to address this problem are considered to have made a positive contribution.

### International Terrorism

Since the dramatic attacks on the World Trade Center in New York City in September 2001, European capitals have also been the victims of high-profile terrorist attacks by Islamist radical groups, with significant loss of life. The most dramatic instances were attacks on Spanish commuter trains in 2004, on the Brussels airport and metro in March 2016, and on multiple locations in France in 2015 and 2016. Alongside these more widely publicized events, a larger number of smaller terrorist incidents have occurred, although the number of casualties from terrorist incidents in the EU is relatively low, in part due to successful anti-terrorist measures.

Following the November 2015 Paris attacks, increasing concern arose about a rising number of radicalized, "homegrown" youth involved with terrorist organizations. These incidents have fed Islamophobic sentiments across Europe, and fears were used by right-wing politicians to mobilize popular sentiments against asylum seekers. Apart from the domestic spillover of the terrorist actions, these events also brought increased attention in Europe's capitals to the roots of the problems. The risks generated by failed or failing states, socio-economic dislocation, ideological radicalization, and civil wars in various African and Middle Eastern countries came more sharply into focus as geopolitical concerns of national and EU leaders. Already in 2005 the EU had adopted a counterterrorism strategy, which involves preventative measures as well as engagement with other international partners, with an important role played by **Europol**, but concerns continued as to whether European security services were adequately coordinating their activities.

As in the regional sphere, these examples illustrate the mixed capacity of the EU to exert effective international influence. In part, this is due to the intractable nature of the problems being addressed and because of the changing nature of security and foreign policy challenges, which require cooperation with a wider variety of international partners that may not share the EU's basic value commitments. Through the use of strategic partnerships, the EU hopes to more effectively leverage its influence with rising global powers. At the same time, the effects of international crises, such as the one in Syria, have also had a critical impact on domestic politics in Europe, making the EU more vulnerable to the destabilizing effects of international conflict.

## Debate: Relations with Russia and the Ukraine Crisis

The relationship with Russia is among the most important, but in many instances among the most contentious, foreign policy issues in the EU. Various member states have widely diverging priorities relating to this issue. The 2004 and 2007 enlargements brought into the EU countries that had previously been under Soviet or, before that, Russian dominance. Some of these countries exhibit particular distrust of Russia, most notably Poland and the three Baltic states, Estonia, Latvia, and Lithuania. On the other hand, since its reunification in 1991, Germany has maintained quite positive relations with Russia, at least up until the Ukraine crisis in 2014. Along with Germany, other countries such as France and the Netherlands also have benefited from very strong trade and/or investment links to Russia, while other countries, such as the Baltic states, felt vulnerable to Russian economic pressure because, until recently, they received 100 per cent of their gas imports from there. Sweden and the United Kingdom have shown particular concern about Russian human rights violations, while the leaders of other nations have been more willing to overlook such issues, given the strong economic interdependencies. When EU member states were able to agree on a package of sanctions against Russia following the latter's annexation of the Ukrainian region of Crimea in February 2014, veteran EU observers were quite surprised. However, over time, divisions about the EU's policy toward Russia are re-emerging, as the EU considers how long to extend sanctions and whether and how to re-engage with Russia.

The EU remains Russia's most important trading partner (see Table 18.1), and the EU continues to be highly dependent on imports of oil and gas from Russia. In the 1990s there was widespread hope that the new Russian Federation would pursue a path of economic and political reform that would bring it into the mainstream of European development, as understood by the EU. And indeed, in 1997 a Partnership and Cooperation Agreement (PCA) between the EU and Russia went into effect. After 2007, it was extended on an ad hoc basis while (so far unsuccessful) negotiations were under way to come to a new agreement. The PCA proclaimed the "paramount importance of the rule of law and respect for human rights" and "the establishment of a multi-party system with free and democratic elections" as the basis of the relationship. In 1999, in an unusual step, the EU articulated a common strategy toward Russia (European Union, 1999), and Russia reciprocated a year later with the Medium-term Strategy for Development of Relations between the Russian Federation and the European Union (2000–10). Neither document has been updated since.

In 2003 Four Common Spaces of cooperation were agreed on between the EU and Russia, relating to economic cooperation; freedom, security, and justice; external security; and research, education, and culture. In 2004, the European Union invited Russia to join the European Neighbourhood Policy (see Chapter 16), but Russia refused this offer, not wishing to sign on to a made-in-Brussels initiative that would relegate it to an equal status with other "smaller" partner countries. Russia was the first country identified by the EU as a strategic partner, in 1998, which signalled the equality of the partners and the **sovereignty** of each. Within the framework of the strategic partnership, the EU and Russia established multiple venues for interaction, including a semi-annual summit involving the highest political leadership of the EU and Russia. In June 2010, the EU and Russia announced a new initiative, the Partnership for Modernization, intended to assist the Russian government in its effort to modernize and diversify its economy. However, from the beginning there was Russian resistance to the EU's attempt to include issues of political modernization (rule of law, human rights, democratic governance) in the concept.

Despite these concrete initiatives, neither Russia nor the EU developed a clear strategic vision for the relationship. Over time, Russia expressed more and more irritation at the EU's efforts to export its version of European norms and values. Russia objected to the EU's insistence on enforcing its market competition rules when the Russian gas monopoly, Gazprom, operated in the EU, while the **European Commission** investigations reflected EU beliefs about the political use of energy-export pricing and the anti-competition actions of Gazprom. In order to deal with underlying differences between the EU and Russia, issues of contest were increasingly redefined as technical issues, in an effort to make them less politically charged and more amenable to compromise. While some progress was made in terms of visa facilitation (i.e., making visas easier to get), the Russian side understood the EU to be placing repeated technical obstacles in the way of visa-free travel itself.

The deepest problems between the EU and Russia, however, stemmed from policies of the two parties in the shared neighbourhood, which refers to countries, formerly part of the USSR, that are now independent states and situated close to both Russia and the enlarged EU (Ukraine, Moldova, Belarus, Georgia, Armenia, and Azerbaijan). When the EU launched its Eastern Partnership policy in 2009 (see Chapter 16), Moscow reacted tepidly. However, over time the Russian leadership came to understand that if these countries moved closer to the EU, Russia's leverage could decline. The Russian leadership responded by reinforcing its own regional integration efforts, involving a regional **customs union**, which became the Eurasian Economic Union in 2015.

The Russian annexation of Crimea in February 2014 was viewed by the EU, as well as by other Western countries, as a blatant violation of Ukraine's sovereignty and of international law. A freeze in relations between the EU and Russia ensued. Efforts to fashion a compromise, initiated by German Chancellor Angela Merkel and French President François Hollande, led to conclusion of the so-called Minsk II protocol in February 2015, but the terms of that agreement have not been fulfilled on either the Russian or Ukrainian side. Russia's annexation of Crimea has remained an issue of severe disagreement between Russia and the West. East Ukraine is, at the time of this writing, still largely outside the control of the Ukrainian government in Kiev, with allegations of continuing support for rebel activity from Russia.

As a result, deep uncertainty remains in Brussels and in many European capitals as to how to deal with Russia. Disagreements have begun to emerge over how long sanctions should be left in place, about whether to engage the Eurasian Economic Union in dialogue, and whether normalized relations should be re-established, despite outstanding and deep objections to Russian actions in Ukraine, including Crimea. In early 2016, EU member states agreed on a policy of selective engagement when this serves EU interests, but the meaning of this statement is undefined and unclear. As long as the EU-Russia standoff continues, division between member states is likely to increase as the risks of re-escalation persist, as important economic ties deteriorate, and as other regional crises, such as the threat of radical Islamist terrorism and the Syrian conflict, could benefit from cooperation between Russia and the West. No clear path forward is evident.

Troubled relations between the EU and Russia since 2014 indicate that the geopolitical changes ushered in by the collapse of the USSR in 1991 still have a critical impact on the EU's capacity to realize its goal of peace and stability in Europe. Economic and energy interdependence between the EU and Russia have not provided the hoped-for foundation for positive political relations. The EU's transformative power in Europe, exemplified through the enlargement process, has not been effective with Russia. The continuing debate over how to deal with Russia reveals a tension between the EU's economic interests in engaging Russia and its normative commitments, which include defence of Ukraine's territorial integrity and continuing efforts to promote liberalizing reform through the Eastern Partnership policy. As tensions between the EU and Russia have grown, Russia has sought to compensate by intensified economic and political relations with China, making evident the challenge that the EU faces as the global constellation of power shifts.

## Conclusion

At the same time that the EU faces unprecedented internal challenges (the **Euro Area financial crisis** and its aftermath, a rise in **Euroskepticism** and nationalist tendencies, and Brexit), its external environment also seems fraught with dangers. The stability of the post-Soviet order in Europe has, with the eruption of the Ukraine crisis and continuing frozen conflicts in other states, proven to be more fragile than anticipated, placing in question the initial goal of the European integration project, i.e., avoiding war on the European continent (Theme 1 of this book). In addition, in the face of new challenges, namely continuing instability in the Middle East and the rising power of China and other BRICS countries, the EU has struggled to increase its capacity to act in a unified manner as a foreign policy actor. Differing member state positions have created difficulties in generating **common positions** in many arenas, thus highlighting the weaknesses of the EU's governance model, which falls short of a true federal state, since member states retain significant autonomy in the foreign policy arena (Theme 2 of this book).

Nonetheless, the EU has had some notable successes in exerting its influence both regionally and globally. On the regional level, this has included a common sanctions policy in response to Russia's annexation of Crimea, maintained despite economic costs to member states. Actions to stabilize the border between Moldova and Ukraine, mediating efforts following

Russia's intervention in Georgia, and the promotion of democratization and good governance in the West Balkans and in some Eastern Partnership countries are other indicators of success. The EU has also certainly become a global actor in the field of trade and economic relations. In other arenas, as well, the EU has proven a capability to "make a difference"—for example, in efforts to prevent Iran from developing nuclear weapons, in civilian missions in Africa, and in terms of climate change policy. Nonetheless, the EU has not yet established itself as a real global force. The continuing importance of individual member states' leadership has been, in some cases, a resource that the EU has been able to harness but, in other cases, an obstacle to unified action.

## References and Further Reading

Carerra, S., S. Blockmans, D. Gros, and E. Guild. 2015, December 16. The EU's response to the refugee crisis. *CEPS Essay No. 20*. Brussels: Centre for European Policy Studies

Casier, T. 2008. "The new neighbours of the European Union: The compelling logic of enlargement?" In *The boundaries of EU enlargement: Finding a place for neighbours*, edited by J. DeBardeleben, 19–32. Basingstoke, UK: Palgrave Macmillan. https://doi.org/10.1057/9780230591042_2.

DeBardeleben, J. 2009. "The impact of EU enlargement on the EU-Russian relationship." In *A resurgent Russia and the West: The European Union, NATO, and beyond*, edited by R.E. Kanet, 93–112. Dordrecht, Republic of Letters Publishing.

Delegation of the European Union to Canada. 2016, June 9. Mogherini welcomes close EU-Canada cooperation. https://eeas.europa.eu/delegations/canada/4037/mogherini-welcomes-close-eu-canada-cooperation_en.

European Union. 1999, June 24. *Common strategy of the European Union of 4 June 1999 on Russia. (1999/414/CFSP)*. http://trade.ec.europa.eu/doclib/docs/2003/november/tradoc_114137.pdf.

European Union. 2003, December 12. *A secure Europe in a better world: European security strategy*. Brussels: European Union. https://europa.eu/globalstrategy/en/file/10/download?token=ubYn8qBQ.

European Union. 2016. *Shared vision, common action: A stronger Europe: A global strategy for the European Union's foreign and security policy*. http://eeas.europa.eu/archives/docs/top_stories/pdf/eugs_review_web.pdf.

Forsberg, T., and H. Haukkala. 2016. *The European Union and Russia*. Basingstoke, UK: Palgrave Macmillan.

Hill, C. 1993. "The capability-expectations gap, or conceptualizing Europe's international role." *Journal of Common Market Studies* 31 (3): 305–28. https://doi.org/10.1111/j.1468-5965.1993.tb00466.x.

Howorth, J. 2010. "The EU as a global actor: Grand strategy for a global grand bargain." *Journal of Common Market Studies* 48 (3): 455–74. https://doi.org/10.1111/j.1468-5965.2010.02060.x.

Keukeleire, S., and T. Delreux. 2014. *The foreign policy of the European Union*. 2nd ed. Basingstoke, UK: Palgrave Macmillan.

Krickovic, A. 2015. "When interdependence produces conflict: EU-Russia energy relations as a security dilemma." *Contemporary Security Policy* 36 (1): 3–26. https://doi.org/10.1080/13523260.2015.1012350.

Lane, D., and V. Samokhvalov, eds. 2015. *The Eurasian project and Europe: Regional discontinuities and geopolitics*. Basingstoke, UK: Palgrave Macmillan. https://doi.org/10.1057/9781137472960.

Manners, I. 2002. "Normative power Europe: A contradiction in terms?" *Journal of Common Market Studies* 40 (2):235–58. https://doi.org/10.1111/1468-5965.00353.

Menon, R., and E. Rumer. 2015. *Conflict in Ukraine: The unwinding of the post-Cold War order*. Cambridge, MA: MIT Press.

Nielsen, K.L. 2013. "EU soft power and the capability-expectations gap." *Journal of Contemporary European Research* 9 (5): 723–39.

Nye, J. 2004. *Soft power: The means to success in world politics*. New York: Public Affairs.

Renard, T. 2016. "Partnerships for effective multilateralism? Assessing the compatibility between EU bilateralism, (inter-)regionalism and multilateralism." *Cambridge Journal of International Affairs* 29 (1): 18–35. https://doi.org/10.1080/09557571.2015.1060691.

Smith, K.E. 2014. *European Union foreign policy in a changing world*. 3rd ed. Cambridge: Polity Press.

Woolcock, S. 2014. "EU policy on preferential trade agreements in the 2000s: A reorientation towards commercial aims." *European Law Journal* 20 (6): 718–32. https://doi.org/10.1111/eulj.12101.

Wurzel, R.K.W., and J. Connelly. 2011. *The European Union as a leader in international climate change politics*. London: Routledge.

## Review Questions

1. Is the EU a geopolitical actor? Discuss how you would define the term. Consider how the EU may be similar or different in its geopolitical role from countries such as Canada or the US.

2. Is soft power (particularly normative power) an effective tool in dealing with geopolitical challenges? Discuss particularly in regard to the EU's relations with Russia and Ukraine.

3. How important is the relationship to the US for the EU? Discuss areas where the US and EU share geopolitical interests and areas where they differ, as well as variations in EU member state positions.

4. Should the EU focus its geopolitical concerns primarily on its immediate neighbourhood, or should it aspire to having an influence on a global level? Explain the reasons for your answers and consider counter-arguments.

5. Discuss areas where Russia and the EU have shared interests, and areas where their interests diverge.

## Exercises

1.  Familiarize yourself with definitions of "geopolitics" in different theories of international relations. What is the realist perspective on the EU as a geopolitical power? What is the liberal perspective? What is the constructivist perspective? Which perspective do you find holds the most explanatory power for explaining the EU's evolution to date?
2.  How could a UK exit from the EU affect the geopolitics of the EU? What might Brexit entail for the EU's self-conception and changing position as an international actor?

# 19

# Conclusion

EMMANUEL BRUNET-JAILLY, ACHIM HURRELMANN, AND AMY VERDUN

The primary goal of this textbook has been to introduce nearly 70 years of history of the European Union (EU) and to explain its current political system and policy-making processes. We have sought to illustrate that the EU has developed into a political system that has increasingly federal features, even if it falls short of being a federation. None of these developments are without challenge, and the path ahead is far from clear. The preceding chapters have detailed the expansion of the EU's institutions, legal system, and governance, as well as the history of ideas and theories about the **European integration** process. The book has also discussed 10 policy areas, so as to provide a nuanced overview of the EU's day-to-day activities. Finally, we have discussed two overarching challenges to the EU, namely, the democratization of its internal processes and the expansion of its geopolitical role. In this concluding chapter, we return briefly to what we have learned from each chapter and draw lessons from the achievements, problems, and future challenges of the EU.

In the introductory chapter of this book, we spelled out three themes that sum up the foundations and the logic of operation of the EU project. Theme 1 refers to the EU as a system of policy-making. It points out that the EU was created out of the ashes of World War II to guarantee peace based on a mixed economic system that combines market-making with social inclusion and market correction. Theme 2 addresses the institutional structure of the EU; it emphasizes that the EU is neither an international organization nor a federal state. Theme 3 focuses on the legitimation of the EU. Traditionally, it has been underscored primarily by the positive economic effect of European integration, but this strategy of maintaining legitimation—producing what has been labelled a "**permissive consensus**"—has over the past two decades been increasingly challenged in intensifying public debates about the EU's democratic quality. The deepening and widening of EU integration in recent decades—the addition of more member states and the expansion of EU powers above and beyond the core areas of economic policy—have added to these legitimation challenges.

As our 10 policy chapters illustrate, the idea that economic integration alone is at the core of the EU is no longer accurate: the policy spectrum of the EU is nearly as vast as that of its constituent member states. EU policies have often originated in and evolved out of an iterative, ill-timed process of expansion. Indeed, and perhaps ironically, EU policies have often developed further during and after crises. In this process, the EU has progressively become a policy instrument for European governments for the resolution of issues "bigger" than those that any one single member state can deal with in isolation. In fact, there have repeatedly been controversies between the EU and its member states. These conflicts have in the past decade often dominated media headlines (for instance in debates about the **Euro Area financial crisis** and the refugee crisis). Nevertheless, these instances of disagreement should not overshadow the achievements of the governments of the member states, which have continued to deepen integration. Other than the government of the United Kingdom, member state governments have done so because they have been convinced that the EU serves their national economic and political self-interest.

This concluding chapter draws some lessons from the preceding chapters about the nature of the European project within the context of the above-mentioned three themes. The chapter thus sums up this book's historical, institutional, and policy-oriented tour of the construction of the EU. In the end, how does our team of experts assess the construction of the EU collectively across these three themes? What perspectives emerge for the EU's future development?

> *Theme 1: To what extent does the EU still reflect the fact that the EU was created out of the ashes of World War II to seal peace in Europe, by fostering economic interdependencies in a mixed economic system that is neither state controlled nor left to an unconstrained market?*

Our review of the EU's history, institutions and law, but especially the discussion of the Union's market and trade policies, as well as its agricultural, environmental, and regional policies, suggest that the EU is possibly the world's largest regulating polity in existence today. Its institutions follow a logic of diversity that encompasses multiple forms of governance and policy-making attuned to the requirements of different policy areas. This diversity in EU governance has been created, in large part, in order to accommodate the different perspectives and preferences of the member states.

The most notable success of European integration has been the creation of the **Single Market**, as well as the associated policies on external trade and—more recently—monetary integration. In these policy areas, **supranational** institutions dominate policy-making; the jurisprudence of the **Court of Justice of the EU** has played an important supportive role. As anticipated by the original architects of European integration, the Single Market has created strong interdependencies among EU member states, which indeed make the prospect of war between them appear remote. Recent economic challenges have not undermined the Single Market. Even in the case of the financial crisis, the EU's anti-crisis measures have consisted of a further strengthening of the supranational and integration agenda. In trade policy, the signing of the **Comprehensive Economic and Trade Agreement (CETA)** between Canada and the EU illustrates not only the dominant importance of the **European Commission**'s supranational strategy but also the increasing pressures from the member states and their citizens to democratize trade policymaking by allowing for more democratic consultation and engagement.

In addition to the abolition of trade barriers through strategies of **negative integration**—including the **mutual recognition** of national regulatory regimes—the creation of the Single Market has also entailed the *production of EU-level rules* (positive integration) aimed at achieving a variety of social purposes, from product safety to environmental **sustainability**. In the process, the EU has developed a diverse and innovative regulatory toolkit. Environmental and energy policy is an example of a policy area in which the EU has pioneered new regulatory approaches (such as the Emissions Trading Scheme), which have turned the EU into a world leader in the fight against climate change.

In contrast to regulatory policies, the EU's attempts at market correction through *redistributive policies*—involving financial transfers—have been more fragmented. In part because of the limited size of the EU budget, agricultural and regional policies have remained the only major fields in which the EU applies redistributive strategies. The EU's agricultural policy achieved its original ambition of stabilizing food supplies, but led to overproduction and thus was criticized for its negative impact on world markets; recent reforms have seen the emergence of a "rural development" paradigm that many observers in other countries (including Canada) view as exemplary. Regional policies, started as a small area of **intergovernmental** partnerships, have evolved over a 40-year span to become an ambitious system for supporting regional development through investments in infrastructure and human capital.

The main fields of social policy, such as health care, pensions, unemployment insurance, and support for the poor, have remained, by contrast, largely in the realm of member states. Although pan-European standards and systems of non-binding coordination between member states exist, each state has to define—and fund—its own social policy regime. The way in which this policy area is governed thus emphasizes the interconnection between EU and member state governance. In member states—or specific policy areas within them—that are traditionally characterized by a liberal model of social policy with low levels of generosity, the EU adds to the social protections enjoyed by the citizens. In such contexts, most notably in the United Kingdom, it is sometimes even accused of overregulating. By contrast, in member states or policy sectors that have traditionally been characterized by high levels of social protection, the EU's mixed-economy model may imply pressure toward liberalization and deregulation. These pressures are especially strong if the member state in question has adopted the euro and hence must coordinate its economic policies with the other economies of the **Euro Area**.

Such pressures for liberalization emerging from EU policy have in recent years contributed to opposition to European integration, particularly in Southern Europe and most pronouncedly among parts of the population that have suffered the most from the recession, such as the unemployed and others who depend on social transfers. One of the main challenges for the future development of the EU will be the updating and further development of its mixed-economy model to address the concern that it is working only for the "winners of globalization" (e.g., the young or middle-aged, well-educated, geographically mobile professionals). This objective will require coordinated activities by EU institutions and by the member states, as the EU's supranational institutions do not have the power (competence) to implement a European mixed-economy model entirely on their own. In other words, EU and member state governance, and supranational and inter-governmental processes in the EU, cannot be considered in isolation. This insight brings us to the next theme.

*Theme 2: Given that the EU's achievements go far beyond similar attempts anywhere else in the history of the world, does it remain appropriate to characterize the EU as neither an international organization nor a full-fledged federal state?*

There can be no doubt that the EU is the most deeply integrated regional organization anywhere in the world. And yet the chapters in this book consistently emphasize that it has not become a full-fledged federal state. Federalist ideals, shared by some of the EU's founding fathers, have been frustrated by disagreements between member states over the larger institutional architecture of the EU, such as the relative powers of the Commission, **Council**, **European Council**, and Parliament. These disagreements have resulted in the creation of complicated procedural mechanisms that limit the transfer of policy competences from member states to the supranational institutions and require a **consensus**-oriented style of EU policy-making in which even small coalitions of member states possess veto powers.

As discussed in the institutional and governance chapters (Chapters 3 to 6), even when the **ordinary legislative procedure (OLP)** is applied—which would allow for **qualified majority voting (QMV)** in the Council and a simple majority in the Parliament—EU policy-making usually resorts to informal mechanisms (such as the so-called trilogues) that seek to construct a broad consensus both within and between the EU's legislative institutions. In sum, for idealists, the federal project for Europe is still in the works.

At the same time, the EU has indeed progressed much beyond a typical international organization. For instance, in its justice, freedom, and security policies, it has taken a leap forward into supranational governance, thanks to the standardization of an EU framework for managing borders and migration. Also, in the face of the multiple veto points that exist in its political system, the EU in practice often turns out to be a surprisingly successful decision-maker that relies on a multitude of modes of governance, which have made it possible to push the integration process forward in spite of opposition. This phenomenon is discussed in detail in the governance chapter (Chapter 6), which explains that because member states have granted additional powers to the EU while simultaneously refusing to increase the EU budget, the EU is forced to develop innovative governance mechanisms. By means of ongoing and recurrent processes of institutional innovation, including modes of governance that focus on coordinating policies and sharing best practices, it has been able to develop policies with a significant effect on European society.

Despite these adaptations, the EU's peculiar character as more than an international organization yet less than a federal state nevertheless implies challenges for the functioning of its political system. While its consensus-oriented style of policy-making has helped maintain the member states' support for European integration, as neither national elites nor citizens have much desire to see the EU acquire statehood, it has severely hampered the development of some EU policies. For instance, any expansion of the EU budget, which might help the EU develop policies that address the concerns of the "losers of globalization" (for instance, people who are unemployed or work in low-skilled, low-paying jobs), is vehemently resisted by the richer member states (especially Germany), which fear the development of a "transfer union." Similarly, member states in Eastern Europe have resisted attempts to develop an EU-wide scheme for the relocation of refugees, which would have eased pressures on border states in the **Schengen Area** (such as Greece and Italy) as well as states that have seen a particularly large influx of refugees (such as Germany or Sweden). Likewise, there is consensus in the foreign and defence policy as well as **geopolitics** chapters in this book

(Chapters 9 and 18) that the EU remains a rather weak actor on the global scene, as it is too complex, does not speak with one voice, has weak political legitimacy to represent all of its citizens in these matters, and lacks centralization in its decision-making apparatus. In these fields, the EU faces the task of reforming its institutional structure to increase its ability to deal with situations of *realpolitik*, such as the recent confrontation in Ukraine.

The character of the EU as an "unidentified political object" (as it was labelled by former Commission President Jacques Delors) also complicates the democratization of the EU. As explained in the democracy chapter (Chapter 17), democratization is an area in which considerable progress has been made, in particular by the strengthening of the **European Parliament's (EP)** legislative powers. Nevertheless, the EU's consensus-oriented policy processes, which often work behind closed doors, make it difficult to secure democratic accountability and to increase meaningful participation of EU citizens and representative organizations. State-based models of democracy prove difficult to apply to the EU system, but alternative ideas such as **demoi-cracy** thus far lack resonance in the citizenry. These considerations take us to the last theme.

> *Theme 3: In light of the issues that have been raised over the last 20 years with regards to citizenship and democratic participation, can the EU continue to base its legitimacy primarily on economic outcomes? In other words, does the fundamental choice to focus on economic integration remain a successful legitimating strategy?*

In the post–World War II era, the strategy was to construct European integration so as to promote peace and economic prosperity. The EU focused on economic integration, which was expected to solidify support for the overall integration project. Some have described this process of legitimizing the integration process by way of securing positive economic effects as focusing on "output legitimacy." As the discussion in this book shows, this strategy worked very well for many years. Increased economic interdependencies in the Single Market not only greatly contributed to achieving the original goal of peace-building, but also helped to turn the EU into an area of prosperity that neighbouring states and their populations have been eager to join. In recent years, however, the EU's output-based legitimation strategy has faced two challenges. First, a sequence of crises linked to core EU policies raised doubts about the material benefits of EU membership. The Euro Area financial crisis pointed to a major tension between the rules of **Economic and Monetary Union**—which demanded austerity policies in the states most severely hit by the crisis—and the political and social realities on the ground. Protestors in the streets criticized the EU for a lack of solidarity with those who were losing their jobs and seeing their state structures crumble. The refugee crisis, triggered by the entry of more than one million immigrants into EU territory, raised concerns about the EU's ability to control its external borders, pacify conflicts in its neighbourhood that give rise to refugee movements, and agree on a fair burden sharing between member states. Many citizens felt threatened by the influx of refugees and other migrants, and perceived them as a source of competition for low-skilled jobs and scarce state resources. In light of these challenges, the significant financial transfers that the EU provides in the form of agriculture and regional funds hardly resonated in public discussions and have not resulted in much legitimacy gain.

The second challenge to the EU's traditional model of economic legitimation originates from increasing demands for more democratic participation and greater transparency. The **Brexit** referendum in the United Kingdom, resulting in the decision to initiate that state's withdrawal from the EU, is in many ways the clearest indication that economic legitimation alone is no longer sufficient for the EU. With good reasons, the "remain" campaign in the referendum emphasized the negative economic consequences of Brexit. But the arguments of the "leave" campaign—many of them framed in terms of British identity, national **sovereignty** and democracy—were ultimately more compelling for a majority of the citizens who participated in the referendum. The Brexit referendum has encouraged **Euroskepticism** in other member states, who have long presented similar arguments.

The example of Brexit shows that "input legitimacy," which is grounded in the participation of citizens, has gained importance in the EU. Yet this does not mean that the EU's "outputs" have become irrelevant. Rather, the EU faces the dual challenge of increasing both its output and input legitimacy. On the output side, it will need to find ways to more effectively address the concerns of its citizens, especially by providing tangible benefits for the aforementioned "losers of globalization." There are also a number of policy successes that the EU could exploit more systematically to build its legitimacy. One example is its successful sustainability agenda, as detailed in the chapters on environmental and **regional policy** (Chapters 12 and 13). The regional policy chapter also notes the benefits of setting up more transparent local-regional partnerships, which require much clearer, data-generating projects, driven by multilevel and multi-sectorial cooperation. These strengthen local democratic agendas, which may result in adjustments in the EU's broader institutional architecture. On the input side, the EU requires further democratic reform. The EU needs to make explicit efforts to explain the workings of the EU to European citizens who perceive it as elitist and complicated. Many are unaware of the existing opportunities for political participation. Given these difficulties, another strategy for reform would involve trying, once again, to simplify the decision-making processes. This is a challenge, because the last time a major overhaul of the EU decision-making rules was attempted, with many access points for citizens, the end result was a draft constitution that was subsequently rejected by citizens in two national referendums. Thus, despite the need for reform, the exact path to get there remains unknown.

To sum up, our book contends that the EU is a peace-driven, mixed system, which developed as a market-maker, but also a regulator of social inclusion and market-correction policies. It is neither a federal state nor an international organization but a polity that rules thanks to complex modes of **multilevel governance** and partnerships. Its legitimacy was originally based on peace-building and economic integration. In the future, new forms of legitimacy originating in "**smart, sustainable and inclusive growth**" (to quote the EU's own **Europe 2020** agenda) and greater democratic transparency and engagement, will need to supplement these traditional considerations.

# Glossary

**Accession treaty:** A treaty that finalizes a country's accession to the EU. The treaty is concluded between the accession state and all current EU member states.

*Acquis communautaire:* A French term that refers to the cumulative body of EU law currently in force, consisting of all treaties, legislation, court decisions, and international agreements. All member states are bound to comply with the *acquis communautaire.* Candidate states must incorporate the *acquis communautaire* into their domestic legal system before they can join the EU.

**Anti-dumping:** A set of measures that can be taken by the European Commission in the context of the Common Commercial Policy to respond to non-EU companies that export a product to the EU at prices lower than the normal value of the product. These measures usually take the form of a duty.

**Area of Freedom, Security, and Justice (AFSJ):** The label that the EU has given to its policies related to justice, security, migration, and borders.

**Banking Union:** A set of policies developed in the context of Economic and Monetary Union that places responsibility for the supervision, resolution, and funding of banks and bank failures at the EU level. It applies to banks of Euro Area member states and to non–Euro Area banks if their member state has opted in.

**Bicameral legislature:** A legislative body that has two branches, chambers, or houses. In the EU, the European Parliament and the Council of the EU can be described as forming a bicameral legislature.

**Brexit:** An abbreviation for "British exit"; the term refers to the United Kingdom's decision to withdraw from the EU (as per the result of a referendum held on June 23, 2016).

**BRICS:** An informal group of states comprising the Federative Republic of Brazil, the Russian Federation, the Republic of India, the People's Republic of China, and the Republic of South Africa. These major emerging national economies started meeting in 2006 and represent about a quarter of global GDP and 42 per cent of the world's population.

**Candidate state:** A European country that has been formally recognized by the EU as a candidate for EU membership. Candidate states must pass far-reaching reforms to domestic legislation before they can be admitted to the EU.

**Capital Markets Union (CMU):** A plan launched by the European Commission in 2016 to increase the integration of capital markets in the EU.

**Cassis de Dijon:** A landmark ruling by the Court of Justice of the EU that established the principle of "mutual recognition": if a product is legally marketed in one member state, the product should normally be considered legal in other member states as well.

**Climate and Energy Packages:** A set of EU policies that set specific goals to reduce the EU's contribution to greenhouse gas emissions, and policy mechanisms to achieve these goals.

**Cohesion policy**: The formal name of the EU's regional policy that seeks to address regional economic disparities and to promote smart, sustainable, and inclusive growth through targeted investments in physical infrastructure and human capital.

**Cold War**: A state of geopolitical tension, from 1947 to 1991, between countries that were part of the Western alliance (United States, Western Europe, and its NATO allies) and the Eastern alliance (Soviet Union and the Warsaw Pact countries).

**Command-and-control**: An interventionist approach to environmental legislation focused on setting binding standards for environmental quality (command), followed by strict monitoring and enforcement (control).

**Committee of Permanent Representatives (COREPER)**: An institution composed of representatives of the member states permanently located in Brussels. COREPER is charged with managing intergovernmental relations between the member states and preparing meetings of the Council of the EU.

**Common Agricultural Policy (CAP)**: A set of EU policies to stabilize the food supply, guarantee the economic viability of farming through agricultural subsidies (direct payments to farmers), and promote rural development in the EU.

**Common Commercial Policy (CCP)**: The EU's policy on trade with non-EU countries; it encompasses managing the EU's common external tariffs, concluding trade agreements with non-EU states, and employing commercial instruments in the context of the EU's existing trade agreements.

**Common Foreign and Security Policy (CFSP)**: The EU's policy framework for dealing with issues of foreign, security, and defence policy. The CFSP encompasses the EU's Common Security and Defence Policy (CSDP). The CFSP is governed through rules that are more intergovernmental in character than regular EU policies.

**Common Market**: A term used in the 1950s, 1960s, 1970s, and early 1980s that has since been replaced by the term "Single Market."

**Common position**: A draft legislative proposal by the Council in the third stage of the ordinary legislative procedure, aimed at producing a compromise with the European Parliament on a contentious piece of legislation.

**Common Security and Defence Policy (CSDP)**: The EU's policy framework for defence policy issues, including civilian and military intervention in international crises (see also "Common Foreign and Security Policy").

**Competition policy**: A set of policies to secure free competition between companies in the EU's Single Market, inter alia, by reviewing mergers and acquisitions, sanctioning the establishment of cartels or the abuse of a dominant market position, and limiting state aid to companies.

**Comprehensive approach**: An inclusive approach in the EU's Common Security and Defence Policy, characterized by the mix of military and civilian instruments.

**Comprehensive Economic and Trade Agreement (CETA)**: An international economic agreement between Canada and the EU (provisionally applied as of 2017), covering tariff barriers, government procurement, investment protection, intellectual property, and regulatory cooperation. It includes an Appellate Tribunal to deal with investor-state disputes.

**Conditionality**: Legal, administrative, economic, and political reforms that an EU candidate state must have made as a condition for membership (see also "Copenhagen Criteria").

**Consensus**: A constellation in which all decision-makers support a certain decision or action, or at least do not object to it.

**Convergence criteria (Maastricht)**: A set of criteria (spelled out in the Maastricht Treaty) that EU member states must meet in order to join EMU. These include upper limits for budgetary deficits, public debt, inflation rates, and long-term interest rates, and participation in the Exchange Rate Mechanism for at least the last two years prior to joining.

**Copenhagen Criteria**: A set of conditions that candidate states must meet before their accession to the EU. These include stable political institutions that guarantee democracy, the rule of law, human rights, and minority protection; a functioning market economy that can cope with competitive pressures in the EU's Single Market; and adoption and effective implementation of the *acquis communautaire*.

**Coordination**: A form of non-binding intergovernmental policy-making; it consists of setting common policy targets and peer-reviewing member state policies without binding EU legislative measures.

**Council**: See "Council of the European Union."

**Council of Europe**: A regional organization, separate from the EU, which seeks to promote human rights, democracy, and the rule of law in Europe. It was set up in 1949 and currently has 47 member states. Canada was granted official observer status in 1996.

**Council of the EU**: One of the EU's core legislative institutions; the Council of the EU (or "Council" for short) is an intergovernmental institution that brings together ministers from each member state, meeting in various formations (depending on the policies discussed). The Council presidency rotates between member states on a half-yearly basis. Formerly referred to as Council of Ministers.

**Court of Justice of the EU (CJEU)**: The EU's judicial institution; the CJEU is tasked with interpreting EU law to make sure it is applied in the same way in all EU countries and with settling legal disputes between national governments and EU institutions.

**Crisis management**: In the context of the EU's Common Security and Defence Policy, a military or civilian intervention—such as peace-making or post-conflict stabilization—in an international crisis or emergency.

**Customs union**: An area of free trade with a common external tariff (common import duties).

**Decision**: A type of EU secondary law; a decision is a flexible legislative instrument that is binding for specific addressees.

**Decoupled payment**: In the context of the Common Agricultural Policy, an agricultural subsidy to farmers that is not tied to production.

**Delors Report**: A proposal by a committee chaired by European Commission President Jacques Delors in 1988 that formed the basis for the establishment of the Economic and Monetary Union.

**Democratic deficit**: A prominent theme in academic and political discourse. This term captures a list of reasons why the EU is insufficiently democratic.

**Demoi-cracy**: A model of democracy that takes the diversity of the EU's political community—the existence of various national *demoi* (peoples)—as a starting point and seeks to develop consensus-oriented political institutions that protect the integrity of these *demoi*.

**Demos**: The Greek word for "people"; used in discussions about democracy in the EU to denote a political community of citizens united by a shared identity. Plural: *Demoi*.

**Diplomacy**: The profession, activity, or skill of maintaining international relations, typically by a political entity's representative abroad.

**Direct payments**: Subsidies paid to farmers under the EU's Common Agricultural Policy. All direct payments are now integrated in a "Single Farm Payment."

**Direct effect**: A core principle of EU law established by the Court of Justice of the EU. Direct effect means that EU law can create rights and obligations for citizens (and not just for the member states) that are enforceable in court.

**Directive**: A type of EU secondary law; a directive establishes binding objectives, which the member states are obliged to transpose into domestic legislation. Directives are commonly used to harmonize the laws of the member states on a particular matter, so that the same rules and standards apply uniformly throughout the EU.

**Directorate-General (DG)**: An administrative unit in the European Commission responsible for a specific task or policy area.

**Dublin Regulation**: A piece of EU legislation in the area of asylum policy; it stipulates that refugees need to register and claim asylum in the first EU member state they land in.

**Economic and Financial Affairs Council (ECOFIN)**: The Council configuration that brings together the member states' finance ministers or equivalent.

**Economic and Monetary Union (EMU)**: Arrangements built on the Single Market that enabled the completion of the four freedoms, in particular free movement of capital and the creation of the single currency, the euro. EMU consists of a supranational monetary policy, set by the European Central Bank, for member states that are part of the Euro Area.

**Emissions Trading System (ETS)**: A cornerstone of the EU's policy to combat climate change; the ETS is a cap-and-trade system applied to high-emission industries that disburses a limited (and shrinking) number of emissions permits that can be traded between companies.

**Energy security**: The uninterrupted availability of energy at an affordable, predictable, and fair price.

**Energy Union**: A 2015 EU initiative launched to move toward achieving energy security, liberalization of energy markets, and climate targets.

**Enlargement**: In the EU context, the accession of new states to the EU.

**Enlargement fatigue**: Sentiments in public opinion in existing EU member states that are characterized by increasing opposition toward further enlargement.

**Environmental Action Programme (EAP)**: A document defining the future orientation of EU policy in the environmental field and suggesting specific proposals that the Commission intends to put forward over the coming years.

**Euratom**: European Atomic Energy Community, one of the three original European Communities. Euratom was established in the Treaty of Rome in 1957; it aims to create and develop the peaceful use of atomic energy in Europe. It is legally distinct from the EU but has the same members. In January 2017 the UK indicated that it was also seeking to leave Euratom.

**Euro Area**: The EU member states using the euro as their currency.

**Euro Area financial crisis**: (also referred to as the "sovereign debt crisis" or "Euro area crisis"): A crisis between 2010 and 2016 in which various Euro Area member states were unable to refinance their government debt or unable to bail out their financial sector (i.e., Greece, Ireland, Portugal, Spain, and Cyprus). To assist these countries, other Euro Area member states and the IMF provided financial support and in return demanded national reforms, monitored by a "troika" of three institutions (the European Central Bank, the European Commission, and the International Monetary Fund).

**Europe 2020:** The EU's 10-year growth strategy adopted in 2010, which established the goal of "smart, sustainable and inclusive growth."

**European Arrest Warrant (EAW):** A mechanism under the EU's Area of Freedom, Security and Justice that commits member states to surrender citizens to other EU member states if they are wanted in relation to significant crimes or to serve a prison sentence for an existing conviction.

**European Atomic Energy Community:** See "Euratom."

**European Central Bank (ECB):** An independent central bank that sets monetary policy for the Euro Area.

**European Coal and Steel Community (ECSC):** The first European Community, created by six Western European states (West Germany, France, Italy, the Netherlands, Belgium, and Luxembourg) through the Treaty of Paris in 1951; the ECSC subjected the member states' coal and steel production to a supranational regulatory regime.

**European Commission:** The main executive body of the EU, which also possesses the monopoly of legislative initiative in most policy areas. The Commission is a supranational body composed of one commissioner per member state, each with a portfolio of responsibilities, tasked with promoting the general interest of the EU.

**European Council:** The summit meeting of heads of state or government of the member states, tasked with defining the general political directions and priorities of the EU. The European Council is headed by a president serving a 2.5-year term.

**European Court of Human Rights (ECtHR):** An international court set up in 1959, which rules on individual or state applications alleging violations of the civil and political rights set out in the European Convention on Human Rights (ECHR). The ECtHR is not an EU institution; it is governed by the Council of Europe.

**European Defence Community (EDC):** Proposed by Jean Monnet and launched in 1951 by the French head of government, René Pleven, this proposed Community was meant to allow for the rearmament of West Germany in a supranational framework (as opposed to having that country join NATO). The EDC would have had the same member states as the ECSC. All member states signed it, but it ultimately failed due to the fact that it was not ratified by the French National Assembly.

**European Deposit Insurance Scheme (EDIS):** A proposed policy, forming part of Banking Union, that would insure deposits in European banks against bank failure.

**European Economic Area (EEA):** The Single Market of the EU member states and three of the four EFTA countries (Iceland, Liechtenstein, and Norway). The agreement ensures that non-EU countries can be part of the EU Single Market; they have to adopt all EU laws but have exemptions in the area of agriculture and fisheries (see also "Single Market").

**European Economic Community (EEC):** One of the three original European Communities, established in 1957 through the Treaty of Rome by the same states that had established the European Coal and Steel Community. It aimed to promote economic integration between member states, mainly through the establishment of a Common Market and a custom union. The EEC was later renamed European Community (EC) and was merged with the EU in the Treaty of Lisbon.

**European External Action Service (EEAS)**: Diplomatic service of the EU, headed by the High Representative of the Union for Foreign Affairs and Security Policy.

**European Free Trade Association (EFTA)**: A free trade agreement formed in the 1960s by European states that did not want to join the European Communities. Most states have since joined the EU, but EFTA remains as a separate institution with four member states (Iceland, Liechtenstein, Norway, and Switzerland).

**European integration**: The process of establishing common institutions and policies in Europe, bringing European states closer together. The EU is the most prominent institutional result of European integration; the Council of Europe is another example.

**European Neighbourhood Policy (ENP)**: An EU policy that aims to improve the EU's relations with countries in its eastern and southern neighbourhoods; the ENP is based on bilateral agreements on closer economic and political cooperation but does not provide the participating states an explicit membership perspective.

**European Parliament (EP)**: One of the core legislative institutions of the EU; the EP is composed of 751 elected Members of the European Parliament (MEPs). Its primary roles include passing laws together with the Council of the EU, adopting the budget with the Council of the EU, deciding on international agreements and enlargements, scrutinizing the executive institutions, and approving the nominations for the members of the European Commission.

**European Rate Mechanism (ERM)**: A system that ties the currencies of non-Euro Area member states to the euro, and determines exchange rates.

**European Regional Development Fund (ERDF)**: One of the structural funds set up in the context of the EU's regional policy to support regional economic development.

**European Social Fund (ESF)**: One of the structural funds set up in the context of the EU's regional and social policy to support employment and labour mobility; education, skills, and lifelong learning; social inclusion; and efficient public administration.

**European Social Model**: A vaguely defined set of values and institutions that are said to define a European approach to social policy, characterized by a higher degree of solidarity and more generous social programs than in North America.

**European Stability Mechanism (ESM)**: An intergovernmental institution set up by Euro Area member states in the context of the Euro Area financial crisis to provide loans to Euro Area member states that experience sovereign debt crises.

**European System of Central Banks (ESCB)**: The institutional framework for monetary policy in the Economic and Monetary Union; it consists of the European Central Bank working together with the national central banks of the member states.

**Europeanization**: A concept in EU studies that describes how the EU impacts the member states. It can refer to a top-down process in which research focuses on how the EU shapes institutions, processes, and policies in the member states; or to a bottom-up process in which research examines how member states and other domestic actors shape the EU and its policies.

**Europol**: The European Union Agency for Law Enforcement Cooperation headquartered in The Hague (Netherlands). It plays a front-line role in coordinating the EU member states' fight against terrorism and cross-border crime. It also collaborates with non-EU states and international organizations.

**Euroskepticism**: A political opinion, manifested in parties and social movements, which explicitly opposes the European integration project, often because of concerns about the dilution of national sovereignty and identity.

**Federalism**: A political system composed of multiple political levels (usually a federal level and multiple regional subunits), each of which possesses its own legislative, executive, and judicial institutions. The decision-making competences of each level are defined in a constitution, which cannot be unilaterally amended by any one level. Federalism can also refer to the theory or advocacy of reaching a federal political system.

**Fiscal federalism**: (1) The sharing of critical functions between the different levels of government (federal and lower levels), e.g., providing public goods and services, income redistribution, and macroeconomic stabilization; (2) Identifying welfare gains for its different parts; (3) Taxation at different levels of government; (4) Use of instruments of fiscal policy for redistribution at both federal and lower levels of government.

**Five Presidents' Report**: A programmatic report by the presidents of the European Commission, European Council, European Parliament, European Central Bank, and Eurogroup proposing the next steps in the development of Economic and Monetary Union.

**Foreign direct investment (FDI)**: An international investment whereby a resident entity in one economy seeks to obtain a lasting interest in an enterprise resident in another economy.

**Foreign policy**: The strategies chosen by a country or political entity to safeguard its interests and to achieve its goals in its regional or global environment.

**Four freedoms**: Freedom of movement of goods, services, persons, and capital.

**Freedom of movement (of people)**: The right of EU citizens to travel between EU member states without restrictions or barriers, and to take up employment or establish a company in another member state. Freedom of movement is one of the core principles of the EU's Single Market.

**Frontex**: The European Border and Coast Guard Agency (formerly the European Agency for the Management of Operational Cooperation at the External Borders of the Member States of the European Union), which provides support to national authorities in the monitoring and controlling of the EU's external borders.

**General Affairs Council (GAC)**: The configuration of the Council of the EU that discusses overarching concerns not restricted to any specific policy area; member states are usually represented by their foreign minister or European affairs minister in this Council configuration.

**Geopolitics**: A framework for the analysis of power in international relations that takes into account spatial or geographic contexts.

**Global financial crisis**: The 2008–09 global financial crisis is considered the worst of its kind since the Great Depression of the 1930s. It started in July 2007 with a loss in confidence in US sub-prime mortgages and related financial instruments, causing foreclosures and an international banking crisis. It worsened in September 2008 when stock markets became severely volatile. It led to a deep economic recession in 2009 and triggered the start of the sovereign debt crisis in the Euro Area in late 2009.

**Governance mode**: The specific configuration of strategies and tools that the EU uses to reach policy objectives; these might include the exercise of authority where permitted by the treaties, financial transfers where there EU has the necessary resources, as well as non-hierarchical approaches such as information sharing or coordination between member states.

**Grand theory**: A theory that aims at a higher level of understanding about the nature of the political system but does not concern itself too much with the details of the empirics. Advanced in first instance by scholars such as the sociologist C. Wright Mills in the 1960s (see also "Mid-range theory").

**Green payment**: In the context of the Common Agricultural Policy, a payment disbursed to farmers on the condition that they undertake practices that are beneficial to the climate and to the environment.

**High politics**: Political issues that relate to the exercise of power and are deemed to be politically central to national sovereignty, including the politics of foreign and military affairs.

**Intellectual property (IP)**: A work or invention that is the result of creativity, such as a design, to which one has rights and for which one may apply for a copyright, trademark, or patent.

**Intergovernmental / intergovernmentalism**: In EU decision-making, processes whereby member states, as opposed to supranational institutions, play the most important role in determining policy outcomes. An intergovernmental theory of European integration is one that privileges the role of states in describing and explaining the integration process.

**Intervention agencies**: In the context of the Common Agricultural Policy, national agencies responsible for price intervention.

**Investor State Dispute Settlement (ISDS)**: A component in bilateral trade agreements concluded by the EU; it establishes a system through which individual companies can sue countries for alleged discriminatory practices.

**Joint action**: In the context of the Common Foreign and Security Policy, the exercise of coordinated action by member states to commit resources for an agreed objective.

**Justice and Home Affairs (JHA)**: The former label used for the EU's policies related to justice, security, migration, and borders. The name was introduced when the policy area became Pillar III of the EU in the Maastricht Treaty; it was replaced by the name Area of Freedom, Security, and Justice (AFSJ) in the Lisbon Treaty.

**Kyoto Protocol**: An international agreement concluded in the context of the United Nations Framework Convention on Climate Change, which commits its parties by setting internationally binding emission-reduction targets.

**Lisbon Strategy**: Launched in 2000, this strategy for the EU's economic and social policy, set itself a goal to become "the most competitive and dynamic knowledge-based economy in the world" by 2010. Strongly influenced by the "social investment" paradigm and broadened by the notion of social policy beyond its traditional focus on social protection, it included social promotion and human capital development. It introduced new mechanisms to coordinate the member states economic and social policies.

**Lisbon Treaty**: The most recent major reform of EU primary law that came into effect in December 2009. The Lisbon Treaty gave the EU a unified legal personality by abolishing the previous pillar structure. It contained major institutional reforms, such as the creation of the post of the President of the European Council. It also contained reforms that strengthened the European Parliament and other democratic mechanisms.

**Low politics**: A term used for policies that are relatively technical in nature and do not normally elicit great public interest (such as product regulation).

**Maastricht Treaty**: A major reform of EU primary law that came into effect in November 1993. The Maastricht Treaty formally established the EU, alongside the previously existing European Communities (European Coal and Steel Community, European Community, Euratom). It first established the EU's Common Foreign and Security Policy and EU policies in the area of Justice and Home Affairs. It also created the institutional foundations for Economic and Monetary Union.

**MacSharry reforms**: A major reform of the Common Agricultural Policy that started the shift from product support (through price intervention) to producer support (through direct payments).

**Market-based style of environmental regulation**: The utilization of market principles to encourage environmentally friendly policies (see, for example, "Emissions Trading System").

**Mid-range theory**: A theory that seeks to integrate empirical insights with modest theoretical understanding (see also "Grand theory").

**Multiannual Financial Framework (MFF)**: The EU's seven-year budget plan that sets the parameters for each year's budget. Decisions concerning the MFF are characterized by tough bargains among member states and between intergovernmental and supranational institutions in the EU.

**Multilateralism**: International cooperation of multiple countries to address or solve a given issue.

**Multilevel governance / multilevel system**: A theoretical framework for research on the EU that focuses on the interactions between the EU level, the national level, and the sub-state level.

**Mutual recognition**: A principle in EU law that requires member states to respect each other's regulatory policies. Applied to the trade in goods, the principle states that member states must normally allow goods that are legally sold in another member state to also be sold in their own territory.

**Negative integration**: A form of integration that involves the removal of barriers between the member states (see also "Positive integration").

**New institutionalism**: A label used for a group of theories developed in the 1990s that reintroduced institutional analysis against the backdrop of the dominance of behavioural approaches in earlier decades.

**Neofunctionalism**: A theory of regional integration that emphasizes how integration processes can develop their own dynamics (most importantly, through processes of spillover between policy areas) and hence spiral out of the control of the member states.

**Non-discrimination**: A core principle of European integration, stating that citizens of the member states must be treated in the same way regardless of their nationality. The principle has also been applied to other relevant differences, such as gender or age.

**Non-tariff barriers**: Barriers to trade that do not originate in tariffs; the most important non-tariff barriers in the EU today result from the regulation of products (e.g., technical standards) or production processes (e.g., environmental or workplace safety rules).

**Open Method of Coordination (OMC)**: A mechanism developed in the area of social and employment policy to coordinate member state policies. The procedure entails a four-step process, whereby the EU level defines policy guidelines and targets, while member states formulate and implement their policies within this framework.

**Opinion**: A decision by the Court of Justice of the EU on the legality of a proposed agreement between the EU and a third country. EU institutions such as the European Parliament may request an opinion before the proposed international agreement enters into force.

**Opt-out**: A clause in the EU treaties or in EU legislation, which allows member states to refrain from participation in certain political actions.

**Ordinary legislative procedure (OLP)**: The normal procedure for most legislation of the EU, in which the European Parliament acts on an equal footing with the Council. The OLP was built on the co-decision procedure introduced by the Maastricht Treaty. It requires that legislation proposed by the Commission can be amended and must be approved by both the Council and the European Parliament.

**Paris Treaty**: The treaty that established the European Coal and Steel Community. It was signed in 1951, came into effect in 1952, and expired in 2002.

**Permissive consensus**: A term first introduced in 1970 by Lindberg and Scheingold, who described the European integration process as passively approved of by public opinion.

**Pillars of the EU**: A system of organizing the EU, established in the Maastricht Treaty and abolished in the Lisbon Treaty, that distinguished (I) the European Communities (European Coal and Steel Community, European Community, Euratom), (II) the Common Foreign and Security Policy, and (III) Justice and Home Affairs. Pillars II and III were based on intergovernmental cooperation method, whereas Pillar I was based on the Community integration method.

**Politicization**: A concept in studies used to describe the (growing) contestedness of EU-related issues in the population.

**Positive integration**: The creation of binding EU-level rules (normally in the form of legislation) that replace previously existing member state laws with a view to deeper integration (see also "Negative integration").

**Primary law**: In EU law, the name given to legal acts of the highest order. The EU's primary law is constituted by the EU Treaties.

**Public procurement**: The process by which public entities (such as governments) purchase work, goods, and services from companies.

**Qualified majority voting (QMV)**: A mode of decision-making in the Council of the EU; QMV requires that at least 55 per cent of the member states, representing at least 65 per cent of the EU population, support a proposal for it to pass and become law. QMV is the standard decision rule of the Council under the ordinary legislative procedure.

**Recommendation**: In EU law, a non-binding legislative act. The Commission often makes recommendations to the member states, or other institutions, as to how to move forward to achieve goals in a particular area where either binding legislation is not within the EU's competence or the necessary support in the Council or Parliament for a binding legislative act cannot be achieved.

**Reference for a preliminary ruling**: A procedure exercised before the Court of Justice of the European Union. Under this procedure, national courts are required to request a decision from the CJEU whenever a case before them rests on an undecided question of EU law. The reference for a preliminary ruling therefore offers a means to guarantee legal certainty by uniform application of EU law.

**Refugee crisis**: A crisis that culminated in Europe in 2015–16 (after building up over many years), when more than one million refugees and other undocumented migrants arrived in EU member states, mostly fleeing war and terror in Syria and other countries. This influx was considered a crisis in part because of the sheer number of people, the casualties and hardship related to their journey, as well as the difficulties that the EU had in finding the appropriate policy response.

**Regional policy**: See "Cohesion policy."

**Regulation**: A type of EU secondary law. A regulation is a legal act that is immediately enforceable simultaneously in all member states (meaning that it does not first need to be transposed into national law). A regulation is binding in its entirety for all natural and legal persons in the EU.

**Renewable energy**: Power generated from natural resources that can be naturally be replenished. Examples are energy from sunlight, wind, tides, geothermal heat, and biomass.

**Schengen Area**: The territory of member states that are signatories to the Schengen Agreement. At the time of this writing, the area encompasses 22 EU member states and four non-EU states. Member states of the Schengen Area have abolished internal border controls (between each other), though such controls may be temporarily reintroduced in emergency situations.

**Schuman Plan**: An official statement made on May 9, 1950, by the French foreign minister, Robert Schuman, proposing to pool French and West German coal and steel production.

**Second-order national election**: An influential characterization of European Parliament elections that points out that many voters approach these elections primarily as a relatively non-consequential opportunity to express an opinion about member state politics. According to this view, the second-order character of EP elections explains why turnout may be low and the campaign dominated by national issues.

**Single Farm Payment (SFP)**: The consolidated direct payment to farmers under the Common Agricultural Policy.

**Single Market**: An area of free movement of goods, services, persons, and capital among the EU member states. Also referred to as the Internal Market or (formerly) Common Market. All EU member states are part of the Single Market. Three of the four EFTA countries also form part of it through their membership of the EEA. Switzerland has not joined the EEA but has made bilateral agreements so it can also be part of the Single Market.

**Smart, sustainable, and inclusive growth**: The core objective of the EU's Europe 2020 growth strategy; it refers to a form of economic growth which prioritizes investments in education, research, and innovation while creating new jobs and combating poverty within all countries of the EU.

**Social partners**: Employer and employee representatives at the EU level; their perspectives are incorporated into EU social policy-making.

**Soft power**: A form of power in the international sphere that derives not from military resources but from economic, cultural, and other non-material factors—such as ideas, discourse, and example-setting—that may appeal and attract.

**Sovereign debt crisis**: See "Euro Area financial crisis."

**Sovereignty**: In international relations, national sovereignty refers to the principle of supreme power or authority of the state. In concrete terms, it means that states have the right to determine their internal affairs without outside interference.

**Spillover**: In the theory of neofunctionalism, the term is used to describe a situation in which regional integration in one policy sector creates pressures to integrate in another, connected sector.

**Supranational / supranationalism**: In EU decision-making, processes that are controlled by institutions that represent the EU as a whole, rather than the member states, and are designed to express the common European interest.

**Supremacy (also called primacy)**: A core principle of EU law that states that EU law takes precedent over the law of the member states. The principle was established by the Court of Justice of the EU and is affirmed in Declaration 17 of the Lisbon Treaty.

**Sustainability**: The ability to utilize a resource within a given territory without damaging future resources or the environment's ability to reproduce that resource.

**Tariffs**: Taxes on imports or exports.

**Third country nationals (TCNs)**: Persons who are not EU citizens.

**Treaty of Rome**: The Treaty that established the European Economic Community and the European Atomic Energy Community (Euratom); signed in 1957, came into effect in 1958.

**Treaty on European Union (TEU)**: A core element of the EU's current primary law; defines the EU's core values, aims, and institutions. The TEU was first drawn up as part of the Maastricht Treaty.

**Treaty on the Functioning of the European Union (TFEU)**: A core element of the EU's current primary law; defines the EU's powers and decision-making processes in a large range of policy fields.

**TTIP (Transatlantic Trade and Investment Partnership)**: A proposed trade agreement between the EU and the United States, with the aim of promoting trade and multilateral economic growth. Negotiations started in July 2013.

**Trilogue**: A system of informal consultations between the European Commission, the European Parliament, and the Council of the EU that takes place in the context of the ordinary legislative procedure. The goal of the trilogue is to produce a compromise on a specific piece of EU legislation, if possible without going through all three stages of the OLP.

**Unanimity**: A form of decision-making that requires explicit support by all decision-makers (such as member states in the Council of the EU).

**Welfare system**: A system dedicated to maintaining the well-being and equality of citizens by providing for those in need through government assistance, policy, and regulations.

**Werner Plan**: An early blueprint for the Economic and Monetary Union, proposed by a committee chaired by Luxembourg's prime minister and finance minister, Pierre Werner, in 1970.

**World Trade Organization (WTO)**: An international organization that oversees the global trade in goods and services.

# Appendix: Research Resources

EMMANUEL BRUNET-JAILLY, ACHIM HURRELMANN, AND AMY VERDUN

Research on European integration can make use of a wide variety of sources. Most primary sources (e.g., legal or policy documents, party manifestos, statistical data) are available on the Internet. There is also a large body of scholarly literature on EU studies, which includes book publications and journal articles. This appendix provides sources that might be useful for students who are doing research on EU institutions, legislation, current policies, or democratic life; sources for EU-related socio-economic data; as well as a list of some of the most important scholarly journals focusing on European integration.

## EU Institutions

The **Europa website** (europa.eu) is the official Web portal of the EU. Offered in 24 languages, it contains basic information about the EU. It also houses the websites of the EU institutions and provides links to EU legislation and other policy documents.

Each EU institution has its own website on the Europa platform; these include the **European Commission** (https://ec.europa.eu/commission/index_en), **Council and European Council** (http://www.consilium.europa.eu/en/home/), **European Parliament** (EP, http://www.europarl.europa.eu/portal/), **Court of Justice of the EU** (https://curia.europa.eu), and **European Central Bank** (http://www.ecb.europa.eu/home/html/index.en.html). These websites contain information about the institutions' personnel and administrative structure, and current policy processes and priorities, as well as important policy documents.

In addition, the **rotating presidency of the Council** sets up its own website, hosted by the government that holds the current presidency (for instance, the Maltese presidency in the first half of 2017 established the website https://www.eu2017.mt/en/Pages/home.aspx). This website informs visitors about Council meetings and other activities of the current presidency.

## EU Law

The texts of the EU treaties (primary law), legislation passed by the EU (secondary law), as well as case law by the Court of Justice can be researched using the **EurLex database** (http://eur-lex.europa.eu). The website has a differentiated search function that makes it possible to search for specific pieces of legislation or all legislation passed in a given issue area. When working with the EU treaties, it is important to refer to the most recent, consolidated version (i.e., the version that incorporates all amendments passed to date)—unless your research has a historical focus.

For ongoing legislative processes, the **EP's Legislative Observatory** (http://www.europarl.europa.eu/oeil/home/home.do) is a helpful resource. Its "procedure files" trace the steps of each bill and contain documents produced in the process (such as the Commission's legislative proposal, EP Committee reports, or Council positions on the bill). The Legislative Observatory also allows for research on legislative processes that have been concluded or abandoned, going back to 1994.

## EU Policies

The websites of the EU institutions contain a wealth of information about the diverse range of EU policies covered in this book. The **European Commission website** is particularly useful; its list of topics (https://ec.europa.eu/info/topics_en) is a good starting point that leads to detailed descriptions of EU policies, including official policy documents, publications for a wider audience, and press releases. For each topic, this website also links to other EU institutions with information on the same topic.

An important resource for research on various policies is the EU's website on its **budget** (http://ec.europa.eu/budget/index_en.cfm). It includes figures on the Multiannual Financial Framework (MFF) as well as the yearly budgets. The website provides an interactive tool that allows researchers to look up various revenue categories (including contributions per member state) and expenditure items (http://ec.europa.eu/budget/figures/interactive/index_en.cfm).

Another useful tool is **Agence Europe** (https://agenceurope.eu/en/home.html). It is a daily newsletter, which provides online full-text access to the **Bulletin Quotidien Europe** (French edition) and **Europe Daily Bulletin** (English edition). Students can use a free trial. A very helpful supplement is its **Europe Documents**, which consists of analytical reviews and presentations of the rotating presidencies. It may also include full reproduction of reports. It has been in place since the early days and can be used for research about historical time periods.

## Social and Economic Data

A number of EU websites contain useful statistical data. A good starting point is **Eurostat**, the EU's statistical agency (http://ec.europa.eu/eurostat). Its website includes not only publications but also a large database that allows researchers to run customized searches for data in a variety of fields, including demographics, regional development, economy and finance, trade, environment, and energy.

Some EU institutions have their own databases. The Commission's Directorate-General (DG) for Economic and Financial Affairs runs the **Annual Macro-Economic Database** (AMECO, http://ec.europa.eu/economy_ finance/ameco/user/serie/SelectSerie.cfm), which contains important indicators on the gross domestic product, labour costs, trade flows between member states, and government debt and deficit. This database is the reference point for procedures relevant to the Economic and Monetary Union, such as the European Semester. The European Central Bank also has its own database, called Statistical Data Warehouse (SDW, http://sdw.ecb.europa.eu/); it contains a broad range of macroeconomic statistics, including data on interest rates and exchange rates.

In addition, a number of Commission Directorates General (DGs) provide publications with statistical data, although they do not offer searchable databases. For instance, the DG for Trade publishes its own **trade statistics** (http:// ec.europa.eu/trade/policy/countries-and-regions/statistics/) and the DG for Regional and Urban Policy has its own website for data on the various **European Structural and Investment Funds** (https://cohesiondata.ec.europa.eu/).

## Democratic Life and Public Opinion

The EU-level political parties, as well as the party groups in the EP, all have their own websites, which provide information on programmatic standpoints, leadership personnel, and current events. Links to the **EP party groups** are prominently posted on the EP website (http://ec.europa.eu/ transparencyregister/public/homePage.do); if a group is associated with an EU-wide political party, the group's website will provide a link.

For interest groups, civil society organizations, and lobbying firms active in Brussels, the EU's **Transparency Register** (http://ec.europa.eu/trans parencyregister/public/homePage.do) is a useful resource; it lists information on more than 10,000 organizations active in Brussels.

Public opinion data on European integration is systematically collected in the **Eurobarometer** (http://ec.europa.eu/COMMFrontOffice/ publicopinion), which is based on public opinion surveys, financed by the European Commission, that are conducted every six months in all member states, as well as current candidate countries. The surveys contain questions on items such as trust in the EU, desired policy priorities, or strength of European and national identities. Eurobarometer data allows for comparisons both between member states and over time. In addition to written reports, detailed data tables are accessible on the Eurobarometer website;

the function "Eurobarometer Interactive" allows researchers to selectively extract data on the question(s) in which they are interested.

## Media Sources

A number of major English-language news sources provide good coverage of EU politics; these include, for instance, the *Financial Times* (https://www. ft.com), *The Economist* (https://www.economist.com/), and *The Guardian* (https://www.theguardian.com/international). There are also some specialist news sources focusing primarily on EU politics; these include the Europe edition of the weekly **Politico** (http://www.politico.eu/) and **EUObserver** (https://euobserver.com), as well as the blog **EurActiv** (www.euractiv. com/). Students researching current events and decision-making processes in the EU are advised to follow reporting in these sources. The news channel **France24** (www.france24.com/en/), in English, has two shows that specialize in EU politics: *Talking EUROPE* interviews EU elected and public officials, and *EUROPE Now* profiles EU member states.

## Scholarly Sources

While the above contain useful primary sources for EU-related research, it is important to relate your research to the scholarly literature in EU studies. The titles provided as further reading at the end of this textbook's individual chapters are a good starting point for researching this literature. In addition, students are advised to review articles in scholarly journals that specialize in EU politics. The most widely used journals in this category are the *JCMS: Journal of Common Market Studies* (http://onlinelibrary.wiley.com/ journal/10.1111/(ISSN)1468-5965), the *Journal of European Public Policy* (JEPP, http://www.tandfonline.com/toc/rjpp20/current), *European Union Politics* (EUP, http://journals.sagepub.com/home/eup), the *Journal of European Integration* (JEI, http://www.tandfonline.com/loi/geui20), and the *European Law Journal* (ELJ, http://onlinelibrary.wiley.com/journal/10.1111/ (ISSN)1468-0386).

In addition to these EU-focused journals, EU-related research is also frequently published in a number of **political science journals with a more general focus**, for instance, *West European Politics* (WEP, http://www. tandfonline.com/toc/fwep20/current), *Comparative European Politics* (CEP, https://link.springer.com/journal/41295), and many more. Depending on the research topic, useful scholarly literature can also be found in more **specialized journals** that focus for instance on a specific policy field (e.g., *European Journal of Migration and Law*, http://booksandjournals.brillonline.

com/content/journals/15718166) or a specific region (e.g., *South European Policy and Politics*, http://www.tandfonline.com/toc/fses20/current).

## Think Tanks

There are a number of think tanks that focus on EU politics. Their policy papers and other publications may be useful, especially for research on relatively recent political developments (scholarly journals, because of their peer-review policies, often take longer to publish articles that reflect on recent events). Major think tanks in this category include **Bruegel** (bruegel.org/), the **Centre for European Policy Studies** (CEPS, https://www.ceps.eu), the **Centre for European Reform** (CER, www.cer.eu), the **European Trade Union Institute** (ETUI, https://www.etui.org/), the **European Policy Centre** (EPC, http://www.epc.eu/), **Notre Europe/Jacques Delors Institute** (http://www.delorsinstitute.eu/), the **Robert Schuman Centre for Advanced Studies** at the European University Institute (http://www.eui.eu/DepartmentsAndCentres/RobertSchumanCentre/Index.aspx), and the **Centre for Economic Policy Research** (CEPR, http://CEPR.org), including its useful policy portal (http://voxcu.org) that provides policy analysis and commentary by economists.

## Canada-EU Relations

There are various useful resources for those studying the EU from Canada. The EU is studied in many Canadian universities. Many researchers have collaborated through the **Canada-Europe Transatlantic Dialogue** (https://labs.carleton.ca/canadaeurope). Canadian-based scholars or those interested in being connected to a network of Canadian scholars, graduate students, and professionals who study the EU are members of the **European Community Studies Association-Canada** (ECSA-C, http://www.ecsa-c.ca/). Its young researchers are further organized in the **Young Researchers Network** (YRN, www.ecsac-yrn.ca). Other useful sources are the websites of the **Delegation of the European Union to Canada** (https://eeas.europa.eu/delegations/canada_en), which is the official EU diplomatic representation in Canada, as well as its counterpart, the **Mission of Canada to the European Union** (www.canadainternational.gc.ca), which is the Canadian "embassy" to the EU.

# Index

Tables and figures indicated by page numbers in italics